Female Terrorism and Militancy

This edited volume provides a window on the many forces that structure and shape why women and girls participate in terrorism and militancy, as well as on how states have come to view, treat, and strategize against them.

Females who carry out terrorist acts have historically been seen as mounting a challenge to the social order by violating conventional notions of gender and power, and their participation in such acts has tended to be viewed as being either as a passive victim or a feminist warrior. This volume seeks to move beyond these portrayals, to examine some of the structuring conditions that play a part in a girl or woman's decision to commit violence. These include economics, the need to protect oneself, and the degree of popular support that female participation receives in a given society. Amidst the contextual factors informing her involvement, the volume seeks to explore the political agency of the female terrorist or militant. Several of the articles are based on research where authors had direct contact with female terrorists or militants who committed acts of political violence, or with witnesses to such acts.

This book will be of great interest to students of terrorism and political violence, gender studies, and security studies in general.

Cindy D. Ness is Director of Programs at the Center on Terrorism at John Jay College of Criminal Justice, and a practicing psychotherapist. She holds a doctorate from Harvard University in Human Development and Psychology.

Contemporary terrorism studies

Understanding Terrorist Innovation
Technology, tactics, and global trends
Adam Dolnik

The Strategy of Terrorism
How it works, why it fails
Peter Neumann and M.L.R. Smith

Female Terrorism and Militancy
Agency, utility, and organization
Edited by Cindy D. Ness

Female Terrorism and Militancy

Agency, utility, and organization

Edited by Cindy D. Ness

 Routledge
Taylor & Francis Group

LONDON AND NEW YORK

First published 2008
by Routledge
2 Park Square, Milton Park, Abingdon, Oxon OX14 4RN

Simultaneously published in the USA and Canada
by Routledge
270 Madison Ave, New York, NY 10016

Transferred to Digital Printing 2008

Routledge is an imprint of the Taylor & Francis Group, an informa business

Typeset in Garamond by Wearset Ltd, Boldon, Tyne and Wear
Printed and bound in Great Britain by Antony Rowe Ltd,
Chippenham, Wiltshire

British Library Cataloguing in Publication Data
A catalogue record for this book is available from the British Library

Library of Congress Cataloging in Publication Data
Female terrorism and militancy : agency, utility, and organization / edited by
Cindy D. Ness.
p. cm. – (Contemporary terrorism studies)
1. Women terrorists. 2. Political violence. 3. Violence in women. I. Ness,
Cindy D., 1959–
HV6431.F423 2007
363.325082–dc22

2007022946

ISBN10: 0-415-77347-4 (hbk)
ISBN10: 0-203-93726-0 (ebk)

ISBN13: 978-0-415-77347-8 (hbk)
ISBN13: 978-0-203-93726-6 (ebk)

Especially for Viola Ness: Grandmother, Mother and Friend

Contents

Notes on contributors   ix
Acknowledgments   xiv

Introduction   1
CINDY D. NESS

1 In the name of the cause: women's work in secular
   and religious terrorism   11
   CINDY D. NESS

2 Women fighting in *jihad*?   37
   DAVID COOK

3 Beyond the bombings: analyzing female suicide
   bombers   49
   DEBRA ZEDALIS

4 (Gendered) war   69
   CAROLYN NORDSTROM

5 The evolving participation of Muslim women in
   Palestine, Chechnya, and the global jihadi
   movement   84
   KARLA CUNNINGHAM

6 Black widows and beyond: understanding the
   motivations and life trajectories of Chechen female
   terrorists   100
   ANNE SPECKHARD AND KHAPTA AKHMEDOVA

7 The black widows: Chechen women join the fight
for independence – and Allah   122
ANNE NIVAT

8 Palestinian female suicide bombers: virtuous
heroines or damaged goods?   131
YORAM SCHWEITZER

9 Martyrs or murderers? Victims or victimizers? The
voices of would-be Palestinian female suicide
bombers   146
ANAT BERKO AND EDNA EREZ

10 Girls as "weapons of terror" in Northern Uganda
and Sierra Leonean armed groups   167
SUSAN MCKAY

11 From freedom birds to water buffaloes: women
terrorists in Asia   183
MARGARET GONZALEZ-PEREZ

12 Women and organized racial terrorism in the
United States   201
KATHLEEN M. BLEE

13 The portrayal of female terrorists in the media:
similar framing patterns in the news coverage of
women in politics and in terrorism   217
BRIGITTE L. NACOS

Index   236

Contributors

Khapta Akhmedova is Professor of Psychology, Chechen State University, Russia, and Coordinator of the Psychosocial Rehabilitation Program of Medecins Du Monde.

Anat Berko holds a PhD in Criminology from Bar-Ilan University and is a Research Fellow with the Institute for Counter-terrorism (ICT), at the Interdisciplinary Center in Herzliya, Israel. She also lectures in the Centers Lauder School of Government, Diplomacy and Security, at a seminar at the Center of Excellence–Defence Against Terrorism in Turkey and for Nato and PIP (Partnership for Peace countries) military and police forces. Dr. Berko serves on Israel's Counter-Terrorism Team, the Israeli Council for National Security, as an advisor to senior-echelon governmental decision-makers. An expert on suicidal terrorists, she is widely covered in the Israeli and international media. Her book *The Path to Paradise: the Inner World of Female and Male Suicide Bombers and their Dispatchers* (2007) has been just published by Praeger. Dr. Berko completed her military career in the Israeli Defense Forces as a Lieutenant Colonel.

Kathleen M. Blee is Distinguished Professor of Sociology at the University of Pittsburgh. She is the author of several books, including *Inside Organized Racism: Women in the Hate Movement* and *Women of the Klan: Racism and Gender in the 1920s*, and numerous articles on the far-right, organized racism, gender, poverty, and group violence. She is currently writing one book on social-movement formation and another on the microdynamics of hate violence.

David Cook is Assistant Professor of Religious Studies at Rice University specializing in Islam. He did his undergraduate degrees at the Hebrew University in Jerusalem, and received his PhD from the University of Chicago in 2001. His areas of specialization include early Islamic history and development, Muslim apocalyptic literature and movements, historical astronomy and Judeo-Arabic literature. His first book, *Studies in Muslim Apocalyptic*, was published by Darwin Press in the series Studies in Late Antiquity and Early Islam. Two further books, *Understanding Jihad* and *Contemporary Muslim Apocalyptic Literature*, were published during 2005. Cook has completed a manuscript on the theme of martyrdom in Islamic civilization for Cambridge University Press (due to be released in October 2006), and is working on a book (together with Olivia Allison) on the policy aspects of suicide attacks for the United States.

Karla Cunningham is a Political Scientist at RAND and is responsible for research on Middle East politics, terrorism, Islamism, and insurgency. Recent projects have concentrated on the Iraqi insurgency, the 2006 Israeli war with Lebanon, and Islamist radicalization. She has published extensively on female terrorism and counter-terrorism, as well as on Islamic fundamentalism, democratization, and economic development. Dr. Cunningham previously worked at SUNY Geneseo and as an intelligence analyst within the Department of Defense and as an inspector with the United States Customs Service. She received her PhD in 1997 from the University at Buffalo.

Edna Erez is Professor and Head of the Department of Criminal Justice at the University of Illinois at Chicago. She has a Law degree (LLB) from the Hebrew University of Jerusalem and PhD in Sociology/Criminology from the University of Pennsylvania. Professor Erez has published extensively in professional journals in criminology and legal studies (altogether over 100 articles and book chapters). She received over one million dollar in grants from state and federal sources in the US and overseas, and she has served on review panels of the National Institute of Justice evaluating proposals in the areas of violence against women, victims, and comparative criminology. Among her recently completed or ongoing funded research projects are a national study on violence against immigrant women and systemic responses, policing domestic violence in the Arab/Palestinian community in Israel, women in terrorism, victims of terrorism, and terrorism, crime and the Internet.

Margaret Gonzalez-Perez is originally from Louisville, Kentucky, where she earned undergraduate degrees in political science and Spanish literature. She earned her PhD in Political Science from Louisiana State University in 1994. Her areas of specialization are comparative politics and international relations, with particular research interest in terrorism, ethnic conflict, and regionalism. She is currently an Associate Professor at Southeastern Louisiana University, where she has taught courses in international relations, international organizations, international law, international political economy, European politics, Middle East politics, and politics of developing nations since 1995.

Susan McKay, PhD, is a psychologist, nurse, and Professor of Women's and International Studies at the University of Wyoming in Laramie,

Wyoming, USA. For almost two decades, she has taught and researched issues focused upon women, girls, and armed conflict, women and peacebuilding, and feminist issues in peace psychology. Recent books include *Where Are the Girls? Girls in Fighting Forces in Northern Uganda, Sierra Leone, and Mozambique, Their Lives During and After War* (2004) and *The Courage Our Stories Tell: The Daily Lives and Maternal Child Health Care of Japanese–American Women at Heart Mountain* (2002). McKay's current research has been funded by UNICEF West Africa, the Rockefeller Foundation, and the Oak Foundation to study issues related to formerly abducted girl soldiers in Northern Uganda, Sierra Leone, and Liberia who return from fighting forces with children. She is past President of the Division of Peace Psychology of the American Psychological Association.

Brigitte L. Nacos received a PhD in political science from Columbia University, where she teaches courses in American politics and government. Among the books she authored are: *Terrorism and the Media: From the Iran Hostage Crisis to the World Trade Center Bombing* (Columbia University Press, 1994); *Mass-Mediated Terrorism: the Central Role of the Media in Terrorism and Counterterrorism* (Rowman & Littlefield, 2002); *Terrorism and Counterterrorism: Understanding Threats and Responses in the Post-9/11 World* (Longman, 2006). She is co-author (with Oscar Torres-Reyna) of *Fueling Our Fears: Stereotyping, Media Coverage and Public Opinion of Muslim Americans* (Rowman & Littlefield 2007).

Cindy D. Ness is Director of Programs at the Center on Terrorism at John Jay College of Criminal Justice in New York City, and a practicing psychotherapist. Her research interests include female youth violence in inner-city communities, political violence by females, and the ethnographic study of public institutions. She holds a doctorate from Harvard University in Human Development and Psychology and she is currently ABD at the University of Pennsylvania in anthropology. She is a former member of the Academic Advisory Council of the National Campaign Against Youth Violence. Representative publications on women and violence include a forthcoming book entitled *Why Girls Fight: Female Youth Violence in the Inner City* (New York University Press) and an article in the journal *Daedalus* entitled "The Rise in Female Violence," among others.

Anne Nivat's book about the Chechen conflict, *Chienne de Guerre*, won the Albert Londres Prize, France's highest award for journalism, and has been translated into many languages. She also wrote *Algerienne* and *View from the Vysotka*. Ms. Nivat has been the Moscow correspondent for the French newspaper *Liberation* and has contributed articles to *Newsweek*, *US News & World Report*, *USA Today*, the *New York Times*, *Washington Post*, *International Herald Tribune* and other foreign and US periodicals, as well as appearances on CNN, PBS, and numerous television and radio broadcasts in Canada and Europe.

Carolyn Nordstrom is Professor of Anthropology, University of Notre Dame. Her principal areas of interest are political violence and peacebuilding, gender and children, transnational criminal systems, and globalization. She has conducted extensive fieldwork worldwide, with long-term interests in Southern Africa and South Asia. Her books include: *Global Outlaws: Crime, Money and Power in the Contemporary World*; *Shadows of War: Violence, Power and International Profiteering in the 21st Century*; *A Different Kind of War Story*; several monographs, including *Girls and Warzones, Troubling Questions*; and the edited volumes: *Fieldwork Under Fire: Contemporary Stories of Violence and Survival*; *The Paths to Domination, Resistance, and Terror*, as well as several dozen articles. She has recently been awarded John D. and Catherine T. MacArthur and John Simon Guggenheim Fellowships.

Yoram Schweitzer is a researcher of international terror at The Institute for National Security Studies (INSS). Schweitzer has had a career in the Israeli intelligence community as well as in the academic world. He has lectured and published widely on terror-related issues, and serves as a consultant for government ministries on a private basis. Schweitzer's current research involves extensive meetings with failed suicide terrorists and their operators in an effort to analyze their motivations and objectives. Schweitzer's recent publications on these issues are: as co-author, along with Shaul Shay, of *Globalization of Terror: the Challenge of Al-Qaeda and the Response of the International Community* (2003). Co-author of Memorandum 78 entitled: *Al Qaeda and the Internationalization of Suicide Terrorism* published by The Jaffee Center for Strategic Studies (2005). Editor of Memorandum 84 entitled: *Female Suicide Bombers: Dying for Equality?* published by The Jaffee Center for Strategic Studies (2006).

Anne Speckhard, PhD, is Adjunct Associate Professor of Psychiatry at Georgetown University Medical School. She is chair of the NATO Human Factors & Medicine Research and Technology Experts Group (HFM-140/RTG) on the Psychosocial, Cultural, and Organizational Aspects of Terrorism, and also serves as co-chair of the NATO–Russia Exploratory Team – Social Sciences Support to Military Personnel Engaged in Counter-Insurgency and Counter-Terrorism Operations. She is a member of the United Nations Roster of Experts for the Terrorism Prevention Branch Office, a member of the European Consortium on Political Research Standing Group on Extremism and Democracy, and was previously awarded a Public Health Service Research Fellowship in the US Department of Health & Human Services. She has provided expert consultation to numerous European governments as well as the

US Department of Defense. Dr. Speckhard has been working in the field of posttraumatic stress disorder (PTSD) since the 1980s.

Debra Zedalis is the Deputy to the Garrison Commander at West Point, NY. Prior to this assignment, Ms. Zedalis was a student at the US Army War College and worked for the US Army in Europe. Ms. Zedalis also serves as an adjunct professor at the State University of New York, New Paltz. Ms. Zedalis holds a masters degree in Strategic Studies from the US Army War College, a masters degree in Business Administration from Syracuse University, a bachelor of arts in Managerial Psychology from the University of Kentucky and is a member of Phi Beta Kappa.

Acknowledgments

The Publishers would like to thank Taylor & Francis for granting permission to reprint the following from *Studies in Conflict and Terrorism*, 28(5) (2005):

"In the Name of the Cause: Women's Work in Secular and Religious Terrorism." Cindy D. Ness.

"Women Fighting in *Jihad*?" David Cook

"(Gendered) War." Carolyn Nordstrom

"The Black Widows: Chechen Women Join the Fight for Independence – and Allah." Anne Nivat

"Girls as 'Weapons of Terror' in Northern Uganda and Sierra Leonean Rebel Fighting Forces." Susan McKay

"Women and Organised Racial Terrorism in the United States." Kathleen M. Blee

"The portrayal of Female Terrorists in the Media: Similar Framing Patterns in the News Coverage of Women in Politics and in Terrorism." Brigitte L. Nacos

Reproduced by kind permission of Taylor & Francis Group plc, www.taylor andfrancis.com.

Introduction

Cindy D. Ness

In the fall of 2004, I was given the generous opportunity by Bruce Hoffman to guest edit a volume of the journal *Studies in Conflict in Terrorism*. The volume was intended as a scholarly consideration of the participation of women and girls in terrorist and militant groups.[1] In the broadest sense, it was meant to provide a window on the many forces that structure and shape why women and girls participate in terrorism, as well as on how states have come to view, treat, and strategize against them. Until that time, there had only been one scholarly book written on the subject – *Women and Terrorism* (1996) by Neuberger and Tiziana – published nearly a decade earlier. The book examined the motivations of Italian female terrorists of the 1970s, including how they understood their actions in retrospect. While thoughtful and informative, the volume could in no way claim to do justice to the subject as a whole given its narrow focus. The few full-length general works on the topic, written by journalists (i.e., Morgan, 1989; McDonald, 1991), were even more dated. While achieving some popular acclaim, these accounts were neither driven by data nor did they provide a critical level of analysis.

For all intents and purposes, the *female terrorist* had not been treated as a legitimate subject for serious inquiry before Wafa Idris, the Palestinian Red Crescent paramedic, blew herself up on Jaffa Road in downtown Jerusalem on January 27, 2002. This was the case, even though several of the most active left-wing terrorist groups of the 1960s and 1970s, ones central to ushering in the era of modern terrorism, were co-created or co-led by women – Ulrike Meinhof of the Bader–Meinhof group, Leila Khalid and Fusako Shigenobu of the Popular Front for the Liberation of Palestine (PFLP), and Adriana Faranda of the Red Brigades held leadership positions in their respective organizations. A quick look at major Western newspapers following Idris' attack might have left one thinking that Idris was the world's first female suicide bomber, despite the fact that Sana'a Mouhadly, a member of the Syrian Social Nationalist Party (SSNP), had earned that distinction in 1985. Mouhadly detonated an explosive-laden vehicle, which in addition to killing her, killed two Israeli soldiers and injured two others. Over the next few years, females carried out four more of the 12 suicide missions undertaken by the SSNP aimed at pushing Israeli troops out of Southern Lebanon.

Girls and women[2] have in fact carried out suicide bombings disproportionate to their numbers in all of the secular terrorist groups that have made serious use of the tactic, from Mouhadly to the present. Any student of suicide terrorism is well aware that the Kurdistan Workers Party (PKK), the first group in the 1990s to employ suicide bombing as a strategic weapon in an ethno-separatist struggle, used females to carry out 11 of its 15 suicide missions in Turkey. Despite the high percentage of females used by the SSNP and PKK in suicide missions, however, it is also well known that most female suicide bombers have belonged to the Liberation Tamil Tigers of Eelam (LTTE) – LTTE women have perpetrated between 30–40 percent of the organization's more than 200 suicide bombings. Unlike many other secular or religious terrorist groups that use women to carry out suicide bombings, however, LTTE females have, for the most part, never been second-class martyrs – their deaths have consistently occasioned the same symbolic representation and ritual celebration as their male counterparts. Although far less central to rebel operations compared to girls and women in the LTTE, Chechen females were involved in 22 of the 28 suicide attacks undertaken since that struggle's beginnings. Initially a purely secular struggle that was infused with religious significance as it became more radicalized, the use of females by Chechen rebels set the stage for religious Palestinian and Salafi terrorist groups to make use of females, as well. What then accounts for female terrorists being understudied by scholars and distorted in the media given the extent of their participation in both New Left and post-New-Left terrorism?

First, as typical social roles and expectations associated with females virtually negate their potential for aggression, females who carry out terrorist acts, whether fighting for secular or religious ends, have historically been seen as violating conventional notions of gender and power – even if only temporarily, their behavior represents a challenge to the social order. Denied the potential to be a violent actor, females have been sensationalized or simply ignored when they have taken to armed resistance. Second, the number of females who engage in terrorist acts has always been small compared to males. While reference to Islamic female warriors in the sixth century or political assassinations by Russian female revolutionaries in the late nineteenth century are commonly cited to strengthen the claim that females have a long and rich connection to armed resistance and to terror, these events and others like them in reality represent isolated incidents of female-perpetrated political violence and not a well-established pattern – indeed, the iconic stature of the female terrorist/militant is easily and conversely redrawn to suggest that she is nothing more than a "fluke."[3] However, numbers alone do not tell the whole story.

Even as female participation in militant groups engaging in terrorism increased dramatically over the last two decades – in some secular groups females comprise more than 30 percent of the fighting force – the centrality of girls and women to the day-to-day survival and wider mission of such organizations still virtually went unnoticed. Perhaps more critical than absolute numbers is the fact that, barring the rare exception, men have typically dominated the power structures of terrorist/militant groups. Indeed, although females serve as unit commanders in many groups that engage in terrorism, unlike their male counterparts, they are still viewed as being pawns of male decision-making because they have not made it into the inner circle of leadership. Lastly, female terrorists/militants have received limited attention because, until recently, they have been active in countries not centrally tied to Western national interests. Suicide missions carried out by Palestinian females in Israeli cities were integral to Western nations taking notice. After the successful attack by Wafa Idris and the dispatch of three more Palestinian female suicide bombers in relative quick succession, the idea that females were capable of inflicting unapologetic carnage, and subsequently, were of great strategic importance to terrorist operations across the globe, was indelibly lodged in the Western subconscious.

With this awakened sense of the female terrorist/militant's existence and utility came a considerable increase in the attention she received; however, at first it was largely one-dimensional in nature. At one end of the spectrum, observers constructed the contemporary female terrorist/militant as trapped by cultural circumstances or as a "romantic dupe" who had been manipulated into violent acts by a male lover or male relative. The female Palestinian suicide bombers who successfully completed suicide missions from January 2002 through January 2004 were initially characterized as being women on the fringe of society who pursued their suicide mission as a way to restore their honor or that of their family (i.e., Davis, 2003; Victor 2003). At the other end of the spectrum, and equally reductive, were observers who constructed the female terrorist/militant as a "liberated" feminist actor embracing violence as a way to achieve respect in a sexist society – an old argument that cast female aggression as a move from the feminine to the masculine. Violence within this framework was characterized as an equal-opportunity employer and the females who resorted to it as being even more dangerous than their male counterparts. It was through girls and women serving as terrorist combatants, or through the far more rare occurrence of them blowing themselves up, that gender equality was seen as being granted expression. Females in secular groups were more prone to the latter stereotype, although it has also been questionably argued by some that females in religious groups have entered the struggle as a desperate measure to achieve equality.

While it is true that instances of both the above scenarios exist, in and of themselves, they could not explain the extent of female participation in political violence around the globe over the last three decades; the mobilization of thousands of girls and women as combatants in secular terrorist groups cannot so easily be accounted for. Moreover, it is inaccurate to perceive females as only following orders when political conflict turns violent.

Pauline Nyiramasuhuko, the Rwandan national minister of family and women's affairs, and the first woman to be charged with genocide and crimes against humanity for ordering the rape and murder of countless Tutsi men and women, stands out as an example, albeit an extreme one, of violent leadership by a woman. Several of the authors in this book, based on research that put them in direct contact either with females who committed or intended to commit an act of terrorism, or with persons who bore witness to such actors, explore the political agency of the female terrorist/militant, amidst the contextual factors, some coercive, that inform that agency.

It is important to note that, like the stories of girls and women that grace the pages of the earlier journal volume I edited, this expanded book also does not begin or end on a note of feminist politics, even when such goals are espoused in the ideology of the groups they are affiliated with. Indeed, though more subtle secondary gains sometimes follow women's engagement in non-traditional roles, the chapter brought together here, consistent with findings in the literature, offer little evidence of gender rights being advanced in the surrounding society in which females carry out terrorism. Nor do any of the chapters offer evidence that true gender equality exists even within the terrorist or militant organization itself. To be sure, it is a commonplace of political violence that, in the name of the cause, traditional mores can be overridden without making a fundamental, or even long-term, alteration in a society's values regarding gender relations. Leila Khaled's observation of more than 20 years ago, that nationalism is the first cause, seems particularly relevant to the majority of politically violent struggles today in societies that do not have egalitarian gender-role expectations to start with. As proof, rather than being welcomed back as heroes, females in contemporary secular terrorist groups have experienced great obstacles to reintegrating back into their communities. This said, while the increased numbers of girls and females participating in militancy and terrorism may not indicate a trend in gender reform, it does speak of a major transformation in the pattern of participation by females in political violence that needs to be understood – participation which at times is entered into voluntarily and at other times against a girl or woman's will. This volume attempts to move beyond the portrayal of the female militant/terrorist as either passive victim or feminist warrior to include some of the structuring conditions, like economics, war-zone realities – including the need to protect oneself – and the degree of popular support that female participation enjoys in a given society, conditions that play a significant role in a girl or woman's decision to commit violence. It seeks to understand the growing sense of legitimacy that girls and women carrying out violence are being granted in the political arena.

Since the publication of the journal volume, the most singular development related to the involvement of females in terrorism/militancy has been the increasingly liberal position taken by Islamic terrorist groups regarding the right and obligation of females to engage in *jihad* against the enemy.

Although Wafa Idris entered the annals of Intifada history as the first Palestinian female suicide bomber, Fatah's Al Aqsa Martyrs Brigade likely sent her to deliver a bomb to a male operative, not detonate one herself. The continued recruitment of female suicide bombers by Fatah, aimed both at reinvigorating its significance on the Arab street as well as moving bombers across Israeli checkpoints, essentially served to pressure Hamas and Islamic Jihad to follow suit or lose influence over the course of political events. Initially more serendipitous than calculated in the Palestinian context, the shock value of the female terrorist, the intensified media coverage she guaranteed, and the operational advantages she offered made it virtually impossible for Islamic religious groups to continue to deny her participation.

With the appearance of Wafa Idris, clerics seeking to provide a cloak of religious permissibility for females undertaking suicide missions engaged as they had not before in a debate which, for all intents and purposes, bowed to practical considerations – 16 months after Idris, the Palestinian Islamic Jihad, in association with al-Aqsa Martyrs Brigade, sent Hiba Daraghmeh to blow herself up at the entrance of a shopping mall in the Israeli city of Afula. The rhetorical strategies used to justify what in reality represented a significant break with accepted gender norms and social practice was in fact not so different in kind from the rhetorical strategies employed by secular groups, although relying on different symbolic meanings to do so.[4] It is important to note that, while religious martyrdom was no longer off-limits to females, it did not equate with Islamic terrorist groups making a place for females in their organizations. Whereas, in secular groups, girls and women are more apt to be afforded a diverse organizational presence, in religious terrorist groups the only identities open to females remained carrying out support functions for male operatives or being sent on suicide missions.

While Chechen rebel leaders may have been first to invoke Islamic ideology to justify the use of females in suicide bombing, it is noteworthy that, in direct interviews with the family and friends of Chechen women who carried out attacks, religious motives have not been credited with being a significant driving factor. Although it is true that women in black chadors with bombs strapped to their torsos were displayed prominently in media coverage of the Dubrovka theatre siege, a call for an Islamic state was not part of the Chechen struggle as it was originally defined – Chechen nationalism and independence were identified as being the main objectives. The institution of Islamic rule as a unifying theme only appeared as the prospects of rebel forces grew dimmer and Islamic fundamentalists offered their support. The adoption of radical Islam as a guiding ideology in the Chechen struggle was initially, at the very least, a tactical decision. While radical Islam has emerged as more of a home-grown phenomenon in the Palestinian conflict, even in this context religion does not appear to be the central catalyst motivating females to kill. As a number of chapters in this volume will argue, not unlike men, women act in response to personal tragedy and the impulse to exact revenge, the trauma associated with living in a conflict zone, and networking opportunities that provide them with the necessary means to undertake a suicide mission (See Speckhard and Akhmedova, this volume, Chapter 6, and Schweitzer, this volume, Chapter 8).

The participation of women in al-Qaeda-"associated" organizations has almost exclusively come about through their being married to or the relative of an active male operative. Prior to the war in Iraq, women's roles were basically limited to providing logistical support for attacks carried out by men. However, with the war came new realities requiring new strategies and even the barriers to women carrying out suicide operations in the most radical fundamentalist groups were removed. Indeed, while he was alive, Al-Qaeda in Iraq's Abu Musab al-Zarqawi was known to be a great supporter of female involvement in martyrdom operations. To expand the element of surprise, insurgent groups in Iraq have dispatched females considered to be less and less likely of carrying out a suicide operation, for instance, younger female operatives and even a 62-year-old grandmother – they have also begun to recruit a new type of suicide bomber – European female converts to Islam who have married radical Islamic men, as in the case of the Belgian woman, Muriel Degauque. Within such groups, the criteria for who can become a female suicide bomber appears to have widened to include any female who has the likelihood of circumventing security measures. Although these Salafi-oriented groups have begun to send women on suicide missions, doing so has led to no discernable shift in the structure of gender relations that these groups support – in essence, females have been allowed the privilege to kill or be killed but still cannot participate as a working member of the group.

Conversely, while al-Qaeda proper has been rumored to be training squads of women to engage in violent *jihad* since 9/11, to date it is not known to have dispatched any females on a suicide mission. Al-Qaeda's online women's magazine, *Al Khansa*, is reputed to be a vehicle for recruiting women to this end; however, thus far, women have continued to provide supportive functions only. As no al-Qaeda spokesperson has commented on the issue of women participating in *jihad*, it is not possible to determine the group's official position on the matter other than by deducing it from its actions to date.

The 13 chapters that follow, including seven from the guest-edited volume of *Studies in Conflict and Terrorism*, offer coverage of key themes that, taken together, begin to suggest the complexity of issues involved in the conduct and representation of terrorism/militancy carried out by females. On a cautionary note, in approaching the subject one must avoid the tendency to assign different causal explanations to the same violent behavior in male and female terrorists/militants, the consequence of which has been to imply that what motivates females and males to commit political violence is necessarily different and, by extension, to dichotomize the emotional states and motives that respectively underlie similar behavior. For example, though the death of a husband or brother is typically cited as what leads many female suicide bombers to strike, the loss of a relative in the family history of a male terrorist is far less commonly cited, though likely no less common. Similarly, the external manipulative agent that recruits a female for a suicide bombing, unlike for male recruits, is viewed as the prime mover behind her action, though observers have noted that male *shahids* are subject to intense indoctrination and social pressure too. While it is crucial to understand the dynamics that gender contributes where terrorism and militancy is concerned, it seems equally important not to let what sets the sexes apart blind us to what is generic to both of them. The chapters in this compilation hopefully will go far to illustrate that, while differences distinguish, similarities abound.

To place the topic in context, in the first chapter I provide a brief history of the involvement of females in the conduct of modern terrorism. I then embark on a discussion of the different ideological mindsets that account for females being more likely to become involved in terrorism associated with ethno-separatist rather than religious concerns, with an eye to the fact that the trend shows unmistakable signs of changing. Lastly, I examine the structure of logic or systems of contention that secular and religious groups employ in attempting to legitimize women and girls offering themselves up as martyrs, and a discussion of specifically what mechanisms they share for doing so.

Then David Cook, a professor of religious studies, looks at the classical Islamic religious and legal literature to contextualize the arguments being made for females participating in *jihad* in contemporary times. He illustrates how radical Muslims seeking to widen their appeal have modified earlier conclusions and have made it possible for women to participate together with men on the battlefield and in martyrdom operations.

After this, Debra Zedalis, Deputy to the Garrison Commander at West Point, in an update to her widely circulated report from 2004, *Female Suicide Bombers*, goes on to discuss female suicide bombings that have occurred since that time. Her analysis considers a wide range of factors including the importance of organizations and community support, recruitment, global expansion, and data gaps.

In Chapter 4, Carolyn Nordstrom, an anthropologist well known for her ethnographic research in war zones, writes about the impossibility of dividing women and girls into "combatants" and "non-combatants," given that fighting is no longer relegated to the battlefield. In her chapter she asks and tries to answer the question: what in this context is a female soldier? She illustrates how the debate about whether women should be allowed to serve in militaries and in combat obscures the ugly truth that to be female in a war zone today is to *be* on the frontlines.

Karla Cunningham, a political analyst at the RAND Corporation then reviews female participation in three Islamist settings – Palestine, Chechnya, and the Global Jidahi Movement – and points to an important evolution over the past six years that links women and *jihad* in a new manner.

While women have been involved in political violence in countries with a large Muslim population over the years, she delineates how the tradition of women in *jihadi* movements is very different from the one related to secular causes.

Anne Speckhard, Adjunct Associate Professor of Psychiatry, Georgetown University Medical Center and Psychological Consultant for Advances in Health, and Khapta Akhmedova, Professor of Psychology, Chechen State University, Russia, and Coordinator of the Psychosocial Rehabilitation Program of Medecins Du Monde, report on the results of a three-year study collecting interviews from family members, close associates, and hostages of 30 female Chechen suicide bombers – so called "Black Widows." The study reports on demographic descriptors as well as the psycho-social motivators for embarking on this path. Among its many findings, the study found that deep personal trauma and the desire for revenge, within the context of a nationalist battle, were the strongest motivating forces behind Chechen female suicide terrorism.

In Chapter 7, the journalist Anne Nivat, who has reported widely on the Russian–Chechen conflict based on her extensive travel in the region, traces the Chechen rebel sieges of the Dubrovka Theater in Moscow and the elementary school in Beslan back to the meaning it holds for women in the region. She interviews women who proclaim their willingness to serve as martyrs, as well as the sisters, friends, and mothers of some of the young women who died in the commando operation at Dubrovka Theater.

Yoram Schweitzer, a researcher of international terror at The Institute for National Security Studies (INSS), then discusses the two opposing approaches that have been posited to explain the involvement of Palestinian women in suicide bombings. One approach, appearing primarily in the Arab and Muslim media, has cast Palestinian women as heroines and as virtuous, while the Western and more dominant approach has presented them as socially deviant and as "damaged goods." In response to these approaches, Chapter 8 seeks to present a more balanced position regarding the personal and organizational factors that propelled several Palestinian female suicide bombers to take or attempt to take such a drastic step. The author's perspective is largely based on personal interviews with Palestinian women in Israeli prisons who either embarked on a failed suicide mission or served as chaperones to male suicide bombers. Male recruiters and dispatchers of women involved in suicide bombings were interviewed as well.

Anat Berko, Research Fellow with the Institute for Counter-terrorism (ICT), at the Interdisciplinary Center in Herzliya, Israel, and Edna Erez, a professor and chair of the Department of Criminal Justice at the University of Illinois at Chicago, examine the accounts of female would-be-suicide-bombers whose missions were either thwarted, failed, or were not carried out because the woman changed her mind. The data were derived from in-depth interviews of seven Palestinian women detained or incarcerated in Israeli prisons for attempting suicide bombing.

In Chapter 10, Susan McKay, a professor of women's studies, expands the definition of terrorism to include many of the acts that girl soldiers carry out in guerrilla warfare against civilians. After situating girls' involvement as child soldiers in fighting forces as a global phenomenon, she focuses upon girls as actors in two fighting forces: the Lord's Resistance Army (LRA) in Northern Uganda and the Revolutionary United Front (RUF) in Sierra Leone. Her chapter is based on extensive fieldwork conducted in both countries.

Margaret Gonzalez-Perez, an Associate Professor at Southeastern Louisiana University, examines the roles that women play in Asian terrorist groups in the context of whether a group has a domestic or international orientation. The chapter argues that women are often more drawn to domestic terrorist groups because these organizations oppose the state and the societal gender restrictions that the state maintains. Conversely, the chapter argues that women are far less active in international terrorist movements because these groups oppose external forces, such as imperialism or globalization, and any change within their own state, including with respect to gender roles, is incidental to its primary objective of combating foreign political, economic, or societal influences.

In Chapter 12, Kathleen Blee, a professor of sociology who has written extensively about women involved in hate movements, then goes on to explore women's involvement in racial violence associated with the major organized white supremacist groups in the USA – the Ku Klux Klan, white-power skinheads, and neo-Nazis – through the lens of terrorism. Beginning with the immediate post-Civil-War era through to the present, she considers two specific dimensions of terrorism: the intended target and how violence is organized. She concludes her chapter with a proposition about the relationships among women's participation, definitions of the enemy, and the organization of terroristic violence in the US white supremacist movement.

And, lastly, Brigitte Nacos, a journalist who has written extensively on terrorism and the media, offers a comparison of the framing patterns in the news about women in politics and the entrenched stereotypes in the coverage of female terrorists. She demonstrates similarities in the depiction of these legitimate (women in politics) and illegitimate (women in terrorism) political actors. She argues that the implementation of anti- and counterterrorist policies must not be influenced by the mass-mediated images of female terrorists because they do not reflect reality.

My hope is that this book will provide connections and parameters for future discussion, as well as new questions where female terrorism and militancy is concerned.

Notes

1 I will consider militant or guerrilla groups that do not reject in their philosophy, or in their practice, the killing of innocent civilians as engaging in terrorism. Examples include the Liberation Tamil Tigers of Eelam (LTTE), Euskadi Ta Askatasuna (ETA), and the Lord's Resistance Army, to name a few. Although these and many other nationalist groups direct their violence primarily at government targets, as compared to "pure" terrorist groups that condone attacking non-government targets, since the former often aims to instill terror in the civilian population, I include them, as well.
2 As it is being used here, a female under the age of 18 is considered a girl. There are reports of several girls aged 17 undertaking suicide missions. In militant groups that engage in terrorism, girls commonly take part in spreading terror among civilian populations from as young as age 10.
3 Neither is the strong tradition of female leadership in New-Left groups operating over 30 years ago representative of the gender hierarchy of most terrorist organizations today.
4 An unsigned fatwa issued shortly after Hawa Barayev, the first Chechen female suicide bomber, struck, and another issued by the High Islamic Council in Saudi Arabia a year later, were cited to bolster the Palestinian case.

References

Davis, Joyce (2003) *Martyrs: Innocence, Vengeance, and Despair in the Middle East* (New York: Palgrave Press)
MacDonald, Eileen (1991) *Shoot the Women First* (New York: Random House).
Morgan, Robin (1989) *The Demon Lover: On the Sexuality of Terrorism* (New York: W.W. Norton & Co.).
Neuberger, Luisella De Cataldo and Valentini, Tiziana (1996) *Women and Terrorism* (London: Macmillan Press).
Victor, Barbara (2003) *Army of Roses: Inside the World of Palestinian Women Suicide Bombers* (Emmaus, PA: Rodale Press).

1 In the name of the cause

Women's work in secular and religious terrorism

Cindy D. Ness

Since 1968, the year when modern international terrorism is widely accepted as having been ushered in, the means by which terrorist acts have been carried out, and the justifications for them, have undergone significant changes.[1] In the post-Cold-War era, terrorism has had two different faces: one secular and one religious.[2] Throughout the 1980s and 1990s, women and girls participated almost exclusively in the former because of the intense significance that religious extremism places on females remaining in traditional roles. Overall, the number of secular ethno-separatist struggles that women and girls were involved in during this period increased dramatically. Yet, despite the breadth of their participation in insurgencies and terrorist activities around the world for well over 20 years, the United States has had great difficulty in thinking of females as agents of aggression. This difficulty is plainly captured in a comment by George W. Bush on 4 April 2002 about the third Palestinian female suicide bomber, Ayat Akhras.[3]

Bush said, "When an 18-year-old Palestinian girl is induced to blow herself up and in the process kills a 17-year-old Israeli girl, the future is dying"; the implication being that when a woman straps explosives onto her body and pushes a button that results in her being ripped into a thousand pieces, it is a qualitatively different matter from a man doing the same thing (Shamsie, 2002) – the gender of the bomber being the critical factor here, not the act itself. It is only as women and girls have become involved in struggles that are seen as having a direct effect on national interests, and because 9/11 has made suicide terrorism seem infinitely closer, that the United States has been forced to open its mind to the idea that females do commit such acts.

The intention of this chapter is, first, to provide a brief history of the involvement of females in the conduct of modern terrorism, and, with that as a backdrop, to discuss the different ideological mindsets that account for females being more likely to become involved in terrorism associated with ethno-separatist rather than religious concerns, with an eye to the fact that the trend shows unmistakable signs of changing. Second, it will consider the structure of logic, or systems of contention, that secular and religious groups employ in attempting to legitimize women and girls offering themselves up as martyrs, and to discuss specifically what mechanisms they share for doing so. The chapter turns its attention to female suicide bombing because it constitutes a distinct expression of female militancy, in that females transgress gender norms, not only by taking life, but also by embracing their own death and, in the process, counter existing core symbolic structures delimiting gender while, at the same time, creating new ones.

In line with this last undertaking, this chapter will focus on the Sri Lankan nationalist-based Liberation Tigers of Tamil Eelam (LTTE) because there, more than in other secular struggles, females have consciously been integrated into the group's philosophy, and they have also figured centrally in carrying out its suicide missions. Hamas and Islamic Jihad will be the religious example because, in shifting their position on the permissibility of females becoming martyrs (after several Palestinian women with the backing of the more secular Al-Aqsa Martyrs Brigade blew themselves up), these two groups present a unique opportunity to observe in the making the process by which female participation is legitimized.

The chapter begins with the premise that females who participate in violent terrorist acts violate conventional notions of gender and power – with few exceptions, violence is cross-culturally considered a male arena – and therefore take as its point of departure that any social group that sanctions female violence, whether secular or religious, must explain itself to itself. The rhetoric that is mobilized is viewed as the ground on which female participation rests. Although the precipitant for incorporating women and girls into political violence is almost invariably tactical, the justification that sustains their participation must be found in the cultural – in the proximal sense, because females who commit violence flout ingrained gender roles and boundaries, they must in all other ways "belong" to their social world, the organization of which is predicated on a host of structural arrangements and deeply felt moral beliefs; in the distal sense, because violent behavior by females must be made to fit within a collectively shared past where it can draw its sustenance from symbols that transcend time, so as not to "appear contingent upon a projected aim" (Schalk, 1997a, 154). In short, the thesis of this chapter (the last section, in particular) is that secular and religious terrorism, although seeking to create significantly different worlds – one modern, the other traditional – fall back on many of the same rhetorical strategies to justify females engaging in political violence, especially the rhetoric of martyrdom. Said another way, in both the secular and the religious case, even if only temporarily, females who enter into armed resistance represent a challenge to the social order, and thus, their violent acts must be reframed or rhetorically repackaged before they can be accepted. In the end, this chapter argues that it is essential that society find a rhetorical (or symbolic) sanction for violence by women before that violence can be encouraged and mobilized.

Female militancy in early modern terrorism

Although the typical terrorist of the 1960s and 1970s was a male in his twenties, usually of comfortable working-class or upper-middle-class origins, as anyone with an abiding interest in the subject of terrorism knows, several of the most active left-wing terrorist groups during this period had a strong female presence (Weinberg and Eubank, 1987, 247).[4] The name Ulrike Meinhof, female co-leader of the Baader–Meinhof group, progenitor to the Red Army Faction, became associated with the whole era of anti-imperialist protest turned to violence (Taylor and Quayle, 1994, 136). Leila Khalid, of the Popular Front for the Liberation of Palestine (PFLP), took part in several hijackings that drew world attention to the Palestinian cause (Arquilla and Ronfeldt, 1999, 59), arguably becoming the international icon of armed struggle and resistance of the time. The Japanese Red Army (JRA) was founded and led by Fusako Shigenobu until her arrest in Japan in November 2000 (Jenkins, 1999, iii). Approximately 20 of the 60 Red Brigade defendants who stood trial for the 1978 kidnapping of Aldo Moro were women – Adriana Faranda being the most well known (Weinberg and Eubank, 1987, 243).

From modern terrorism's beginnings, women have tended to be more active as leaders and members of groups that have worked to overturn traditional values rather than those seeking to restore old ones – stated another way, they have been less likely to play an active role in right-wing groups that idealize the past and incorporate sexism as part of their political ideologies (Handel, 1990, 197).[5] By their very nature, left-wing groups are ideologically more suited to justify and advocate women assuming combatant and other non-traditional roles because they premise that fundamental problems in the political and social institutions of society require a radical break with the past (Ardovini-Brooker, 2000, 258–259). Such was the thinking behind the "anti-imperialist" politics of the Weather Underground as articulated by its female members in the following quotation:

> the struggle against sexism demands the destruction of the American state, and ... the immediate personal nature of sexism requires struggle against men who enforce that oppression as well as its institutions.
>
> (*Ms.* Magazine, 1974, 105)

Interestingly, some of the most virulent "anti-imperialist" resistance groups of the period in which women played significant roles arose in Western nations (Gurr, 2000) where feminist struggles were simultaneously being waged – a convergence that greatly influenced the development of a unique brand of female militancy.

That said, although it is important to recognize the relatively greater influence that women held in such groups, and the greater involvement they had in carrying out violence, it is critical to not lose sight of the fact that, historically, even the most politically violent left-wing groups of the day (1960s and 1970s) were not entirely able to divest themselves of widely held beliefs about gender embedded in the culture surrounding them. Interview transcripts cited in Neuburger and Valentini (1996) are an excellent source of information regarding the attitudes that were actually held by Italian female and male terrorists active in Marxist/Communist armed resistance (as opposed to the group's stated revolutionary goals), and among other things, documents how women in the movement were perceived by their male counterparts and how they perceived themselves:

> there was no female commander and in any case aptitude for command is masculine ...
>
> (Bruno Laronga, *Prima Linea*)

> In the armed struggle women had to win equality because[,] and let us not forget it, violence has always been masculine and women have always been subjected to it.
>
> (Mario Ferrandi, *Prima Linea*)

> I am sure that for a woman to give up motherhood is terrible, the idea of not marrying because there is not time for it is terrible. A man does not have motherhood at stake. In a word, women think it over three times as much before joining the armed struggle.
>
> (Mara Aldrovandi, *Reparti Comunisti d'Attacco*)

> The women lost their true character, they were just women combatants; it was the men who mostly ran things ...
>
> ("F" a female terrorist)
> (Neuburger and Valentini, 1996, 17–19)

Thus, although the declared intention of Western left-wing radical groups to extend equality to gender relations is in sharp contrast with the tenets of right-wing groups, and indeed provided women with an avenue to engage in political violence, what actually took place between men and women in these terrorist groups was rife with contradiction.

In considering female militancy during this period, it is also important to take into consideration that while "new-left" terrorist groups fashioned themselves as "representing the people," their ranks were relatively small. Ironically, although these groups are known for their strong female presence, the absolute number of females that were engaged in them was rather limited compared to the number that would play a role in future struggles[6] – nor is there reason to believe that these groups could have recruited females in substantial numbers given that they lacked broad-based support or the extensive infrastructure necessary to enlarge their operations (more later about the role that popular support plays in sanctioning the use of females to carry out political violence). Indeed, despite their populist message, "new-left" terrorist groups neither curried nor sustained widespread favor among the populace, certainly not to the extent that many ethno-separatist and radical Islamic groups achieved subsequently – for example, according to a study conducted by the Palestinian Center for Research and Cultural Dialogue, were a popular election to be held today, 31 percent of the people surveyed would vote for Hamas, 27.1 percent for Fatah, 3 percent for Islamic Jihad, and 3 percent for the secular Popular Front for the Liberation of Palestine (Musleh and Shomaly, 2004). Thus, notwithstanding their high profile, in actuality, radical "new-left" women actually represent too small a sample from which to derive generalizations that could be considered representative of female militants.

Female militancy in more conservative societies

In primarily concentrating on leftist terrorist groups based in Western nations thus far, this chapter does not mean to imply that women living in conservative societies do not participate in political violence. On the contrary, it is well known that females were active in Palestinian liberation groups as underground fighters (Reeves, 1989, 189) during the two decades prior to the rise of religiously motivated terrorism associated with radical Islam. Two of the four Palestinian terrorists who, in May 1972, hijacked a Sabena Airlines plane in Brussels and forced it to land at Lod Airport, were women. Until the early 1980s, women in the PFLP had their own training camps in Jordan and in Lebanon, as well as separate women's sections that were counterpart to the existing male ones (Khaled, 1995). Before clerics prohibited their participation, females were involved in perhaps as many as five of the early suicide operations against Israel in Southern Lebanon (*Jane's Intelligence Review*, 2000).[7]

Rather, in cultures where gender roles are traditional, it is that much more incumbent on women and girls to improvise techniques by which they can carry out their missions while still adhering to the gender dictates of the dominant social structure. A review of the literature on women militants in traditional societies reveals a pattern whereby women combatants are viewed as equal to men in issues relating to the struggle, but not outside of it (Khaled, 1995; Helie-Lucas, 1999, 275). Indeed, it is a well-established truth of political violence that, in the name of the cause, common mores can be overridden without ultimately changing a society's fundamental values regarding gender relations.[8,9]

Khaled's observation of 20 years ago, that nationalism is the first cause, indeed seems equally relevant to the majority of politically violent struggles today in societies that do not embrace egalitarian gender-role expectations to start with. Where the two collide, nationalist aspirations take priority over feminist ones; the frequently cited reason being that equality between men and women cannot be realized under conditions of oppression, although a more trenchant analysis of the situation would include the reluctance that movement leaders and their surrounding societies have shown toward fundamentally challenging the structure of gender relations.[10]

Although some would argue that violence undertaken by secular ethno-separatist groups does not officially constitute terrorism, but more properly falls under the heading of guerrilla warfare, it is my view that many ethno-separatist groups fit within the chronicle of female terrorism that is laid out here. As McKay suggests (this volume, Chapter 10), much of the violence that is perpetrated by these groups is done with the intent of spreading terror in civilian populations, which in essence satisfies the definitional standard of terrorism. Moreover, females have and continue to engage in meting out ethno-separatist violence in large numbers, and several such groups have played an important role in the development and refinement of suicide bombing at the hands of women.

Whereas earlier "anti-imperialist" sentiment emerged predominantly in Western nations, most if not all of the secular ethno-separatist movements of the 1980s arose in non-Western societies. These groups were far more organizationally sophisticated and programmatic about recruiting female militants than the earlier secular terrorist groups. The introduction of women and girls into combat generally came about in response to logistical demands: the mounting number of casualties, the intensified crackdowns by government, and the ability of women to escape detection more easily than men. The Kurdistan Workers Party (PKK), The Shining Path, the Liberation Tigers of Tamil Eeelam (LTTE), and the Revolutionary Armed Forces of Columbia (FARC) were greatly strengthened by the influx of women and girls into their ranks, and might not have been able to sustain themselves had they not opened their doors to them.

If women and girls were initially admitted into a wider range of roles based on necessity, however, their participation gradually became integrated into the organizational structure of many such groups. Over time, the more that women and girls engaged in these less conventional roles, the more conventionality they came to assume, a theme that will be taken up in short order. As of today, females account for 30–40 percent of the fighting force in many ethno-separatist groups and serve in a wide range of leadership positions, although unlike in new-left groups, women rarely reach the highest rungs of power in them.

A central feature that distinguishes female militancy in ethno-separatist groups from their involvement in other political violence is the extent to which abduction and coercion are used as tools of recruitment. For example, McKay in Chapter 10 of this volume writes:

> during the war in Mozambique (1976–1992), the Frelimo government force recruited and gang-pressed girls to fight in the war against Renamo rebel forces. Frelimo recruiters arrived with buses at schools where they asked girls to volunteer for the military. When few agreed,

girls were forced onto buses and taken to a military base where they met with other "recruited" girls and began military training.

It is fair to say that coercive recruitment is a staple of many ethno-separatist groups, and that many females who have come to regard themselves as militants or terrorists in such struggles were initially forced to join. Although it has been argued by Victor (2004) that, in many cases, male relatives or key operatives were critical in manipulating a Palestinian female suicide bomber to martyr herself, there is no data to suggest that a formal policy of forced recruitment exists in radical Islamic groups, and certainly not one that is on par with the degree of coercion in ethno-separatist groups. The number of active females in radical Islamic groups is in fact negligible in comparison to their numbers in ethno-separatist groups.

Another feature that sets female militancy in ethno-separatist groups apart from other types of political violence is their employ of youths. Scholars concur that the use of girls and adolescents, both in a supportive capacity (as menial labor and as "wives," for example) and as combatants, is a widespread phenomenon (this volume, Chapter 10). Many females who have gone on to leadership positions have literally grown up in ethno-separatist organizations.

That said, coercion alone is not sufficient to explain the comparatively large numbers of females who have engaged in ethno-separatist struggles. Rather, the widespread poverty and lack of economic opportunity that historically have afflicted Third-World nations set the stage for females to enlist in rebel movements en masse – in essence, whereas ideology led females to associate themselves with the politically violent "new left," social opportunity has played a central role for many Third-World females.

On the most fundamental level, being part of a rebel force ensures that one's need for food and shelter are met. Such groups also afford females the chance to acquire potentially valuable skills that can later be transferred to civilian life; in addition to serving as combatants, females fill a range of roles that include intelligence gathering, disseminating propaganda, and acting as liaisons to the community; and, through these roles, develop confidence that they otherwise might not have. This is not to say that ideology plays no role in the decisions of females to enlist in these groups, but rather that there is an appeal beyond the immediate struggle. Lastly, in societies where gender roles are tightly regulated by tradition, female soldiers are afforded a degree of status, which, if only for the short run, provides some respite from the "machismo" attitude of their society (Kirk, 1997).

However, here too is found consensus among authors that women have been denied the status proportionate to their real role in the struggle (Khaled, 1995; Kirk, 1997; Helie-Lucas, 1998). For example, Kirk notes that, at its height, the fighting force of the Shining Path was 30–45 percent female, and females held prominent positions throughout the organization. However, placing these facts in context, she says: "It 'does not mean that it is feminist,' to the contrary 'It has a highly patriarchal structure, with the founder, Guzman, at the pinnacle'" (Kirk, 1997). Despite their importance to the cause, whether in traditional or non-traditional societies, the position of females engaged in political struggle is compromised due to their gender.

Lastly, although they have not been afforded much attention until recently, females have figured prominently as suicide bombers in secular struggles over the last 20 years, The LTTE, the first major secular group to follow Hizbollah in carrying out suicide terrorism (Schweitzer, 2000), has, since 1987, far exceeded Hizbollah in casualties and incidents. Although the reasons for using females in suicide missions have evolved from a variety of considerations, both secular, and most recently, religious militant groups have all traded on gender expectations that revolve around the idea that females by nature are averse to committing violence – as such they have been particularly successful in slipping through tight security arrangements under a number of guises. Indeed, over a relatively short period of time, females have come to carry out a disproportionate percentage of such missions (Schweitzer, 2000), their participation clearly being part of a military strategy aimed at inflicting maximum damage. It was only as a result of suicide attacks by Palestinian females in Israel, however, that the idea of the female suicide bomber finally entered into Western popular consciousness.

Female militancy in religious terrorism

The 1980s marked a critical juncture with regard to terrorism, the substance of which had a significant effect on female participation. It is well recognized that as new-left terrorism went into decline, Islamic terrorism began its ascendancy. The 1979 Iranian revolution, held up to Muslims around the world as a pan-Islamic movement, was intent on accepting nothing less than the worldwide implementation of Shari'a (Hoffman, 1999, 43). Force and violence were not only acceptable, but were seen as necessary for accomplishing the revolution's ends. The introduction of modern suicide terrorism by Hezbollah in 1983 was to become the trademark of other radical Islamic groups, as well as non-Muslim secular groups, adding significantly to the increased lethality of both secular and religious terrorism that would characterize the coming decades.

Two defining qualities of religious terrorism for the next 20-plus years were its lack of female participation and the specific ideology that deterred it. The analysis of fundamentalist thinking by Helie-Lucas has particular purchase for explaining the exclusion of women and girls. She describes the world that religious fundamentalist movements fight against as a world characterized by sexual disorder, one in which females are seen as encroaching on the male domain (1999, 280). According to Helie-Lucas, the fundamentalist agenda in essence incorporates a twofold mission: trying to maintain the border of the nation-state and its attending ethnic identification, but also defending the domain of masculinity (1999, 280). From this perspective, foreign powers are viewed as insurgents that must be kept out in order to maintain national survival. Hoffman (1998) has argued that violence in such a world becomes a rite of purification through which the intruding power must be purged or else society itself will be defiled.

Although female sexual purity is crucial to the underlying purity of society within a fundamentalist framework, paradoxically, at least until recently, women and girls were not considered pure enough by many to be offered up as suicide bombers in Islam – nor were other acts of political violence by women looked on favorably.[11] Historically, the waging of holy war was placed squarely on the shoulders of men.[12] Given the strict gender demarcation of the public and private sphere in Islam, the resort to violence by women and girls, rather than constituting a restorative act, amounted to a sign of cultural fragmentation. Along these lines, a woman could only hope to attain the honor associated with martyrdom on the battlefield through her sons or her husband.

It is important to note, as well, that this interpretation of the appropriate role of religious Islamic women and girls in war and terrorism has not been consistently held to either. Under Khomenei, veiled battalions of female Iranian soldiers took up arms, first in the Iranian Revolution and then in the Iran–Iraq War (Reeves, 1989). When it came to defending the Islamic Republic, Khomenei and his fellow clergy conceived of Shi'a women as "warriors of Islam" (Reeves, 1989). This thinking all but disappeared after Khomenei's death, only to emerge as a subject of fierce clerical debate within the Islamic world over the last several years when political considerations seemed to demand the participation of women.

Chechen women were the first Islamic females to engage in militancy following this virtual moratorium, and have helped to clear the way for other Islamic females to engage in *jihad*. In June 2000, Hawa Barayev blew herself up in the name of Allah.[13] Her act, besides inflicting damage on Russian targets, was designed to further radicalize the fight for independence. Hoping to disgrace men into action, she characterized them in her parting words as passive – the resort to violence by women in right-wing or religious groups is often rhetorically used to shame men, with no such parallel existing in violent left-wing groups.[14] Following Barayev's death, violence by Chechen women only grew. Of the seven suicide bombings by Chechen separatists in 2003, six were carried out by women.

Dubbed "Black Widows" because many lost their husbands, sons, or brothers to the war, the motivation of Chechen female militants has largely been characterized in terms of their grief and revenge, rather than their political agency. In truth, however, there is a dearth of information about these women and about the larger tactical considerations that inform their violence. Although they were first to put a semi-religious face on female suicide bombing in any organized fashion, it is not at all clear how religion factors into their actions or how it came to do so. Really all that is known about these women is that they have become a very effective "front line" in the Chechen struggle, have carried out the majority of Chechen suicide attacks over the last year and a half, and had a major presence in the Moscow theater and Beslan school attacks that resulted in hundreds of casualties.

That the conflict with Russia began as a secular struggle for independence (Chechnya declared itself an independent secular state in 1991 and religion was largely repressed under the Soviet Union) and only became radicalized in Islamic terms as casualties increased, explains the relative ease with which women came to participate in what only later was characterized as "jihad." Chechnya's turn to Wahhabism, fanned by Arab mercenaries, appears to be more the product of political compromise to secure funding than of a Chechen commitment to Islamic belief. A month after Barayev's suicide, Chechen rebels issued an unsigned fatwa sanctioning female suicide bombers:

> The young woman who was – inshaa-Allah – martyred, Hawa Barayev, is one of the few women whose name will be recorded in history. Undoubtedly, she has set the most marvelous example by her sacrifice. The Russians may well await death from every quarter now, and their hearts may appropriately be filled with terror on account of women like her. Let every jealous one perish in his rage! Let every sluggish individual bury his head in the dirt! She has done what few men have done.
> (Unsigned fatwa, July 2000)[15]

Hawa Barayev's suicide and the fatwa that supported it are important markers in the development of female participation in religious terrorism in that they represent trial balloons for gauging the reaction of more traditional Islamic societies to the idea of females seeking martyrdom (Cook, 2005). Rather than being met with unified opprobrium, Barayev's act spurred debate, which gradually grew into acceptance of the idea. In essence, Barayev's act set a precedent, which could be used to legitimize such acts in the future. The following year (August 2001), with the Chechen example as its backdrop, the more conservative High Islamic Council in Saudi Arabia issued its own fatwa encouraging Palestinian women to become suicide bombers.

Although, to date, Al Qaeda has not publicly sanctioned the use of female militants in direct combatant activities, anecdotal reports suggest its increasing readiness to move in that direction. Although there is no hard evidence to support this, anecdotal reports have surfaced that imply such a trend. For example, in March 2003, *Asharq Al-Awsat*, a Saudi-owned paper, published an interview with a woman calling herself "Um Osama," the mother of Osama. Claiming to be the leader of the women Mujahedeen of Al Qaeda, Um Osama stated:

> We are preparing for the new strike announced by our leaders and I declare that it will make America forget ... the September 11 attacks.

The idea came from the success of martyr operations carried out by young Palestinian women in the occupied territories. Our organization is open to all Muslim women wanting to serve the [Islamic] nation ... particularly in this very critical phase.

(Al Jazeerah News, 2003)

Whoever Um Osama really is, her words underscore a recognized reality, namely, that were Al Qaeda to deploy female operatives, these women would have an easier time evading security measures. Most important to note is that the prohibitions that kept Islamic females from participating in *jihad* have been significantly loosened and fewer hurdles, religious or cultural, stand in the way of their involvement now. As such, there is good reason to assume that it is only a matter of time before Al Qaeda exploits this resource.

Rhetorical strategies for justifying females engaging in martyrdom

This section considers the concept of martyrdom as framed by the secular LTTE, and the radical Islamist groups, Hamas and Islamic Jihad, paying particular attention to the core rhetorical strategies that each uses to confer martyrdom status on females. The analysis that scholar Peter Schalk advances with regard to the LTTE in large part serves as the foundation for my own analysis concerning Hamas and Islamic Jihad. The specific contribution of this chapter, beyond fleshing out Hamas and Islamic Jihad's thinking along these lines, lies in the development of the idea that secular and religious militant groups utilize surprisingly similar rhetorical strategies to condone females carrying out suicide missions. When breaking with conventional behavior where gender relations are concerned (women committing violence and appropriating martyr status), the secular terrorist group and the religious terrorist group alike must historicize itself in such a way that its actions are not viewed as a rupture from "decent" behavior but, rather, a transition whereby an old gender value is seen as being given new expression (Schalk, 1997a).

Although advocating markedly different blueprints for structuring society, the LTTE on the one hand, and Hamas and Islamic Jihad on the other, both rely heavily on the traditional past in some form or fashion to confer legitimacy on female suicide bombers. As Schalk explains with regard to the secular LTTE, "new things in an old culture have to still be rationalized with reference to old values if they are not to appear anomalous" (1994, 177). He suggests that secular groups attempt to do this by calling up the vision of a glorious cultural past – that is, an imagined "golden age" before the perceived historical social and cultural degradation of a people took place. Religious movements do this par excellence by introducing the new as an extension of "the sacred" – suicide terrorism, for example, is cast as a new form of waging *jihad*, an act of righteous standing in Islam. To maintain continuity with a culture's collective identity, the source, although not necessarily the form, of that which is "new" is "found" in the past. In essence, each group, whether secular or religious, must ask itself, 'What do we need of the distant and even the recent past to sanction female martyrdom in the present and the future?'

Thus, what would otherwise be interpreted as aberrant behavior becomes contextualized in a history of accepted ideas. The female martyr is constructed as embracing culturally accepted gender norms at the same time that she steps outside of them – she is modest, chaste, and a purveyor of family honor in her personal life, whereas she is fierce, courageous, and the equal of men in the name of the cause.

It is critical, however, to keep in mind that the collective past is a social construction. Social remembering is a discursive process that is as much about the present as it is about invoking or re-telling history. Although depending on a connection with actual events, the collective past is nonetheless always in a state of revision. Schalk (1997b, 38), in the context of LTTE, argues that, tradition, as a marker, is "constructed and imagined or invented" to serve a function at different times (1997b, 38). To this end, he argues that memory plays an important role in its capacity to supplant history – "What is in the memory is identity" and "it is the inflation of memory as history" (1997b, 38) that makes the contemporary act a signifier of the past (and renews and confirms it). In such negotiations, female martyrdom gets recast in terms of historical experiences, both near and distant, whose details, simultaneously memorialized and lost to time, come to evoke the feeling that a related claim in the present carries truth.

In essence, the logic that the suicide bomber qua female martyr narrative engenders is built on a trans-historical structure that resounds deeply, lends itself to being imagined and embraced communally, and creates participation structures that encourage increasing violence. The seemingly universal social and psychological inclination to "perform" tradition is a useful tool in uniting popular support behind these groups and in attracting new followers. Were the surrounding populace to conceive of female suicide bombing as wholly alien and offensive to basic cultural sensibilities, it would undermine the critical mass of popular support that such groups require to carry on their militant activities.

With these ideas in mind, the next section illustrates something of how LTTE, Hamas, and Islamic Jihad have each come to rationalize female suicide bombing. Unfortunately, what is known about the martyrdom ideology of these groups is mostly limited to their public statements because it is difficult at best for observers to have direct contact with persons in the leadership structure of these organizations or with female militants themselves. Even when such rare exchanges occur, observers remain outsiders and there is good reason to suspect that the access they receive is structured so that they disseminate the group's chosen message rather than reveal its inner workings.

The secular case

LTTE was formed in 1976 under the leadership of Velupillai Pirabaharan (Hoffman and McCormick, 2004) to counter what were deemed to be discriminatory practices by the Sinhala majority and with the purpose of creating an independent Tamil state in the north and east of the island – the group was constituted four years after British Ceylon was re-named Sri Lanka in the language of Sinhalese. The integration of women and girls into fighting proceeded slowly so as not to offend the cultural values and sensibility of the society at large. On its Internet homepage, where its philosophy and historical narrative are laid out, the LTTE talks of how expectations regarding the role of females in military combat within Tamil, and within Hindu culture, had to be adjusted to accommodate the present circumstances (LTTE homepage, 1995–2004). It underscores that, like in most cultures, Tamil and Hindu culture glorifies motherhood and not the participation of women in combat. Thus, it explains that females were initially relegated to non-combatant roles as nurses, doing administrative work, and in the kitchen. The document exhibits the LTTE's understanding of the power that established tradition has, and the need to pay homage to it.

However, in Hindu mythology, there is also a tradition of women who participate in battle, and more recently, of female cadres in the Indian National Army – formed during World War II by nationalists seeking India's independence from the British Empire. Interestingly, like the later LTTE, it had its own organized suicide squad. It is in the context of this historical line that Schalk suggests the idea of war and peace as the concern of both sexes gets rationalized, and through it, the notion of a Tamil female "martial psyche" is established (1994, 174); the female LTTE fighters of today become, in essence, the latest expression of females waging battle in that line. In the LTTE philosophy, the flow of time between Sathyabama, Krishna's wife fighting by his side, and the making of a Tamil Tigress, is portrayed as an unfolding that is both natural and predictable. The more contemporary vision, which connects liberation on the national front with liberation of Tamil women (part of the stated LTTE vision), is then superimposed by the LTTE on the more transcendent one. It is important not to forget, however, as Schalk points out, that, although a narrative makes sense, it is not necessarily true, although it does suggest a permanent collective identity (1997b, 38).

Schalk argues that the LTTE frames the new social role of fighting women qua liberated women as mitigated by the classical Tamil concept of *karpu* – learned behavior or restraint – a value suggestive of chastity. Indeed, on all occasions other than when their military projects are coordinated, the sexes remain segregated within the LTTE. Females live in separate camps, run their own military organization, and plan their own projects. Marriage is also prohibited for women before the age of 25. Schalk contends that the incarnation of an LTTE female warrior as a kind of "secluded armed virgin" (Schalk, 1994, 179) makes her martial actions more acceptable to the popular understanding of correct female behavior, removing certain gender distinctions, although leaving other ones safely in place. Although these accommodations have not wholly stifled the debate over whether the role of female, armed freedom fighter is "natural," they have gone far toward minimizing the sense that such behavior will lead to a major disruption in the social order as it is known.

According to Joshi (2000), the average age of recruits in the LTTE's Black Tiger suicide unit has ranged between 14-to-16 years old, and 30-to-40 percent of the LTTE's suicide terrorism has been carried out by females (the group's secular nature permits it to create such statistics). To date, females have carried out more suicide bombings in its name than in the name of any other group. Unlike in radical Islamic groups, martyrdom has not been differentially scripted for male and female cadres. There does not appear to have been any point in the organization's history when females were refused the distinction of martyr once they were permitted to engage in combat. Although the group has been in a relatively peaceful phase since signing a cease-fire in February 2002, prior to that, for example, suicide bombers of both genders would take their last meal with LTTE leader Prabhakaran. After their deaths, the honorific title of "ma~virar," or "Great Hero," would be applied to both equally.

It is important to note that Adele Balasingham, a sociologist and wife to Anton Balasingham, a close political advisor to Prabhakaron, contests the assertion by Schalk that LTTE maintains the concept of the "armed virgin." Balasingham draws the female martyr as a wholly willing subject. Nor, given the secular nature of the group's belief structure (in contrast to radical Islamic groups), is the promise of a blissful afterlife the incentive to kill or be killed. Rather, the act of defending Tamil life against its perceived enemies is cast as the driving force – martyrdom in this framework is "knowing" what is deemed a purposeful death. Balasingham writes, "It is in the context of the redemption of the collective life at the expense of individual life that martyrs are honored" (2001, 289). Nor do women seek martyrdom to become pure after meeting with some degradation, as has been suggested with regard to several of the Palestinian female recruits (Victor, 2004). Nor is the grief and revenge of the Chechen female suicide bombers cited as a major justification. It could be argued that the motivation of LTTE females to embrace killing and death, compared to other militant groups is, for these reasons, most fully constructed in political terms.

Yet, at the same time that the LTTE organization celebrates females for their valor, it also goes to pains to maintain the image of them as caring and soft outside of combat. As Balasingham writes, "behind the appearance of every uniformed female fighter, is a tender, gentle and passionate young women with all the qualities attributed to femininity" (2001). LTTE female combatants are constructed not as abandoning their femininity but, rather, as suspending it on a situational basis – they maintain the innate qualities of femininity as recognized by the culture that surrounds them, even as they kill. Every militant group must similarly find a way to expand the definition of femininity to include the conduct of violence.

The religious case

Although the Israeli–Palestinian conflict has produced over 150 suicide bombings, the large majority of them during the Second Intifada alone, before 27 January 2002, females had not carried out any of them. Although in disagreement about the permissibility of suicide terrorism, Sunnis and Shi'as both took the position that holy war should be left to men. As noted earlier, the Palestinian struggle's long secular roots were infused with religious aims only after the Iranian Revolution. The shift carried great significance for the topic at hand, because at the heart of religious fundamentalist policies stands the interpretation of women's roles. Prior to the shift, Palestinian women had been engaged in combat against the British dating back to the 1930s. For the next three decades, they remained an active part of the movement to reclaim Palestinian land, culminating in their systematic military training under the auspices of the Al-Nakbah women's movement in the 1960s.

Although there are instances of women being labeled martyrs in early Islamic history (the first person to suffer death for Islam was actually a woman, Sumayah Zawjat Yasir[16]) – 15 until over a year into the Second Intifada – the dominant interpretation of the classical religious and legal canon was that women were unsuited for the mission.[17] Such a call to duty was not thought to befit feminine nature. Koranic teachings largely relegated women and girls' lives to the domestic sphere. The relatively few accounts of women engaging in direct combat in the classical literature were historically understood as uncommon acts of valor under uncommon circumstances legitimized on that basis alone.

What female involvement existed at the beginning of the Intifada was scaled back and more tightly controlled once terrorist organizations took a leading role in the uprising, a little over a year into it. In particular, Hamas and Islamic Jihad were quick to gain power in the streets as the insurrection became more organized and radicalized. Both organizations moved in to fill the economic vacuum that arose as Israel increasingly cordoned the Palestinian territories off, jerryrigging what semblance of a social service infrastructure they could muster. Not surprisingly, the emphasis on religious practice grew enormously under these organizations, as did the authority and influence of Islamic clerics. The pressure on females to follow a strict code of modesty was also much more widely felt. Yet, despite the ascendancy of conservative forces, there were females who both took to the streets and served as accomplices as the world outside their windows crumbled. Initially, at demonstrations, females remained at a distance from young males, although over time they came to occupy supportive roles such as providing boys with stones, serving as lookouts, or even throwing stones themselves. So as not to flout social customs, females had to uphold normative ideals, although at the same time try to convince society of their distinguished contribution to the struggle when that was permitted. Behavior that would have been taken for immodesty given the conservative gender arrangements of Palestinian Muslim society took on different meaning as the "occupation" progressed.

The Second Intifada was even more dominated by Hamas and Islamic Jihad as they took the lead in suicide terrorism. Arafat, who initially had been reluctant to embrace suicide missions, eventually had to change tack as his grip on public opinion and the street loosened. Some suggest that in an effort to resolve his floundering control over the Palestinian Authority, he reached out to engage women in the struggle. In a break with Hamas and Islamic Jihad, on 27 January 2002, he convened a crowd of reportedly more than a thousand women and invited them to join the armed resistance against Israeli occupation. Beyond designating these women as his "army of roses," he took the additional step of calling for their participation in suicide missions with the words, "shahida all the way to Jerusalem" (Victor, 2004). Indeed, it was on the same afternoon as Arafat's speech that Wafa Idris became the first female to blow herself up in the name of the Palestinian struggle.

The participation of Palestinian females in suicide missions, however, was not as sudden as it appeared. Women had been used by Palestinian terrorist organizations during the Second Intifada to support suicide attacks by men. For example, the Hamas operative who carried out the Sbarro restaurant bombing on 9 August 2001 was driven to his destination by Ahlam Tamini, the same woman who on 30 July 2001 set off a small explosive charge hidden in a beer can at a Jerusalem supermarket. Hamas also sent Iman Asha to detonate an explosive device at a Tel Aviv bus station on 3 August 2001. Neither of these women, however, intended to die, nor did they, in the course of carrying out their operation.

Having no religious stricture to bar them, Al-Aqsa Martyrs Brigade, part of Arafat's secular Fatah group, began recruiting females for suicide missions at the beginning of the Second Intifada. In relatively quick succession, Al-Aqsa initiated and subsequently claimed responsibility for the first four female suicide bombings between the period of January and May 2002, and was reputed to have started a special unit for female suicide bombers named for Wafa Idris. However, although the trajectory leading up to the bombings provides a critical context for understanding the cultural and political forces in play and the events that unfolded, it is not Arafat's rhetoric that the author takes as the primary concern. Rather, it is the rhetorical turns (grounded in religious argumentation) used by Hamas and Islamic Jihad to justify females waging "*jihad*," that is of specific interest.

Indeed, after some initial ambivalence, Hamas and Islamic Jihad, in conjunction with a long list of high-ranking clerics throughout the Islamic world, went on public record to express strong support for women carrying out suicide missions and their eligibility for martyrdom status. Doing a complete about-face from his earlier stated views on the subject, Hamas leader Abd al-Aziz Rantisi described the attacks as the most important "strategic weapon" of the Palestinian resistance (Rantisi, 2002). He stated, "There is no reason that the perpetration of suicide attacks should be monopolized by men" (as quoted in *Suicide Terrorism: Rationalizing the Irrational Strategic Insights*, III, 8, August 2003). Clearly, it was not an epiphany that led to such a highly unconventional reading of the body of religious doctrine, but seeing the tactical and symbolic advantages that female suicide bombers had for the struggle. Yet Sheikh Hassan Yussef, a Hamas leader in the West Bank, insisted otherwise, noting, "We do not act according to the opinion of the street or of society. We are men of principle ... [and act] according to what our religion dictates" (as quoted in *Al-Sha'ab* (Egypt), 2002).

So as not to appear to be overturning normative values, especially those surrounding gender relations, these otherwise forbidden acts by women were redrawn in three ways. First, they were rationalized as desperate measures for desperate times. In this context, although the bombings symbolized a deviation from proper gender roles, Hamas, like LTTE, left intact the traditional understanding of what proper gender roles in normal times should be. The female bombers were essentially characterized in terms of their military function as defenders of Islam, not by their stepping outside of accepted social norms, which would tend to undermine it.

Second, the bombings were historicized in the context of women militants in the past, with the recent women militants seen as completing their path. Like the LTTE, Hamas selectively appropriated early Islamic history so that the current situation could be analogously framed with reference to the traditional past. For example, Sheikh Abu Al-Hassan based his sanction of female suicide bombing on well-known "acts of female Jihad" during the raids led by the Prophet Muhammad:

> The Prophet's aunt came down from the women's citadel, and fought a man from among the infidels who had climbed up the citadel. She killed him, but took care to protect Islamic morality by refraining from stripping and disarming him.
>
> (As quoted in *Afaq Arabiya* (Egypt), 2002)

Lastly, the female suicide bomber was elevated to a level in which she was in some way made awe-inspiring – there was talk of the purity and beauty that Wafa Idris exuded with her bomb strapped to her body. In this sense, she and her deed become transcendent, and any contingency associated with her being female was relegated to the background. Dareen Abu Aisheh, the second female Palestinian suicide bomber, was celebrated for her deep piety.

Hanadi Jadarat, the sixth female Palestinian suicide bomber, was touted for her unusual "brilliance." Rather than being disgraced, these females were idealized, their missions built on one another, and in so doing, created a kind of chain event, which encouraged the incidence of future acts.

To make the breach with traditional gender arrangements more palatable to Palestinian society, clerics speaking on the matter also made adjustments to the suicide bomber narrative where needed. For example, women would not receive the same reward as men upon entering paradise. A woman was said to have one eternal husband because it fit her nature.[18] Initially, Sheikh Yassin, the spiritual leader of Hamas, asserted that women were only allowed to act in such a mission if chaperoned by a man (*Al Sharq al-Awsat* (London), 2002), although several days later (*Al Sharq al-Awsat* (London), 2002) he rescinded his first statement and issued a second one saying that women could proceed alone if not unaccompanied for more than 24 hours.

A superficial consideration of the eight Palestinian females who have successfully carried out suicide missions could lead to the interpretation that who gets selected also inadvertently serves to reinforce traditional gender values and norms in Muslim society. It has been suggested that each suicide bomber was chosen because in some way she failed to meet or deviated from gender expectations, and that each was motivated by the thought of restoring her honor (Victor, 2004). For instance, Andalib Suleiman al-Taqatiqah (#5) and Reem al-Riyashi (#7) were said to have been involved in extramarital affairs, and Wafa Idris (#1) was divorced and unable to bear a child. The implicit message was that terrorist organizations do not cross the line to recruit "true" Muslim women.

To determine the merit of this position would require more data, not only about female bombers but about the selection and motivation of male bombers as well. Nevertheless, to show that these eight females were exploited or sought out their suicide missions in desperation still would not explain the reported interest that Palestinian female youths across a wide spectrum of demographics express in becoming martyrs. As Hamas senior leader Abd al-Aziz al-Rantisi has stated:

> thousands of our women are looking forward to the day on which they can make a sacrifice on behalf of the children, women and elderly who are being killed daily. ... This is a craving, a wave of craving among women.
>
> (As quoted in an interview granted to CNN, 2004)

The framing of female suicide missions as a form of sacrifice has been a successful rhetorical strategy to define the act in terms consonant with accepted gender expectations and, as such, to make the act more palatable to society. Rather than being perceived as a display of female inhumanity, which Palestinian society would be hard pressed to accept, a female who offers her life in this context is seen as engaging in the most profound form of selflessness. Giving life to a Palestinian state is privileged even over motherhood. This at least seems to be the working principle for women who do not leave children behind.

Of the eight female Palestinian suicide missions, the populace least embraced the one carried out by Reem al-Riyashi. The only female bomber sent by Hamas to date, Riyashi was a mother of two children, one an infant, the other three years old. The sense of her death as a selfless act was mitigated by the impact that it would have on the two young children she was leaving behind. [19] The disapproval that was voiced stands as an indication that, although Palestinian society has widely accepted the use of female suicide bombers, there are limits to what it will tolerate where females are concerned. Such operations, and the groups that back them, cannot exist without a critical mass of popular support. Thus, if it is in fact true that there are countless women and adolescents who are willing to carry out suicide missions in the future, it seems reasonable to assume that they will continue to be selected with public opinion in mind.

Conclusion

This chapter has tried to provide a multifocal discussion and analysis of the involvement of females in the conduct of modern terrorism. Starting with a brief historical overview of the subject organized around major trends, it went on to consider the different ideological mindsets that account for why females have overwhelmingly been associated with ethno-separatist terrorist groups rather than religious ones. Given the shift of the last decade, whereby females have become more accepted if not enthusiastically welcomed by terrorist groups fueled by religious extremism, it then took a comparative look at the rhetorical strategies used by both types of groups (secular and religious) to legitimize female participation in violence, particularly suicide bombing. The chapter's intent has been to contribute to a deeper understanding of how such groups and the societies they depend on for popular support create, define, and reinforce new social spaces and categories that facilitate such operations.

Despite the very different worlds that secular and religious terrorism have sought to create, one modern, the other traditional, based on an extensive review of the literature, this author found that both kinds of groups fall back on many of the same rhetorical strategies. Both kinds of groups, while sanctioning a deviation from proper gender roles, leave intact the traditional understanding of what proper gender roles in normal times should be. The reproduction of normative gender values is critical to achieving the popular support base necessary for sustaining a culture of female martyrdom.

This chapter concludes that, to avoid their forbidden acts appearing alien to cultural sensibilities, secular and religious groups redraw the behavior of females who commit violence in three ways: both types of groups rationalize female behavior as desperate measures for desperate times; each historicizes the acts of contemporary female militants in the context of female militants who came before them; and, lastly, such acts are justified by elevating the female suicide bomber to a level in which she becomes awe-inspiring – whether due to her beauty, brilliance, or piety. In this sense, the deed and she become transcendent and any contingency associated with her being female is relegated to the background.

It is important to underscore here that there is little convincing evidence in the literature that female involvement in religious terrorist organizations represents a progressive trend in gender relations, because, despite their resort to violence, females appear to be no less bound to traditional codes. The observation appears no less relevant for secular struggles except in cases where a widely supported women's liberation movement already exists.

In the end, this chapter calls for greater research on women and girls engaged in terrorism and other political violence. This author believes that there is a pressing need to study how factors that have traditionally been taken into account when studying males who commit terrorism conspire to affect women, in addition to analyzing those factors that are gender-specific to women. Such inquiry would be of practical significance where counterterrorism efforts are concerned and would undoubtedly provide further insight into terrorism in general.

Notes

1 Modern international terrorism is widely accepted as having been ushered in on 23 July 1968 when the Popular Front for the Liberation of Palestine (PFLP) hijacked an Israeli El Al plane in Rome – the pilot was forced to fly to Algiers but there were no fatalities. From that point forward, hijackings, bombings, and kidnappings of elites for ransom became the métier for terrorist groups to show their strength and make their agendas known on the international stage. Whereas the threat of violence initially sufficed to achieve these ends, by 1972 deadly force was on a meteoric rise that continued its ascent until 1979 (Lessor *et al.*, 1999, 32). Terrorists of this period were frequently described as coming to terrorism through an intellectual commitment to radical politics rather than social deprivation or religious fervor (Taylor and Quayle, 1994, 136). Most groups considered themselves to be populist movements – their platform was anti-imperialist, anti-capitalist, and, almost always, anti-American. Accordingly, terrorist activities of this period bore the label of "ideological terrorism." Although all terrorism has an ideological foundation, it is terrorism associated with an intellectual secular tradition rather than a sacred one that characterizes the terrorism of this period.
2 Terrorist activities of ethno-separatist groups, both then and now, tend to be less international in scope (Hoffman, 1998, 42). In line with their raison d'être, the political agenda of this type of group is more narrowly focused on a single nation-state and routinely articulated in the confines of its social space. The assassination by ETA terrorists of Aldo Moro, the Spanish Prime Minister, and his bodyguards in 1973, for instance, brought unprecedented attention to the Basque separatist cause. In cases where the separatist group views itself to be under foreign occupation by a power whose interests are supported by other nation-states, like the Palestinians in the Middle East, separatist struggles by

their very nature become international. The PLFP and the JRA attack at Lod Airport had Marxist, anti-capitalist, and separatist underpinnings, and was an international incident because it took place on Israeli soil and many of its victims were Puerto Ricans on a pilgrimage to the Holy Land (Lessor *et al.*, 1999, iii). The common denominator among ethnic-separatist groups demanding their own rival states, or radical political ones wishing to topple and replace an extant government with a more progressive one in its image, was the secular nature of their struggles.

3 Although the title refers specifically to women in order to make use of a play-on-words, this chapter recognizes the participation of girls and adolescents as combatants in violent struggles around the world, and that their acts meet the definition of terrorism (see McKay, this volume, Chapter 10) – beyond perpetrating death or harm, they are symbolic and seek to instill fear, in addition to being aimed at non-combatants.

4 Not an insignificant number of the post-colonial groups waging the struggle for nationhood favored socialism as their old rulers were capitalists (Lessor *et al.*, 1999, 97). Of the 13 terrorist groups most active in 1968, the majority were ideologically Marxist–Leninist. The remainder were ethno-nationalist separatists fighting to win greater representation or separate statehood for ethnic minorities. These included: the Basque, ETA (Euzkadi Ta Askatasuna); the Catalan, Terra Liure (Our Earth); the Breton, Liberation Front in France; and the Fronte Paesanu Corsu di Liberazione (FPCL) – interestingly, some of the most virulent separatist struggles of the day brewed within Western nations (Gurr, 2000).

5 A wide range of American right-wing extremist groups have successfully encouraged female involvement over the last several years to the point where many, like the Aryan Resistance Movement (ARM), boast separate sister organizations (Women for Aryan Unity). Yet, the concept of gendered difference is still central to the philosophy of these groups. See Blee (2002) and Dobratz and Shanks-Meile (2000) for a close analysis of changing women's roles in such groups. David Duke was supposedly the first Klan leader to welcome women as equal members (ADL, 1988b, 84, as noted in Dobratz and Shanks-Meile (2000, 88)). See Blee (1991) with regard to how women's roles have been relegated historically in such groups. For a broader discussion, see Sarkar and Butalia (1995).

6 Compared, for example, to later ethno-separatist groups such as the Sandinista National Liberation Front (FSLN) in Nicaragua, the Farabundo Marti National Liberation Forces (FMLN) in El Salvador, the Guatemalan National Revolutionary Unity (URNG) in Guatemala, and The Shining Path in Peru. In many of these struggles, women make up 30 percent of the fighting force and serve not only as combatants but also in leadership roles with men under their command. For example, FARC is estimated to have 18,000 fighters with 45 percent being female. In some cases, women and girls joined of their own free will and in other cases their initial entry to the group was involuntary.

7 According to Beyler (2003), as noted in the Merari database, on 9 April 1985, Khyadali Sana drove a car with bombs that exploded near an IDF convoy in Bater Al Shuf Jezzin, killing two soldiers and wounding two others. On 9 July 1985, Kharib Ibtisam carried out a suicide attack at a SLA post in the Ras Al Bayda security zone, wounding several though killing none. On 11 September 1985, Khaierdin Miriam carried out a suicide attack in Hatzbaya, Lebanon, on a SLA checkpoint, wounding two people. On 26 November 1985, Al Taher Hamidah carried out a suicide attack on an SLA checkpoint, in the Falous village of Jezzin, in South Lebanon, On 17 July 1986, Norma Abu Hassan carried out a suicide attack in Jezzin Lebanon targeting Lebanese agents. On 14 November 1987, Shagir Karima Mahmud detonated an explosive charge in

Beirut, killing seven people and injuring 20. On 11 November 1987, Sahyouni Soraya carried out a similar attack at Beirut airport, killing six and injuring 73. The last two charges were reportedly activated by a remote control, leaving it open to question whether these women intended to die during their mission. On 20 April 1985, with almost no chance of escape, Loula Aboud opened fire on Israeli soldiers so her comrades could get away.

8 According to Khaled:

> within these organizations, women were equal to male comrades in terms of rights and duties, but this arrangement did not carry over to social responsibilities. The everyday social world was treated as a personal concern that was outside of the domain of the struggle for independence.
>
> (1999)

Several authors have noted the tendency for women to be only equal with men in issues relating to the struggle, but not in everything (Khaled, 1995; Helie-Lucas, 1999). There is a consensus among authors that, although military action provides an opportunity for women in ethno-national political struggles to demonstrate that they are able to perform the same duties as men on the national liberation stage, it alone cannot give women their liberty until their society is liberated (Khaled, 1995, 1999; Helie-Lucas, 1999).

9 The notable exceptions where the struggle for national rights and women's rights in leftist groups have been linked together do not fit within this theory – in the 1960s and 1970s in societies where there was an active feminist and student protest movement, the dynamics within radical political groups were more progressive. The liberation of women's roles, for example, was seen as integral to the new social order being fought for by the Weather Underground in the United States (Jacobs, 1997). Linda Evans and Susan Rosenberg were active agents in carrying out several bombings aimed at protesting policies of the United States to which the group was opposed (Jacobs, 1997). Although Khaled and other women revolutionaries have argued that all women are oppressed in all societies, there is evidence that societies with more egalitarian gender relations to start with are more likely to accommodate women's gains in status outside of the movement.

10 For example, women participated in the Algerian armed struggle but, due to long-standing cultural values and the failure of the new regime to support women's individual rights, their role receded after independence (Helie-Lucas, 1999). More recently, Khaled has argued that the problem of women's rights cannot be solved while Palestinians are under occupation as they have no real authority to make laws that could be adopted and enforced by a state (1995).

11 For example, until the Erev Crossing bombing at the hands of Reem al-Rayishi, Hamas had been unwavering in its position against using females to carry out suicide missions. Al-Rayishi is said to have approached Hamas on several occasions before Sheik Yassin personally agreed to the mission. Yassin noted, "For the first time, Hamas used a female fighter and not a male fighter." Yassin told reporters, "It is a new development in resistance against the enemy. ... Resistance will escalate against this enemy until they leave our land and homeland" (JPost.com, 2004). Hamas also turned away Dareen Abu Aisheh, the second female Palestinian bomber, and subsequently she was taken up on her offer by Al-Aqsa Martyrs Brigade.

12 For further explication, see the chapter by David Cook in this volume.

13 Hawa Barayev was the cousin of Arbi Barayev, a militant leader in the struggle. Also see Pravda (2003).

14 Women have goaded men by calling them "eunuchs."

15 The Islamic Ruling on the Permissibility of Martyrdom Operations: Did Hawa Barayev Commit Suicide or Achieve Martyrdom? Although unsigned, the fatwa is widely accepted as being the statement of Chechen militants.
16 Sumaya was one of the first seven people in the Prophet's inner circle to declare her faith to Islam. She was killed when she refused to publicly relinquish her faith. Her death was avenged, which the Prophet is said to look well upon.
17 For further explication, see the chapter by David Cook in this volume.
18 The implication is that, as it fit her nature, she was satisfied with that arrangement.
19 It is important to note that Reem al-Riyashi was thrown out of her home several months before the attack for having an affair with a neighbor and disowned by her family, and even her lover.

References

Afaq Arabiya (Egypt). January 30, 2002. As cited in MEMRI: Inquiry and Analysis Series, No. 83: *Wafa Idris: The Celebration of the First Female Palestinian Suicide Bomber* (Part I). Online, available from: http://216.239.39.104/search?q=cache: 0mAtNzDg3GUJ:www.memri.org/bin/articles.cgi%3FArea%3Djihad%26ID%3 DIA8302+%22according+to+what+our+religion+dictates%22&hl=en (accessed September 12, 2004).

Al Jazeerah News. 2003. "Bin Laden Has Set Up Female Suicide Squads: Report," *Arab News*, Dubai, March 13, 2003. Staff writer. Online, available from: www.aljazeerah.info/News%20archives/2003%20News%20archives/March%202 003%20News/13%20News/Bin%20Laden%20has%20set%20up%20female%20 suicide%20squads%20%20aljazeerah.info.htm (accessed October 12, 2004).

Al-Sha'ab (Egypt). February 1, 2002. As cited in MEMRI: Inquiry and Analysis Series, No. 83: *Wafa Idris: The Celebration of the First Female Palestinian Suicide Bomber* (Part I). Online, available from: http://216.239.39.104/search?q=cache: 0mAtNzDg3GUJ:www.memri.org/bin/articles.cgi%3FArea%3Djihad%26ID%3 DIA8302+%22according+to+what+our+religion+dictates%22&hl=en (access September 20, 2004).

Anti-Defamation League (ADL). 1988b. *Extremist on the Right*. New York: ADL.

Ardovini-Brooker, Joanne. 2000. "Terrorism," in *Encyclopedia of Women and Crime*, Nicole Rafter (ed.). Phoenix: Oryx Press, 258–259.

Arquilla, John and Ronfeldt, David. 1999. *Networks, Netwar, and Information Age Terrorism in Countering the New Terrorism*, Lessor, Ian, Hoffman, Bruce, *et al.* (eds). California: RAND.

Balasingham, Adele. 2001. *The Will to Freedom: an Inside View of Tamil Resistance.* Mitcham: Fairmax Publishing.

Basu, Amrita. 1997. "Hindu women's activism and the questions it raises," in *Appropriating Gender: Women's Activism and Politicized Religion in South Asia*, Amrita Basu and Patricia Jeffrey (eds). New York: Routledge, 3–14.

Beyler, Clara. 2003. *Chronology of Suicide Bombings Carried out by Women*. Online, available from: www.ict.org.il (accessed October 9, 2004).

Blee, Katherine. 1991. *Women of the Klan: Racism and Gender in the 1920s*. Berkeley: University of California Press.

Blee, Katherine. 2002. *Inside Organized Racism: Women in the Hate Movement*. Berkeley: University of California Press.

CNN interview. January 23, 2004. As cited in Intelligence and Terrorism Information Center at the Center for Special Studies: Special Information Bulletin, January 2004. Online, available from: http://64.233.161.104/search?q=cache: CZKjrZY6FM0J:www.intelligence.org.il/eng/tr/erez_2_04.htm+%22thousands+ of+our+women+are+looking+forward+to+the+day%22&hl=en (accessed 10.20.30).

Dobratz, Betty and Shanks-Meile, Stephanie. 2000. *The White Separatist Movement in the United States: White Power, White Pride*. Baltimore: Johns Hopkins Press.

Gurr, Ted. 2000. *Peoples Versus States: Minorities at Risk in the New Century*. Washington, DC: United States Institute of Peace.

Handel, Joel. 1990. "Socioeconomic profile of an American terrorist: 1960's and 1970's." *Terrorism*, 13, 195–213.

Helie-Lucas, Marieme. 1999. "Women, nationalism, and religion in the Algerian liberation struggle," in *Rethinking Fanon: the Continuing Dialogue*, Nigel Gibson (ed.). Amherst, NY: Humanity Books.

Hoffman, Bruce. 1998. *Inside Terrorism*. New York: Columbia University Press.

Hoffman, Bruce. 1999. "Terrorism, trends and prospects," in *Countering the New Terrorism*, Lessor, Ian, Hoffman, Bruce, Arquilla, John, *et al.* (eds). Santa Monica, CA: RAND, 7–35.

Hoffman, Bruce and McCormick, Gordon. 2004. "Terrorism, signaling, and suicide attack." *Studies in Conflict and Terrorism*, 27(4) (July–August), 243–281.

Jacobs, Ron. 1997. *The Way the Wind Blew: a History of the Weather Underground*. London/New York: Verso Press.

Jane's Intelligence Review. October 20, 2000. Online, available from: www.janes.com/ security/international_security/news/usscole/jir001020_1_n.shtml (accessed September 14, 2004).

Jenkins, Brian. 1999. "Foreword," in *Countering the New Terrorism*, Lessor, Ian, Hoffman, Bruce, Arquilla, John, *et al.* (eds). Santa Monica, CA: RAND, iii–xiv.

Joshi, C.L. 2000. "Sri Lanka: Suicide Bombers." *Far Eastern Economic Review*, June 1, 2000. Online, available from: http://216.239.39.104/search?q=cache:aEKqRESw CTEJ:www.essex.ac.uk/armedcon/Countries/Asia/Texts/SriLanka011.htm+joshi+ %22far+eastern+economic+review%22+2000+recruits&hl=en (accessed September 2, 2004).

The Islamic Ruling on the Permissibility of Martyrdom Operations: Did Hawa Barayev Commit Suicide or Achieve Martyrdom? Online, available from: http://64.233.161.104/search?q=cache:PRvfixqkL2IJ:www.religioscope.com/pdf/ martyrdom.pdf+did+hawa+barayev+commit&hl=en (accessed December 17, 2004).

Israel Ministry of Foreign Affairs. January 2003. "The role of Palestinian women in suicide bombing," as quoted in Julian Madsen, *Suicide Terrorism: Rationalizing the Irrational Strategic Insights*, Volume III, Issue 8 (August 2004). Online, available at: www.ccc.nps.navy.mil/si/2004/aug/madsenAug04.asp#references.

JPost.Com. 2004. "Report: Yassin Personally Authorized Woman Bomber." January 15 2004. Online, available from: www.jpost.com/servlet/satellite? pagename=JPost/JPArticle/ShowFull&cid=1074140311992&p=1008596981749 (accessed October 12, 2004).

Khaled, Laila. 1995. "Arm the spirit." Online, available from: www.pflppal.org/ opinion/interviews/khaled/arm.html (accessed August 25, 2004).

Khaled, Laila. 1999. "I made the ring from a bullet and a pin of a hand grenade."

Online, available from: www.pflp-pal.org/opinion/interviews/khaled/made.html (accessed August 25, 2004).

Kirk, Robin. 1997. *The Monkey's Paw: New Chronicles from Peru*. Amherst: University of Massachusetts Press.

Lessor, Ian, Hoffman, Bruce, Arquilla, John, Ronfeldt, David F., Zanini, Michele, and Jenkins, Brian Michael (eds). 1999. *Countering the New Terrorism: Implications for Strategy in Countering the New Terrorism*. Santa Monica, CA: RAND.

LTTE Homepage. 1995–2004. "Women fighters of the liberation struggle." Online, available from: www.eelamweb.com/faq (accessed October 13, 2004).

Ms. Magazine. 1974. Attributed to Women of the Weather Underground, February, 105, as specified in *The Columbia World of Quotations* (1966). Online, available at: http://64.233.161.104/search?q=cache: kN5m3FSWRkUJ:www.bartleby.com/66/88/2688.html+%22ms.+magazine%22+ 1974+%22the+struggle+against+sexism %22&hl=en&client=safari (accessed March 24, 2005).

Musleh, Isam and Shomaly, Walid. 2004. "Fluctuations Of Palestinian Public Opinion in Response to Israeli Measures." Paper presented at the Annual Meeting of the Association for Israel Studies, The Hebrew University, Jerusalem, June 14–16, 2004. Online, available at: http://64.233.161.104/search?q=cache:RFC-qJKfM3R4J:www.aisisraelstudies.org/2004CONPAPERS/Palestinian%2520Publ ic%2520Opinion%2520in%2520Response%2520of%2520Isreal.doc+%22pales-tinian+center+for+research%22&hl=en (accessed October 9, 2004).

Neuburger, Luisella De Cataldo and Valentini, Tiziana. 1996. *Women and Terrorism*. New York: St Martin's Press.

Pravda. 2003. *Shamil Basayev Trains Female Suicide Bombers,* May 15. Online, available at: http://64.233.161.104/search?q=cache:7giMcf5AHgJ:english.pravda.ru/world/20/93/374/9995_suicide.html+%22trains+female+suicide+bombers%22& hl=en (accessed September 12, 2004).

Rantisi, Abd al-Aziz. 2002. On "Al Jazeera This Morning," Al Jazeera (Doha), May 20, 2002, as quoted in Madsen, Julian, *Suicide Terrorism: Rationalizing the Irrational Strategic Insights*, Volume III, Issue 8 (August 2004). Online, available at: www.ccc.nps.navy.mil/si/2004/aug/madsenAug04.asp#references (accessed October 7, 2004).

Reeves, Minou. 1989. *Female Warriors of Allah: Women and the Islamic Revolution*. New York: E.P. Dutton.

Sarkar, Tanika and Butalia, Urvashi. 1995. *Woman and Right Wing Movements: Indian Experiences*. London: Zed Books.

Schalk, Peter. 1994. "Women fighters of the Liberation Tigers in Iliam: the martial feminism of Atel Palac." *South Asia Research*, 14(2) (Autumn), 1–22.

Schalk, Peter. 1997a. "The revival of martyr cults among Ilavar." *Temenos*, 33, 151–190.

Schalk, Peter. 1997b. "Historisation of the martial ideology of the Liberation Tiger of Tamil Ealam (LTTE)." *South Asia: Journal of South Asian Studies*, 20(2), December 1997, 35–72.

Schweitzer, Yoram. 2000. "Suicide Terrorism: Development and Characteristics." Online, available at: http://216.239.39.104/search?q=cache:dC0eKo26pHwJ: www.ict.org.il/articles/articledet.cfm%3Farticleid %3D112 +schweitzer+yoram+ suicide+terrorism+2000+development+and+characteristics&hl=en (accessed October 12, 2004).

Shamsie, Kamila. 2002. "Exploding the myths." The *Guardian*, 27 April 2002.

Taylor, Maxwell and Quayle, Ethel. 1994. *Terrorist Lives*. London: Brasseys.

Victor, Barbara. 2004. *Army of Roses: Inside the World of Palestinian Suicide Bombers.* Emmaus, PA: Rodale Press.

Weinberg, Leonard and Eubank, William. 1987. "Italian women terrorists." *Terrorism: An International Journal*, 9(3), 241–262.

Yassin, Sheik Ahmed. 2002. As quoted in *Al Sharq al-Awsat* (London), 31 January 2002.

Yassin, Sheik Ahmed. 2003. As quoted in *Al Sharq al-Awsat* (London), 2 February 2002.

2 Women fighting in *jihad*?

David Cook

Introduction

The following account appears in the chapter on the subject of *jihad* in al-Bukhari's authoritative collection of the Prophet Muhammad's traditions:

> The Messenger of God would enter into the house of Umm Haram daughter of Milhan, and she would feed him (Umm Haram was married to 'Ubada b. al-Samit.). So the Messenger of God went into her, and she fed him and began to pick the lice off his head. The Messenger of God fell asleep and then woke up, laughing. She said: Why are you laughing? He said: People from my community [Muslims] were shown to me fighting in the path of God, sailing in the midst of the sea like kings on thrones. She said: O Messenger of God, pray to God that I might be one of them! And so the Messenger of God prayed for her ... and she sailed the seas during the time of Mu'awiya b. Abi Sufyan [661–80], and fell from her mount when she disembarked and perished.[1]

This tradition is an odd one. The Prophet Muhammad is shown participating in regular intimate encounters with the wife of another man, who was not present during these encounters, who would then pick the lice off his head, implying that he was in close physical contact with her. To put it mildly, this description is unusual and in direct contravention to Muslim law concerning the relations between men and women who are not married or related to one another.

However, this tradition also raises the issue of women fighting in *jihad* and becoming martyrs. According to the usual interpretation, women are not permitted to fight in *jihad*, but were told that their *jihad* was a righteous pilgrimage to Mecca (*hajj*).[2] It is not surprising that what was in classical times (and even today) a very dangerous trip to the holy city would constitute the equivalent to fighting. However, in light of the continually growing numbers of Muslim women participating in radical Islamic, and especially nationalist radical Islamic (such as Palestinian and Chechen), groups there is a need to examine the Muslim sources and legal literature concerning this subject, and compare them to the realities of modern warfare.

Classical background

In order for an issue to gain legitimacy for religious Muslims, it must have historical depth. This means that some traditions from the Prophet Muhammad or historical examples from his close companions must be pressed into service. With regard to women fighters, this can mean that either statements of the Prophet enjoining or allowing women to fight must be found, or examples of women close to the Prophet must be adduced.

Examples of women companions of the Prophet Muhammad fighting in the *jihad* are also available from both classical and contemporary accounts. For example, the moralist figure 'Abd al-Ghani b. 'Abd al-Wahid al-Maqdisi (d. 1203) in his small treatise *Manaqib al-sahabiyyat (The Merits of the Women Companions {of the Prophet Muhammad})* describes two women from the time of the Prophet Muhammad who fought in his wars.[3] One of them, Nusayba daughter of Ka'b (also known as Um 'Umara), is said to have gone out to help the wounded during the Battle of Uhud (626), which was the Prophet's major defeat, but then took up a sword and received 12 wounds. She is quoted as saying that there were four women with her – she took up a sword, whereas another, who was pregnant at the time, had a knife, and they fought alongside the men.[4] Another of the women cited by al-Maqdisi was Safiya, the aunt of the Prophet Muhammad, who during the Battle of the Khandaq (627) took refuge in one of the strongholds of Medina together with other Muslim women and children. At a particular time, some Jews attacked their stronghold, and one of the Jews climbed the wall and came into the fort. Safiya took up a sword and cut off his head, and threw it back at the Jews outside, who hastily dispersed.

Clearly women did take part in the fighting. Modern Muslim feminists have managed to gather more names of women who fought during the time of the Prophet. 'Aliyya Mustafa Mubarak, in her collection *Sahabiyyat mujahidat*, has assembled a list of 67 women who, according to her, fought in the wars of the Prophet Muhammad or immediately afterward in the great Islamic conquests.[5] However, when the list is examined, it becomes apparent that many of the women participated in battles in a supporting role, usually by accompanying the fighters,[6] encouraging the men, or by providing medical care and assistance after the fact.[7] Comparatively few of the women she cites actually went out on the battlefield.

From the citation at the beginning of this chapter, it is known that different women did participate in the great conquests. Again, the information concerning the nature of their participation is limited. Umm Haram does not appear to have done anything more substantial than sail on a boat; whether she actually participated in any campaigns is doubtful. From later times (approximately from the ninth through eleventh centuries) we know of a category of women known as the *mutarajjulat*, women who act or dress like men. These women were cursed by the Prophet Muhammad, who grouped them together with men who acted or dressed like women (probably effeminates or passive homosexuals).[8] However, the grouping of these two categories together does not necessarily mean that the *mutarajjulat* were lesbians (because condemnations of lesbians used a different word), but more probably that these were women who participated in the world of men and dressed like men. Although there are few historical anecdotes about such women, there are a number of accounts in literary folk tales that indicate they fought in battles.[9]

Women and the classical *jihad* material

There is a very large heritage of treatises on the subject of *jihad* from classical Islam. Despite the periodic attempts of Muslim apologists to claim the contrary, this is entirely militant and warlike material. Women do not play a major role in these treatises, with one important exception, which will be noted later. However, it is clear from stray traditions that they were aware of the high spiritual merit accorded to the (male) *jihad* fighter, and wanted to participate in the fighting. For example, in one of the minor collections of tradition emanating from the border regions close to the Byzantine Empire from the ninth century is found this very interesting tradition:

> A woman came to one of his [Muhammad's] sessions and said: I am a delegate of women to you. By God, there is not a single woman who has heard of my going out or did not hear who does not support what I say. God is the Lord of men and women, Adam was the father of men and women and you are the Messenger of God to men and women. God has ordained *jihad* for men – if they are wounded they gain a reward, if they die their reward is granted by God and if they are martyred then "they are living with their Lord, well-provided for" [Qur'an 3:169], while we stay at home, taking care of their mounts and do not get to participate in any of this.[10]

Unfortunately, her protest was met by the Prophet Muhammad telling her that the reward given to men in *jihad* would be given to women if they obeyed their husbands and kept to their houses. Thus this attempt by women (if it was such) to join in the fighting process during the classical period was still-born.

Likewise, the Shi'ite tradition is very reluctant to accord women a role in *jihad*. The tenth-century jurisprudent Ibn Babawayhi reports that both men and women have a *jihad*, but that "the man's *jihad* is to sacrifice his wealth and his blood until he is killed in the path of Allah, but the *jihad* of the woman is to endure suffering at the hands of her husband and his jealousy [of her]."[11] Just as with the Sunni tradition, the word *jihad* is completely reinterpreted for the woman; they might gain similar spiritual benefit for performing it, but the action performed is without topical connection to fighting.

It is clear after reading the *jihad* literature that there was a very good reason why men would want to keep women from the battlefield. For the male fighter, the women of paradise were a major attractant, as seen from the earliest books on *jihad*. Earthly women represented a tie that bound them to this world, whereas the whole focus of the fighter was supposed to be on the next. *Jihad* fighters should not be distracted by having a wife or a family; they should be part of the living dead. The *jihad* book of Ibn Abi al-'Asim (d. 900) says:

> The Messenger of God said: One of the prophets prior to me used to raid, and said: No man who has built a house and has not dwelt in it, or who has married a woman and not entered into her should accompany me, nor any man who has any need to return.[12]

All of the primary elements of civilization – building a home, marrying, and living with a woman – should be decisively rejected by the fighter. Thus odd customs are found such as "marriage ceremonies" on the battlefield between the Muslim soldiers and the women of paradise (the houris), or visions of them just prior to battles.[13] Traditions like these make it doubtful that women would have been particularly welcome in the Muslim ranks (although no doubt there were women camp-followers, etc.).

From the fifteenth century comes the great *jihad* composition of Ibn al-Nahhas al-Dumyati (d. 1414) in which he takes an extreme misogynist view, seeing earthly women as the primary temptation preventing men from setting out for *jihad*:

> If you say [wanting to avoid *jihad*]: My heart is not comfortable parting from my wife and her beauty, the companionship I have close to her and my happiness in touching her – even if your wife is the most beautiful of women and the loveliest of the people of the time, her beginning is a small drop [of sperm] and her end is a filthy corpse. Between those two times, she carries excrement, her menstruation denies her to you for part of her life, and her disobedience to you is usually more than her obedience. If she does not apply kohl to her eyes, they become bleary, if she does not adorn herself she becomes ugly, if she does not comb her hair it is disheveled, if she does not anoint herself her light will be extinguished, if she does not put on perfume she will smell bad and if she does not clean her pubes she will stink. Her defects will multiply, she will become weary, when she grows old she will become depressed, when she is old she will be incapacitated – even if you treat her well, she will be contemptuous towards you.[14]

This classical book has been consistently popular throughout the Muslim world since the time of its composition – since it was regularly cited in the later *jihad* literature – and has been translated into Urdu and Uzbek during the recent past by radical Muslims.

Contemporary legal literature

It is hardly surprising that classical Muslim legal literature contains very little material concerning the issue of women participating in *jihad*. However, changing attitudes toward women in the Muslim world and the emergence of "Islamic feminism" has made the issue far more immediate. From the beginning of the 1990s, Muslim writers discussing *jihad* have regularly included a section on the issue of women fighting. Probably the most impressive of these has been Muhammad Khayr Haykal, whose three-volume *al-Jihad wa-l-qital fi al-siyasa al-shara'iyya* (*Jihad and Fighting According to the Shar'i Policy*), written in 1993, covers in an exhaustive manner all of the major and many of the minor issues of *jihad*. In volume two he covers the question of who is eligible for fighting, the definition of which traditionally has been reduced to six categories (Muslim, adult, sane, free, male, and able-bodied). While listing these categories off he stops at "male" and asks the pointed question of whether the tradition stating that women's *jihad* was the pilgrimage to Mecca (discussed earlier) *actually* forbade women from participating in the fighting process, or whether it was merely a statement that gave them a peaceful opportunity to gain the same merit as men did in *jihad*? Haykal distinguishes between the two types of *jihad*: *jihad* as *fard kifaya* (where the obligation of *jihad* is upon part of the Muslim community) and *jihad* as *fard 'ayn* (where the obligation of *jihad* is upon each and every one of the members of the Muslim community), and states that in the instance of *jihad* being *fard kifaya* there is no necessity for women to fight, but they should have that option if they wish to volunteer. Under the condition of *fard 'ayn* women would have to fight.[15]

After examining the classical sources, Haykal comes to the following conclusions: the number of women who joined male fighters was small, their purpose was not to fulfill any obligation of *jihad* on their part, and they served an auxiliary function. The number of times that women actually bore arms and fought together with the men was extremely limited. According to the legal sources, if the necessity for *jihad* is incumbent upon the entire Muslim community, then women do have the option of fighting.[16] But most still say that even in extreme circumstances women fighting remains an option, not an obligation.[17]

But then Haykal asks the question of whether there is a place for women in the regular army of an Islamic state, and, surprisingly, he says yes in a most direct manner:

> From this we believe that it is incumbent upon the Islamic state to prepare training centers for women so that they can learn the use of

arms and methods of fighting in them. This is because as long as it is possible that *jihad* could become *fard 'ayn* upon the woman, it is incumbent to train her for this eventuality so that she will be prepared to fulfill this obligation.[18]

This is quite a revolutionary conclusion and departs significantly from what the medieval (and modern) commentators have said on the subject. It seems that Haykal's sole reason for making this statement was that it *might* be possible for women to have to fight some day (hypothetically), so it is necessary that they be made ready for that eventuality. However, it is interesting to realize to what extent a writer such as Haykal – whose command of the legal and historical literature is near total – is willing to disregard it and make the exception the rule.

Radical Muslims associated with Chechnya (especially from the onset of the Russian re-occupation in 1999) also explored the possibility of women fighting. As noted later, the Chechen conflict has been the one in which women have been most closely associated with actual fighting. Interestingly, they came to much less revolutionary conclusions than did Haykal. Their article, "Sisters' Role in Jihad" (written by Sister AI), after the manner of the classical material, emphasizes that women have a supporting role and should not go and actually fight unless called for:

> the situation in the Ummah [Muslim community] is not that desperate yet that sisters are called to fight. Those sisters who voluntarily want to join the fighting for reward from Allah are advised to not go unless the leader of Jihad in that place calls sisters to fight.[19]

All of the activities mentioned in this article (raising *mujahid* children, medical assistance to fighters, encouragement, prayer) are traditional in nature and do not go even as far as Haykal did.

The Syrian writer Nawaf al-Takruri who, in his repeated editions of *al-'Amaliyyat al-istishhadiyya fi al-mizan al-fiqhi* (*Martyrdom Operations in the Legal Balance*), has dealt with most of the legal questions associated with suicide attacks, covered the question of women suicide attackers in the fourth edition. The fact that the earlier editions did not cover this question demonstrates the relative newness of the practice. Al-Takruri accepts Haykal's ideas concerning women fighting in the *jihad*, and despite their revolutionary nature, takes them as his starting point. However, as he reviews the literature concerning women fighting during the time of the Prophet Muhammad (summarized earlier) he does not mention the secondary role of women at all, but emphasizes only their personal and violent participation in the fighting process.

But even al-Takruri recognizes that fighting is different than participating in a martyrdom operation. He quickly brings out the source of his difficulty: the probability that a woman, in order to effectively carry out a martyrdom operation, would have to dress in an immodest fashion. He notes that, whereas a woman has the advantage of being less suspect than a man, for a woman to carry the amount of explosives necessary to carry out an effective operation she would have to either wear so many clothes that she would stand out (hence nullifying her initial advantage) or else carry a minimal amount of explosives and dress in an immodest fashion. This is no small matter for him because, he explains to his readers, he agonized over this section of the book more than any other, and in the end was not able to come to a conclusion. Although he states that the necessity of fighting *jihad* often nullifies parts of the *shari'a* (giving examples), in good conscience he cannot mandate immodest dress for a woman (which for him means exposing her lower legs and arms).[20]

Al-Takruri cites six *fatwa*s allowing women to participate in martyrdom operations: by Yusuf al-Qaradawi (the famous TV and radio personality), three faculty at al-Azhar University in Egypt, Faysal al-Mawlawi of the European Council for Research and Legal Opinion (based in Dublin),[21] and Nizar 'Abd al-Qadir Riyyan of the Islamic University of Gaza (Palestine).[22] It is significant that the more conservative Jordanian, Syrian, and Saudi religious leaders are completely absent from this list. One can see that the question of women participating in suicide attacks has become associated with the Egyptian–Palestinian and consequently more progressive side of the Muslim world. If the Syrian al-Takruri agonized over the participation of women, for the conservatives the idea was anathema.

Fatwas in action: Chechnya and Palestine

Although al-Takruri wrote his book with the intention of supporting suicide attacks against Israel, *'Amaliyat* still has a decidedly academic and detached quality to it. This quality persists to some extent with regard to the Chechens. There is some irony in the fact that, although the separatists in Chechnya – whether nationalists or radical Muslims – have produced more women suicide attackers than any other conflict (with the possible exception of the Kurdish PKK) in any Muslim countries, the *fatwa* designed to legitimize their behavior is decidedly ambiguous. On 10 June 2000, Hawa Barayev, a close relative of several prominent Chechen commanders, drove a truck filled with explosives into a building housing Russian Special Forces and killed 27 of them (according to the accounts of the Chechen separatists). This event occasioned the "Islamic Ruling on the Permissibility of Martyrdom Operations: Did Hawa Barayev Commit Suicide or Achieve Martyrdom?," which has since become one of the chief documents used by radical Muslims to prove that "martyrdom operations" are in accord with Muslim law.[23] The irony of the matter was that women's participation in *jihad* is not mentioned even once in the *fatwa*, most probably because it was written by "a council of scholars from the Arabian Peninsula" (i.e., Wahhabis from Saudi Arabia) who did not want to think about the implications of women participating in martyrdom operations.[24] However, some radical websites have ascribed "The Islamic Ruling" to Yusuf al-'Ayyiri (killed 2003), in which case it can be related to his later discussion of women and *jihad* (see later).

There is also some ambiguity with regard to the Palestinian *fatwa* literature enjoining women's right to participate in suicide attacks. Comparatively speaking, the Palestinians have come late to the issue of women's martyrdom operations, and despite the *fatwa* of Nizar al-Riyyan (cited earlier), probably only began to choose women attackers out of desperation. This desperation was not the lack of qualified male suicide attackers, but most probably the desire to skew the profile of the typical suicide attacker that the Israeli intelligence and security forces had developed. In addition to al-Rayyan, other Palestinian religious leaders are known to have dealt with the question of women's martyrdom, such as Dr. Salam Salamah, again of the Islamic University of Gaza, who cited Umm 'Umara (see earlier), who lived during the time of the Prophet Muhammad, as an example of someone who asked for martyrdom but was not granted it.[25] There is no evidence in the historical sources for this, however, as she is merely said to have fought together with men at Uhud.

However, as with al-Takruri, there are some discordant voices. The reward aspect of the female martyr has confused Hamas. Male martyrs traditionally received extravagant sexual rewards in heaven, but in the classical sources no such rewards are specified for women. On 18 January 2002, the Hamas website was asked the pointed question:

> I wanted to ask: what is the reward of a female martyr who performs a martyrdom operation; does she marry 72 of the houris?
>
> [*answer*] ... the female martyr gains the same reward as does the male, with the exception of this one aspect [the houris], so that the female martyr will be with the same husband with whom she dies. "And those who have believed and their progeny, followed them in belief, We shall join their progeny to them. We shall not deprive them of any of their work; every man shall be bound by what he has earned" [52:21]. The one who is martyred and has no husband will be married to one of the people of Paradise.[26]

Because this reward is significantly less attractive than that of a male martyr, it is clear that the question has not been fully answered and the subject remains to be developed. In retrospect, it seems that the ideological preparations for women's suicide attacks among Palestinian radical Muslims have yet to be fully fleshed out. At the time, Ahmad Yasin (founder and ideological leader of Hamas) voiced the same reservations as Nawaf al-Takruri was to do in his *al-'Amaliyyat al-istishhadiyya* (cited earlier), and stated that no woman should be allowed to go out for *jihad* without a male chaperone, for which he was criticized by some in the Palestinian media.[27] Popular pressure eventually forced Yasin to retract his critique, and since that time Hamas has embraced the idea of female suicide attackers. Other conservatives have also demonstrated some flexibility in this manner.

Yusuf al-'Ayyiri and the Saudi Arabian al-Qaeda

One of the most unusual and unexpected changes in Saudi Arabian radical Islam is the willingness of certain revolutionary writers to embrace the idea of women fighting in *jihad*. Yusuf al-'Ayyiri, who was one of the ideological leaders of the Saudi Arabian branch of al-Qaeda prior to his death at the hands of security forces in June 2003, penned a document entitled *Dawr al-nisa' fi jihad al-'ada' (The Role of Women in the Jihad against Enemies)*.[28] Like his intellectual predecessors, al-'Ayyiri begins his pamphlet (18 pages long) with a discussion of the low state of the Muslim world and the general necessity for *jihad* in order to redeem the honor of Islam and to "raise the Word of God to the highest." He states that women are frequently one of the main reasons why men find it difficult to fight *jihad*. Just like Ibn al-Nahhas and others cited in this chapter, he notes that women tie men to this world, create familial responsibilities and make them hesitate to go out to fight. However, he does not take the misogynist turn that Ibn al-Nahhas did or emphasize the sexual rewards awaiting men in paradise. Instead, he appears to want to bring women into the *jihad* process rather than allowing them to remain on the sidelines.

In order to accomplish this, like all of those cited earlier, he brings examples of women fighters from Islamic history. Al-'Ayyiri offers the examples of eight women, all except one of them fighters (like Um 'Umara), but he does not only draw from those who lived during the time of the Prophet Muhammad, but selects several who lived during medieval times. Seven of these are actual fighters. Thus, al-'Ayyiri deliberately focuses in his selection on women as fighters, rather than in a supportive role. He continues to the present day and gives examples of four contemporary women fighters, among them Hawa Barayev and three others from the Afghan war against the USSR. Again, all of them participated in actual violence.

However, al-'Ayyiri at the end of his pamphlet avoids making the revolutionary call of women to the battlefield that seems to be the tone of his pamphlet until then. Instead, he merely states that women should take the earlier examples to heart when they know that their husbands or sons are going to fight *jihad*, and not be obstacles. This comparatively muted conclusion is much more startling because, in his final paragraphs, al-'Ayyiri very casually destroys two of the principal blocks against women actually fighting in *jihad*: that they would need the permission of their parents and that, according to al-Bukhari, women's *jihad* is the performance of the *hajj* ritual. He states unequivocally that because *jihad* at this present time is a *fard 'ayn* it is incumbent on women as well as men, without regard to parental permission. And as for the idea that the *hajj* supercedes *jihad*, he cites a tradition that enumerates the importance of various activities, and lists them in the following order: prayer, *jihad*, and respect toward parents. With these two comments he has laid the intellectual ground for the full participation of women in *jihad* among radical Muslims.

It is difficult to say why al-'Ayyiri did not take the final step and actually call for women to participate in *jihad*. Perhaps within the conservative context of the Saudi Arabian society he felt that he could not make such a call. Comparing his earlier work (if indeed he wrote it), "The Islamic Ruling" cited earlier, to this pamphlet, one perhaps could note a pattern of indirect suggestion. Nominally "The Islamic Ruling" was supposed to answer the question of whether Hawa Barayev committed suicide or not. Although the document exhaustively covers the question of martyrdom operations and their legality, the author does not even once deal with the question of women participating in such actions. But perhaps the choice of Barayev, given the fact that she was hardly the only Muslim (Chechen, Palestinian, or other) available about whom one could ask the question of whether the martyrdom operation they initiated was Islamically legitimate, indicates a desire to open women up to consideration. If this was indeed the case, then perhaps al-'Ayyiri in this document desired to indirectly destroy the religious and intellectual impediments to women participating in *jihad* without being too direct. Although this is speculative, and to date radical Saudi Muslims have not demonstrated a desire to follow up on his work,[29] it is possible that in the future a further weakening of the taboo against women fighting in *jihad* will be seen among radicals.

Conclusions

Classical Islamic sources are fairly negative about the role of women in *jihad*. Although some historical anecdotal evidence is available, it is clear that, for the most part, women did not fight in pre-modern times. This is reflected in the conservative genre of Muslim law. However, it is equally clear that radical Muslims – among whom al-Takruri must be numbered – have been attempting to legitimize women's participation in *jihad*. These attempts are qualified by a number of problems: questions of reward for martyrdom as well as issues of gender division and sexual purity noted earlier. The legal issues raised here are too recent for the outsider to know whether this revolutionary change in *jihad* will be accepted by the larger Muslim community.

It is significant to note that the locations where women participate in martyrdom operations on a large scale (Chechnya and Palestine) are two of the more secularized and well-educated areas in the Muslim world. Chechnya, especially after living for decades under the secular Soviet regime, has a severe lack of Islamic knowledge. To date, women fighting in *jihad* have only been a factor in these nationalist–Islamic resistance movements (Palestinian and Chechen), but not in other globalist radical Muslim warfare. With the exception of al-'Ayyiri, al-Qaeda does not appear to have promoted the use of women in *jihad*, let alone in suicide attacks, although, as a result of the legal discussions conducted by these other radical Muslim groups, there do not seem to be a serious ideological impediments remaining for them to attack. One suspects that the reasons for the non-appearance of women among al-Qaeda attackers is simply the social conservatism that prevails in Muslim societies. If al-Qaeda and other globalist radical Muslim groups do allow women to fight in *jihad*, one suspects that the initial trial attempts will be drawn from expatriate Muslim communities, Palestinians or Chechens.

A woman's right to join men on the battlefield (or other locations in which *jihad* is waged), to fight using their methods, in sharp contradistinction to the classical sources, can only be seen as a radical change in Islam and, as such, has been treated with suspicion by Muslim conservatives. However, it is also clear that the radicals have been able to establish a fairly strong intellectual and religious case for women fighting.

Notes

1 'Abdallah b. Isma'il al-Bukhari (d. 869), *Sahih* (Beirut: Dar al-Fikr, 1991), III, p. 265 (no. 2788).
2 For example, al-Bukhari, *Sahih*, III, p. 264 (no. 2784).
3 Al-Maqdisi (d. 1226), *Hadith al-ifk wa-yalihi min Manaqib al-nisa' al-sahabiyyat* (Damascus: Dar al-Basha'ir, 1994), p. 59.
4 Ibid., pp. 53–54.
5 'Aliyya Mustafa Mubarak, *Sahabiyyat mujahidat* (Beirut: Dar al-Kutub al-'Ilmiyya, n.d.).
6 Al-Bukhari, *Sahih*, III, p. 292 (no. 2879).
7 Ibid., pp. 292–293 (nos. 2880–2883).
8 Al-Bukhari, VII, p. 72 (no. 5886); for discussion, see Everett Rowson, "The effeminates of early Medina," *Journal of the American Oriental Society*, 111 (1991), pp. 671–693.
9 See Carole Hillenbrand, *The Crusades: Islamic Perspectives* (Edinburgh: Edinburgh University Press, 1999), pp. 348–349; *Alf Layla wa-layla* (trans. Richard Burton, London, 1885–1886), II, pp. 114–119 (story of 'Umar al-Nu'man which can be dated to the time of the Crusades), V, 277–283; and the Kirghiz epic of *Manas* (trans. Walter May), *Manas* (Moscow and Bishkek, 1995), I, p. 297, as well as popular Persian tales such as *Samak-i Ayyar*.
10 Muhammad b. Sulayman al-Masisi (d. 859), *Juz' fihi min hadith Lawin* (Riyad: Maktabat al-Rushd, 1998), p. 125 (no. 113); compare the fuller versions in Ibn Abi al-Dunya (d. 894), *Mudarat al-nas* (Beirut: Dar Ibn Hazm, 1998), p. 144 (no. 173); Ibn Bishran (d. 1039), *Amali* (Riyad: Dar al-Watan, 1997), pp. 28–29 (no. 11); Ibn 'Asakir (d. 1173), *Ta'rikh Madinat Dimashq* (Beirut: Dar al-Fikr, 1995–2000), VII, pp. 363–364.
11 Ibn Babawayhi (d. 991), *Man la yahduruhu al-faqih* (Beirut: Dar al-Adwa', 1992), III, p. 316.
12 Ibn Abi al-'Asim (d. 900), *Kitab al-jihad* (Medina: Maktabat al-'Ulum wa-l-Hikam, 1989), I, p. 141 (no. 11).
13 Ibn al-Mubarak (d. 797), *Kitab al-jihad*, p. 38 (no. 22), 117–118 (no. 142), 124–125 (no. 150); and see also Ibn Abi Zaminayn (d. 1009), *Quduat al-ghazi* (Beirut: Dar al-Gharb al-Islami, 1989), p. 242.

14 Ibn al-Nahhas al-Dumyati (d. 1414), *Mashari' al-ashwaq ila masari' al-'ushshaq* (Beirut: Dar al-Basha'ir al-Islamiyya, 2002), I, p. 129 (no. 60); see also I, pp. 215–217.

15 Muhammad Khayr Haykal, *al-Jihad wa-l-qital fi al-siyasa al-shara'iyya* (Beirut: Dar al-Barayiq, 1993), II, pp. 995–997.

16 Ibid., pp. 1013–1018. Unfortunately, my copy of Haykal suffers from a blank page where he gives the details that would support this conclusion, but it is one that accords with my own.

17 Ibid., pp. 1019–1022.

18 Ibid., p. 1024.

19 "Sisters' Role in Jihad." Online, available at: www.qoqaz.co.za/html/articlessistersinjihad.htm.

20 Nawaf al-Takruri, *al-'Amaliyyat al-istishhadiyya fi al-mizan al-fiqhi* (Damascus: al-Takruri, 2003), pp. 208–213.

21 One should note that this organization was founded by al-Qaradawi and is intellectually dominated by him.

22 Ibid., pp. 212–223.

23 For example, see www.animal-cruelty.com/sister_hawaa.htm, "Sister Hawaa' Barayev Martyrdom Attack on a Russian Military" [sic].

24 See my "Suicide Attacks or 'Martyrdom Operations' in Contemporary *Jihad* Literature," *Nova Religio*, 6 (2002), pp. 7–20 for a full discussion of this text.

25 Taken from memri.org (28 October 2003), cited from the Palestinian newspaper *al-Hayat al-Jadida* (28 October 2003).

26 Kataeb-ezzeldeen.com/fatwa (no. 3) (10 November 2002); for the legality of women conducting "martyrdom operations," see al-Takruri, *'Amaliyyat al-istishhadiyya*, pp. 208–223.

27 See memri.org, "Inquiry and Analysis," nos. 83–85 (12–14 February 2002): "Wafa Idris: the Celebration of the First Female Palestinian Suicide Bomber."

28 It is available at e-prism.com.

29 For example, the appearance of the Saudi Arabian radical Muslim journal *al-Khansa'* (aimed at women) does not encourage them to actually take part in fighting.

3 Beyond the bombings

Analyzing female suicide bombers

Debra Zedalis

It is a woman who teaches you today a lesson in heroism, who teaches you the meaning of Jihad, and the way to die a martyr's death ... It is a woman who has shocked the enemy, with her thin, meager, and weak body ... It is a woman who blew herself up, and with her exploded all the myths about women's weakness, submissiveness, and enslavement.[1]

(*Al-Sha'ab* Editorial, 1 February 2002)

Looking back, it is hard to pinpoint when the world first noticed the recurring, violent use of female suicide bombers. Female suicide bombing began in 1985 with 16-year-old Khyadali Sana in Lebanon; however, since 1985, the ever-increasing death toll associated with numerous attacks in multiple countries by a variety of organizations has elicited worldwide attention. Although validated data is not available, a conservative estimate of the carnage is approximately 600 dead and 800 wounded in eight countries by 49 female suicide bombers. Of particular concern is the increasing lethality of the attacks, with 485 deaths occurring in 25 bombings since 2002. The Institute for Counter-Terrorism (ICT) states that the "number of casualties is constantly increasing, due to the increase in overall suicide attacks and due to the improvement and sophistication of suicide attacks as the subject gains more attention."[2]

Terrorism experts note that suicide terrorism is the most aggressive form of terrorism,[3] that terrorist organizations increasingly rely on suicide attacks to achieve major political objectives,[4] and that suicide bombing campaigns coexist with regular insurgent tactics.[5] These insights are particularly relevant in analyzing suicide bombing by females. Although experts caution against predicting an epidemic of female violence, many are concerned that the practice is escalating.[6] Female suicide bombers fascinate the public, and obtain media coverage not afforded male suicide bombers. For these reasons, the June 2004 publication, *Female Suicide Bombers*, predicted that terrorist organizations would continue to employ female suicide bombers.[7]

Analyzing female suicide bombings is fraught with problems, however. In addition to having a small sample size and being unable to obtain direct information from successful bombers, problems with stereotypes, projection of intention, political use of the information, and media hype cloud the issue. This chapter reviews the 2004 report, analyzes recent utilization of female bombers, and provides additional insight into this modern "weapon."

Initial analysis

The 2004 research discussed the characteristics of female suicide bombers, their use, and strategic assessment. In 2003, the Institute for Counterterrorism noted that one of the major challenges in studying female suicide bombers was that "there are not enough reports with descriptions of the cases, there are not enough documentation ... there are not enough testimonies."[8] Although the case number has increased, there is still difficulty in obtaining and objectively assessing this weapon.

Female suicide bombers rose in importance because they provided a tactical advantage, increased the number of combatants, received enhanced media coverage, and maximized psychological impact. In terms of analyzing character traits, the only characteristic that typified most bombers was that they were relatively young. In terms of identification, recruitment and deployment, female suicide bombers had much in common with their male counterparts. The 2004 analysis indicated that "the selection of women for suicide operations and the methods used to persuade them ... are similar to those employed for men."[9] In terms of recruitment, females, like males, were young and had experienced the loss of a close friend or family member to armed struggle. Additionally, in terms of religious or patriotic orientation, the "... motivations are the same: they do believe, they are committed, they are patriotic and this is combined with a religious duty."[10]

A major difference between male and female suicide bombers, which is consistently evident, is the increased media coverage of females, since "women who kill or threaten to kill are hot news."[11] This media attention, which also serves as a "horrible advertisement,"[12] may improve recruitment and is one of the strategic reasons terrorist organizations deploy women. As early as 2003, experts worried that media focus would "... lead to more women ... and attract disproportionate publicity."[13] From the first female suicide bomber to the last, media attention, especially on the life of the woman herself, has continued to be a major focus.

The 2004 report noted two implications for future change – the religious approval of female suicide bombers and the possibility that the bombings were being supported, financed and directed by a global network. These changes had a major impact, as "religious terrorism is a particular potent form of violence."[14] The report found that "the most important factor is the organization."[15] Organizational support is critical in suicide bombing; suicide bombers are not individual random weapons. Organizations that support suicide bombing choose the bombers and the targets and then provide the bombs, the training, and all support functions to ensure the bombing is successful. The strategic recommendations from the 2004 report included discouraging community support for female suicide bombers; eliminating terrorist financing; reducing the terrorist organization's base of support through developmental programs;[16] reviewing schools supported by terrorist organizations; deterring alienated youth from joining a terrorist organization; and discrediting terrorist groups, for, "without popular support, a terrorist group cannot survive."[17] Finally, three predictions were made:

1 terrorist organizations will continue to use suicide bomber tactics and employ female suicide bombers;
2 the use of female suicide bombers will increase; and
3 the next "first" would be the first Al Qaeda female suicide bomber.[18]

Were the predictions correct?

Recent activity

Review of female suicide bomber data from June 2004 until March 2006 indicates that all three predictions were valid. Terrorist organizations continue to successfully employ female suicide bombers. Suicide bombings were "carefully planned and executed as a part of a precise political strategy"[19] as the "use of the least likely suspect is the most likely tactical adaptation for a terrorist group under scrutiny."[20] There were 12 attacks in six countries, expertly executed with body belts (5 December, 2005), explosive vests (9 November, 2005), and grenades (9 October, 2005); on buses (16 July, 2005) and airplanes (24 August, 2004); in children's stores (5 March, 2005), medical establishments (9 October, 2005), metro stations (31 August, 2004) and checkpoints (14 January, 2004). The "least likely suspects" elaborately disguised themselves as being pregnant (26 April, 2006), members of the police force (5 December, 2005), injured (14 January, 2004), or male (28 September, 2005). In addition to those who were successful, reports indicate that at least 20 unsuccessful bombers are in Israeli custody[21] and more than 40 female terrorists have been arrested since 2000.[22] Thus, the number is rising and the "upsurge in the number of female suicide bombers has come from both secular and religious organizations."[23] Female suicide bombers' adaptability continued as the new "weapons" included the first mother, the first females bombing airplanes, the first female Al Qaeda bomber, and the first female Caucasian bomber (who was also an Islamic convert – another first). The first Al Qaeda "milestone, was, sadly, claimed by an unnamed woman who bombed an American compound in Tall Afar [Iraq] on September 28, 2005, killing five civilians."[24]

Recent activity – implications of change

The 2004 publication discussed potential changes such as clergy approval, the blurring between nationalism and religiosity, and global organizational support. These three factors continue; however, motivation (national and religious) and organization appear even more critical today.

While some experts note that "more efforts are being made to analyze and understand the process of recruitment, indoctrination and motives,"[25] others state that understanding motivation "is difficult as there is no single overriding motivation but rather a number of motivations working in concert."[26] Christoph Reuter, in *My Life is a Weapon*, focuses on the role of religion:

> Notwithstanding the pretense of traditional religion in which their actions are traditionally cloaked, suicide bombers are quintessentially modern ... and exploit only selected aspects of religion ... for in Judaism, Christianity and Islam, the power over human life belongs exclusively to God.[27]

Mia Bloom, in *Dying to Kill*, notes that "suicide terror plays a greater role in ethnic disputes as targeting the other side is easier when they belong to a different race, ethnicity, religion, or nation."[28] However, Scott Atran states that "ethnicity alone may not be enough; religion may also be needed to cement commitment," and he cites a comparison of ethnic Palestinians and ethnic Bosnians which indicates that Palestinians are much more likely to use religious sentiments to express hope for the future by being willing to die for the group, whereas the Bosnians do not express religious sentiments, hope, or a willingness to die. He concludes by noting that "martyrdom" will more likely endure in religious ethnic groups.[29] Additionally, to motivate suicide bombers, the "modern-day culture's marketing techniques use a creative reinterpretation of theology that lends religious legitimacy to the attackers' suicides."[30] Thus, religious and ethnic motivations continue to be touchstones for suicide bomber recruitment and commitment. The religious approval of using females, combined with praise of women "martyrs," increases the recruitment pool of suicide bombers.

The vital importance of organizations is acknowledged, for it is well known that suicide bombers do not act alone: "it is the organization, rather than the existence of grievances, that determines the occurrence and scope of suicide attacks."[31] However, the "problem is that little is known about the organizations behind the attacks, which consequently make a robust analysis very difficult if not impossible."[32] So, while agreement exists that any counter-offensive must target the groups recruiting, training, and deploying suicide bombers, the reality is that there is very little credible information about these organizations or their recruitment and training methods. What is known is that "nations under attack face a set of largely autonomous groups and cells pursuing their own aims."[33] In Hamas, for example, groups preparing for the attacks are divided into tiny cells called *unqud* (bunches of grapes) whose cadres only know the members of their own cell.[34] While general information (e.g., organizational identity, key/influential leaders, etc.) may be known, specific data such as the location of "safe houses" where the bombers are sheltered and trained is not readily available. This lack of specific information hampers the ability to prevent the recruitment, training, and deployment of suicide bombers. In 2003, the Palestinian Islamic Jihad (PIJ) launched a public campaign to recruit women; reports are that PIJ now has a well-trained network of female operatives who identify and recruit potential candidates.[35] The Muzhakhoyeva case (of a failed Chechen bomber) emphasized the importance of the organization in recruitment, training, motivation, and deployment of human bombers; her testimony revealed that the process of putting a female suicide bomber in place is long and detailed.[36]

In terms of global expansion, the growth of the al-Qaeda network has allowed suicide attackers to detach themselves from specific local or regional problems.[37] This expansion is aided by the "fundamental role of the internet, which as global jihad scholar Reuven Paz has noted, has turned into an open university of jihad."[38]

> Even more ominous, Islamic Jihadi groups are now networked in ways that permit "swarming" by actors contracted from different groups who home in from scattered locations on multiple targets and then disperse. Multiple coordinated suicide attacks across countries and even continents are the adaptive hallmark of al-Qaeda's continued global web making.[39]

Of all the changes, this globalization of terror via network swarming is most disturbing and has major strategic impact.

Recent activity – strategic assessment

The 2004 strategic assessment discussed profiling, organizational and individual analyses, community support, and the probability of increases in number and types of bombers.

According to the 2004 report, there is little information available with which to draw up profiles of female suicide bombers; that situation has not changed. In fact, for both males and females, "the vast spread of suicide terrorism suggests that there may not be a single profile."[40] Reuter quotes work done by Kahlil Shikaki, a Palestinian expert in survey research, and notes that:

> The presupposition that the attackers consist solely of fanatical, single uneducated men from the slums is simply wrong; women and secular people are just as likely to blow themselves up. Neither is the

unchanging misery of their living conditions a crucial factor; if it were half the Somali population would have already blown itself up.[41]

Research has shown that "suicide terrorists exhibit no socially dysfunctional attributes or suicide symptoms."[42] Additionally, Reuter reports that Israeli analysts have spent years working on a profile for a "typical suicide assassin" to conclude that there just isn't one. He quotes Ariel Metari of Tel Aviv University as stating there is no way to draw a narrow profile of today's would-be attacker.[43] Analyses of the 9–11 bombers revealed that "they didn't exhibit the kind of profile that would have made it even remotely possible to predict what they planned to do. In fact, for years they fell within the everyday spectrum of normality."[44] In restricting the analyses to women, no profile has been found, and "the selection of candidates for suicide operations and the methods used to persuade them are similar to those employed for males."[45]

> But are suicide bombings committed by women different than those committed by their fathers, husbands, sons, and brothers? No, they are not different because women despair as much as men and want to fight for the freedom of their people just as their male counterparts do. Yes, they are different because women often stand as boundary stones at the dawn of a new escalation in a conflict.[46]

While profiling focuses on individual characteristics, more experts agree that a complete analyses must also focus on the organization. While some maintain that it is "almost impossible to discover who exactly is behind an attack and how the chain of command operates,"[47] others assert that "understanding and parrying suicide terrorism requires concentrating on organizational structure, indoctrination methods and ideological appeal of recruiting organizations rather than on personality attributes of the individuals recruited."[48] In actuality, individual motivations and organizational processes must both be equally studied to exploit "soft spots" and stop suicide bombing.

Initial recruitment is a critical organizational role and "Ricolfi observes that the clustering of Palestinian suicide volunteers in a few towns suggests the importance of peer pressure."[49] In addition to recruitment, organizations obtain resources and services, procure weapons, provide the technical "know how" of weapon use, gather intelligence, select the target, handle public relations, and do the overall decision making and strategic planning.[50] While the individual bomber "stories" captivate audiences, the organizations are focused on achieving a strategic objective and these organizations "adapt to changing political circumstances and are sensitive to the reactions of suicide operations."[51] In decision-making and strategic planning, even though women have been used as human bombs, there is no indication that women are involved in higher-level positions. Analysis indicates that "the

Chechen terrorist attacks as well as those in Israel appear to be entirely directed by men."[52] Will women begin to play more than an operational role? Can the use of women as merely throw-away weapons (as suicide bombers) be exploited to diminish potential female recruits?

There are many players in this bombing tragedy – individual bombers need organizations; however, organizations that use humans as weapons would not exist without community support. Given the daily report of suicide bombings, one might suspect that communities have reached the saturation point in supporting this brutal weapon; however, indications are that support may be increasing in some geographical areas. One author wonders how any "society can come to tolerate and, and indeed foster, a practice so opposed to the survival instinct; it is difficult to imagine how the collective psychology supporting suicide attacks can be maintained indefinitely."[53] A March 2004 Pew Research Center survey indicated that nearly half of Pakistanis and substantial majorities in supposedly moderate Muslim countries (e.g., Morocco and Jordan) now support suicide bombings as a way of countering the application of military might.[54] The continued use of suicide bombings in Iraq, which have killed thousands of non-combatants, indicate that this support is not lessening. While one may wonder at the logic of a community "death wish," Pape notes that "suicide terrorists' political aims, if not their methods, are quite often mainstream; they reflect quite common, straight-forward nationalist self-determination claims of their community."[55] Therefore, strategically, one must convince the community that it is not in their best interests to support organizations (and, therefore, individuals) that use suicide bombers. "The domestic environment will have an enormous impact on whether suicide bombing continues to be used, whether it is abandoned, or whether there is an explosion in the number of organizations using suicide terror to mobilize the population and increase their bases of support."[56]

Given improved communication via the Web, enhanced organizational capabilities, and increasing community support, female suicide bombing is likely to continue.

> Emboldened by the strategic successes of suicide-sponsoring terrorist organizations and increasing support and recruitment among Muslim populations, Jihadi groups believe they are able to mount a lengthy war of attrition. Religious ethnic groups offer a good foundation for sustaining resource-deficient insurgencies."[57]

This is because they are "core" elements in providing resources (manpower, dollars, weapons) to allow engagement in a lengthy war. Not only do organizations continue to receive large numbers of willing volunteers, but the time needed to train them has dropped dramatically.[58] Of note is that "every suicide campaign from 1980–2001 has had as a major objective – or its central objective – coercing a foreign government that has military forces in what they see as their homeland to take those forces out."[59] As a result, resources are provided (recruits, equipment, training) so efficiently and motivation so focused on the foreign enemy, that bombings have increased and the lethality of those attacks has increased.

These same overall components influence female suicide bombers. While the numbers vary by organization, location, and reporting sources, all agree that the use of women has increased. In terms of Palestinian suicide bombers, one report states that 40 terrorists have been arrested,[60] another says there were 59,[61] and a third lists 35 caught prior to an action.[62] In "Cross Regional Trends in Female Terrorism," the author notes that female involvement with terrorist activity is widening ideologically, logistically, and regionally as pressures are creating a convergence between individual women, terrorist organizations, leaders, and society.[63] Objectively assessing the components of this problem (individual, organization, community, recruits, training, and resources) would predict continuing and increasing acts of female terror.

Analytical gaps

Obtaining data and objectively analyzing female suicide bombers is not easy. The 2004 paper cited the small number of cases, which precluded in-depth analyses or projections. Although the number has increased, the questionable information, media misinformation, female stereotypes, political reporting, and limited intelligence on individuals and organizations make strategic assessment difficult. Although male and female suicide bomber data has not been analyzed or compared for accuracy, media coverage of male suicide bombers indicates that men receive less individual attention, perhaps in part because there are so many male suicide bombers that the public may have lost interest in knowing each and every one's personal story. Finally, when the media do focus on male suicide bombers, just as in the case of female suicide bombers, the report attempts to proffer Westernized rationales to explain suicide bombing.

The most important source in explaining motivation would be the bomber herself but "those who could tell us their stories – those who went through with this death act – cannot share their thoughts and motivation."[64] In some cases videotapes or written messages are prepared before the act, but these messages, scripted by the sponsoring terrorist organizations, do not provide individual insight but merely mouth the latest political rhetoric. Those who have failed to successfully carry out their mission also provide questionable information. "Interviews with would-be suicide attackers who failed or were foiled are an intrinsically unreliable source,"[65] as a person's belief at the time of the event may differ from a rationalized belief once they are captured. The motivation the second before pressing the bomb's button may vary drastically from the ascribed motivation the second after the bomb failed to explode – this information (or rationalization) is time-fungible: "The women themselves have left few clues as to their state of mind and reports of the rare ones who have surrendered are dubious because of their need to gain the favor of the authorities who detain them."[66]

In addition to the lack of reliable source data, much has recently been written about media reporting and female stereotypes. Without a doubt, female assassins are used because of the media coverage. Suicide bombing as a "strategy of communication" largely depends upon mass media to achieve its goals[67] and, as a Hezbollah representative noted, "The media is part of the war – CNN is more important than airplanes."[68] While suicide bombing, now a daily event, is no longer novel, the use of women continues to inspire more print as media sensationalizes prominent cases. However, the major difference is not just the amount but also the type of coverage.

Media coverage of women suicide bombers is being studied. Tellingly, articles about women project the intention of the bomber, speculating on why this woman killed herself and others; media stories focus on tales of loss, dishonor, humiliation, and coercion as reasons for this death-bringing decision. "Even though women are playing traditional male roles of combat and terrorism and the actual definition of terrorism rests on a political motivation, women are consistently depicted as apolitical non-actors forced into violence through personal circumstances."[69] The problem is that media interpretations frame the analyses to meet both political and societal needs. One analyst noted that

> media coverage, particularly in the West, appears to actively search for alternate explanations behind women's participation in ways that do not parallel the coverage of male suicide bombers, whose official ideological statements are taken at face value.[70]

Two authors note that our societal shock, controversy, and interest in the "new" phenomena of female terrorism can be explained by the fact that female violence had not previously been accurately portrayed[71] and that society's conception of war, violence, and death is based upon our gender stereotypes.[72] The warnings against inappropriately analyzing a situation based upon gender stereotypes ring true today. In a recent symposium on the "She Bomber," one panelist stated:

> A person harbors a multitude of male and female identifications. To accept the issue of gender in this limited way is precisely to buy into terrorism's concreteness and literality. If we take this bait, we will not be able to tackle this problem.[73]

Finally, the answers obtained result from the questions posed – what if the wrong questions are being asked?

> The media is particularly useful in its framing and myth-making functions. In selecting and highlighting some of the events or issues and making connections among them so as to promote a particular

interpretation, evaluation and/or solution, the media provides stories that make sense of a society for a society.[74]

The stories may fit our need to understand gender or violence, but do these stories and questions build the objective framework required to objectively analyze the problem?

> The questions not being asked about women terrorists are important silences. Not all rape victims are terrorists. Not all desperate widows commit suicide and those that do usually do not kill others in the process. Terrorism is a political act, yet no one has stopped to ask what women's political goals are.[75]

Beyond myth-making and gender-based projections, another key gap is the understanding of suicide bomber behavior. When suicide bombings first occurred, many bombers were seen as mentally unstable, poor, or depressed. While that assessment has now been proven false, there is still a debate on whether analysis should focus on individual characteristics, environmental structure, or organizational attributes.

Analyses of individual characteristics as well as environmental structure are often a direct result of cultural orientation. For example, "Americans overwhelmingly believe that personal decision, success, and failure depend upon individual choice, responsibility and personality"[76] and psychologists have attempted to reconstruct suicide bomber recruitment methods based upon their experience in treating members of Western sects.[77] This "individual-focused" analysis may not hold true across cultures. One of the major analytical errors cited is the

> tendency for people to explain human behavior in terms of individual personality traits, even when significant situational factors in the larger society are at work. This attribution error leads many in the West to focus on the individual suicide terrorists rather than the organizational environment which produces them.[78]

The key is the organization, not the individual.

In analyzing female suicide bombers, the media hype, gender stereotyping, and personal "stories" obscure the environmental and organizational data. Finally, even if individual and organizational information are available, there is still a data gap:

> For while models do tell us something about motivations, they are completely incapable of explaining why these attacks begin at a particular time and in a particular place; why they spread throughout the world in very specific patterns; why some militant organizations have employed them while others haven't.[79]

"While these attacks have become ubiquitous, real intelligence on what is committing them, and where, and why, is only gradually emerging from the shadows of false political assumptions and plain ignorance."[80] The shortage of intelligence about organizational methods and individual motivation has created a vacuum in developing a way to defuse this human bomb. The amorphous nature of the global terrorist network combined with the use of the Web to recruit activists has "hampered the tracking efforts of intelligence agencies."[81] Finally, in "Mishandling Suicide Terrorism," Atran states that, while "billions of dollars have been allocated to countermeasures associated with protection, mitigation, and preemption, there is scant evident of serious effort or funding to understand why individuals become, or to prevent individuals from becoming, terrorists in the first place."[82] With all that is not known, can projections for female suicide bomber activities be made?

Projections

Future bombings will:

1   continue to use Islamic converts who will have a tactical advantage of "blending in" (e.g., will "look Western");
2   include multiple targets, with bombings being either sequential or simultaneous;
3   continue to focus on "high value" targets (e.g., a high number of casualties and high media attention);
4   continue to use the Web for recruitment as well as operations;
5   include women in strategic-level positions; and
6   use young girls or pregnant women.

Finally, within the US, right-wing terrorist groups may use female suicide bombers.

The December 2005 female suicide bomber in Iraq was a Belgian woman who married and converted to Islam, her husband's faith. Terrorist experts note that European women who marry Muslim men are now the largest source of religious conversions[83] and *The Times* noted that "Al Qaeda recently appealed for white converts to become suicide bombers because it was easier for them to travel and evade detection."[84] After the December 2005 bombing, the Belgian government arrested individuals in the same terrorist cell:

> The backgrounds of those arrested show that the problem of Islamic terrorism is no longer confined to immigrant communities – 7 were Muslim converts of native Belgian origin, 2 were Belgians of North African origin, 2 were Tunisians, and 3 were Moroccans.[85]

In September 2005, three months before the first "Western White Woman Suicide Bomber,"[86] Nancy Kobrin, when discussing the "She Bomber," stated: "It is no longer *if* but *when* – when will we have Caucasian converts to Islam or second generation (fill-in-the-blank of the Arab/Muslim country) American/Canadian female suicide bombers? It is only a matter of time."[87]

The 9/11 bombings in New York City – two buildings, two planes, the perfect timed execution – has become the al-Qaeda signature. A 2003 publication, "Cross Regional Trends in Female Terrorism," accurately predicted that a logical progression for women would be tandem suicide bombings.[88] Recent attacks, including the failed female suicide bomber in Jordan, used multiple bombers to explode either simultaneously or sequentially. The multiple bombers are not limited to al-Qaeda. Two Chechen female suicide bombers on two separate airplanes successfully killed using tandem bombings. Finally, the most recent adaptive behavior has been to have the first bomber detonate and then another bomber, who is moving with the massed, fearful crowd trying to escape the bombing, detonates the second bomb. This new modification ensures a higher kill rate.

Suicide bombing is gauged most successful when many people die. To achieve this high kill rate, terrorist organizations use multiple bombers, go after highly populated areas, and pick soft targets such as restaurants, clubs, and hotels:

> The most popular target was public crowded areas. Open spaces are more accessible. The second target is public transportation. Public transportation, mainly buses, is targeted because of the concentration of people in a small space, usually closed so the blast effect is maximized.[89]

A recent example of tandem bombings in a populated environment was the bombing of the police academy in Iraq. The two female suicide bombers were most likely students at the academy; one exploded in the crowded cafeteria while the second exploded during the police roll call.[90] This attack not only killed and wounded many (27 dead; 32 wounded), but it also sent a strategic message by striking police and police recruits within their own building. The desire for a high kill rate is almost as simple as a cost–benefit analysis: "Suicide attackers are likely to have a very focused motivation: to take as many enemy lives as possible. For them it is the main benefit that justifies the high cost of their action, namely their death."[91] In March 2005, a failed PKK female suicide bomber stated: "The target was the bus. I had my bag and student uniform. There were too few people [on the bus] and a police officer was there. If there were more on the bus, I would have done it."[92]

The use of the Web to recruit suicide bombers is well-documented. A 2005 Italian report notes:

> The Web has confirmed its role as a preferential vehicle for the so-called "thought and word jihad" setting out to cultivate and disseminate a radical ideological context capable of wining new recruits over to the fundamental cause. New acolytes now being sought are the female

public for which a specific on-line journal, *Ali-Khansa*, has been launched in recent months.[93]

In addition to the use of the Web, future female participation will not only be at the tactical level, as a human bomb, but might well increase to the strategic level:

> The new global jihad will be using the world of women as the springboard for its quantum leap: female suicide bombers, recruited via the web as well, with the job of taking the attack to the very heart of the West.[94]

> Although women as leaders of terrorist organizations are rare, they did exist. In Germany, the Red Army Faction (a.k.a. the Baader-Meinhof Gang) and the Red Brigades had women leaders and co-founders, as did Prima Linea in Italy. In addition, the Japanese Red Army, and the Weather Underground (later the Symbionese Liberation Army) all had women leaders at one time or another.[95]

Additionally, women have often been leaders in the Tamil Tigers; in 1990 the LTTE had the first female commander of a rebel unit.[96] Although, to date, the number of female leaders has been small, this may change as it is predicted that the number of women engaging in terrorist activities will increase significantly, and women will be participating on a strategic level, planning and facilitating a large number of attacks.[97] Female leaders, however, will most likely occur in secular terrorist organizations; thus far, there have not been, nor are there likely to be in the near-term, female leaders in Islamic terrorist organizations.

The 2004 paper stated that there were few boundaries left for females to cross. In January 2004, the world saw the first "mother" whose last pictures showed her holding her young son on her left arm and her weapon in her right hand. Two other boundaries do exist – young girls or pregnant women. An Israeli soldier discussed the use of children being trained for martyrdom[98] and Palestinian TV specifically advocated that children should sacrifice their lives for Jihad in the fight against Israel:[99]

> A Palestinian psychologist, Dr. Massalha, studied Palestinian children aged 6 to 11 and reported that over 50 percent dream of becoming suicide bombers wearing explosive vests. Mass indoctrination of children and young adults by a multi-modal methodology emanating from media, schools, pulpit and street has been eminently successful in helping to generate this abundance of suicide bombers for future generations.[100]

Using girls as suicide bombers makes tactical sense as "girls are less suspect than boys and less often subjected to body searches."[101] The number of girl "soldiers" could be quite large for, from Colombia to Kosovo to Chechnya to Israel and Africa, girls are in fighting groups. Between 1990 and 2003, girls were part of fighting forces in 55 countries, and participated in 38 armed conflicts in Africa, Asia, Europe, Middle East and the Americas.[102]

Finally, another new boundary to cross would be a pregnant female suicide bomber. On April 26, 2006, a Sri Lanka female suicide bomber disguised herself as a pregnant woman en route to the hospital. As of this date, no pregnant bomber has been used; however, "a flesh and blood pregnant suicide bomber seems to be a horrific, but somehow logical, continuation of the phenomenon."[103] A pregnant suicide bomber, who would take her own life as well as her child's, would be a powerful statement as to the determination of the bomber. Such an act, however, could also have negative consequences if the public and supporting community would refuse to accept such rationale and condemn the act (and the organization that sponsored the killing of an innocent child).

Specifically looking at potential terror in the US, "Cross-Regional Trends in Female Terrorism" findings were that:

1   the emerging trend in the US is the growing mobilization of female members, particularly via use of the Internet;
2   women now make up 25 percent of the right-wing groups in the US; and
3   women are as much as 50 percent of the new recruits.

Given that domestic terror remains the most likely source in the US, the trend is noteworthy.[104] The report stops short of projecting an attack in the US by females aligned with right-wing organizations. However, the global terrorist network, increased use of the Internet for recruitment and planning, and the growing use of female suicide bombers indicate that this US trend bears scrutiny.

In reviewing these projections, it is clear that while female suicide bombers continue to be creatively used, many more ways exist to frighten the public, obtain media coverage, and kill large numbers of innocent people:

> Suicide terrorist organizations are better positioned to increase expectations about future costs by deliberately violating norms in the use of violence. They do this by crossing the thresholds of violence, by breaching taboos concerning legitimate targets, and by broadening recruitment to confound expectations about limits on the number of possible terrorists.[105]

Way ahead

The frequency of suicide bombing and the death it causes impels us to seek ways to limit, then eliminate, this weapon. A two-pronged attack, focused on the organization as well as the individual, is a needed first step. Additionally, the use of all elements of national power (e.g., diplomatic, economic, informational, and military) is also required. Suicide bombing will continue to be used as long as it is successful – a counter strategy must crush its success in recruitment and execution.

The nexus between the organization and the individual is the recruitment process; to successfully stop suicide bombers, recruits must become nonexistent: "The first line of defense involves understanding and acting on the root causes of terrorism so as to drastically reduce the receptivity of potential recruits mostly though political, economic, and social action programs."[106]

Suicide bombing can only exist if you have volunteer bombers; volunteer bombers are encouraged or dissuaded by their community. "Whatever the basis for community support for organizations that sponsor terrorism, that support needs to be the long-term focus of attention. For without community support, terrorist organizations can no more thrive than a fish out of water."[107] It will be necessary to "develop strong, confidence-building ties and mount communications campaigns to eradicate support from these communities. The most useful intelligence comes from places in the community where terrorists seek to establish and hide their infrastructure."[108] This foreknowledge of a terrorist organization's logistical base or infrastructure can help to pre-empt successful execution.

By focusing intelligence, information operations, and military response against the terrorist organization, the actual training and deployment of suicide bombers of both genders can be lessened. A key component will be the "synchronization of intelligence as operations for whoever has better intelligence is the winner."[109] So, part of the goal of successfully shutting down the organization is to force the terrorists to pay more attention to their own organizational security than to planning and carrying out attacks. The goal is to actively shrink the time and space in which suicide bombers and their operational commanders, logisticians, and handlers function.[110]

As noted in the 2004 publication, the US must use a variety of approaches to deal with female suicide bombers. First and foremost, the US cannot act alone. A top US State Department counter-terrorism official stated: "Despite the continued violence we see, there's a growing recognition and a realization among civilized societies and countries and individuals that we have got to bond together."[111] US engagement should include operations that are diplomatic, economic, informational, and military.

Diplomatically, "the US must work in concert with the international community to address historical and personal grievances, whether perceived or actual."[112] A case study of Turkey and the PKK provides insight on actions that could be taken, and noted that Turkey addressed the situation by creating stable governing structures for the Kurds, improving agriculture and education, and massively investing in the geographical area.[113] The US needs to continue diplomatic pressure on countries that support terrorist organizations, and should ensure that international funding for these organizations is blocked. Finally, the US needs to work to convince Muslim communities to stop supporting religious schools and charities that feed terrorist networks.[114]

Economically, in addition to freezing funds to terrorist organizations, the US should target economic support to areas that habitually provide female suicide bombers: "It seems paradoxical that the groups offering the most comprehensive social welfare services are also the most ardent proponents of suicide bombing."[115] Organizations, such as Hamas, provide financial support to the families of suicide bombers – the suicide bombers, the families, and the communities all know this. "Democratic nations that fight terrorism must discretely help others in these societies to compete with rather than attempt to crush such programs for the bodies, minds, and hearts of the people."[116]

In today's environment, a major weapon is information. "Given the increased role played by the internet, efforts should foster alternative peer groups in cities and cyberspace, showing the same commitment and compassion towards their own members as terror groups seem to offer."[117] In addition, information operations should debunk terrorists' arguments in recruiting suicide bombers. Interestingly, "Mark Tessler, who coordinates long-term surveys of Muslim societies, finds that Arab attitudes toward American culture are most favorable among young adults – the same population that terrorist recruiters single out – regardless of their religious orientation."[118] This favorable attitude needs to be cultivated through a variety of media. Finally, on the negative side, Reuven Paz noted that European jihadists act not to achieve a clearly specified goal but to oppose a perceived global evil; 14 Arab countries say they have volunteered to fight against "international evil" rather than for Iraq.[119] Again, media can assist by providing specific goals and challenging the mantra of "international evil." The story needs to bring the issue home – not in a global, generic sense, but in areas from which the suicide bombers are recruited.

Experts seem to agree that the answer is not a completely military response. In fact, "repeated suicide actions show that massive counterforce alone does not diminish the frequency or the intensity of the suicide attack."[120] Additionally, "military actions alone rarely work for long. Although decapitation of terrorist organizations can disrupt their operations temporarily, it rarely yields long-term gains."[121] However, military action, used in concert with other weapons, can be successful. In the PKK example, "the Turkish military hit the rebels hard, crushing the PKK, closing down international support and eventually arresting its leader."[122]

The use of women as human weapons will continue. Future female suicide bombings will continue to adapt and seek maximum deaths, exposure, and shock. Key to our success in combating female suicide bombers will be our knowledge and understanding of the organization and the individual. This knowledge is only as good as the questions we ask.

Notes

1 Karla J. Cunningham, "Cross-Regional Trends in Female Terrorism," *Studies in Conflict and Terrorism*, 26, 2003, p. 183.
2 Ophir Falk, Yaron Schwartz, Eran Duvdevany, and Eran Galperin, "The Suicide Attack Phenomenon," January 10, 2005, p. 4. Online, available from: www.ict.org.il/articles/articledet.cfm?articleid=526 (accessed: 13 March 2006).
3 Robert A. Pape, "The Strategic Logic of Suicide Terrorism," *American Political Science Review*, 97, 3, August 2003, pp. 3–4.
4 Ibid., p. 1.
5 Mia Bloom, *Dying to Kill: the Allure of Suicide Terror*, New York: Columbia University Press, 2005, p. 79.
6 Olivia Ward, "The Changing Face of Violence," *Toronto Star* (Canada), 10 October 2004. Online, available from: search.epnet.com/login.aspx?direct=true&db=tsh&an=6FP2307378099 (accessed: 25 February 2006).
7 Debra Zedalis, "Female Suicide Bombers," *Carlisle Papers in Security Strategy*, June 2004, p. 12.
8 Clara Beyler, "Messengers of Death, Female Suicide Bombers," February 12, 2003. Online, available from: www.ict.org.il/articles/articledet.cfm?artieid=471 (accessed: September 5, 2003).
9 Zedalis, "Female Suicide Bombers," p. 8.
10 Greg Zoroya, "Her Decision to be a Suicide Bomber," *USA Today*, April 22, 2003, section A, p. 1. Database online, available from Lexis-Nexis (accessed: September 5, 2003).
11 Melanie Reid, "Myth that Women are the Most Deadly Killers of All," *Herald* (Glasgow), January 29, 2002, section A, p. 14. Database online, available from Lexis-Nexis (accessed: September 5, 2003).
12 Mark Danner, "Taking Stock of the Forever War," *New York Times Magazine*, September 11, 2005, p. 48.
13 Reid, "Myth that Women are the Most Deadly Killers of All."
14 Zedalis, "Female Suicide Bombers," p. 9.
15 Jessica Stern, *Terror in the Name of God*, New York: HarperCollins, 2003, p. xxiii.
16 Rex A. Hudson, "The Sociology and Psychology of Terrorism: Who Becomes a Terrorist and Why?" Library of Congress, September 1999. Database online, available from Lexis-Nexis (accessed: September 5, 2003).
17 Ibid.
18 Zedalis, "Female Suicide Bombers," pp. 12–13.
19 Bloom, *Dying to Kill*, p. 144.
20 Ibid.
21 Jabin T. Jacob, "Female Suicide Bombers: a Political Perspective," No. 1118, September 1, 2003. Online, available from: www.ipcs.org/ipcs/kashmirLevel2.jsp?action=showView&kValue=1127&subCatlD=1022&mod=g (accessed: March 20, 2006).
22 "Suicide Bomber Was Children's TV Show Hostess," Israel National News, 23 September 2004. Online, available from: www.israelnationalnews.com/news.php3?id=69329 (accessed: February 22, 2006).
23 Bloom, *Dying to Kill*, p. 143.
24 James Joyner, "Suicide Girls," January 18, 2006. Online, available from: www.tcsdaily.com/article.aspx?id=011706D (accessed: March 15, 2006).
25 Roger McDermott, "Russia Ponders Female Suicide Bombers," *Chechnya Weekly*, 5, 43, November 24, 2004. Database online, available at: www.jamestown.org/publications_details.php?/volume_id=396&article_id=2368913 (accessed: March 17, 2006).

26 Yoni Fighel, "Palestinian Islamic Jihad and Female Suicide Bombers," October 6, 2003. Database online, available at: www.ict.org.il/articles/articledet.cfm?articleid=499 (accessed: March 17, 2006).
27 Christoph Reuter, *My Life is a Weapon*, New Jersey: Princeton University Press, 2004, p. 16.
28 Bloom, *Dying to Kill*, p. 79.
29 Scott Atran, "Mishandling Suicide Terrorism," *The Washington Quarterly*, 27, 3, Summer 2004, p. 77.
30 Ibid., p. 13.
31 Nabi Abdullaev, "Women to the Forefront in Chechen Terrorism," *International Relations and Security Network*, March 8, 2005. Online, available at: www.isn.ethz.ch/news/sw/details.cfm?ID=9781 (accessed: March 21, 2006).
32 Claudia Brunner, "Female Suicide Bombers – Male Suicide Bombing? Looking for Gender in Reporting the Suicide Bombings of the Israeli–Palestinian Conflict," *Global Society*, 19, 1, January 2005, p. 44.
33 Scott Atran, "Trends in Suicide Terrorism: Sense and Nonsense," presented to World Federation of Scientists Permanent Monitoring Panel on Terrorism, Erice, Sicily, August 2004, p. 1. Online, available at: www.sitemaker.umich.edu/satran/files/atran-trends.pdf (accessed: March 18, 2006).
34 Reuter, *My Life is a Weapon*, p. 88.
35 Fighel, "Palestinian Islamic Jihad and Female Suicide Bombers," p. 1.
36 McDermott, "Russia Ponders Female Suicide Bombers."
37 Reuter, *My Life is a Weapon*, p. 17.
38 Assaf Moghadam, "The New Martyrs Go Global," *Boston Globe*, November 18, 2005.
39 Atran, "Trends in Suicide Terrorism: Sense and Nonsense," p. 3.
40 Pape, "The Strategic Logic of Suicide Terrorism," p. 2.
41 Reuter, *My Life is a Weapon*, p. 10.
42 Atran, "Trends in Suicide Terrorism: Sense and Nonsense," p. 9.
43 Reuter, *My Life is a Weapon*, p. 109.
44 Reuter, *My Life is a Weapon*, pp. 7–8.
45 Yoram Schweitzer, "Female Suicide Bombers for God," Tel Aviv University, the Jaffee Center for Strategic Studies, 88, October 9, 2003. Online, available from: www.e-prism.org/images/female_suicide_bomber_tel_Aviv_Note_88.doc (accessed: March 2, 2006), p. 2.
46 Brunner, "Female Suicide Bombers – Male Suicide Bombing?," p. 44.
47 Reuter, *My Life is a Weapon*, pp. 140–141.
48 Atran, "Mishandling Suicide Terrorism," p. 80.
49 Jon Elster, "Motivations and Beliefs in Suicide Missions." Online, available at: www.hf.uio.no/ifikk/forskning/seminarer/vitenskapsteori/gamle-sider/2004-v/Elster-paper.html (accessed: April 27, 2006), p. 6.
50 Assaf Moghadam, "Palestinian Suicide Terrorism in the Second Intifada: Motivations and Organizational Aspects," p. 76.
51 Bloom, *Dying to Kill*, p. 88.
52 Ward, "The Changing Face of Violence."
53 Reuter, *My Life Is a Weapon*, p.p. 11, 15
54 Atran, "Trends in Suicide Terrorism: Sense and Nonsense," p. 11.
55 Pape, "The Strategic Logic of Suicide Terrorism," p. 7.
56 Bloom, *Dying to Kill*, p. 81.
57 Atran "Trends in Suicide Terrorism: Sense and Nonsense," p. 8.
58 Reuter, *My Life Is a Weapon*, pp. 113–114.
59 Pape, "The Strategic Logic of Suicide Terrorism," p. 7.

60 "Suicide Bomber Was Children's TV Show Hostess," Israel National News, 23 September 2004.
61 "Attack by Female Suicide Bomber Thwarted at Erez Crossing," June 29, 2005. Online, available from: www.mfa.gov.il/MFA/Terrorism-+Obstacle+to+Peace/Terrorism+and+Islamic+Fundamentalism-/Attac+by+female+suicide+bomber+thwarted+at+Erez+crossing+20-Jun-2005.htm (accessed: March 8, 2006).
62 Falk, "The Suicide Attack Phenomenon."
63 Cunningham, "Cross-Regional Trends in Female Terrorism," p. 185.
64 Zedalis, "Female Suicide Bombers," p. 1.
65 Elster, "Motivations and Beliefs in Suicide Missions," p. 20.
66 Ward, "The Changing Face of Violence."
67 Brunner, "Female Suicide Bombers – Male Suicide Bombing?," p. 30.
68 Reuter, *My Life is a Weapon*, p. 73
69 Jessica West, "Feminist IR and the Case of the 'Black Widows': Reproducing Gendered Divisions," *Innovations – A Journal of Politics*, 5, 2004–2005. Online, available from: www.acs.ucalgary.ca/~innovate/issues/2005spring/Inv2005spr-2.pdf (accessed: April 1, 2006), p. 8.
70 Terri Toles Patkin, "Explosive Baggage: Female Palestinian Suicide Bombers and the Rhetoric of Emotion." Online, available from: www.highbeam.com/doc/1G1:130469595/Explosive+baggage~C~+female+Palestinian+suicide+bombers+and+the+rhetoric+of+emotion.html?refid=SEO (accessed: April 7, 2006).
71 Ward, "The Changing Face of Violence."
72 West, "Feminist IR and the Case of the 'Black Widows': Reproducing Gendered Divisions," p. 6.
73 Glazov, Jamie, "Symposium: the She Bomber," *Front Page Magazine*, September 9, 2005.
74 West, "Feminist IR and the Case of the 'Black Widows': Reproducing Gendered Divisions," p. 5.
75 Ibid., p. 9
76 Atran, "Trends in Suicide Terrorism: Sense and Nonsense," p. 10.
77 Reuter, *My Life is a Weapon*, p. 8
78 Atran, "Trends in Suicide Terrorism: Sense and Nonsense," p. 9.
79 Reuter, *My Life is a Weapon*, p. 9.
80 Ibid., p. 6.
81 Falk, "The Suicide Attack Phenomenon," p. 3.
82 Atran, "Mishandling Suicide Terrorism," p. 73.
83 Craig S. Smith, "Raised Catholic in Belgium, She Died a Muslim Bomber," *New York Times*, December 6, 2005, A10.
84 Anthony Browne, "Western White Woman a Suicide Bomber," *The Times* (London), December 1, 2005.
85 Atran, "Mishandling Suicide Terrorism," p. 73.
86 Browne, "Western White Woman a Suicide Bomber."
87 Glazov, "Symposium: the She Bomber."
88 Cunningham, "Cross-Regional Trends in Female Terrorism," p. 182.
89 Falk, "The Suicide Attack Phenomenon," p. 5.
90 "Update 15: Two Female Suicide Bombers Kill 27 in Iraq," Associated Press, December 6, 2005. Online, available from: www.forbes.com/work/feeds/ap/2005/12/06/ap2371791.html (accessed: February 26, 2006).
91 Elster, "Motivations and Beliefs in Suicide Missions," p. 18.
92 NATO Center of Excellence Defence Against Terrorism (CoE-DAT), Defense

Against Suicide Bombing Course, interview with failed PKK female suicide bomber, Ankara, Turkey, March 2005.

93   Gian Marco Chiocci and Claudia Passa, "Al-Qa'ida is Now Recruiting Female Terrorists in Italy," *World News Connection*, March 4, 2005. Online, available from: search.epnet.com/login.aspx?direct=true&db=tsh&an=EUP200503040000 35 (accessed: March 8, 2006).

94   Ibid.

95   Foreign Policy Association, *Commentary: Women and Terrorism*, January 15, 2003. Online, available from: www.fpa.org/newsletter_info2478/newsletter_ info.htm (accessed: August 13, 2006).

96   Reuter, *My Life is a Weapon*, pp. 60–61.

97   "The Emergence of Female Suicide Militants," February 25, 2006. Online, available from: www.crimelibrary.com/terrorists_spies/terrorists/palestinians/ 10.html.

98   Hoffman, Bruce, "The Logic of Suicide Terrorism," *The Atlantic Monthly*, June 2003. Online, available from: www.theatlantic.com/doc/200306/hoffman (accessed: March 1, 2006).

99   Burdman, Daphne, "Education, Indoctrination, and Incitement: Palestinian Children on their Way to Martyrdom." Online, available from: taylorand francis.metapress.com/(afupjdjhmnlbp52lumhzjm55)/app/home/contribution.asp? referrer=parent&backto=issue,4,8;journal,13,21;linkingpublicationresults, 1:108550,1 (accessed: March 8, 2006), p. 97

100   Ibid., p. 106.

101   McKay, Susan, "Girls as 'Weapons of Terror' in Northern Uganda and Sierra Leonean Rebel Fighting Forces," *Studies in Conflict and Terrorism*, 28, 385–397, 2005, p. 387.

102   Ibid.

103   Brunner, "Female Suicide Bombers – Male Suicide Bombing?," p. 36.

104   Cunningham, "Cross-Regional Trends in Female Terrorism," pp. 177–178.

105   Pape, "The Strategic Logic of Suicide Terrorism," p. 5.

106   Atran, "Trends in Suicide Terrorism: Sense and Nonsense," p. 4.

107   Atran, "Trends in Suicide Terrorism: Sense and Nonsense," p. 10.

108   Hoffman, "The Logic of Suicide Terrorism."

109   Ibid.

110   Ibid.

111   Mazzetti, Mark, "Insurgent Attacks on Iraqis Soared in 2005, Report Says," *New York Times*, April 29, 2006, A7.

112   Atran, "Mishandling Suicide Terrorism," p. 85.

113   Ali Wyne, "Suicide Terrorism as Strategy: Case Studies of Hamas and the Kurdistan Workers Party," *Strategic Insights* 4, 7 (July 2005).

114   Atran, "Mishandling Suicide Terrorism," p. 84.

115   Reuter, *My Life is a Weapon*, p. 66.

116   Atran, "Mishandling Suicide Terrorism," p. 84.

117   Scott Atran and Jessica Stern, "Small Groups Find Fatal Purpose Through the Web," *Nature*, 437, September 29, 2005, p. 620.

118   Atran, "Mishandling Suicide Terrorism," p. 73.

119   Atran and Stern, p. 620.

120   Atran, "Trends in Suicide Terrorism: Sense and Nonsense," p. 1.

121   Pape, "The Strategic Logic of Suicide Terrorism," p. 14.

122   Wyne, "Suicide Terrorism as Strategy: Case Studies of Hamas and the Kurdistan Workers Party Strategic Insights."

4 (Gendered) war

Carolyn Nordstrom

The Road
The road is thronged with women; soldiers pass
And halt, but never see them; yet they're here —
A patient crowd along the sodden grass,
Silent, worn out with waiting, sick with fear.
The road goes crawling up a long hillside,
All ruts and stones and sludge, and the emptied dregs
Of battle thrown in heaps. Here where they died
Are stretched big-bellied horses with stiff legs,
And dead men, bloody-fingered from the fight,
Stare up at caverned darkness winking while.
   (Siegfried Sassoon (1983), written August 1916 – on the way to make a
         night attack on Quadrangle trench beyond Mametz village)

Betrayal

Barbara Ehrenreich (1997, 1) observed in her book *Blood Rites*: "Some years
ago I had occasion to need a theory of war. The occasion, fortunately, was
only a literary one." I, too, found that I needed a theory of war, but, unfortunately, mine was not a literary need, but one born of seeing war's frontlines. The first time I discovered the need for a theory of war was in the
early 1980s in Sri Lanka, when the island suffered wave after wave of escalating political violence. I had at my disposal numerous theories of war
provided by scholarly and military treatises, but, upon seeing war first-
hand, I found none fit. Most reflected the same view of war as the opening
poem: silent women thronging roadways, never seen, while men fight and
die.
   I have spent half of the last 25 years since that time conducting ethnography in various war zones of the world, and I have never yet met Siegfried
Sassoon's silent women waiting by the road of war. I have met many hundreds of women under attack and fighting back as best they could. They do
not quietly and patiently wait its end, sick with fear – they fight for it,
fearful or not.

... *Losing women*

I lost and found women in war for the first time in Sri Lanka in 1983, when I was at the center of the riots against the Tamils that took thousands of lives and destroyed one-sixth of the country's infrastructure in seven days. I had seen rioters beat and kill women on the streets; and I had seen women join in violent mobs. Yet in the days and months following the riots, I watched the accounts of the riots systematically exclude women, either as victims or as perpetrators. In the end, the official version of the riots was that "men in trousers" were responsible for the attack on Tamils. If I had not been on the streets for those seven days, I might well have accepted this "reasonable" version. One iconic representation of women did circulate widely: "the pregnant women disemboweled by terrorists." This icon is intended as a call to arms, and appears worldwide. This pregnant woman, always nameless as befits her iconic status, has been killed in every city and country at war I have been in; and, although such atrocities do occur, the use of this image as an icon effectively obscures all the many women and girls who die and fight without recognition.

The reporting on the riots in Sri Lanka improved little over time, and the stereotypes continued: rioters (adult male) and victims (identified as mass casualties, generally nameless). Worse, attitudes and policies were formed on this misinformation that tended to foment ongoing cycles of violence. I first thought that the erroneous views were the result of a lack of information: how many impartial researchers conduct viable research in the midst of a firefight? When violence erupts, few people take notes and most people take sides. I further assumed that the policies based on erroneous information — policies doomed to fail because they were based on fictions and not facts — would embrace more accurate information should it become available. But the first time I publicly presented my research on the political violence, another view began to form. People from the audience stood up, incensed, to challenge my data: "How can you say that women were involved in violence?" For others, I was being offensive by saying some youths participated in the violence, or that trusted members of the community harmed children. "Females don't join mobs, they are only assaulted by them!" The list of offenses went on. It did not matter that I had witnessed these events personally, talked to the people involved. The offense was speaking of these things.

... *Losing women soldiers*

The riots marked a turning point in Sri Lanka's political violence, and over the next two years the armed conflict between the government and the armed Tamil groups escalated. The government's atrocities were so severe that, by 1986, Amnesty International cited the Sri Lankan military as one of the worst human-rights violators in the world. As I followed the course of the war, I realized there was little in-site research in the Tamil regions under government siege, and even less about women fighting. In 1985, I made a trip to the Tamil regions of Jaffna and Trincomalee to do ethnography among female guerrillas. Once in Jaffna, I discovered that there were not three or four guerrilla armies (as was commonly presented), but 33 at that time. It was, I thought, a remarkable opportunity to study different groups' rules, roles, and treatment of female soldiers.

One picture galvanized my study. The day I arrived, I was approached by several of the major armed factions who wanted to know who I was and what I was doing in Jaffna. Few people came to the area at that time; I was told I was the second non-military person to travel to Jaffna in two years, the first being a BBC correspondent. In introducing me to the situation, I was given some political literature. On the cover of one of the group's publications was a picture of a young female guerrilla soldier in fatigues, AK-47, and full combat gear. It was the quintessential photo of a young woman soldier, and it was effective because it was riveting: she was beautiful, glowing with health and confidence. She smiled at the viewer with an openness that spoke of the commitment to fight for the justice that had been taken from her. The photo was brilliant: somehow it captured that she fought for the right to be a normal woman, in love, starting out on life, career, family – all in a grainy black and white reproduction. It was the story I was looking for: the "qualia" – the essential experience – of being a female guerrilla soldier. I began my search for her, for the sisterhood of soldiers.

I never found the young soldier. In a profound irony, I never would: of the 33 armed groups, only one allowed women into the forces, and they did not allow women to hold combat positions.[1] The public photo hid a private reality of far different values: no woman donned combat fatigues, carried an AK-47, held military rank. No female guerrillas existed.

Years later I ran across the same picture: it was a young woman from Central America. Her picture had been borrowed to adorn the cover of a guerrilla group half a world away in a war she would not be allowed to fight in.

...Finding women (non-)combatants

My study of female guerrillas ended before it began. But walking down the road in Jaffna that day, I discovered a deeper truth. It is not one that graces political literature. I was on a dirt road outside the city center when I came across a young teenage girl tied to a barbed wire fence. She had been beaten and killed. She was bound to the fence standing up, with her arms stretched out beside her tied to the wire – in a position reminiscent of both a prisoner and a crucifixion. She was not "just" dead; she was intended to be a message to the larger public. No one removed her body, although to leave it out in the open without normal burial procedures was a painful affront.

Her story was common and silent against the public fanfare of non-existent females guerrillas. Women and girls were not allowed military positions or equipment, but they transported messages, munitions, supplies, and food. They were a backbone of the war: running arms, procuring survival necessities, acting as communications systems, doing reconnaissance. This fact was not lost on the government troops. Unarmed, operating without the support of a military action, and often working alone, girls and women were easy targets. Troops caught, raped, and killed these girls and women with far less risk than they would encounter against an armed Tamil soldier. They left them in public sites as a terror-tactic and a warning.

It was at this point that I realized the whole discussion about women serving in the military is moot, and it is dangerous. In war, women are serving whether they are in a recognized military unit or not. They carry out primary functions of war, they are central targets, they are tortured and killed in numbers as great as, and often greater than, males ... and they are generally unarmed. There is a profound irony in this: women in many locales are denied access to military combat positions because, ostensibly, it is too dangerous. This leaves them vulnerable to attack without weapons, training, and backup.[2] My focus rests with a world today where the majority of battle deaths are civilians, and wars rage across community centers, not remote battlefields. In such a world, the unarmed *are* the frontlines. Women at the epicenters of political violence who are not part of a formal military are fighting, uniformed or not.

The discussion about women serving in the military is dangerous in its ability to silence the story of the dead girl on the fence, and all those like her – the poem at the beginning of this chapter asks the reader to imagine a war where women are silent stragglers on the backlines of wars men fight; the dead girl tied to the fence speaks to the reality of war in the contemporary world where 90 percent of all war-related deaths are non-combatants, the majority women and children. It is this that leads me to speak of betrayal as part of the "theory of war." She – and the hundreds like her in Jaffna, the thousands like her throughout Sri Lanka, and the millions like her worldwide – is betrayed by militaries that target women, but refuse to give them the means to defend themselves, as I have already suggested. She is betrayed by the media who delete such casualties from the public spotlight. And she is betrayed by scholars and theoreticians who continue to focus primarily on the military, the political, the institutional, and the masculine in addressing political violence. This silence is not haphazard. It is as political and as ideological as proclaimed manifesto and public creed. The fact that this girl was murdered and strung on a fence in the face of 70,000 conventions proclaiming human rights is possible because of this silence.

Destruction

I am hard put to find statistics on the number of women and girls killed in contemporary wars worldwide. Perhaps because it is a number militaries are not proud of, it is expunged from public databases. Perhaps because the killing of so-called non-combatants violates all international war protocols, these figures are actively hidden. Or, possibly, people who walk the front-lines do not collect statistics, and those who collect neutral data are not likely to walk the frontlines. I suspect the numbers are far higher than most analyses indicate.

Why should women and children be targeted by dirty war tactics? First, if the goal of dirty war is to produce terror in order to undermine political will, then the maiming and murder of the most vulnerable members of society are postulated to produce the most terror. The message is twofold: terror seeks to condemn the leaders of the victims for not being able to protect them – what right do they have to govern? The second reason women and children figure heavily in terror warfare is that they tend to be less mobile then men. Women are usually responsible for their homes, crit-ical subsistence, and the young, and thus tend to be more directly tied to a set locale. It has been my fieldwork experience that in attacks, women gener-ally search out and try to carry their children (and sometimes the infirm and elderly), and are thus among the slowest to flee. They are thus among the most likely to be caught by troops, by bullets, and by bombs. Home and hearth, mothers and children, tend to represent the heart and core of virtu-ally all societies. Attacks that hit at this center are constructed as the ulti-mate insult: "if 'we' can take out 'your' homes and 'your' families – what kind of protector, soldier, military, government, person, are you?"

"Who" is targeted is a more difficult question to answer. The question runs aground in the shoals of shallow description and poor theory that accepts a "nameless mass" of "non-combatant" casualties. In general, both state militaries and non-state guerrilla groups publicly uphold the tenets of just war theory that states the only legitimate targets in war are military ones. To explain civilian casualties, the notion of "collateral damage" – acci-dental civilian deaths – emerged. For the notion of collateral damage to hold, civilians *in general* had to comprise the casualties. If more poor or rich, women or men, children or adults, religious opposition groups or ethnic minorities, journalists or human rights activists, were killed – intentional targeting would be implied, and the accidental part of the killing would be called into question. A war cannot be just if any non-combatant group is intentionally targeted. Thus, the generalized category "non-combatant deaths" evolved as an undistinguished mass. This mass hid a multitude of military sins. In supporting a "Kiplingesque just-so story" of "just war," a deeper truth is hidden: to pull a trigger, drop a bomb, or torture a person, first a soldier has to select the target. The notion of "mass" in casualties is a sham. Which women are selected for kidnapping, forced labor, rape, torture, murder? Are they more likely to be the landed, the urban, the educated, or the poor, the peasants, and the disenfranchised? Are they more likely to be political, or just the opposite, to be alienated from politics, and thus from the means to armed revenge? Are the casualties most likely to be adult women, or are the elderly, the youth, and infants more likely to die? It is in the patterns of targeting that scholars can begin to explore the manifestations of power: who, exactly, constitutes a threat. Power is imminently discerning.

What, then, is theory?

Academic theory suffers under these burdens: even the most honorable theorist can do little if the only data she or he has access to has been collected by military and political officials with vested interests (and who walks the frontlines counting casualties?), and then further edited by media sources with other vested interests – in much the way the women, children, religious officials, elites, and elderly were edited out of the riots in Sri Lanka in 1983. Without a way to evaluate and critique existing data, a theorist at best produces theory based on faulty foundations, and at worst unwittingly perpetuates perspectives based in vested interests. "For the sake of intellectual responsibility," write Addelson-Payne and Watson-Verran (1998, 181), "academic theories require test." If analyses talk predominately about soldiers when the majority of war-related actors and casualties are non-combatants, these analyses are not theory; if they talk about the thoughts and actions of men alone in wars where women are critical to defense, survival, and targeting (as they are in all wars today), they do not constitute theory – for these mask the realities of the human condition rather than illuminating them.

Ethnography, although not the ultimate solution to the dilemma, provides one answer: by conducting long-term, in-depth studies within war zones, rather than relying solely on second-hand data, and by following all sides of a conflict and not relying on a necessary association with one side (as is the case in military and political associations), ethnography provides the tools to assess conventional "wisdom," political "facts," and military "statistics." It is observation, and not the printed word, that in this instance takes the mantle of empirical and theoretical objectivity.

Fighting back

The story circulates along informal channels: across backyards, alongside byways, between towns, throughout provinces. "She" had changed the course of the war. She was a poor, a desperately poor, village woman in the proverbial "anywhere" village of the frontlines. She had no schooling, no military training, no uniform, no weapons ... she had no name. She was the collateral damage of the eons. The war had rolled across her doorstep numerous times: troops came and demanded food, supplies, and recruits; they raped, maimed, and killed to ensure no one challenged them. They burned the villagers out when they left to make sure no one could gather the means to fight back. "She" had experienced the worst of the war. One day soldiers re-entered her village and demanded "more." She stood up, grabbed an axe, and hacked a soldier to death. She threw down the axe, spit, and walked off.

She broke the mystique of military control. Some say this marked the beginning of the end of the war.

The raging debates of whether women should be allowed to serve in militaries, and in combat, obscure an ugly truth: to be female today in a war zone is to *be* the frontlines. But women generally enter the battle armed with little more than their intelligence and values – they are often denied access to the weapons and training they require to fight back. So they create.

Literature, movies, and media have created an image of war as "fighting." Only fighting. It is easy to forget in the adrenaline rush of a two-hour movie or a media sound bite on exploding bodies and weapons that people live their lives amid these explosions. They must eat, sleep, find food and clothing, work, care for loved ones, and craft resistance. What, in this context, is a female soldier? A woman who acquires a weapon to shoot those who threaten her home; a woman journalist who risks her life traveling to the front to document the war; a nurse who remains on the frontlines even though she knows there is a death-threat on her because she is providing critical medical services; a woman who walks across land-mined battle-grounds to carry food and essential supplies to a besieged town?

... Two women

Graca. Maybe she was a nurse, or an unofficial combatant in her home town under siege. Or maybe she was a jack-of-all-trades – the ultimate survivor making sure others also survive. I ran into her in the public health office in Mozambique during the height of the war: she was taking some vaccines and medicines out to a community under attack. She asked if I wanted to come along, and introduced herself as Graca. "Grace" was an appropriate name, I soon learned. The ride to the battle zone was several hours, and to this day, I have never experienced a ride like that. "Some call it Hell's Corridor, others Demolition Lane, some just call it Shit," she explained, an assault rifle casually laid across her lap as she drove. The road was lined with burned-out carcasses of cars that had been attacked by troops, guerrillas, bandits, and profiteers. It was pockmarked with large potholes from landmines, mortars, and pernicious weather. No one undertook repairs; such work was lethal. It looked like a scene out of a science fiction movie about Armageddon. As soon as we left town, Graca apologized as she pressed the gas to the floor and began to drive at very high speeds, and erratically, down the road: "This is the only way to avoid attack." I wondered what the difference was between dying in an attack or in a spin out from hitting a landmine pothole. As we careened around holes and skidded around corners at break-neck speeds, Graca calmly explained to me about the kinds of attacks taking place. As is common worldwide today, unarmed townspeople were being attacked by the same collection of soldiers, guerrillas, bandits, and profiteers who were attacking the cars along this road. A desperate, starving, beleaguered population – what was left of it – depended on people like Graca for their survival.

Graca brought not only medicines, food, weapons, and other essentials, she brought hope and a will to fight. This woman was like seeing tomorrow: people said when Graca was there they believed, at least for that moment, that tomorrow could – would – come. "Grapefruit," Graca exclaimed, and I thought she was having a momentary pang of food longing, common in war zones where food is one of the first casualties. I had not seen a grapefruit for months, and frequently dreamt about fruit. She slammed on her brakes, took a corner at a ninety-degree angle skid, and fishtailed down a tiny road that had been invisible seconds before. We skidded to a stop before a dilapidated shell-pocked building. "We run grapefruit out of here," Graca explained. Run grapefruit? I had heard of running diamonds and guns, but grapefruit? I realized that in a land awash with weapons, bought with commodities like blood gems (gems used to purchase military equipment), war made food more scarce, and more valuable, than arms. It was not unusual for a person to trade an assault weapon for a meal. "To survive, we need to be able to purchase at least a bit of food, medicines, petrol, and the like. Grapefruit sells across the border (in South Africa), and with the profits we buy essentials." We loaded up her car with grapefruit and roared back down the road. When we arrived at her destination, I could not find the town. It had been attacked so many times, nothing remained but people trying to eke out a seemingly impossible living. One man invited me to his "place" to talk. We sat on a fallen tree trunk in the open air that served as a chair, and, seemingly, a house: "How can we rebuild and rebuild, time and again?" he asked. "How many times can a person try to put together a house again, replant their crops, get tools after losing them all yet again to another attack? When do we stop believing in tomorrow? Why bother?" I pointed out that he was "bothering": as we spoke, he was digging in the dirt at his feet, dropping in seeds Graca had brought. "Yeah," he said, "Graca and her kind don't let us give it up. I can't believe she's still alive," he mumbled under his breath. "They say she has guardian spirits, they won't get her." Graca was the survival line to a number of communities like this one. Almost no one outside of the ubiquitous troops and bandits traveled these roads – and without people like her, no food, no arms, no supplies, and little hope entered these frontline towns.

Leenda. A large woman in camouflage pants and a t-shirt came up and she and Graca threw their arms around each other in a warm embrace. Leenda, Graca told me, was one of the commanders in the area. She was tough, jovial, and beloved. Leenda walked about, showing me the area, as she talked about the battles taking place. In this war, the rebels were backed by neighboring apartheid governments and were credited internationally with the majority of the severe human-rights abuses taking place. Leenda fought with the government. Maybe. In the truth of war – versus the pretty media accounts – who one fought with and for were far more nebulous and contested than conventional military lore would have it. Leenda, and all those like her, shaped the realities of the war far more than the power elite would ever wish – the latter were in the safety of the capitals, while all the Leendas of the war managed the frontlines. Leenda pulled no punches in discussing the war. She was brutally frank about who was killing whom, why, and how. She outlined the atrocities done by the rebels, and by her own troops. She talked of the fact that her outfit had not been paid in months, and that supplies rarely made it out to the frontlines. She had a mandate to protect the population, but she also had a mandate to protect her troops: if they had guns, and were starving, should she stop them from "requisitioning" food and supplies from the communities they fought to protect? Should she shoot a soldier she caught raping young girls during his last attack? Should she point out to me the propaganda put out by both the rebels and the government that was patently untrue, even if it supported her? Leenda crafted the morals of the war in stride, in situ; not the generals in safe offices in military headquarters, not politicians ensconced in their well-protected offices, not the judges or human rights advocates. Leenda, and all those like her walking the frontlines with the weapons to enforce their decisions, defined the war. No journalists came to take her story, no television crews shoot footage of her decisions in battle. Leenda had been in the center of the worst of war: she led attacks, carried children to medical attention whose legs had been blown off by landmines, buried her friends. She fought not because she wanted power or liked command – she fought because her home had been destroyed and she hated war. "You see this," she said sweeping her arm to encompass the area around us,

> this is life? The children have no school, the teachers have been killed, the clinic burned down, the nurses shot. The crops have been razed, the water sources polluted, and every home looted. Nothing to eat, little to hope for. What are we fighting for? This is what we bring? I want no part of politics, I want our life returned to us.

I watched Graca and Leenda hug as they said goodbye to each other. Graca in a traditional Africa wrap, Leenda in fatigues. Both fighting the war together. Who was a soldier?

Graca and I got in her car to continue on our journey, and I noticed she no longer had her assault rifle. I remembered one distraught woman telling me earlier in the day that her home had been attacked four times, and each time she had been burned out, losing everything including her crops and food. "How can I find the hope to plant a fifth time, to rebuild my home for my remaining children. I don't even have a gun to try to protect my family," she cried. I figured now she did. Again, I thought, who were the soldiers?

Regeneration

The war that Graca and Leenda were fighting in Mozambique in 1990 had taken over a million lives and displaced over one-third of the population from their homes. I spent several years in Mozambique during this time, and with the permission of the Ministry of Health, traveled nationwide, visiting a number of frontline locations. I met Graca's and Leenda's equivalents in province after province. Mostly, they were like Graca: women outside of formal militaries fighting without the back-up, the weapons, and the supplies afforded by militaries. A site in central Zambezia in a diamond-rich mining area (always the worst hit by vicious fighting) provides a good example. Arriving in such a location looks much like a scene from a post-Apocalypse script: farmlands razed, water sources polluted with dead bodies, standing structures bombed into a combination of tilting half-walls and strafed rubble. The formal institutions of society are bombed, looted, and closed, and the professionals that ran them are gone, either killed or forced to flee. In many towns I visited, 25 or more people were dying a day of starvation. Gunshots from the opposing forces rang out from the bush nearby. Landmines were buried along roadways, water sources, agricultural areas, and service buildings. These locales, especially those rich in minerals or other strategic goods, changed hands between the government and rebel forces with frequency, and each battle took a further toll on civilian society.

Yet, as I walked amid the rubble and suffering, I found that average people in fact resisted war with tremendous conviction, and the means by which they resisted was in large part by rebuilding the core institutions of society. Many people told me that it is in refusing to fight, and in rebuilding society, that war is defeated. This made them even more threatening targets for militaries.[3]

In this town in central Zambezia I met a nurse who was threatened with death by soldiers. She pretended to flee after her healthcare facility was looted and burned, but stayed in hiding to hold "midnight clinics." She buried the medicines she had been able to flee with in a burned field, and informed the civilian population when and where she would hold clinics. She had to move the site every several days to avoid detection by troops, and often held them in the middle of the night. The nurse was not the only unsung warrior of the town: by day, several women ran "the school under the tree." Even though the schools had been bombed out, these women held classes under shade trees, teaching pupils to write and do arithmetic with sticks in the dirt. Given the troops' strategies of undermining society by targeting service institutions, teaching was an act of military resistance and courage. Contrary to urban conceptions that tend to see pupils forced to go to school, these children clamored for education: it provided a site of sanity and development in the midst of war's chaos. The list of people fighting the war by rebuilding societies continued: at night I attended ceremonies to help the severely war-traumatized. Women, for example, who were kidnapped by rebel forces, and forced to act as porters, sexual providers, and laborers at military bases under the worst of conditions – and who managed to escape – were provided with healing ceremonies. Throughout the length and breadth of Mozambique, people explained to me that if the mental and emotional assaults of war were not treated along with the physical damage of violence, war-traumatized people would be unable to participate in daily life in a healthy way, and this would undermine the very ability of society to regenerate. In another example, women banded together to set up "women's banks." Banks tend to be non-existent on the frontlines. So women pooled financial resources and made loans to one another. This allowed the initial development of trade, industry, and agricultural activities in the midst of institutional collapse. Such stories continue. But these suffice to show that the frontlines are neither Hobbesian pits of violent self-interest, vacuous wastelands of aimless war-traumatized, nor decimated stretches of civilians cowed into terrorized inaction. Neither are devoid of females fighting – whether they are recognized by any formal military or not.

Do political treatises rebuild shattered societies? They are necessary, but not sufficient: they allow the space to forge healthy societies. Peace does not equate to peace accord. Peace accords are political and military documents; they do not rectify collapsed institutions, nor cull the violence embedded in society. If people are war-traumatized, so too are the institutions they populate. Peace is more than an end to violence, it is a freedom from oppression, fear, and misery born of political bloodshed.

A critical question then becomes: if peace accords do not rebuild essential institutions, and if they do not reweave the core threads of a nation's social fabric, what, or who, does? In much the same way that women outside the military carry out many of the core activities of war and defense on the frontlines, women outside of formal governmental institutions also carry out many of the core activities of constructing peace.

At the height of the war in Mozambique (or Angola, Bosnia, Sri Lanka, or any other war zone I have been in), women were among the first refugees to return to war-decimated lands. They braved landmines and rogue soldiers to plant and harvest essential foods. They helped to set up trade routes to bring in essential supplies. Women are instrumental in rebuilding the less-tangible institutions of society, in addition to starting clinics, schools, and informal financial systems; women often institute security networks, dispute-resolution councils, and support groups for the war-afflicted. They play key roles in reintegrating the war-maimed, soldiers, and the tortured back into daily society; in counseling a generation of traumatized children; in redesigning families who have lost members to war; and in re-establishing peaceful ideals over those of violent revenge. Such women are as little recognized as Graca. Who stands in the embers of war and documents the patient rebuilding of society's structures, the careful revitalizing of war-damaged lives and institutions? Yet this rebuilding is critical to a society's survival if it is not to revert to ongoing cycles of violent conflict.

What, again, is theory?

I began this chapter by quoting Ehrenreich's first line of her book *Blood Rites*: "Some years ago I had the occasion to need a theory of war." She follows with the observation:

I soon found that there are no theories of war or – depending on what you are willing to accept as a "theory" – far too many of them. Ask a scholar for an explanation of war, and he or she will most likely snicker at your naivete in expecting that something so large and poorly defined could even be explained. Ask a nonspecialist, however, and you will get any of a dozen explanations, each proffered with utter confidence: It is because of our innate aggressiveness ... or because of innate male aggressiveness ... or because of imperialism and greed ... or over-population and a shortage of resources ... or it is simply a manifestation of unknowable evil. Our understanding of war, it occurred to me, is about as confused and uninformed as theories of disease were roughly 200 years ago.

(1997, 1–2)

Our understanding of war may well be poorly developed – but this development is not random: what we believe to be true about war furthers a set of beliefs we believe to be true about our world: the world of power, gender, representation, force, and ultimately, the human condition.

Theory purporting to describe war that does not address the realities of war – theories that delete any of war's casualties or perpetrators, heroes or villains – is not theory, it is ideology. One might argue that war is *supposed* to be about militaries, and that justifies deleting non-combatants, women, children, the infirm, rogues, and "collateral damage" from astute analysis. But writing about what is supposed to be is neither data nor science.

If non-combatant women comprise such a large part of today's war's frontline actors – if their actions are critical to the nature, manifestation, and outcome of war – why are they deleted from the majority of English publications available on war? Several answers come to mind:

- Leaving women out is a holdover of archaic theories based on the trench warfare of World War I, where indeed the majority of battlefield deaths were male soldiers.
- Proponents of a just war theory are embarrassed by the sheer number of non-combatant female casualties that attend to war and by the brutality to which they are subjected, and find it more convenient to delete these realities from consideration than to grapple with them.
- Women are purposely expunged from analysis as this allows tactical targeting of civilian communities and non-combatant women to take place with impunity through invisibility.

This question is complicated by an additional factor: the role of non-combatant women is not only deleted from considerations of violence, but from considerations of peace-building as well. Why should women's actions in forging peace be equally invisible in traditional analyses of the war/peace continuum? A fourth answer joins the list of the previous three:

- Women's role in war violates conventional notions of power.

To explain: the regeneration of peaceful society is crucial to instituting peace processes. As Aretxaga (1997, 4–5) writes:

> Republican women ... do, of course, want peace. That is not the issue. The question for them is what exactly peace means. Defining peace, like defining war, means delineating the terms for a particular kind of society and a particular political structure. Peace and war are not so much two opposed states of being as they are multifaceted, ambiguous, mutually imbricated arenas of struggle.

If such peace-building is critical to peace accords, it must begin *before* the accords can be crafted, not after. It must begin in the epicenters of political violence, and that is in the homes and communities of general society. It is here too that peace is first crafted: not just in the acts of diplomats and generals.

Such a view of power and political transformation clearly violates top-down approaches to power. It is antithetical to government and diplomatic control. It is threatening to the idea that power is encoded in organized institutions. And it is distasteful to realist versions of military and political bases of power. A more critical understanding of power is a point central to Susan Strange's book, *The Retreat of the State*:

> Another reason why power has been rather superficially treated in the literature of international political economy may be the tremendous concern – one might almost call it an obsession – with the role of hegemons in the system. This has tended to exclude all other questions relating to the nature and use of power in the world system.
>
> (1996, 21)

On a more performative level, de Certeau has devoted considerable analytical focus to uncovering the ways violence, hegemony, resistance, and transformative power operate in daily life and in phenomenological culture. In a poetic example from Oscar Lewis to illustrate his theoretical assertions that power is indeed manifest in the daily dynamics of the average and the unknown, he captures the aspects of power I am discussing here. The only thing left to de Certeau is to add "women" as well as "men" in his statement:

> Manuel, a vagabond peasant in the slums of Mexico City, was already designating a cultural revolution when, thinking he was a piece of shit, he barely (but wasn't it "laughable") ... he dreamed to "find the appropriate words" to "sing the poetry of life," to "express the lowest passions in the most beautiful way" ... "win the fight against [him]self." "Men

who can write of these things make the world more habitable." A few
poetic words, and *perhaps* the world as it is lived begins to change.

(1997, 12)

Conventional modernist worldview postulates the necessity of states where
the best and brightest rise to the top to fashion governing institutions that
keep the Hobbesian masses in check. Civilization proceeds from elite institutions; from the few, and mostly from the male. Threats to civilization
come from the undifferentiated many, the masses snarling and snapping in
naked self-interest and irrational emotionalism. War is instigated by the
dangerous other; it is solved by the elite military commanders, the visionary
politicians, and the educated diplomats. All these groups rely on the tools
and theories crafted by scholars – and thus this group too is postulated as
central to the civilizing process. It is patently obvious to note the gender,
ethnic, political, and nationalistic nature of these power configurations.

Such theories underlie larger worldviews about the nature of power –
about how power *should* be. Part of this equation is the fact that the people
who perpetuate these top-down theories of power are among those who
benefit most from these views, which, unsurprisingly, places them at the top
of the top-down model. Data suggesting that core aspects of political transformation are instituted by and among average civilians – who themselves
create civil *and* moral society, irrespective of the governing institutions or
lack thereof in war – prove unsettling to such conventional approaches. That
many, and perhaps the majority, of these civilians are women who eschew
formal governing structures, formalized civil society groupings, and formu-
lated political theory undermines the most basic ideals grounding conventional theories of power. In sum, then, deleting women casualties from war
obscures the fact that, in current military thought, political will and transformative power are seen to reside in the center of average society, and that
is precisely why it is targeted. Ignoring the role women play in war and
peace-building alike obscures the fact that political transformation will
come to naught if the foundations have not already been laid by average
non-combatants, many of them women, who patiently rebuild destroyed
infrastructures, shattered lives, and impoverished futures.

Notes

1 After some years, several of the major paramilitaries did begin to allow women to
  join their ranks. But this came at a cost: when the author was in Sri Lanka in the
  late 1980s, one of the most popular wisecracks concerned the way the commander
  of one of the major paramilitaries was forced by popular pressure to allow women
  to fight, and his wife joined – but, the wisecrack went, he forced her to stay at
  home in uniform and posted troops (much needed elsewhere) around his house to
  protect her.
2 It is important to note that women are allowed into the military in a number of
  countries and guerrilla groups in the world. Their status varies considerably, from

largely feminized non-combat positions to frontline commanders. Many have argued that even in forces that allow women combat positions, they are excluded from top political and military decision-making positions.

3 For a more complete explanation, see Nordstrom's *A Different Kind of War Story* (1997).

References

Addelson-Payne, Kathryn, and Helen Watson-Verran. 1998. "Inquiry into a feminist way of life," in *Daring to be Good*, edited by B.O. Bat-Ami and A. Ferguson. London: Routledge, pp. 168–182.

Aretxaga, Begoña. 1997. *Shattering Silence: Women, Nationalism, and Political Subjectivity in Northern Ireland*. Princeton: Princeton University Press.

de Certeau, Michel. 1997. *Cultural in the Plural*. Translated by Tom Conley. Minneapolis: University of Minnesota Press.

Ehrenreich, Barbara. 1997. *Blood Rites*. London: Virago.

Nordstrom, Carolyn. 1997. *A Different Kind of War Story*. Philadelphia: University of Pennsylvania Press.

Sasson, Siegfried. 1983. *The War Poems*. London: Faber & Faber.

Strange, Susan. 1996. *The Retreat of the State: the Diffusions of Power in the World Economy*. Cambridge: Cambridge University Press/UNICEF.

5 The evolving participation of Muslim women in Palestine, Chechnya, and the global jihadi movement

Karla Cunningham

Introduction

Muslim women are not new participants within the nationalist, and often violent, conflicts that exist in their respective countries. They have been long-associated with secular nationalist settings in Algeria, Palestine, Turkey and Lebanon. In modern times, women's involvement in Islamic religious violence first appeared during the Iranian Revolution. Their involvement in Islamic religious violence widened in the context of the Chechen movement and then in the Palestinian and Salafi global jihadi movement (GJM), though, by most accounts, their numbers have remained relatively small, though not insubstantial.[1] The evolution of women's political violence from secular to Islamic religious settings[2] is the focus of this analysis.

It has been argued that women's political violence has most frequently been associated with leftist movements, largely because

> [b]y their very nature, left-wing groups are ideologically more suited to justify and advocate women assuming combatant and other non-traditional roles because they premise that fundamental problems in the political and social institutions of society require a radical break with the past.
>
> (Ness, 2005, 355)

Indeed, it has only been since 2000 that women's roles in *jihad* have been significantly considered, discussed, and analyzed within the Muslim world due to their increased involvement in suicide attacks. The majority of these attacks have been perpetrated in the Palestinian and Chechen contexts since 2000, though they have not involved religious conceptions of *jihad*. Instead, the bombings have been nationalistic acts that extrapolate religious symbolism and terminology. Though reference to *jihad* has been made in both the Palestinian and Chechen political arenas, the understanding and use of *jihad* in Palestine and Chechnya differs in important ways from its understanding and use associated with the GJM, as will be discussed shortly. Cook notes that "[t]o date, women fighting in *jihad* have only been a factor in these nationalist-Islamic resistance movements [Palestinian and Chechen], but not in other globalist radical Muslim warfare" (Cook, 2005, 383). However, as will be argued below, women are increasingly involved within the GJM, and this involvement differs from women's participation in other Muslim settings.

Religious discourse, women and *jihad*

Cook (2005) quite rightly notes that, within classical *jihadi* materials, there is little mention of women, but that this began to change in the 1990s due to regional attitudinal changes regarding women and "Islamic feminism" (2005, 377–378). Significantly, in 1993, Islamic scholar Muhammad Khayr Haykal argued that women should be trained to use arms and on how to fight "... because as long as it is possible that *jihad* could become *fard 'ayn* upon the woman, it is incumbent to train her for this eventuality so that she will be prepared to fulfill this obligation" (Haykal, cited in Cook, 2005, 379). In August 2001, the High Islamic Council in Saudi Arabia issued a *fatwa* (religious decree) urging women to join the fight against Israel as martyrs. Finally, by 2003, Saudi Arabian religious scholars such as Yusuf al-'Ayyiri began to clear the way for women to fight in *jihad* by abolishing the traditional restrictions to their participation that included parental permission and performance of the *hajj* ritual.

Central to religious discussions of women's roles in *jihad* is how religious scholars interpret *jihad*. Critical is whether *jihad* is conceptualized as *fard 'ayn*, meaning that *jihad* falls on every individual member of the Muslim community, or whether *jihad* is understood as *fard kifaya*, wherein *jihad* becomes the obligation of only the part of the Muslim community who can successfully wage *jihad* (Cook, 2005, 379, 381–382; Yadlin, 2006, 53).[3] Traditionally, *jihad* has been conceptualized as *fard kifaya*, and the obligation it entails has applied only to a small percentage of male community members. Conceptualizing *jihad* as *fard 'ayn* involves the notion of "total war." This necessitates that every man, woman and child mobilize for conflict, as opposed to limited war involving only adult males, often within a narrow age range. Because Palestinian, Chechen and, increasingly, Salafi GJM leaders frame their conflicts as *fard 'ayn*, Islamic religious and ideological pathways for female participation have been established that have heretofore not existed in the Islamic setting. Nevertheless, the conceptualization of *fard 'ayn* is different for the Palestinian and Chechen cases on the one hand, and the Salafi GJM on the other hand, as will be demonstrated shortly.

While terrorist leaders in the three cases considered here face operational constraints that raise the probability and desirability of female terrorist participation (e.g., males arrests, detention and/or counter-terrorism profiles), they also need to find social sanction within highly traditional Islamic societies for female participation in violent political activities. While nationalists – both secular and Islamist – employ the religious concept of *fard 'ayn* in the Chechen and Palestinian cases, they do so instrumentally. Religious symbolism and terminology becomes a potent ideological force to mobilize society to support violence by armed groups. Women's mobilization,[4] including violent mobilization, within this context is made consistent with cultural norms (Ness, 2005, 356–357, 362), mainly by emphasizing mothering and sacrifice, in the same manner as in non-Islamic settings such as Nicaragua and Colombia. While the use of Islam in this context is a potent symbolic and ideological tool, it is more instrumental and ideological than truly religious. This is in stark contrast to the Salafi process where something more is required than simply showing that female violence is consistent with cultural norms of female behavior. Rather, for the Salafis, women's mobilization, especially for violence, must be shown to conform to *religious norms* of female behavior, and to that end, a great deal of intellectual movement has been applied within Salafi circles.

Shalinsky (1993) provides an intriguing discussion of women's roles in Afghanistan's *jihad* that has direct bearing on the current discussion.[5] During a time of crisis, such as *jihad*, the traditional, and socially sanctioned, focus of women on family and kin becomes *nafs* (self-indulgence/desire) whereas *'aql* (reason) moves from the traditional conceptualization of veiling and concern for family and kin to a willingness to sacrifice herself and her kin (1993, 663, 665).

> Jihad is a special time of transition between the old corrupt society and the new improved society that will emerge. Because it is a liminal or transitional phase, jihad includes a certain amount of disorder or chaos. In such a time, women are "liberated" from many of the traditional norms of gender-appropriate behavior. Contrary to usual norms, they not only must sacrifice their kin, they can even kill the unbeliever.... After the jihad is over ... [women] should relegate themselves to the household and kin network that they have momentarily transcended.
>
> (Shalinsky, 1993, 674)

This perception of *jihad* is consistent with many non-Islamic nationalist movements, and their efforts to mobilize women to support their respective conflicts up to, and including, violent actions. To do this, nationalist leaders have needed to find a way to make women temporarily consistent with violent political action, while simultaneously creating the avenue to return women to their pre-war, and often idealized, traditional social structures.[6] Notably the process Shalinsky describes is not particularly religious; while *jihad* is discussed, its context is consistent with broader nationalist settings from around the world.

Illustrative cases

The three cases that will be reviewed below represent the most active settings regarding Muslim female terrorism since 2000; however, they possess significant differences. First, only two involve actual territory (Palestine, Chechnya) and, in both of those cases, the populations are engaged in a nationalist war against an occupying power. Second, one case is a religious ideological movement (Salafi GJM), but its ties to several terrorist events and its potential for the future make it a significant case. Third, the cases range from secular/nationalist to Salafi religious, reflecting the scope of female participation in *jihad* (Figure 5.1).

Palestine: secular and religious nationalism

The Palestinian case possesses both secular and religious features, but importantly, it is not a part of the Salafi/Wahhabi movement, unlike both the Chechen and Salafi GJM cases. Rather, the Palestinian case resembles traditional nationalist movements, and their goals, most notably, are geographically limited (i.e., to the Occupied Territories) and politically straightforward – gaining political independence from Israel and instituting a Palestinian state. The ideological base of that state could range from secular to Islamic, depending on whether one is considering Fatah or Hamas.

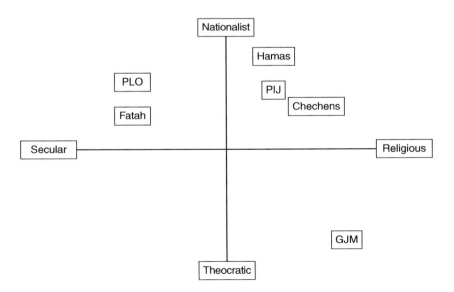

Figure 5.1 Political and ideological range of Islamist groups involved in female suicide attacks since 2000.[7]

There is a long line of Palestinian women who have been involved with terrorist organizations, particularly since the nationalist-based movements began to carry out violent activities in the 1960s. Palestinian secular leaders have historically been willing to include women in an array of roles to gain strategic advantage and for operational reasons. Women have mobilized for several purposes that include, but are certainly not limited to, nationalism, to fill personnel requirements as their male counterparts are killed or arrested, because of the individual and collective impact of occupation, and political activism. However, leaders' strategic objectives and women's mobilizational potential have frequently been stymied by Palestinian society, which has tended to resist expanded roles for women and only allowed such expansion under extreme stress, and then only for limited periods of time. Three visible historical periods exist that include the 1967 war, the first *intifada* and the second *intifada*; within each historical period, women have been mobilized in response to heightened Israeli occupation and/or aggression.

One of the most well-known female terrorists, Leila Khaled, was affiliated with the Popular Front for the Liberation of Palestine (PFLP). Another woman convicted of planting a bomb in a Jerusalem supermarket during 1969, Randa Nabulsi, was sentenced to ten years' imprisonment (Al-Batsh, 2002). While there has been a low probability for women to be used by Islamist terrorist groups, continuing the global trend of lower female representation amongst rightist and/or religious conservative organizations, there is in fact some precedent for such inclusion in Palestine.[8] Nevertheless, most Palestinian women who engaged in political violence from the late-1960s through the late 1980s were almost wholly affiliated with non-religious or more traditionally nationalist movements such as the Palestine Liberation Organization (PLO). Society was also very ambivalent about women's participation and roles within the Palestinian resistance movements during this period.

Women's mobilization during the first *intifada* went through two phases that built upon the structural developments that had occurred since 1967, but was also heavily influenced by complex social forces contending with escalating Israeli violence, heightened national expectations and expanding female roles. Initially, women mobilized as either mothers or warriors, mirroring the events of the 1967 war but also involving more women in a wider array of roles. Women at this time mobilized for a number of reasons, including: personnel shortages, the extension of their involvement with public organizations such as neighborhood committees, which became activist during the conflict, and their support by the Palestinian leadership (Usher, 1993, 38). However, after about a year, the *"Hijab* Campaign" (Hammami, 1990, 1997; Usher, 1993) evolved as a complex reaction to secularist–Islamist competition over nationalism, women's mobilization by secular forces and societal ambivalence over this expanding female public role. The result was that young "warrior" women, whose public but usually non-violent activities challenged social norms of appropriate female behavior, were pushed out of the visible ("unveiled") public ("warrior") realm. In turn, mothers expanded their symbolic and support roles. Thus, by the second stage of the first *intifada* "... only the 'mother' generation played a role in public while younger women were kept at home, the main argument ... being for their safety" (Hammer, 2000, 304). Despite the religious overtones associated with the *Hijab* Campaign and the growing role of Islamist organizations like Hamas in the *intifada*, religion was not a critical component of this conflict, and where religion was injected, it was done so in ideological and instrumental terms.

Women's roles in the second *intifada* have continued to range along the mother–warrior continuum. However, evidence suggests that women have been more heavily attracted to an activist "warrior" stance in this *intifada* than in earlier cases, and that their roles expanded early in the uprising. This process is largely a response to the deeper features of the second *intifada*, the scope of Israel's response, and a reaction to the first *intifada*. Beginning in late 2000 and then escalating throughout 2001, women were increasingly visible participants in a range of violent activities that presaged their role as suicide attackers. For example, Ahlam Al-Tamimi reportedly worked with Mohamed Daghles, a member of the Palestinian Authority security body, and the two are linked to at least two incidents in the summer of 2001. In July, Al-Tamimi appears to have carried a bomb disguised as a beer can into a West Jerusalem supermarket which detonated but did not injure anyone. In August, Al-Tamimi was linked to a Hamas bomber who carried a bomb in a guitar case into a Sbarro pizzaria that killed the bomber and fifteen others. She was arrested by Israel's Shabak in 2001 and charged with extending logistical support to the Hamas cell that attacked Sbarro. On 3 August 2001, Ayman Razawi, 23, a mother of two, was caught before she could plant an eleven-pound bomb packed with nails and screws hidden in a laundry detergent box in a Tel Aviv bus station.

Despite the activities noted above, the prospect of a female martyr remained remote through the first weeks of 2002 – "[t]here have been very few cases of Arab women found infiltrating Israel on a mission to murder civilians" (Reeves, 2002). That perception changed dramatically on 28 January 2002, when Wafa Idris, 28, detonated a twenty-two-pound bomb in Jerusalem that killed her, as well as an 81-year-old Israeli man, and injured more than 100 others. The Fatah-linked Al-Aqsa Martyr's Brigade (aka Al Aqsa Brigades) claimed responsibility for her attack and described Idris as a "martyr." Following the incident, reactions to Idris' bombing were mixed. Sheikh Ahmad Yassin, spiritual leader of Hamas, opposed Idris' action, citing the adequate reserve of personnel – "in this phase [of the uprising], the participation of women is not needed in martyr operations, like men." He went on to note that "[w]e can't meet the growing demands of young men who wish to carry out martyr operations" and "women form the second line of defence in the resistance to the occupation." Yassin later qualified his objection, however, when he added that if a woman wanted to carry out a martyr operation that she should be accompanied by a man if the operation required her to be away more than a day and a night. Sheikh Hassan Yusef, another Hamas leader, noted that there was no *fatwa* that prevented a woman from being a martyr ("We Don't Need Women Suicide Bombers," 2002). Yusef's point mirrored the opinion of Isma'eel Abu Shanab, a leader of Hamas, who also reportedly stated that there is no *fatwa* prohibiting women from carrying out suicide attacks, ostensibly against Israeli occupation in the Palestinian territories (The Middle East Media and Research Institute, 2002).

Between January 2002 and May 2006, there were sixty-seven Palestinian women who sought to be suicide attackers; eight were successful and, of these, five were sent by Fatah, two by Islamic Jihad in Palestine and one by Hamas (Sweitzer, 2006, 25). On 23 November 2006, Fatima Omar Mahmud al-Najar, a 68-year-old with over forty grandchildren, blew herself up on behalf of Hamas in the first suicide attack claimed by the group in almost two years. Interestingly, Hamas has begun to grapple with the role of women in its organization. For example, despite continued resistance to female activism, Hamas' female wing, the Sisterhood, was pivotal in mobilizing female voters in the January 2006 election that resulted in a Hamas electoral victory (Hadid, 2006). Hamas' ability to place a lid on growing female demands for influence is diminishing as a result of three factors: existing socio-political structures that facilitate female mobilization such as the Sisterhood, electoral laws establishing a quota system for female representation and women's involvement in violent political activism during the second *intifada* (Cunningham, 2005).

To summarize, while religion is a factor within the Palestinian setting, its significance differs from both the Chechen and GJM cases. Hamas, the dominant Islamist force, espouses a "traditional" view of Islam that is consistent with nationalist aspirations and the politicized role of Islam within the Middle East and North Africa for the past several decades. Radical Salafi Islam is not present in the Palestinian case, thereby making the Palestinian brand of Islam much more consistent with established understandings of political Islam and nationalism.

Chechnya: nationalism blends with Salafi/Wahhabism

The Chechen case diverges importantly from the Palestinian case and is a useful counterpoint to the GJM case. Information remains scarce regarding women's involvement in the Chechen separatist movement and attention only increased after the introduction of female suicide attacks in 2000. Chechnya has experienced two distinct conflicts: the first Chechen war took place between 1994 and 1996, and the second Chechen war has been ongoing since 1999. The first Chechen war witnessed significant levels of violence and international condemnation of Russia for human rights violations. Russia withdrew in 1996, and in the interim period, while a new government was being installed, it was not possible to fully achieve law and order over Chechen territory. This laid the groundwork for Russia's intervention in 1999. The scope of both wars, and the tremendous costs to civilians, has been instrumental for drawing both male and female participants to the conflict. While there is some evidence that a limited number of women were involved in the first Chechen war as combatants, and that some of these women were Wahhabis (Nivat, 2001), these accounts are almost entirely journalistic. The combination of violent conflict, geographic and cultural constraints, and Russian media controls has significantly limited observer scrutiny of the Chechen wars. Indeed, it was the introduction of female suicide attackers that prompted an increase in observer interest in the second Chechen war.

The first suicide attack undertaken in the Chechen case was by two women, Khava Barayeva and Luisa Magomadova, on 7 June 2000. Since 2000, there have been 112 suicide terrorists, of whom forty-eight were women (43 percent) and sixty-four were men (57 percent) (Speckhard and Ahkmedova, 2006a, 431). Women have been involved with 81 percent of the total suicide attacks involving Chechen rebels (Speckhard and Akhmedova, 2006b, 63), and men working alone have carried out only 18 percent of the attacks (Speckhard and Akhmedova, 2006a, 468).

Speckhard and Akhmedova (2006b) report that all of the women they studied were motivated by ideas associated with violent Salafi Wahhabism following a personal trauma. Salafi thought increased in Chechnya throughout the 1990s just as war broke out with Russia. In contrast, Nivat (2005) argues that, for young women, "the *jihad* is not especially a question of religion, it is just that they understand the revival of Islam in Chechnya as a critical element in the identity-building of the torn region" (2005, 417). For the mothers of some of the female suicide attackers, their daughters were driven by despair and a lack of "dialogue" between Chechen civil society and the Russians (Nivat, 2005, 416).

These differing perspectives on the roots of female violence in the Chechen setting illustrates that the highly nationalist features of the Chechen conflict have become religiously infused. The secular nationalist aspects of the Chechen war generated a pathway to violence for women that better resembles Palestine than the GJM. Because the Chechen case remains highly nationalistic, women have never been precluded from political violence. However, their inclusion evolved slowly and was prompted by the protracted and costly ramifications of war with Russia on operations and personnel. Further, prior to the Chechen wars, women were fairly "modernized," in keeping with former Soviet gender policies that emphasized female education and employment. The Chechen case emphasizes nationalism and separatism "which is linked ideologically to the global Salafi jihad but finetuned to fit local circumstances" (Speckhard and Ahkmedova, 2006a, 440). Women's participation in the conflict is more consistent with women's roles in the traditional nationalist and Islamic nationalist settings such as Palestine with respect to general societal features. However, what differentiates the Chechen case, and what makes it an important bridge between the nationalist and religious Islamic nationalism of Palestine and the Salafi movement, is the influence of Salafis within the Chechen case, and their role in terrorist violence. While Chechen society has not necessarily embraced the Salafi religious mantle, those engaged in terrorist activities on behalf of the Chechens have embraced this religiosity. Further, this religiosity is no longer merely symbolic and instrumentalist; it is intrinsic and essentialist. Thus, in Chechnya, society possesses one type of nationalism/Islamism and the terrorists who have largely evolved during the second war with Russia (since 1999) employ the very different perspective of Salafism.

Chechnya provides the link between the nationalism of the Palestinian case and the Salafism of the GJM case by blending these two dimensions. For both the Palestinians and Chechens, the wars they face are viewed as total (or *fard 'ayn*) but the importance of religion in these contexts differs from the *fard 'ayn* conceptualized by the Salafi GJM, as will be discussed in the next section. For the Palestinians and the Chechens, *fard 'ayn* permits and even necessitates female political violence but it remains conceptualized and rooted in nationalist discourse. Religious justifications for female political violence have been unimportant in the Chechen case and Palestinian religious leaders have been willing to issue *fatwas* permitting female suicide attacks to lend a religious justification to political contingencies and operational constraints. In stark contrast, religious justifications have been slow to emerge in the Salafi GJM, but their emergence, and the context within which they have emerged, suggests a very different basis for potential female violence, and signals how the Salafi GJM understands the conflict it finds itself embroiled within.

Salafi jihadis and female violence

Perhaps the most interesting change in female terrorism and political violence involving Muslim women centers around the growing discourse and activism among Salafi *jihadis*, a group that is frequently viewed as being uniquely hostile to women. The GJM has undertaken two phases with respect to female political violence that merit attention, and to a great extent these phases are now running concurrently. The first phase involves establishing the intellectual basis for female political violence. The second phase involves the recruitment, training and, to a limited extent, the operationalization of female militants.

Many of the pertinent features of the intellectual phase were discussed in the introduction of this analysis, but to summarize, Islamic leaders have been eradicating intellectual and religious obstacles to female participation in suicide attacks for years, either overtly or through their silence, and this discourse has included even the most radically conservative Wahhabi movement (Cook, 2005). The implications of this intellectual step cannot be overstated or underestimated. The willingness of Salafi *jihadists* to include women in their movement in a violent capacity symbolizes the expanding sense of threat that this movement perceives, and signals a hardening of their intellectual and religious position. This is because the inclusion of women, and the religious justification necessary to facilitate this process, indicates that they now conceptualize the battle they are waging as constituting *fard 'ayn*. Rather than weakening the movement, women's inclusion signifies its religious authenticity and the totality of the threat they are confronting. If women are required to participate in *jihad*, the entire community is seen to face an existential threat; instead of constituting the primary mechanism that distracts men from participating in *jihad*, women now become a critical component of demonstrating to society – using religious justifications – the totality of the war they are waging. The result is a deepened legitimization of *jihad* and a reinforcement of its need for violence.

Alongside efforts to develop the intellectual and religious justifications necessary to support female participation in the GJM have been other efforts to expand female participation with respect to their overall numbers, roles and cross-cultural representation. Ayman Al-Zawahiri is reported to be "an ardent supporter of both the education of women and their participation in military activities," which put him at odds with former Taliban leader Mullah Mohammed Omar (Dickey, 2005, 6). Indeed, Al-Qaeda reportedly has trained women at bases near Jalalabad and Kandahar airports, and has maintained a unit of well-trained and battle-hardened women who have moved between Afghan and Pakistani compounds over the last several years (Dickey, 2005, 6). Over the past two years, Salafis have been reaching out to women through message boards and an online magazine – in August 2004, an Islamic women's group, the Women's Media Bureau in the Arabian Peninsula, reportedly launched a women's Internet magazine, *Al-Khansaa*, geared toward female *jihadis*. The magazine offers advice ranging from fitness to treating injuries to raising future martyrs. Importantly, the magazine takes the position that

> when Jihad becomes an obligation, then the woman is summoned like a man, and need not ask personal permission from her husband nor from her guardian because she is obligated. She need not ask permission in order to carry out a commandment that everyone must carry out.
>
> (Beichman, 2004)

Female suicide attackers have also grown in popularity in Salafi propaganda. While these examples remain fairly small, they serve to illustrate the increased Salafi interest in attracting female participation within their movement.

While Salafi discourse remains overwhelmingly geared toward emphasizing female support roles within the family as the critical component of sustaining the wider *jihad*, there has also been a deepening emphasis on women as *"mujahidat"* – female martyrs – justified by Qur'anic verses and historical examples. Salafi official discourse recounts stories of females involved in *jihad* dating back to the time of the Prophet Muhammad. Though women have been supporters and family members of global Islamist groups like Al-Qaeda for many years, more recently they have also reportedly begun to be trained as combatants ("Mother of Usama") (Al Jazeerah News, 2003). Indeed, since 2003, women have also participated in suicide attacks, and several failed efforts, in Iraq – and, as of 2005, these attacks were claimed by Iraq's Al-Qaeda. Moreover, it would be fair to say that, since 2001, women have been associated with Islamist militancy, largely linked to Al-Qaeda and/or the GJM, in Pakistan, Great Britain, the United States, Jordan, Iraq, the Philippines and Uzbekistan.

Women involved with the Salafi GJM largely fall into three general categories: women who support the movement largely through raising future warriors, women who support *jihadis* by providing safe havens and support, and women who support the GJM through physical violence. Importantly, the first and second categories are blurring with the third, suggesting a significant shift amongst Salafis that may portend growing female violence emanating from this movement. By far, the vast majority of women affiliated with the GJM fall into the first category – and, indeed, this is where Salafi leaders have been most content to keep their female supporters.[9] Yet even here the expanded sense of women's roles in *jihad* becomes readily apparent. Rehima, wife of a powerful member of Pakistan's *Jamaat-i-Islami* and supervisor of one of its *madrassas* for girls, states:

> I named my son Osama because I want to make him a mujahid. Right now there is war, but he is a child. When he is a young man, there might be war again, and I will prepare him for that war. In the name of God, I will sacrifice my son, and I don't care if he is my most beloved thing. For all of my six sons, I wanted them to be mujahedeen. If they get killed it is nothing. This world is very short. I myself want to be a mujahid.... Jihad is when you are attacked, you attack back. This is God's wish. We are not afraid. I am already asking my husband if I can go to Kashmir and train to fight. I will suicide bomb. If there are 20 to 30 non-Muslims, there I will commit martyrdom.
>
> (Addario, 2001, 39)

Over the past two years there have also been a growing number of cases involving women who support *jihadi* males by providing safe havens, support and even citizenship. This has been an especially charged issue in Europe and North America where they have sometimes been labeled the "brides of bin Laden" (Bhatia, 2005). Yet, even amongst this group, there is evidence that efforts have been made to recruit women for violent actions, and in at least one instance, this was successful. Up to forty-seven female

Muslim converts from Belgium, Denmark and Germany were reportedly targeted for recruitment to carry out attacks in Iraq and Pakistan (Rosenthal, 2006). On 9 November 2005, Muriel Degauque, 38, a Belgian woman, blew herself up attacking Iraqi police near Baqubah. Degauque was one of four female suicide attackers tasked by al-Zarqawi; three succeeded in their attacks inside Iraq, while the fourth, Sajida Mubarak al-Rishawi, failed to detonate her bomb inside a Jordanian hotel in November 2005.

Al-Zarqawi was the first Salafi to use women in suicide attacks inside and outside Iraq, and this is not altogether surprising. He was known to be innovative in his tactical style (e.g., initiating beheadings of kidnapped foreigners) – the competitive violent context within which he operated exacerbated personnel issues and operational constraints. Al-Zarqawi was also motivated by a rivalry with Usama bin Laden with respect to gaining notoriety and influence within the broader GJM. Perhaps most interesting was his willingness to employ foreign women and to use a female in his Jordanian operation. With respect to the former, this may be a sign of a lack of indigenous Salafi support, especially during the period in which al-Zarqawi was operating in Iraq, for the GJM, thereby necessitating using more religiously motivated external actors. With respect to the Jordanian operation, the inclusion of the female operative facilitated the group's travel and entry into the establishments that were being targeted. Al-Zarqawi's lead established a precedent for female suicide attacks, with the operational utility of women being demonstrated once again. Moreover, the attacks were consistent with the intellectual evolution of the GJM.

To summarize, the GJM views the war they are engaged in as *fard 'ayn*, which necessitates total social mobilization in support of *jihad*. Importantly, this mobilization has been made consistent with religious norms through an intellectual process that relies upon Qur'anic justification and historical precedent from the period of the rightly guided Caliphs. Women's mobilization and violence has thus been made consistent with both social and religious norms. The violent female now becomes a supporter of her community and, most significantly, upholds her religious obligation through violent action in the same manner as her male counterpart.

Conclusion

In all three cases under consideration in this analysis, participants consider themselves embroiled in *fard 'ayn*; however, its conceptualization diverges significantly between the Palestinian and Chechen cases on the one hand, and the GJM case on the other hand. While the Palestinians and Chechens pay lip service to the idea of *fard 'ayn*, and do conceptualize their respective battles as total war, the religious overtones of the conflicts are largely symbolic. This is in dramatic contrast to the GJM which understands and operationalizes *fard 'ayn* in its fullest religious meaning. The religious obligation of *fard 'ayn* is well-developed in the Salafi GJM setting and, as a result, women can become full partners in a way that is not possible in the current Palestinian and Chechen cases because *fard 'ayn* imposes religious obligations that trump socially entrenched gender norms. The religious necessity of the war gives women rights that are not, and most likely will never be, reflected in nationalist settings where women's participation remains optional.

As a result, there is the potential for Salafi women to enjoy, in some sense, a westernized understanding of political equality, which is ironically inspired by extreme religious conservatism. The implications of this process are significant, as Salafi women are not only included in violence, given their current understanding of the conflict they are embroiled in, but indeed are *religiously obligated* to participate in *jihad* up to and including violent actions. Most significantly, the inclusion of women in this movement, and indeed the need for women's involvement to signify the scope and intensity of the *jihad* the GJM is facing, suggests a hardening of the GJM position. The failure of Western observers to fully appreciate the mobilizational potential of Salafi ideology makes the operational utility and potential impact of these women troubling with respect to counter-terrorism calculations.

Notes

1 There are three Salafi factions – purists, politicos and *jihadis* – who share a common creed but differ over their understanding of the contemporary world and its problems, and thus offer different solutions to those problems. *Jihadis* take a militant position and believe that change can only be achieved through violence. The Salafi movement thus includes a diverse array of people, including Usama bin Laden and the Mufti of Saudi Arabia (Wiktorowicz, 2006, 207).
2 Islam and nationalism are often considered at odds with each other because the former is typically conceived as transcending state borders and the latter is usually assumed to incorporate secularism. Nevertheless, the intersection of Islam and nationalism in the Middle East is often mutually reinforcing rather than merely conflictual (Razi, 1990, 82). While an extensive discourse on this topic extends beyond the intended scope of this discussion, for the purposes of this discussion it is important to be clear how several terms are conceptualized and thus operationalized. Religious (or Islamic) nationalism is understood to mean the

> repoliticization of Islam and the use of Islamic symbols in the political realm. ... Islam "must be seen as the vehicle for political and economic demands, rather than as being itself the 'impulse' behind these demands" to the proponents of Islamic resurgence [the term Tibi assigned to this phenomenon], "Islam is their most convenient, readily available ideological instrument."
> (Tibi, 1987, 68)

Nationalism (or secular nationalism) is conceptualized in broader terms as captured by Smith (1989) wherein nationalism is

> an ideological movement for attaining and maintaining the autonomy, unity and identity of an existing or potential "nation".... As a movement, nationalism often antedates, and seeks to create, the nation, even if it often pretends that the nation already exists.
> (1989, 343)

3 Traditionally, *fard 'ayn* has centered on individual religious duties such as prayer, whereas *fard 'kifaya* involves the entire community and this is historically where *jihad* has been located. Under *fard 'kifaya* every individual does not have an obligation to wage *jihad* as long as a sufficient number of the community are prepared to do so. *Fard 'kifaya* becomes *fard 'ayn* when the Muslim community is under direct threat from an invading/occupying force.

4 The concept of total war, whether Islamic or secular, has been a powerful tool to mobilize both men and women to fight on behalf of nationalist causes throughout the world.

5 Shalinksy studied Farghanachi Uzbek refugees from Afghanistan in Karachi, Pakistan, in 1990 and their use of taped messages and stories (on audio cassette) regarding the Afghani war. Some of these cassettes described women's roles in the conflict and these were frequently listened to and discussed by the women and children Shalinsky observed. Shalinsky is not only interested in examining the "discourse and values that are considered appropriate for a time of jihad" but also "how the concern for social responsibility shifts in focus from ordinary time when women are enmeshed in family to extraordinary time when women are to transcend familial entanglements for the greater good" (Shalinsky, 1993, 661).

6 Central to this discourse is perhaps the most important distinction between secular nationalist and religious nationalist contexts: the women in the former want to be "liberated," in the Western sense of the term, from their traditional roles. They embrace the liberation, whereas oftentimes society and even terrorist and nationalist leaders pay lip service to the idea only to succumb to practical political accommodations in the aftermath of war (Chatterjee, 1989). For others, the "liberation" Shalinsky discusses is forced upon women and, while it is accepted, it is not embraced, and it is neither hoped to, nor intended to, carry over into the post-conflict society. Observers have difficulty understanding that this process is oppositionist and usually essentially tied to nationalist discourse on opposing the "occupying power." Further, this distinction is consistent with larger intellectual barriers to understanding the breadth of female political attitudes and the frequent inability to conceptualize how some women greet being wrested out of the private sphere that they "own" with tremendous disdain. Kandiyoti (1988) captures this idea in the "patriarchal bargain," wherein women often embrace conservatism because modernism offers little benefit. In particular, modern social forms that disengage "sexuality from reproduction and domesticity is perceived by many women as inimical to their best interests, since, among other things, it weakens the social pressure on men to take responsibility for the reproductive consequences of sexual activity" (1988, 284).

7 The acronyms applied in this figure are: Palestine Liberation Organization (PLO), Palestinian Islamic Jihad (PIJ) and the Global Jihadi Movement (GJM).

8 For example, Etaf Aliyan, a Palestinian woman and a member of Islamic Jihad, was scheduled to drive an explosive-laden car into a Jerusalem police station in 1987, but was apprehended before the attack could occur. Had the operation been successful, it would have represented "the first suicide vehicle bombing in Israel" (Sharrock, 1998), and significantly, it would have been perpetrated by a woman.

9 While it is true that much of women's activity in the GJM is non-violent – running women's organizations and groups, participating as girls in Islamist summer camps and *madrassas*, distributing Qur'ans in prisons and schools, creating Islamist non-governmental organizations and charities, participating in Muslim Student Associations (MSAs), and engaging in illegal activities such as fundraising (Ozment, 2004; Scroggins 2005) – such activities can also be viewed as representing a similar radicalization pathway as that taken by men.

References

Addario, Lynsey. 2001. "Jihad's Women." *New York Times Magazine*, 21 October: 38–41.

Al-Batsh, Majeda. 2002. "Mystery Surrounds Palestinian Woman Suicide Bomber." *Agence France Presse*, 28 February. Lexis/Nexis, accessed 6 February 2002.

Al Jazeerah News (2003) "Bin Laden Has Set Up Female Suicide Squads: Report," Arab News, Dubai, 13 March 2003. Online, available from: www.aljazeerah.info/ News%20archives/2003%20News%20archives/March%202003%20News/13%2 0News/Bin%20Laden%20has%20set%20up%20female%20suicide%20squads% 20%20aljazeerah.info.htm (accessed October 12, 2004).

Beichman, Arnold. 2004. "Women's Jihad." *Washington Times*, 11 September. Online, available from: www.washingtontimes.com (accessed 12 October 2006).

Bhatia, Shyam. 2005. "Guilt by Association." *Deccan Herald*, 6 October. Online, available from: www.deccanherald.com (accessed 2 November 2006).

Chatterjee, Partha. 1989. "Colonialism, Nationalism, and Colonialized Women: the Contest in India." *American Ethnologist*, 16, 4 (November): 622–633.

Cook, David. 2005. "Women Fighting in *Jihad*?" *Studies in Conflict & Terrorism*, 28, 5 (September–October): 375–384.

Cunningham, Karla J. 2005. "Women, Political Violence, and Democratization," in William Crotty (ed.), *Democratic Development and Political Terrorism: the Global Perspective* (Boston, MA: Northeastern University Press): 73–90.

Dickey, Christopher. 2005. "Women of Al-Qaeda." *Newsweek*, 12 December. Lexis/Nexis, accessed 12 October 2006: 1–7.

Hadid, Diaa. 2006. "Hamas Women Seek Bigger Political Role." *Seattle Post-Intelligencer*, 24 November. Online, available from: seattlepi.nwsource.com/ national/1107AP_Hamas_Sisterhood.html (accessed 27 November 2006).

Hammami, Rema. 1990. "Women, the Hijab and the *Intifada*." *Middle East Report*, May–August: 24–31.

Hammami, Rema. 1997. "Palestinian Motherhood and Political Activism on the West Bank and Gaza Strip," in Alexis Jetter, Annelise Orleck, and Diana Taylor (eds), *The Politics of Motherhood: Activist Voices from Left to Right* (Hannover: University Press of New England, 1997): 161–168.

Hammer, Juliane. 2000. "Prayer, Hijab and the Intifada: the Influence of the Islamic Movement on Palestinian Women." *Islam and Christian-Muslim Relations*, 11, 3 (October): 300–320.

Kandiyoti, Deniz. 1988. "Bargaining with Patriarchy." *Gender & Society*, 2, 3 (September): 274–290.

The Middle East Media and Research Institute. 2002. "Inquiry and Analysis No. 83: Jihad and Terrorism Studies – Wafa Idris: the Celebration of the First Female Palestinian Suicide Bomber – Part I" (12 February). Online, available from: www.memri.org (accessed 6 March 2002).

Ness, Cindy D. 2005. "In the Name of the Cause: Women's Work in Secular and Religious Terrorism." *Studies in Conflict & Terrorism*, 28, 5 (September–October): 353–373.

Nivat, Anne. 2001. *Chienne de Guerre: a Woman Reporter Behind the Lines of the War in Chechnya.* Susan Darton, trans. (New York: Public Affairs): 187–199.

Nivat, Anne. 2005. "The Black Widows: Chechen Women Join the Fight for Independence – and Allah." *Studies in Conflict & Terrorism*, 28: 413–419.

Ozment, Katherine. 2004. "Who's Afraid of Aafia Siddiqui?" *Boston Magazine* (October). Lexis/Nexis, accessed 18 November 2005: 1–8.

Razi, G. Hossein. 1990. "Legitimacy, Religion, and Nationalism in the Middle East." *American Political Science Review*, 84, 1 (March): 69–91.

Reeves, Phil. 2002. "The Paramedic Who Became Another 'Martyr' for Palestine." The *Independent*, 31 January 2002. Online, available from: www.ccmep.org/hotnews/parameic013102.html (accessed 6 March 2002).

Rosenthal, John. 2006. "German Women Answer the Call (to Jihad)." *Transatlantic Intelligencer*. Online, available from: www.trans-int.com (accessed 12 October 2006).

Scroggins, Deborah. 2005. "The Most Wanted Woman in the World." *Vanity Fair*, 195, 3 (March). Lexis/Nexis, accessed 23 November 2005: 1–10.

Shalinsky, Audrey C. 1993. "Women's Roles in the Afghanistan Jihad." *International Journal of Middle East Studies*, 25, 4 (November): 661–675.

Sharrock, David. 1998. "Women: the Suicide Bomber's Story." The *Guardian*, 5 May 1998. Lexis/Nexis, accessed 30 March 2002.

Smith, Anthony D. 1989. "The Origins of Nations." *Ethnic and Racial Studies*, 12, 3: 340–367.

Speckhard, Anne and Khapta Ahkmedova. 2006a. "The Making of a Martyr: Chechen Suicide Terrorism." *Studies in Conflict & Terrorism*, 29: 429–492.

Speckhard, Anne and Khapta Ahkmedova. 2006b. "Black Widows: The Chechen Female Suicide Terrorists," in Yoram Schweitzer (ed.), *Female Suicide Bombers: Dying for Equality?* Memorandum No. 84, Tel Aviv: Tel Aviv University (August): 63–80.

Sweitzer, Yoram. 2006. "Palestinian Female Suicide Bombers: Reality vs. Myth," in Yoram Schweitzer (ed.), *Female Suicide Bombers: Dying for Equality?* Memorandum No. 84, Tel Aviv: Tel Aviv University (August): 25–41.

Tibi, Bassam. 1987. "Islam and Arab Nationalism," in Stowasser, Barbara Freyer (ed.), *The Islamic Impulse* (Washington, DC: Georgetown University Center for Contemporary Arab Studies): 59–71.

Usher, Graham. 1993. "Palestinian Women, the *Intifada*, and the State of Independence." *Race and Class*, 34, 3 (January–March): 31–43.

Usher, Graham. 1997. "What Kind of Nation? The Rise of Hamas in the Occupied Territories," in Beinin, Joel (ed.), *Political Islam: Essays from Middle East Report* (Berkeley, CA: University of California Press): 339–354.

"We Don't Need Women Suicide Bombers: Hamas Spiritual Leader." 2002. *Agence France Presse*. 2 February. Lexis/Nexis, accessed 6 March 2002.

Wiktorowicz, Quintan. 2006. "Anatomy of the Salafi Movement." *Studies in Conflict & Terrorism*, 29, 3: 207–239.

Yadlin, Rivka. 2006. "Female Martyrdom: the Ultimate Embodiment of Islamic Existence?" in Yoram Schweitzer (ed.), *Female Suicide Bombers: Dying for Equality?* Memoranda No. 84 (Tel Aviv: Jaffe Center for Strategic Studies, August): 51–61.

6 Black widows and beyond

Understanding the motivations and life trajectories of Chechen female terrorists

Anne Speckhard and Khapta Akhmedova

Introduction

The tactic of suicide terrorism was first imported into the Chechen conflict on June 7, 2000 when two women – Khava Barayeva, cousin of well-known Chechen field commander Arbi Barayev, and Luisa Magomadova drove a truck filled with explosives into the temporary headquarters of an elite OMON (Russian Special Forces) detachment in the village of Alkhan Yurt in Chechnya. Unlike many other Muslim areas of the world where the tactic of suicide terrorism has been used – Palestine, Lebanon, Afghanistan, Iraq – Chechen women have carried out acts of suicide terrorism from the beginning of this struggle for independence. Indeed, Chechen female terrorists have participated in a majority of suicide attacks in Chechnya – taking part in 79 percent of the total attributed to terror groups (twenty-two of twenty-eight to date). A total of 42 percent of all Chechen suicide bombers have been women – that is, forty-six women bombers out of a total of 110 Chechen[1] suicide bombers.[2] Table 6.1 shows a complete listing of all suicide attacks attributed to Chechens to date.[3]

The types of suicide terrorism that Chechen women have been involved in have varied – wearing explosive bomb belts, carrying bomb-filled bags, driving cars or trucks filled with explosives, exploding themselves on airplanes, in subways, and on trains. Chechen women also participated in the two largest mass hostage-taking events associated with suicide terrorism to date: the takeover of the Moscow Dubrovka Theater (Nord Ost) and the Beslan school in North Ossetia. Of the forty-six Chechen female bombers, twenty-three successfully detonated their bombs and died by truck, car bomb, or improvised explosive device (suicide belt or bag), and two exploded bombs on airplanes (one was fatally wounded by her bomb and died shortly thereafter in the hospital); two were unsuccessful (both carried bomb-filled bags – one was wounded and the other walked away from her bomb-filled rucksack); and nineteen women took part in the Dubrovka takeover – wearing bombs wrapped around their bodies but did not die by self-detonation.[5] Another two took part in the Beslan school mass hostage-taking and were either killed by their comrades or exploded themselves

Table 6.1 Summary of total number of suicide terror acts attributed to Chechens

	Date of terrorist act	Place of terrorist act	Total terrorists	Women terrorists	Men terrorists	Killed victims	Injured victims	Hostages	Level of terrorists injury
1	June 7, 2000	Chechnya, Alkhan-Yurt military base (Khava Baraeva, Luiza Magomadova)	2	2	0	2	5	0	Dead
2	June, 2000	Chechnya, military checkpoint	1	0	1	?	?	0	Dead
3	July 2, 2000	Chechnya, military base (Movladi)	1	0	1	33	81	0	Dead
4	December 2000	Chechnya, MVD building (Mareta Duduyeva)	1	1	0	?	?	0	Wounded, later dead
5	November 29, 2001	Chechnya, Urus-Martan, military office (Elza Gazueva)	1	1	0	1	3	0	Dead
6	February 5, 2002	Chechnya, Grozny, Zavodskoy ROVD (Zarema Inarkaeva)	1	1	0	23	17	0	Wounded
7	October 23–26, 2002	Moscow theatre	40	19	21	129	644	<800	Dead
8	December 27, 2002	Chechnya, Grozny, governmental complex (Tumrievs family)	3	1	2	83	<200	0	Dead

continued

Table 6.1 Continued

	Date of terrorist act	Place of terrorist act	Total terrorists	Women terrorists	Men terrorists	Killed victims	Injured victims	Hostages	Level of terrorists injury
9	May 12, 2003	Chechnya, Znamenskaya, governmental complex	3	1	2	59	111	0	Dead
10	May 14, 2003	Chechnya, Iliskhan-Yurt, religious festival (Shahidat Shahbulatova, Zulay Abdurzakova)	2	2	0	18	145	0	Dead
11	June 5, 2003	North Osetia, Mozdok military base (Lida Khildehoroeva)	1	1	0	17	16	0	Dead
12	June 20, 2003	Chechnya, Grozny, governmental complex (Zakir Abdulazimov)	2	1	1	6	38	0	Dead
13	July 5, 2003	Moscow, rock festival (Zulikhan Elihadjieva, Mariam Sharapova)	2	2	0	14	60	0	Dead
14	July 11, 2003	Moscow, Twerskaya str. (Zarema Mujikhoeva)	1	1	0	1	0	0	Lived
15	July 27, 2003	Chechnya, Grozny, military building (Mariam Tashukhadjieva)	1	1	0	?	?	0	Dead
16	August 1, 2003	North Osetia, military hospital	1	0	1	35	300	0	Dead

No.	Date	Location							Status
17	December 5, 2003	Southern Russian near Yessentuki, train (Khadijat Mangerieva)	4	3	1	41	<150	0	Dead
18	September 15, 2003	Ingushetia, FSB office	2	1	1	2	31	0	Dead
19	December 9, 2003	Moscow, National Hotel near Duma	1	1	0	6	14	0	Dead
20	February 6, 2004	Moscow subway station Avtozavodskaya	1	0	1	41	<130	0	Dead
21	April 6, 2004	Ingushetia, president's car	1	0	1	2	25	0	Dead
22	August 25, 2004	Airplane TU-134 Moscow-Volgograd (Sazita Jebirhanova)	1	1	0	43	0	0	Dead
23	August 25, 2004	Airplane TU-154 Moscow-Sochi (Aminat Nogaeva)	1	1	0	42	0	0	Dead
24	August 31, 2004	Moscow, subway station, Rijskaya	1	1	0	10	33	0	Dead
25	September 1–3, 2004	North Osetia, Beslan school (Roza Nogaeva, Mariam Tuburova)	32	2	30	330	470	1,120	Dead
26	May, 2005	Chechnya, Grozny	1	1	0	0	0	0	Dead
27	May, 2005	Chechnya, Assinovskaya	2	2	0	0	0	0	Dead
28	July, 2005	Chechnya, Grozny	1	0	1	0	0	0	Dead
			110	46[4]	64	939	2,913	2,043	
			100%	42%	58%				

prior to Special Forces storming the school. The women and the group's leaders were believed to be in conflict about taking school children hostage.[6] Table 6.2 shows the breakdown of Chechen women's activities as suicide bombers by type of attack.

Our study

This chapter reports on data from three groups of respondents. The first includes interviews with close family members or close associates of suicide terrorists reporting on a total of sixty-four suicide terrorists (of the total universe of 110 suicide terrorists). These individuals were interviewed over the course of three years, beginning in March 2003 up to the present (as of this writing, March 2007).[7] The close family and associate interviews were given mainly by mothers, sisters and brothers, aunts and uncles, first cousins, childhood friends, long-term neighbors, and teachers.

The second sample consists of twenty-eight interviews of hostages that were held in the only two known mass hostage-taking events, to date, which involved suicide terrorists. This sample consists of eleven hostages who were held in the October 2002 Nord Ost/Dubroka Theater takeover in Moscow, and seventeen who were held in the September 2004 Beslan school in North Ossetia. The Dubrovka/Nord Ost hostage interviews were collected from the first week of December 2002, five weeks after the terrorist takeover, into the first week of March 2003, four months after the takeover. The Beslan hostage interviews were collected in August of 2005, close to the one-year anniversary of the attack, a time when emotions and traumatic memories were dramatically heightened.[8]

Table 6.2 Chechen women's activities as suicide bombers by type of attack

Type of attack	Number of women involved
Truck and car bombs driven to and exploded at target	7
Attacker carrying explosive device on body and exploding it in a place other than metro, train or airplane (one died in hospital)	10
Mass hostage-taking with bombs strapped to body and rigged for detonation (Nord Ost and Beslan)	21
Metro suicide bombings	1
Commuter train suicide bombings	3
Suicide bombing on airplanes	2
Failed attacks with females carrying a bag filled with explosives	2
Total women involved	46

Lastly, we include for analysis interviews on two would-be suicide terrorists, both women, and interviews with four seriously radicalized individuals who appeared to us to be vulnerable to becoming suicide terrorists[9] (two of these women were from within the group of close family and associate interviews and two from inhabitants of the Chechen refugee camps in Ingushetia).

Thus, our total sample of respondents upon which we base this analysis includes ninety-six respondents and approaches the topic from multiple points of view – trying to understand the bomber's inner psychology and psychosocial state leading to membership in a terrorist group, his or her relationship with that group, and ultimately the reasons for carrying out a martyrdom operation. All of the descriptive statistics that we report here are based upon the sixty-four suicide terrorists that we were able to closely study (post-mortem) through the family member/close associate interviews that we collected in Chechnya. Thirty of these, or 47 percent of our sample of bombers, were females, providing us the opportunity to compare and contrast their actions and what motivated them in comparison to their male counterparts. We augment our descriptions of these specific terrorists (by their family members and close associates) with hostages' observations of the terrorists with whom they spent three days, many of them having ample opportunity to observe the suicide terrorists' behaviors, interactions, and to seriously engage in discussions with them.

Research interview – psychological autopsy method

For the Chechen interviews (carried out in Chechnya), Akhmedova, a clinical psychologist, used a semi-structured format and focused on open-ended questions regarding life events previous to the women becoming terrorists; personality and behavioral changes leading up to the terrorist act; and possible motivations for it. We also included questions regarding what was known about the suicide bombers' recruitment and interaction with the terror group. Moreover, we considered how family members and close associates of the bomber viewed the acts of the terrorist and their views of societal support for this type of act. We also asked questions about the contagion effect of the acts on those persons close to the bomber. This method of "psychological autopsy"[10] is essentially a post-mortem in-depth interview with close associates/family members to reconstruct the bomber's life; significant and formative events in it that led up to the suicide act; focusing on what these respondents know of the bomber's motivations; involvement with the sponsoring group; and emotional, behavioral, and cognitive changes leading up to taking part in a martyrdom operation.

In the case of the hostage interviews (conducted by Speckhard), the focus was on the hostage's response to being held hostage by suicide terrorists (including his or her psychological response, both during the event and following it, which required a psychotherapeutic approach in the interview), and accompanying this, a detailed inquiry into the hostage's recollections about the hostage-takers (including observations of the hostage-takers' actions; the interactions the hostage-takers had with each other and the hostages; conversations with the hostage-takers; recollection of statements made by them; and assessment of how suicidal they appeared in their intentions). In a few cases, some of the hostages had in-depth conversations with one or more of the hostage-takers or were trained health or security professionals, and thus had insightful comments from observing or conversing about the terrorists' motivations, actions, and states of mind.

Results

In general, we found that female Chechen suicide bombers were on average twenty-five years old, with an age range of fifteen-to-forty-five. Many were married and had children. All the women appeared to be indoctrinated into militant jihadist ideology[11] prior to bombing themselves, and they were at least minimally trained and equipped by an organization. All the women were volunteers. Psychological trauma, a desire for revenge, and the nationalist desire to throw an enemy occupier out of their country were the strongest factors motivating them to seek out terrorist organizations that promised a ready and ideologically honorable way (to them) to do so.

The data we possess to date shows only minimal differences between male and female Chechen bombers with regard to demographic variables and to the motivational states that were associated with carrying out suicide terrorism. The main difference that we found has its parallel in the structure of gender relations in the society at large. In Chechen society, males play lead roles and women follow. In large part, this was found to be no less true in suicide operations. This dynamic may have made the crucial difference in the Nord Ost Theater takeover. The women for some reason did not detonate their bombs before gas overtook them. It is possible that they may have been waiting for the order to detonate and were hesitant to do so without being told to.[12] Neither has a Chechen female played a significant leadership role within a terrorist organization, though many of the women in our sample could be described as playing substantive roles.

It should be pointed out that while Chechen society is traditionally Muslim in cultural heritage, women during the seven decades of Soviet rule had equal opportunity to higher education and the majority worked outside of the home – many in professional roles. It would be fair to say that Chechen women have not been subjugated by men in the same way that women under the Taliban were, or women in Middle Eastern cultures may be thought to live now. This said, traditional family structures and the division of male and female responsibilities are present as the norm in indigenous Chechen culture. However, the practice of women covering themselves completely, as is found in some conservative Muslim cultures, has never been a feature of indigenous Chechen culture. Rather, many women in

Chechnya adopted Middle Eastern dress and habits of covering with the introduction of militant jihadist ideology into Chechen society, both during and after the two recent wars (1994–1996 and 1999–2000). This form of dress, used by militant Wahhabi adherents[13] to express religious values, was also embraced by some Chechen woman as an outward sign of having taken on a new identity. By doing so, the women demarcated themselves as "true believers" and separated themselves from the rest of mainstream Chechen culture.

Demographic data

Age, marital status, and childbearing

While we do not have full demographic data on all 110 suicide terrorists, of those whom we conducted specific psychological interviews (*n* = 64; 30 female and 34 male), females were found to range in age from fifteen to thirty-eight. Our sample included fifteen single women (never married), three married, four divorced, seven widows, and one who was married a second time. Thus the label of "Black Widows" is not accurate for this sample (which represents *more* than half of the known universe of Chechen female bombers) as only 23 percent were widows. Comparing the marital status of female to male bombers, the biggest difference was that 12 percent of male bombers were married at the time they went to explode themselves, in comparison to only 3 percent of the females.

In both cases, however, the married bombers – both men and women – left children behind. Doing so was not seen as being in conflict with militant Wahhabi-held values; in fact, to the contrary. Chechen militant Wahhabis are known to believe that it is better to martyr oneself after having fulfilled life obligations, including having children. This is in direct opposition to the practice of Lebanese and Palestinian groups that generally favor(ed) sending unmarried and childless men, and in many cases, refused to send women at all until – at least in the Palestinian case – it became tactically advantageous and perhaps even necessary to do so.

Table 6.3 Marital status and gender, crosstabulation

	Marital status	Females (percent)	Males (percent)	Total (percent)
1	Single	15 (42.9)	20 (57.1)	35 (54.7)
2	Married	3 (10.0	12 (35.3)	15 (23.4)
3	Divorced	4 (13.3	1 (2.9)	5 (7.8)
4	Widow	7 (23.3	1 (2.9)	8 (12.5)
5	Second marriage	1 (3.3)	0 (0)	1 (1.6)
	Total	30 (100)	34 (100)	64 (100.0)

Table 6.4 Children of terrorists

How many children	Frequency	Percent
0	43	67.2
1	7	10.9
2	13	20.3
3	1	1.6
Total	64	100.0

Education

As is true of suicide bombers active in other arenas,[14] the female bombers in our sample were as educated as their peers: 65.3 percent (17/26) had finished high school (ages fourteen-to-sixteen, as per the Chechen system); 11.5 percent (3/26) were currently studying in college (ages seventeen-to-twenty); 4 percent (1/26) had finished college; and 19.2 percent (5/26) had finished their university studies (see Table 6.5). One woman, for instance, was studying history in the university and had planned to become a lawyer before her life was derailed by war.

Socio-economic status

The socio-economic status of the bombers was difficult to assess as nearly all Chechens have been severely impacted by the country's two recent wars. Socio-economic status was rated by Akhmedova according to her assessment of the family's observable living conditions and their self-reported information. Approached this way, only two of the female bombers were viewed as being of truly low economic status in comparison to the general population, although it could certainly be argued that all of the bombers – male and female – were frustrated in their career and educational aspirations. In our sample, there were only six subjects who had jobs[15] and these were all women who ran their own businesses trading

Table 6.5 Education level of suicide terrorists

	Frequency	Percent
High school	48	75.0
College	6	9.4
University	6	9.4
Studying on university or college	4	6.3
Total	64	100.0

Table 6.6 Socio-economical status

	Frequency	Percent
Poor	5	7.8
Middle	45	70.3
Good	12	18.8
High	2	3.1
Total	64	100.0

in the market, an activity that in recent years has been one of the limited ways of surviving the wars in Chechnya. This market activity in fact actually provided the women who went to bomb themselves in the Moscow Dubrovka Theater and at Beslan with an acceptable cover – they told their families they had to travel to get products for their businesses. Thus, their activity and being absent was not considered unusual, or cause for alarm.

Religion

All of the bombers took on the militant jihadist views of the militant Wahhabi terror groups before going to bomb themselves. We investigated this variable and found that less than half of the bombers – male and female – were from previously religious backgrounds. In the case of the females, only four were from traditionally religious families. It is our contention that a religious background can be protective in a number of ways. First, a person with a strong religious faith has a base philosophy, which is likely to offer some psychological buffer and protection to deal with death and other serious traumatic events. Likewise, we argue that existing religious education in a moderate form of Islam makes one less likely to be confused or taken in by the militant jihadist ideology promoting "martyrdom," which is put forward as an appropriate response to traumatic life events by the terrorist groups.

Table 6.7 Employment

	Frequency	Percent
Unemployed	58	90.6
Own business	6	9.4
Total	64	100

Table 6.8 Prior religiosity

	Frequency	Percent
Secular	45	70.3
Traditional religion	19	29.7
Total	64	100.0

Motivational factors

The study, which included looking at the life trajectories of all of the suicide bombers within the sample, showed that ten main variables were commonly found in bombers' lives leading up to their suicide terror acts. Four of these variables were present in all cases and we considered them to represent the main motivations of individuals to commit suicide terrorism in Chechnya:

1   Living under conditions of a nationalistic conflict/war/occupation;
2   A serious *personal trauma* that in nearly every case involved the death, torture, and/or disappearance of a close family member, and often witnessing violence to family members at the hands of Russian forces;
3   Exposure to, and in nearly every case, active *seeking out of militant Wahhabi terror groups*;
4   A message resonating with a *deep personal search* for a) meaning, life purpose, and certainty – amidst chaos; b) brotherhood and lost family ties and c) for the means of enacting revenge (the terror organizations in essence provided this).

These four variables were equally predictive as motivators for becoming suicide terrorists in men and women, although we must point out that, just as in the Palestinian/Israeli conflict, Chechen women, as opposed to Chechen men, may more readily embrace the role of suicide terrorist because the roles of being an active combatant are far less open for them (indeed, they are completely blocked for most Palestinian women).[16] Some of the women in our sample took part in war activities prior to becoming human bombers (see Table 6.9). In these cases, they participated as nurses, couriers, and support personnel, but did not themselves engage in battles. A few stand out given the range of activities they were allowed to carry out. One woman learned to drive and drove a military vehicle for her group (Chechen women rarely learn to drive), and two participated in placing land mines and other improvised explosive devices before becoming human bombers.

Our main finding in the Chechen sample is that deep personal trauma and the desire for revenge within the context of a nationalist battle were the strongest motivating forces behind suicide terrorism. When certain individuals were exposed to groups espousing a militant jihadist ideology, groups who were equipped with explosives to carry out a suicide mission, and groups who provided the opportunity for traumatized individuals to self-recruit, psychological vulnerabilities and needs became fatally matched with opportunity. As these variables in our opinion tell the main story of the bombers' motivations, we devote another longer section below to discussing their interaction in greater detail following our less detailed discussion of the other remaining motivating variables (that most traumatized individuals do not become suicide bombers will also be discussed later).

Six additional variables that were also important and generally or often present in the total sample of both men and women are:

5   *Fugitive status* – choosing when and how to end one's life by enacting a suicide act of vengeance becomes more attractive than risking falling into the hands of the Russians and dying by torture or facing a brutal imprisonment. This would only be true of those who were actively being sought by Russian forces, which was the case for some in our sample. Nearly half of our sample had some prior participation in war activities, with the women providing more support roles (nurses, couriers, cooks, drivers) and the males doing more of the actual fighting.

Both men and women who have been held in so-called "filtration camps"[17] have reported high levels of torture at the hands of Russian forces, and there are also cases of rapes of Chechen women by Russian forces occurring during detention.

6   *Religiosity* – as noted earlier, previous adherence to Sufi Islam, which is the indigenous form of Islam in Chechnya, appears to have been a protective variable. The majority of our sample was "Islamic" in name only and thus more vulnerable to being swayed by militant interpretations of Islam that allow self-bombing. After so many years of Soviet rule, in which all religions were suppressed, many Chechens are only nominally Muslim and know very little about their faith, which makes these individuals much more vulnerable to being convinced by militant religious ideologies than those who had been raised in traditionally religious families. Supporting this hypothesis is the fact that 70 percent of the

Table 6.9 Prior participation in war

	Frequency	Percent
Fighters	14	21.9
Helpers of fighters	15	23.4
No participation	35	54.7
Total	64	100.0

sample of bombers came from secular backgrounds. All of the subjects took on the militant Wahhabi jihadist ideology in full before becoming "martyrs," although we see this as less of an issue of religion than one of searching for answers amidst traumatic conditions and finding an ideology that resonates with deep personal psychological pain. We discuss this in more detail further on.

7   *Nationalism* – many of the nationalist fighter groups became the "terror groups" that turned to suicide operations as a form of fighting against a much stronger and well-defended military opponent.[18] Hence, some of those who would formerly have taken up arms as fighters were now organizationally funneled into other roles, including suicide bombers. Nationalistic motives were difficult to separate out from individual motives of revenge as personal revenge appeared to be more important on the individual level than nationalistic motives, but these were clearly tied together.

8   *Networked recruitment* – this occurred in some cases through family members and close ties, but again the first four variables were already present – networking alone did not appear key. Two men in particular served as strong hubs for networked recruitment: Rustam Ganiev was the hub for equipping at least five female bombers and Arbi Baraev equipped at least two female bombers, while another from his group went to Nord Ost after his death, with his relative Mosar Baraev (see Figure 6.1). In at least four cases, female bombers had married into Wahhabi militant families. After marriage, they took on the covered dress code and were often involved in support roles for the militant activities of their families. Over time, the effect of deep personal traumas (e.g., torture and death of family members), combined with the fact of already being married into a group that provided an ideology and a means for revenge, made it simpler for them to volunteer as suicide bombers. However, it is important to note that many more women who were not already networked into such groups self-recruited in direct response to the experience and psychological devastation caused by gravely traumatic events at the hands of the Russian forces in their personal lives.

9   *Psychological contagion* – this is a variable that is often found to operate among young people, but also occurs in families as well. Essentially, we found in our sample that the suicide action of one family member made a strong impact on another, and in some cases played a large role in influencing the other to consider following the same path. But again, trauma, exposure to jihadist ideology, and a desire to revenge were, in our opinion, the most active variables influencing the contagion effect. It is interesting that psychological contagion associated with suicide terrorism appeared to be greatest for women subjects, but since there were very few cases in our sample that fell into this category, we cannot be sure that the same does not operate on an equal basis for men. Again it

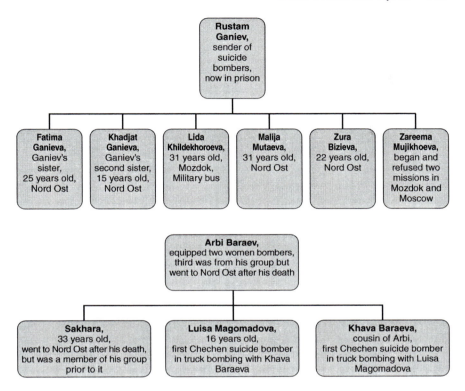

Figure 6.1 Networked recruitment of Chechen suicide terrorists.

is possible that men had more roles open to them so that, when a close friend or family member went on to be a bomber, they might choose to follow them, but follow as an active combatant versus as a human bomber themselves.

10 *Loss of other meaningful roles* – there were a few cases of infertile women in our sample; the majority of the sample was unemployed; the effects of war blocked educational and employment opportunities; and a general feeling of hopelessness created vulnerabilities in certain individuals, which likely could not have been exploited if the first four variables were not in operation.

The lethal mix

In our sample, trauma and the duty to revenge amidst a nationalistic conflict appeared to be the most important motivating variables on the level of the individual. That said, deep personal traumatization or the desire for revenge were not, on their own, either necessary or sufficient variables to motivate an individual along the path to "martyrdom." All of the suicide terrorists in this sample had self-recruited in direct response to deep personal traumatization and 67 percent had commented beforehand to family members that they desired to seek revenge for the death or torture of a family member. Yet none of them could have ended their lives as "martyrs" and killed others on the basis of either trauma or revenge without an ideology to convince them of the righteousness of doing so, or without a group to equip them. (See Table 6.10 for traumatic events suffered and Table 6.11 for the variable of desiring to revenge.)

Nearly all of Chechen society has suffered serious losses and witnessed bloodshed.[19] The question, then, is what caused a very small minority of Chechens to self-recruit to terrorist organizations and ultimately become suicide bombers? Our view is that the presence in society of these terror organizations that are ready to equip and send bombers, along with the militant ideology that they espouse, is the catalyst that causes highly traumatized individuals who desire revenge to activate. Indeed we see in our data that the majority – 87 percent of the bombers – sought out a relationship with terrorist groups only *after* having suffered a deep personal trauma, and those that had contact before usually had it by marriage and these also only activated as bombers in response to traumas and the desire to revenge.

Likewise, it is necessary to say that all Chechens have suffered from the recent wars, but the types of trauma that occurred to the suicide terrorists in our sample were of the types that had touched their lives with unimaginable horror. Many witnessed their family members killed or beaten in front of them, or viewed their corpses with marks of torture upon them, or learned of brutal rapes and dismemberments. The traumatic experiences that led Elza Gazueva, who bombed herself in the Russian forces military command, to self-recruit was described by her sister:

> The soldiers came to their house at night and took away my brother and my sister's husband. They beat them in front of her and bound them

Table 6.10 Traumatic events suffered by Chechen suicide terrorists

	Frequency	*Percent*
More than one family member killed	35	54.7
Father or mother killed	9	14.1
Brother killed	9	14.1
Husband killed	2	3.1
Family member raped by enemy	2	3.1
Family member disappeared after arrest	5	7.8
Family member tortured	4	6.2
Total	64	100.0

Table 6.11 Revenge as a motivator

	Frequency	Percent
Yes	20	66.7
No	10	33.3
Total	30	100.0

and took them away. The next morning the relatives searched for them in the commandant's offices and filtration points (this is where one would normally go to try to buy a loved one back) but in all cases they were told that they were not there. In two weeks their corpses were found on the outskirts of the village. They had many marks of torture on them. After three months my sister tied herself with explosives and went to the commandant's office, there she asked for the commandant and before exploding herself and killing them both she asked him "Do you remember me?" [20]

Militant jihadist ideology as psychological first aid

In our view, the militant jihadist ideology espoused by Chechen terrorist groups, which is not unlike the global militant jihadist ideology currently in vogue, is one that is capable of meeting a traumatized individual at nearly all of his or her points of vulnerability with remedies, albeit short-lived, to his or her psychological pain. Symptoms of psychological trauma such as depression, survival guilt, traumatic bereavement, constant bodily arousal states of fear and horror, feelings of shame, grief and powerlessness, and a sense of a foreshortened future (i.e., feeling that one will not live long) are all "treated" in a short-term "fix" by the militant jihadist ideology which encourages "martyrdom." Table 6.13 shows the serious personality changes that occurred following traumatization in this sample.

How does the militant jihadist ideology offer psychological first aid? First of all, the loss of family members and a need to belong is met by the group offering "Muslim sisters and brothers" in replacement for those loved ones who have been killed. The group is bound by deep ties of loyalty, even a

Table 6.12 Relationship of suicide terrorists with Wahhabi groups

	Frequency	Percent
Before trauma	8	12.5
After trauma	56	87.5
Total	64	100.0

Table 6.13 Post-traumatic changes in suicide terrorists in our sample

	Frequency	*Percent*
Social alienation and isolation	56	87.5
Depression	27	42.2
Suspiciousness	35	54.7
Aggression	21	32.8
Fanaticism	14	21.9
Conflicts	10	15.6
Guilt	8	12.5

willingness to die for each other, which is similar to ties found in families.[21] Likewise, the traumatized initiate who is in a state of depression, confusion, grief, and anger approaches the militant Wahhabi group knowing there he or she can finds simple answers. Clarity and order will be restored and the desire for purity, clear loyalties, and a sense of purpose will be met. The loyalties and ties to the Jamaat (i.e. brotherhood) are presented to him or her as bound by orderly rules, and the group claims to espouse a pure and incorruptible form of Islam, which presents itself as a stark contrast to what is happening all around in the war-torn society where family members can no longer provide, protect, or even keep themselves alive. As a result, all others are repudiated in favor of the new fictive kin – the new "brotherhood." Faith in the state powers, which are clearly corrupt, is rejected, and one's family, who are either dead or powerless to protect them from harm, are left behind, and so on. The group offers solid answers for the self-recruit who can no longer find meaning amidst deep and violent chaos where everything has been thrown into question. Likewise, in deep need of a positive identity, a sense of empowerment and a means of overcoming survivor guilt, which is common after trauma, the suicide bomber is offered purpose by the group (even in death), self-empowerment (short-lived in the case of being equipped as a bomber), and the means to revenge and overcome survivor guilt. Overwhelming grief is met with the promise of reunion with loved ones in paradise following "martyrdom." Guilt and grief over leaving family members behind is met with the promise of being able to bring loved ones to paradise as a result of achieving martyrdom. A sense of a foreshortened future (common to trauma survivors) is met with the promise of greater glory – it is achieved by giving up what might have been a short life anyway. A strong desire for revenge, which is a long-standing duty in Chechen culture, but highly codified, often becomes distorted in the highly traumatized individual into fanaticism. The willingness to revenge ultimately gets generalized to the wider group that includes innocent civilians as targets.[22] This distortion is strongly supported by the group and the group's ideology, which equips the bomber to carry out his or her desire for revenge. Lastly, depression and the desire to die and remove oneself from unbearable emotional pain (i.e. "psych-ache")[23] are replaced by the group's working on all of the above vulnerabilities to transform the traumatized individual into one who not only wants to die for reasons he or she has come to believe are good, but who also wants to use his or her death to kill those people upon whom he or she wishes to revenge.

To the traumatized woman who is troubled, bereaved and guilty, martyrdom can come to be seen as the most honorable choice. A woman who has become alienated, depressed, aggressive, irritable, or dehumanized by the experience of trauma is searching for answers to re-humanize herself, to belong again, and to find meaning amidst painful and overwhelming horror. The group offers her this – but only in the short term. She pays for this comfort with her life. This is what we began to see among the Chechen suicide terrorists as the necessary "lethal mix."

Conclusion

This chapter presents the results of a three-year study collecting interviews from family members, close associates, and hostages of sixty-four Chechen suicide bombers, thirty of them being female suicide bombers – the so-called Chechen "Black Widows." The study analyzed demographic descriptors as well as investigated the life trajectories of Chechen female terrorists and the psychosocial motivators that were activators for embarking on this path. All of the female bombers in our sample self-recruited and took on the militant jihadist ideology prior to bombing themselves.

We found the main motivating variables that underwrite female suicide bombing to be the presence of nationalistic conflict/war/occupation, coupled with serious personal trauma, resulting in a search to find answers for resulting psychological vulnerabilities, combined with exposure to a militant jihadist ideology and a group ready and willing to equip suicide bombers. Lesser variables included lack of previous knowledge about Islam, fugitive status, nationalism, loss of meaningful roles, psychological contagion, and networked recruitment. While psychological trauma was a serious motivating variable, it was not in itself sufficient as a cause for suicide bombing. The necessary condition seems to be access to a terrorist group ready to equip and send a woman on a mission, as well as exposure to a militant jihadist ideology that resonates with the woman's psychological needs; needs that emanate from serious traumatization occurring from war, conflict, and occupation.

Chechen female suicide bombers come from a war-torn country that has developed small pockets of society in which an imported militant ideology in the hands of terrorist organizations has gained significant currency. The leadership in these groups are fanatically desirous to revenge upon Russian military and civilian populations hoping to turn the political tide back that stands in the way of independence, as well as to express their outrage over the widespread death and destruction in their country. The female recruits who come to these organizations are not coerced, but are, in our view, deeply traumatized individuals who sought out organizations on their own accord for answers and to bring meaning to their deep psychological pain. The answers they receive are unfortunately very short-lived and end in their own deaths and the deaths of many innocent civilians.

As Chechen women in the main, and Chechen society as a whole, do not endorse the tactic of suicide terrorism, do not agree with killing innocent civilians, and want peace versus continued conflict to achieve a very unlikely independence in their country, we must do all we can to support this desire. That requires working on a political level to bring an end to severe military, police, and corrupt counter-terrorism activities – torture, kidnap, disappearances, and other forms of illegitimate force that continue to terrorize ordinary Chechen civilians, as well as to work toward derailing terrorist acts intent on hijacking a legitimate political process. The Chechen people have suffered immeasurably in recent years and deserve every effort possible to help them to restore peace and security in their nation. We hope that our study contributes to that possibility.

Notes

1 Chechen groups have used individuals from other nationalities as bombers (i.e. Ingush and Ukrainian male bombers were present in Beslan), but for the sake of simplicity we refer to Chechen bombers as those who acted on behalf of Chechen groups. All of the female bombers acting on behalf of Chechen groups have been from Chechnya.

2 We have classified suicide bombers as anyone who goes so far as to strap on a bomb or drive a vehicle filled with explosives to a target, or who otherwise attempts to detonate an explosive device on an airplane or elsewhere with the aim of dying to kill, irrespective of whether or not the bomber actually died in the attack or was successful in detonating – as that is often not within the bomber's control. We take the point of strapping on a bomb or other type of improvised explosive device, or driving a vehicle loaded with explosives to a target, as enough evidence of seriousness of the intent to commit suicide, and we see the end result, which is often out of the hands of the bomber, as less meaningful than the intent implied by these actions.

3 These numbers are based upon our database of attacks attributed to Chechens as of March 2007. Quantifying the exact number of attacks, gender of bombers, and so on, is difficult, as reports vary by government and news source and the gender of accomplished bombers is not always evident after an attack. In every case we have used the more conservative estimates, as our experience with journalists reporting in and about Chechnya is that they have difficulty getting reports and sometimes rely on rumors. See Table 6.1 for a complete account regarding suicide terror acts attributed to Chechens.

4 We declined to count one of these failed bombers (Zarema Inarkaeva) in our total of suicide bombers because, in her case, she was not aware that she was carrying a bomb which was detonated without her knowledge by remote control from outside of the police station where she had delivered it for her boyfriend. She was thus, in our opinion, not a true suicide bomber. We call attention to her case, but do not consider it a real case of suicide terrorism because she was not willingly or knowingly entering into the act. This is reflected in our total in

Tables 6.1 and 6.2 as well, where only forty-six bombers are considered in the total for female bombers as opposed to forty-seven.

5 There is some controversy as to whether or not the Dubrovka bombers were indeed suicide bombers, as their plan to die by exploding themselves was interrupted by the Russian Special Forces gassing and storming the building. The female bombers died of gunshots to the head after succumbing to the gas. As will be seen in this chapter, we have strong confirmation from many family members, close associates, and hostages of these women's intent to self-detonate, as well as the evidence of their intent in the fact that the women were already clad with suicide belts. Thus, we take their stated intent and their behavior of strapping on bombs as strong enough evidence to classify them as suicide bombers for the purpose of this analysis. We consider this analogous to the many Palestinian bombers currently incarcerated who were thwarted in the last moments before their attempts, but who are also closely studied to understand the psychology and psycho-social aspects of suicide bombers.

6 Speckhard, A. (2005). Unpublished Beslan interviews.

7 For an analysis of our previous work with data studying Chechen suicide bombers, see also: Speckhard, A. and Akhmedova, K. (2006). Black widows: the Chechen female suicide terrorists. In Y. Schweitzer (ed.), *Female suicide terrorists*. Tel Aviv: Jaffe Center Publication; Speckhard, A. and Akhmedova, K. (2006). The new Chechen jihad: militant wahhabism as a radical movement and a source of suicide terrorism in post-war Chechen society. *Democracy and Security*, 2(1), 103–155; Speckhard, A. and Ahkmedova, K. (2006). The making of a martyr: Chechen suicide terrorism. *Journal of Studies in Conflict and Terrorism*, 29(5), 429–492; and Speckhard, A. and Akhmedova, K. (2005). Mechanisms of generating suicide terrorism: trauma and bereavement as psychological vulnerabilities in human security – the Chechen case. In J. Donnelly (ed.), *NATO security through science series: human and societal dynamics, volume 1*. Brussels: NATO Science Series.

8 See also the following for an analysis to date of our previous reports from interviews with the hostages of the Nord Ost mass-hostage-taking operation: Speckhard, A., Tarabrina, N., Krasnov, V., and Akhmedova, K. (2004). Research note: observations of suicidal terrorists in action. *Terrorism and Political Violence*, 16(2), 305–327; Speckhard, A., Tarabrina, N., Krasnov, V., and Mufel, N. (2005b). Stockholm effects and psychological responses to captivity in hostages held by suicidal terrorists. *Traumatology*, 11(2), 121–140; Speckhard, A., Tarabrina, N., Krasnov, V., and Mufel, N. (2005a). Posttraumatic and acute stress responses in hostages held by suicidal terrorists in the takeover of a Moscow theater. *Traumatology*, 11(1), 3–21; Speckhard, A. (2004a). Soldiers for God: a study of the suicide terrorists in the Moscow hostage taking siege. In O. McTernan (ed.), *The roots of terrorism: contemporary trends and traditional analysis*. Brussels: NATO Science Series.

9 Because the authors are both practicing psychologists, we decided that upon coming across anyone seriously considering becoming a suicide terrorist that we would make every clinical effort to dissuade them. In our opinion we were generally successful in offering therapeutic services to help the subjects work through the traumatic experiences that appeared to be a driving motivation for considering enacting suicide terrorism.

10 See Edwin S. Shneidman, *The suicidal mind*, Oxford: Oxford University Press, 1996, in which he discusses the concept of a psychological autopsy following a normal suicide.

11 We have chosen to use the phrase "militant jihad" to refer to the ideology used by Chechen terrorist groups as well as to refer to them as "militant jihadists"

since they themselves refer to "going on jihad." It is important to state that we are well aware of, and have the highest respect for, the religious and completely non-terrorist-related references to the greater jihad in the Koran and sacred writings of Islam as referring to the constant and ever-vigilant need for an inner struggle to master oneself and attain a moral lifestyle, as well as references to the lesser jihad of defending Islamic lands by military force. While having the highest respect for the Koran and sacred writings of Islam, we chose to use the term "militant jihad" in this chapter as a shorthand reference to the common usage found among terrorists groups themselves in referring to their militant activities waged in the name of Islam. In doing so we also follow the shorthand reference made by many counter-terrorism experts referring to the global and local militant campaigns currently waged by terror groups claiming that they are following Islam and who, in the name of Islam, carry out militant attacks primarily against civilian, but also military targets – these made with the objective of causing mass terror, gaining respect, and further recruits among their sympathizers, and thereby influencing the political process.

12 See Speckhard, A., Tarabrina, N., Krasnov, V., and Akhmedova, K. (2004). Research note: observations of suicidal terrorists in action. *Terrorism and Political Violence*, 16(2), 305–327; Speckhard, A. (2004a). Soldiers for God: a study of the suicide terrorists in the Moscow hostage taking siege. In O. McTernan (ed.), *The roots of terrorism: contemporary trends and traditional analysis*. Brussels: NATO Science Series; Speckhard, A. and Ahkmedova, K. (2006). The making of a martyr: Chechen suicide terrorism. *Journal of Studies in Conflict and Terrorism*, 29(5), 429–492; Speckhard, A. and Akhmedova, K. (2006). Black widows: the Chechen female suicide terrorists. In Y. Schweitzer (ed.), *Female suicide terrorists*. Tel Aviv: Jaffe Center Publication.

13 While the label "Wahhabism" denotes a totally other and neutral meaning in the Gulf States and elsewhere in the world, it should be understood that, in Russia, Chechnya, the Caucuses, and the other former Soviet Union republics, this label denotes an ultra-militant form of Islam and refers to militant religious groups that promote jihad and terrorism – so much so that in Russian the word "wahhabist" has become synonymous with terrorist. For the purposes of this chapter, we adhere to the Russian meaning of the word as it is understood in the Chechen context – we refer to Wahhabists in Chechnya as those groups that have formed according to a militant interpretation of Islam which promotes militant jihad and allows for and promotes terrorism. By doing so, we mean no offense to Wahhabists who practice Islam peacefully in other parts of the world (or in Chechnya for that matter), and we fully acknowledge that this term has an entirely other peaceful meaning outside of Chechnya.

14 See Scott Atran (2003). Genesis of suicide terrorism. *Science*, 7 March, 299, 534; also Scott Atran (2004). Mishandling suicide terrorism, *The Washington Quarterly*, 27:3, pp. 67–90, Summer; and Ariel Merari (2003), *Suicide terrorism* (unpublished).

15 Some of the subjects who had worked as rebel fighters prior to becoming bombers (this was 21 percent of the sample) might have received payments for their activities prior to becoming bombers, but they did not have conventional paying jobs.

16 Author's interview (Speckhard) with Palestinian terrorist leader Zubedi, who was a sender of suicide bombers from the Jenin Al Aqsa Martyrs group, made clear that many more Palestinian women than men volunteer as bombers and Zubedi believed this was because other options of fighting are blocked for the women. At the time, he said that his organization refused to send female bombers. Other Palestinian organizations had sent female bombers prior to this.

Reference: Speckhard, A. (2004). Unpublished Palestinian militant interviews. For additional excerpts from these Palestinian interviews, see also: Speckhard, A. and Ahkmedova, K. (2005). Talking to terrorists. *Journal of Psychohistory*, Fall 33(2), 126–156; and Speckhard, A. (2005a). Understanding suicide terrorism: countering human bombs and their senders. In J.S. Purcell and J.D. Weintraub (eds), *Topics in terrorism: toward a transatlantic consensus on the nature of the threat*. Washington, DC: Atlantic Council.

17 A filtration camp is the first point of detention for Chechens arrested in raids and at checkpoints. These "camps" may be simple hold cells, a pit dug deep into the ground with a grate overhead. They are of course cold in the winter, and horrible places to be held. Disappearances often occur when an individual is taken to a filtration camp and torture is widely reported by those who are released as a method of trying to obtain confessions. Family members generally try to obtain release of their loved ones by collecting large sums of money and bringing them as bribes given in exchange for information as to the whereabouts and release of their family member. This has become a bit of a corrupt business among some Russian forces.

18 See The new Chechen Jihad for a discussion of how the rebel movement transitioned during the two wars into making use of terrorism in response to being overwhelmed by a more powerful military force while, at the same time, receiving an influx of funds along with a militant jihadi ideology that supported the move to terrorism. Likewise, see Speckhard, A. and Ahkmedova, K. (2006). The making of a martyr: Chechen suicide terrorism. *Journal of Studies in Conflict and Terrorism*, 29(5), 429–492; and John Reuter (2004). *Chechnya's suicide bombers: desperate, devout, or deceived?*, The American Committee for Peace in Chechnya publication. Online, available from: www.peaceinchechnya.org/reports/SuicideReport (accessed June 1, 2005) about how terrorism was used by these groups to bring the Russian public's attention to war atrocities committed in Chechnya by Russian forces and to attempt to change public opinion and thereby move the political process.

19 In addition to daily fear and daily humiliation, every person in Chechnya has suffered multiple traumatic losses. The Chechen population was decimated by the two wars, with 180,000 Chechens killed and 300,000 fleeing as refugees. One in two Chechens was either killed or ran away as the result of the wars and Chechnya's cities still lie in rubble. For further discussion on this issue, see John Reuter (2004). *Chechnya's suicide bombers: desperate, devout, or deceived?*, The American Committee for Peace in Chechnya publication. Online, available from: www.peaceinchechnya.org/reports/SuicideReport (accessed June 1, 2005).

20 Speckhard, A. and Ahkmedova, K. (2006). The making of a martyr: Chechen suicide terrorism. *Journal of Studies in Conflict and Terrorism*, 29(5), 429–492.

21 This is referred in anthropological literature as "fictive kin." See Atran, S. (2003). Genesis of suicide terrorism. *Science*, 299, 1534-1539, for an additional discussion of this concept.

22 For a complete discussion of the development of fanaticism and generalizing of revenge to include civilian targets in traumatized individuals, see Akhmedova, K. (2003). Fanaticism and revenge idea of civilians who had PTSD. *Social and Clinical Psychiatry*, 12(3), 24–32, in which she reports on a clinical study of over 600 research subjects.

23 "Psychic pain" meaning deeply felt emotions that are painful to the individual. Shneidman coined the term "psyche ache" stating that the best predictor of an individual's propensity to suicide is when emotional pain is experienced as overwhelming and inescapable. Edwin S. Shneidman (1996). *The suicidal mind*. Oxford: Oxford University Press.

7 The black widows

Chechen women join the fight for independence – and Allah

Anne Nivat

On 23 October 2002 there was a full house at the Dubrovka Theater, located in a former Soviet ball-bearing factory on Melnikova Road, Moscow. The hit musical "Nord Ost," a satire about life in Russia during Stalin's time, had been selling out for months and everyone in the audience thought they were lucky to get tickets. But in the middle of the performance, a group of terrorists from Chechnya burst onto the stage and streamed down the aisles. The heavily armed men, accompanied by several women wearing traditional Muslim headscarves and bombs strapped to their waists, took the audience, cast, and staff hostage, threatening to blow everyone up if their demands for an end to the Russian occupation of Chechnya were not met.

Only a few people escaped during the initial siege, and a few more were released during subsequent negotiations, but hundreds remained trapped in their seats, using the orchestra pit as a toilet and eating only vending machine candy. For two days and nights they remained in the custody of kidnappers determined to draw attention to the plight of the Chechen people, who have been fighting for freedom from Russia since the fall of the Soviet Union.

The Russian public were galvanized by this major terror attack on innocent citizens right in the middle of their city. Most shocking of all was the fact that some of the attackers were women. Devout Muslim women, always thought of as subservient and anonymous in their long, flowing chadors, were wearing explosive belts tied with detonator cord. It was a sight that had never been seen or even imagined. The Russian media dubbed them the "black widows." Throughout the crisis, 19 long female silhouettes wrapped in black, their fingers gripping Makarov rifles and detonators, ready and willing to pull the trigger, proved to everyone that the conflict between Russian forces and Chechen freedom fighters was definitely not over.

On all of the Russian government and independent television channels, citizens, politicians, journalists, and political analysts debated and discussed one topic all night long – would President Putin re-examine his policy of military intervention in Chechyna as a result of this event to prevent further terrorist acts in Moscow and elsewhere in Russia? Everyone was shocked that not only had rebels managed to hold off the Russian army and create mayhem in Chechnya for 12 years, but now the war had almost reached the doors of the Kremlin. Even Chechen women had joined the cause!

Emotions ran high among the crowd of onlookers and family members of those being held. Everyone was prepared for a long wait. Not far from the police cordons, four young women walked nervously back and forth, pushing their babies in imposing strollers. "We are not worried about how this hostage-taking will end. We trust President Vladimir Putin," they affirmed in chorus. "We should have finished off those gangsters in Chechnya a long time ago," another one chimed in, whispering as if afraid to be heard.

A little further away, a group of about 50 young, serious-looking people waved banners in front of the television cameras from all over the world. Their signs read: "Down with War," "People are more important than policy," "Stop the Killing," and "Force is not the answer."

The most emotional of them was Marat, a 33-year-old theater technician. "We are here at the request of our colleagues from the theater who are still inside. By telephone, they asked us to organize this small demonstration to avoid the worst outcome, so that this won't end in a bloodbath." Marat had been among the hostages, but escaped with the help of a man from the Emergencies Ministry. "We have to take these kidnappers seriously," he explained. "They are determined. Me, I am of Kazak nationality, a Muslim, but it does not mean I agree with this way of practicing the religion. I don't understand why these men and women are ready to die."

By the third day of the standoff, nearly all of the Russian media had reached a rare anti-Putin consensus. They denounced the fragility of their "allegedly strong" president and criticized his policy with respect to Chechnya. "Until now," the opposition daily newspaper *Nezavissimaya* stated, "the authorities had used Chechnya as a cover for its other problems. Today, Chechnya represents a problem in the heart of Moscow." What's more, this had happened although the government was "using an iron fist."

The federal government "got a punch in the belly from its enemy," who carried out this operation "with astonishing ease," added the reformist daily newspaper *Vremya Novosty*. "However this hostage-taking ends, it will advance the situation in Chechnya," the only independent radio station, Echo of Moscow, dared to predict. According to one of its commentators, Andrei Cherkizov, "they have lied to us for three years, claiming that all was going well down there. Now we can draw our own conclusions."

After the siege had gone on for 56 hours, Russian special operations forces used a gaseous sedative to incapacitate everyone in the theater. About 150 hostages died from complications of the gas and lack of proper aftercare, and all the terrorists were killed before they could detonate their bombs. Their dead bodies were shown on worldwide television. Photographs of the women with bombs still attached to their inert torsos were the most dramatic, their heads leaning back or hanging down, loose-jawed, faces framed by black veils emphasizing their pallor. Four of the women were slumped as if in peaceful sleep on the red velvet seats of the Dubrovka Theater, but they were obviously quite dead. In some cases, a neat bullet hole was apparent in front of the ears or in the middle of the forehead.

"They spoke to us rather nicely," several former hostages said, and they behaved "as normal women." So what would prompt these young women to sacrifice themselves? Most were widows of rebel combatants who had been killed by Russian soldiers. They felt they did not have any more to lose, having already lost a husband, a brother, a father, a son – a life.

Almost two years later, on 1 September 2004, another group of terrorist commandos made their way to neighboring North Ossetia, also a former Soviet Republic now part of the Russian Federation, and raided an elementary school in the small town of Beslan during the traditional celebration of the first day of school. Teachers, students, and parents were taken hostage in what turned out to be a well-planned attack in which weapons and explosives had been pre-positioned in the school building.

So far the terrorist's nationalities are not known for certain, but they were probably Ingush and Chechen, and only two women seemed to be part of this commando squad. According to the Kremlin, about 300 people were held hostage for two days. In fact, there were almost 1,500 people trapped inside the sweltering building, and almost 300 lost their lives.

What really happened inside the Beslan elementary school during the moments just before the first explosion? According to some sources, the two female members of the terrorist group started disagreeing with the commanders of the siege. "You didn't tell us we'd have to kill innocent children," they allegedly complained to their leader. Some of the male hostage-takers agreed with them, and supposedly their leader killed them and detonated some of the explosives they had carefully planted around the room. This noise is what caused the family members and Russian assault forces to storm the building, leading to the massive loss of life.

Talking to the friends and relatives of Chechen female martyrs

In more than five years of reporting on Chechens, the author had never met anyone destined for martyrdom. However, during the summer of 2003, she managed not only to meet these candidates for suicide (or those who proclaim themselves as such), but also sisters, friends, and mothers of some of the young women who had died in the commando operation at Dubrovka Theater. (The author did not meet with relatives of the two women who participated in Beslan because she has not had an opportunity to go to Chechnya since it happened.)

Sitting straight as an arrow on a worn-out sofa, a scarf tied behind her neck, holding a handkerchief with which she kept dabbing her eyes, Yassita was obviously still grieving. She was the mother of Aiza Gazueva, one of the first two Chechen female suicide bombers who martyred themselves on

29 November 2001, in an attack against General Gaidar Gadzhiev, a pro-Russian Chechen chief of the military administration of the Urus-Martan region of Chechnya. "A few months earlier, Aiza's husband had been dragged away by Russian troops in front of her eyes. She had neither father nor brother anymore – no reason to live. She was a loyal woman, to the end," explained her mother between sobs.

In a somber suburb of Grozny, the family of Zareta Bairakova, who died in the Dubrovka Theater at the age of 26, was heartbroken. On the fourth floor of a dilapidated apartment building perforated by artillery shells, her mother, Madni, told the author about the last moments she saw her daughter:

> That Sunday at midday she was in her room praying when a woman I didn't know knocked on our door and asked to see Zareta. "Your daughter knows me well," she claimed. They left the house together. Zareta wanted to accompany her friend to the road. She never returned.

In the photograph album assembled by her mother, Zareta has a pale face and does not appear to be happy. "I knew," regrets Madni, "that she could never be happy. It was tuberculosis. She caught it during the first war. In any case, she did not share anything about her life with me." Today, Madni lives in fear for her elder child too, so she sent her to live in Siberia for several years. "What if the federals kill her too? Anything is possible."

In another village, the mother of Aminat, who was also a member by the Dubrovka commando group, was joined by one of her younger daughters and Animat's best friend. Her pain showed. "Without legitimizing the act of my daughter, I do understand it. It is despair. I only wish she had just said something." These words of sad mothers are trying to express the pain and the incomprehension in front of an ultimate act carried out by young women who obviously had many reasons to be desperate, but did not seem to have enrolled in heavily organized religious training camps by fanatics. From the perspective of the mothers, these daughters had been driven by despair, and lack of dialogue between the "lost" Chechen civil society and the Russian Federal Army "occupying" the territory for five years.

Maaka, 19 years old, had the same pale beauty and slender build of her eldest sister, the terrorist. She seemed to be as angry as her sister was: to have survived a war does not make it easier to live "normally," especially, according to her, when Russia, and the "West" in general, seem *not* to understand what Islam means. These young and despairing women are easy to convince that, by sacrificing their life, they are gaining much more: a room in paradise, which is what the male organizers of the terroristic acts make them believe. Her sister explained, her voice rising in frustration:

> I think that she did that in the name of Allah to stop the war and to save her Muslim brothers, because we are sick and tired of not being

able to live in peace. Yes, I wear the scarf tied under my chin. So what? It is not a reason to treat me like a Wahhabi [Islamic fundamentalist]! Yes, I wear a long tunic because, according to my reading of Koran, the crowned book requires me to wear it, but in what does it matter to anyone else? Aminat wanted quite simply to live as a good Muslim woman and they wouldn't let her. And me – I am an extreme case because I do not have any other recourse. If the situation does not change, if they don't let us live as we want, I would gladly join her in paradise.

Aminat's friend and neighbor, Tamara, another splendid 21-year-old red-head who wore the same vestments as Maaka, pressed a letter from Aminat tight against her chest, then tearfully read it to the author:

Tamara, I left by the will of Allah – you know where. I very much wanted to see you, but that was not possible. Tamara, I stopped crying, and believe me I could not swallow anything or even speak to anyone until had'th [account of Mahomet's words, counsels, and behaviors from the Koran in which the prophet prohibited mourning more than three days]. Then only, with the greatest difficulty in the world, I calmed myself, and also because I know that, soon, Insh Allah, I will find your brother in paradise. Tamara, all that belongs to me is at your disposal. Do not be sad. The difficulties and the strength come from God. Insh Allah, we will find ourselves together in paradise.

With these words, scribbled on a simple sheet of graph paper, Aminat, 28 years old, proceeded on 29 September 2002 to bid farewell to her best friend, Tamara. Less than a month later, on 23 October, the young woman appeared on the television screens of the world as one of 19 women holding hostages in the Dubrovka Theater in Moscow. Curiously, it was also on 29 September that Aishat, 31 years old, left her family in a village south-west of Grozny, umbrella in hand, pretending to leave her parents' house for a few days to go to neighboring Ingushetia. And, as in Grozny, the parents of Zareta, another suicide bomber from the Dubrovka Theater, eerily recall how their daughter left mysteriously, accompanied by a female stranger, on Sunday, 29 September.

Maaka and Tamara tried to explain their *jihad*. "Why aren't we loved in the village? Is it because I learned how to read the Arabic Koran? Why do they act as if I have the plague?" wondered Maaka. Tamara was more vehement:

Since I lost my adored brother, who Aminat loved so much [referred to in her letter], what is there to keep me on this earth? My youth? To do what with it? Since nobody around us acts, we take things into our own hands. Good! Once and for all, the world is starting to be concerned with this conflict. Us, we are not afraid anymore. We've already died.

For these young women, the *jihad* is not especially a question of religion, it is just that they understand the revival of Islam in Chechnya as a critical element in the identity-building of the torn region. For them, not to be allowed to practice their Islam freely is understood as the ultimate attack against who they are, or who they are trying to be: faithful young Muslims.

Tamara turned the page of her best friend's letter to read her own comments, added in clumsy, round handwriting. It started by addressing her beloved elder brother, killed during the war:

> It is such a disgusting world, so unjust. O you my brother, who had always learned how to give me hope, now that you are not here anymore, I want to join you, I want to see you, I want to go to paradise too. I do not want to live in this world.

The last few words are addressed to Aminat: "I am with you. Insh Allah we will meet in paradise, where we will spend a normal life for eternity. I will join you very soon."

Raising her head, she sealed her words with a sad smile:

> Our only desire is to be able to live in peace, to wear a scarf if we want, to study whatever we want, including the Koran, and to perpetuate our families. But here, it is impossible. And if today they accuse us of terrorism and Wahhabism, there is only one culprit – Akhmad Kadyrov!

(Until his assassination in May 2004, Kadyrov was head of the Chechen administration, appointed by the Russian government and elected in December, 2003.) The beautiful red-head stood up. "During the first war, when he was on the side of the rebels, he was the one who inculcated in us to respect the Koran and its primacy above all!"

The very fact that Ahmed Kadyrov, a one-time respected Muslim cleric, became a pro-Russian official illustrates how confusing the situation is in Chechnya where religion only recently started playing a role, after the collapse of the 75-year-old atheist Soviet regime. It is not totally surprising that religion as a new element in the nation-building process of the region has had a strong impact on the young: to them, being a "Wahhabi," despite the fact that they do not really understand what it means, is above all a way to exist, and to exist differently among the vast majority of non-Muslim people within the Russian federation. Many locals do not hesitate to accuse Kadyrov of "having sold himself" to guarantee safety to his entire family and clan. When he was assassinated in May, it surprised nobody in Chechnya. The author even heard people wondering why it had not happened earlier. In such a state of psychological chaos, nobody will be able to stop these young women who are in deep despair and have no fear of death to proceed with more suicide bombings.

Russian public opinion has held them, along with their brothers and fathers, responsible for the chaos that reigns in Chechnya; they are accused of "Wahhabism" (intended as a supreme insult) when they try to practice their faith freely. And, on top of that, the Russian government will not allow the country to become independent. These women feel they have no place to turn. The Chechen independence movement leadership does not offer them any hope of either peace or religious freedom: the extremist rebels, demonstrating political naivete, offer the sort of peace that comes with the death of a martyr, and that is their best offer. Having lived a war-ravaged life, and having no hope of a better one, these women turn to the fate that solves all problems permanently. They have been let down by everyone, and so feel they owe nothing to anyone else. It is a mass psychosis that has been created by uncompromising politicians and a turn toward religious fanaticism. These women feel psychologically abused by the local geopolitical circumstances.

If, in Palestine, the families of the shahids (suicide bombers) are proud of their acts of terror, in Chechnya, the close relatives of the women kamikazes live in fear of being assassinated by their neighbors, the more secular Chechens who want only to live in peace and have this nasty war end. Although all Chechens want peace and independence, only a tiny minority are fighting a religious *jihad*. Those in the majority feel that their valid claim for independence has been poisoned by the linkage with international terrorism, which became especially visible after 11 September 2001, when Russian President Vladimir Putin sided immediately with US President Bush on the "global war on terror."

The Kremlin continues to link Chechens fighting for independence with international terrorists connected with Al Qaeda without providing any proof. For example, right after the Beslan siege Russian officials claimed ten "Arabs" were among the commandos inside the school. The FSB (Federal Security Bureau) had to officially deny the claim two days later. Chechnya's officially elected president-turned-warlord Aslan Maskhadov seems to be losing control of the fight for independence to fundamentalist Islamic terrorists, who decided to abandon the traditional guerilla warfare that has not succeeded in driving out the Russian occupiers and go for cheaper and more effective (in their minds) acts such as the siege of a school, a hospital, or a theater, or suicide bombs in Moscow restaurants and metro stations.

After two years of media hype, the commando operation at Dubrovka Theater, directed by 23-year-old Movsar Barayev, remains an enigma, as does the Beslan school siege. Who were these men and women who sacrificed themselves for the cause of independence for Chechnya? Or was it for some other cause? Did they act on the orders of "hostile foreign forces" as President Vladimir Putin proclaimed a few hours before the final assault? Did they carry out the orders of the "independent Chechen high-command," that is, of President Aslan Maskhadov, of some Al Qaeda commander, or did they act on their own, looking only for a place in history? Who is really behind them? Is it, in the case of Beslan, the Chechen leader Shamil

Basayev, who officially took responsibility, or has he also lost his grip on leadership of the rebels and let some extremists linked to others in the Islamic world take power by exerting terror on innocents?

Interviews with the families of terrorists, such as those the author conducted, which would answer some of those questions, are not allowed to be published in Russia. Many of the questions raised by the independent Russian media remain outstanding as well. For example, how did the hostage-takers get to Moscow? Some arrived by bus, some in a convoy of Jeeps and SUVs with tinted windows. But where did they stay while they concocted their plan? Where did they get and store their weapons? Who were their contacts in Moscow, not only among the Chechen diaspora, but also within the state structures? Were there foreign accomplices?

But, especially, there remains the *critical* question of what to do in Chechnya, where, according to the local public opinion, "they lied to us for three years, claiming that the situation was under control and almost normalized." So far the only official reply has been that the two largest independent television channels, TV5 and NTV, have been closed down by the government for their critical coverage of the crisis. After Beslan, the editor-in-chief of the nationally acclaimed daily newspaper *Izvestya* also lost his job for having conducted an "overly emotional" coverage of the siege.

Although these two major terrorist attacks in two years on Russian soil did not make the Kremlin revise its Caucasian policy, it seems nevertheless to have made obvious to Russian public opinion the many errors and miscalculations of the Russian authorities in Chechnya over the last ten years. First, the immense gap between reality and propaganda was exposed, and this realization has affected Russian public opinion. On 4 September, when many small anti-government demonstrations where taking place in Vladikavkaz, the capital of North Ossetia, another, much larger official demonstration was organized in Moscow (far from the anger of locals in Ossetia) under the banner "against terror."

Since Beslan, more voices have been heard in Russia casting doubts about the reality of the "normalization" in the Caucasus and the end of the "Chechen problem." Now, more people want a quick end to the Chechen problem without holding their president responsible for how bad the situation has become. Vladimir Putin's very high popularity rating (more than 70 percent favorability) dropped only temporarily and infinitesimally after both events because a majority of Russian citizens remained silent in the hopes that their country could find a solution, without "Russia bending its knees" – a phrase used by Putin at the time of his televised "request for forgiveness" to the families of the victims of the attack in Moscow. With the war on terror intensifying, President Putin seems to realize more acutely how important it is to stop the war in Chechnya given the threat it presents to the safety of his country.

On the author's last trip to Chechnya a few months ago, she got the impression that nothing has changed. There is still the same humming of bombers in the distance, the same muddy, rusted armored tanks posted along the roads, the same bored but arrogant manner of the Russian soldiers who stop every vehicle to request papers from the driver, and then demand a bribe whether the documents are in order or not. And there are still innumerable accounts of *zatchistki* (cleansing operations), the same stories told in every village, of masked Russian soldiers who sweep down on the civilian population and kill or drag off the men and boys without explanation or justification. And innumerable pleas for peace from exhausted locals ready to take any compromise in order to achieve it.

It seems, based on the author's experiences in the field, that as long as President Putin does not develop a vision for the future of Chechnya that includes true autonomy, there will be Chechen women driven by despair who are willing to participate in terrorist operations. In fact, since the Dubrovka Theater incident, female suicide bombers have allegedly participated in several more high-profile explosions in Moscow, including a rock concert, a car outside a hotel, a subway car during rush hour, and most recently and most deadly, two commercial planes that were flying from Moscow to the south. (They had bought their way through for as little as 40 dollars each.)

Indeed, Chechen women have been implicated in every terrorist attack in Russia for the last two years, and more Chechen women seem to be participating actively in the separatist-turned-jihadist struggle than in the larger and longer-running Palestinian conflict. Such is the level of desperation and the degree of decimation of the male Chechen population, and the determination of some Chechen women to join their men in "paradise."

8 Palestinian female suicide bombers

Virtuous heroines or damaged goods?

Yoram Schweitzer

Introduction

Although not a new phenomenon, suicide bombings by women attract a dis-proportionately large amount of media scrutiny and academic study in relation to suicide bombing as a whole. Possible explanations for the disproportionate attention that female suicide bombers receive include the seeming incongruity of women, symbols of fertility, and the gift of life, intentionally taking the lives of others. Palestinian female suicide bombers, in particular, have received extensive coverage in the global media due to the relative ease of accessing their families for interviews following a bombing. Israeli policies, which allow media to obtain interviews with suicide bombers imprisoned after failing to complete their missions, have also increased their exposure.[1]

To date, approximately seventy Palestinian women are numbered as having been involved in suicide bombing attempts in Israel – ten of whom actually carried out an attack and died in the process. Indeed, notwithstanding the decline in Palestinian suicide bombings in Israel since the *tahadiya* (the unilateral temporary restraint that was announced in March 2005), two of the eleven suicide attacks were carried out by women. Both of these women were dispatched from Gaza in the span of less than a month. On November 6, 2006, Marwa Masoud, an eighteen-year-old student from the Islamic College in Gaza blew herself up near a group of soldiers, killing herself and slightly wounding one soldier. A few weeks later, on November 23, another female suicide bomber, Fatma Omar al-Najar, a fifty-seven-year-old grandmother with over thirty grandchildren, also detonated herself. Dispatched by Hamas, al-Najar was identified by IDF soldiers who shot at her and foiled her plan before she was able to inflict any casualties, however she did in fact manage to detonate her bomb and injure two soldiers. In addition to the above, a female suicide bomber from the West Bank was apprehended on the way to carrying out an attack in an Israeli city. Moreover, recently published statements by five women associated with the Palestinian Islamic Jihad were suggestive of their intent to engage in such a mission in the future. In May, two mothers thirty-nine-year-old Fatima Younes Hassan Zaq, a mother of eight and pregnant with her ninth child, and Zaq's niece,

thirty-year-old Rawda Ibrahim Younes Habib, a mother of four, were intercepted at the Erez crossing in the Gaza Strip for their intention to perpetrate
a double suicide bombing attack.

While initially the involvement of Palestinian women in suicide bombings was uniformly perceived as abnormal and a social aberration,[2] with time
two opposing approaches have been posited in the media to explain such
attacks. One approach, appearing primarily in the Arab and Muslim media,
has cast female suicide bombers as heroines and pioneers. The more dominant
and "Western" approach has presented female suicide bombers as socially
deviant and, in some measure, as "damaged goods." This chapter seeks to
present a more balanced view of the personal and environmental factors that
propel Palestinian females to engage in suicide bombing and to understand
their doing so within the context of the organizational interests that surround
such bombings. Furthermore, and without questioning the inherent moral
turpitude of the act, it challenges the perception that Palestinian female
suicide bombers are necessarily "damaged goods." The chapter is largely
based on interviews over a two-and-a-half year period that were conducted by
the author in Israeli prisons. The women interviewed either embarked on a
failed suicide mission or served as chaperones to male suicide bombers. Male
recruiters and dispatchers of the women were interviewed as well.

Opposing images: virtuous heroines or "damaged goods"

Palestinian female suicide bombers have typically been portrayed in the
Arab and Muslim media as social heroines and role models: poetic descriptions that emphasize their unique personality and divine qualities are standard. Typically, these women are described as bestowing pride and prestige
on their people, their homeland, and the entire Muslim nation. They have
been compared to glorified historical figures; for example, Wafa Idris, considered to be the pioneer among them, has been described as a modern Joan
of Arc,[3] as possessing the mysterious smile of Mona Lisa, and as a Christ
figure.[4] Other Palestinian female suicide bombers have been presented as
ideal women with supreme qualities of purity, beauty, piety, and rare brilliance.[5] The Arab media has not only praised their acts as unmatched
heroism, but has called upon men to learn from these women and join the
struggle to liberate occupied Arab land and restore Islamic pride.[6]

Against their characterization as heroines, there have been mainly
Western writers who have characterized the women who embark on such
missions as "not whole" women, and even social outcasts. Within this
framing, female suicide bombers are sometimes portrayed as being forcibly
recruited for their missions, since to engage in such violence is outside the
boundaries that define their gender roles. By going on a suicide mission,
women are seen as breaching the accepted moral norms of their conservative
societies, especially when it comes to gender relations. The "aberrant" role
that the woman adopts and the woman's "defects" are the basis for character-

izing her as "damaged goods" – the social and personal "defects" include her being unmarried at a relatively advanced age, being divorced or barren, or having had sexual relations before marriage or an affair during marriage. Other "shortcomings" include belonging to families that carry with them the stain of collaboration, which obligates the woman's sacrifice in order to cleanse the family name. Another anomaly might be a physical defect that lowers a woman's desirability as a wife and prevents her from fulfilling her traditional destiny as a married woman and as a child-bearer. According to this view, the dominant motivation of the woman to sacrifice herself under the banner of the national religious cause is her "defect".

A most prominent example of the "damaged goods" framing by Western media is the recurring reference to Wafa Idris' inability to bear children. Considered to be the first Palestinian female suicide bomber, many attributed Idris' suicide to psychological motives that were caused by her personal circumstances. Idris was married at the age of sixteen to her cousin and was unable to conceive. After nine years of marriage, her husband divorced her and married another woman. Mira Tzoreff, an Israeli researcher, claims that

> while much has been written explaining Idris' deed ideologically, testimony of her friends and family strongly suggests that the motivation for her suicide was personal rather than national or religious. Idris' status as a divorced and barren woman, and her return as a dependant to her parents' home where she became an economic burden, put her in a dead-end situation in a traditional, patriarchal society.[7]

A similar social/personal explanation was given by American journalist Barbara Victor. She too implied that Idris had been driven to her act mainly because she was divorced and barren. Her husband's marriage to another woman, and that marriage resulting in the birth of his child shortly thereafter, was said to bestow an unbearable shame on her at the Ramallah camp in which she lived.[8] Victor argued that only as a result of her growing depression, combined with her religious and nationalistic ideals, did Idris find the reason and determination to carry out the attack.[9]

Victor's book, *Army of Roses*, published in 2003, gained prominence by virtue of it being the first major work on female Palestinian suicide bombers. It describes the story of a relatively small number of women who blew themselves up and a female chaperone of a male suicide bomber. The book received widespread attention and went far to advance the idea that the women who participated in these acts both had few social or personal prospects and were taken advantage of by the militant organizations that preyed on their vulnerability.

In this context, Victor tells the story of Darin Abu Aisha, a student of English literature from the al-Najah University in Nablus, who blew herself up in a car at a roadblock in Israel in February 2002. Aisha died in the attack and her two male chaperones, also in the car, were injured, as were two Israeli policemen. Aisha is presented by Victor as a brilliant woman trapped by her parents' and society's expectations that she marry in conflict with her own personal and academic aspirations. According to Victor, the dilemma lay at the basis of her decision to pursue a path of self-sacrifice in the name of the nation and God.

Victor writes that Aisha suffered social pressure due to her being twenty-two years old and still unmarried. Victor quotes Samira, Aisha's cousin, as saying:

> Sometimes people teased her and called her names because she refused to marry and have children. Her parents suffered because of this. Now they are better because they realize she had other, more important plans.... She knew that her destiny was to become the bride of Allah in Paradise.[10]

According to her close friend, Aisha knew that "her fate as a Palestinian woman was sealed – an arranged marriage, six or seven children, a husband who probably wouldn't have the same hopes or curiosity about life as she did."[11] She was depressed and desperate since she knew that she would be forced to marry her cousin, whom she was ordered to kiss publicly by Israeli soldiers at a roadblock. This event supposedly obligated a marriage between the two since the act was performed before many people and rumor about it had spread; Aisha had been aware of the fact that her refusal to marry her cousin would cast a stain upon her family.[12]

Another female suicide bomber, Ayat al-Akhras, an eighteen-year-old from Dehaisha, was dispatched by a Fatah cell to commit suicide in Kiryat Yovel, Jerusalem, in March 2002. The suicide attack at the supermarket killed two Israelis, including a girl her age. Akhras is presented as someone who sacrificed herself in order to save her family and in order to remove the suspicion of treason that surrounded her father's work with Israelis. Victor here quotes Akhras' friend in explaining Akhras' sentiments:

> She told me there was only one chance to save her family from disgrace ... and that was to become a martyr. By then there was talk around the camp that her father was going to be lynched and their home destroyed. There was no way out for the family.[13]

Another girl, referred to as "Zina" in Victor's book, was the chaperone of a male suicide bomber who blew himself up at the Sbarro Pizza store in Jerusalem, in August 2001. Fifteen Israelis were killed and dozens of people were injured in that attack. "Zina" is presented by Victor as a naive person who was manipulated by her operator and married lover with the promise of a shared eternal life in heaven. Victor also reported that "Zina" gave birth to a son outside of wedlock and that the son was taken from her by her parents. "Zina" was sent from Jordan to the West Bank in order to cover the disgrace. The loss of her child and the promise of her operator/lover to marry her are presented as the events that propelled her to agree to undertake the mission.[14]

Victor's claims are echoed by Anat Berko, an Israeli researcher who interviewed female suicide bombers in Israeli prisons and asserted that none of the seven women who had "exploded" (this number has since grown to ten) could be defined as "normative" within the bounds of Palestinian society.[15] Berko even quotes an Arab–Israeli journalist who accompanied her and described one of the female suicide bombers with the harsh statement "not a shahida but a whore," referring to the woman's illicit relationship with a male. In other words, the bomber was not a woman who died in the name of Allah, but rather, just a prostitute. He added that "it was preferable for her to die rather than be murdered, and as she also took a few soldiers with her, all her sins were forgotten."[16] Kimhi and Even have called this type of suicide bomber the "Exploited Type."[17]

Particularly, given that the pool of successful and would-be female suicide bombers has grown vastly since some of these books and articles were published, it is fitting to examine the validity of the all-encompassing generalization about these women through direct interviews with those who carried out their mission and survived, those who did not carry out their mission, the dispatchers of the women, and the families of the women.

Dispatchers of female suicide bombers

Some of the interviews I conducted in Israeli prisons over a span of two-and-a-half years were with the dispatchers of female suicide bombers who died.[18] Wafa Idris' dispatcher is still unidentified, but among many of the still-imprisoned Fatah members whom I spoke with, the accepted opinion is that Wafa Idris was not dispatched for a suicide mission but rather to just place an explosive device. It is unclear whether Idris was the victim of a work accident or if she ultimately decided to activate the explosive device on her own. The question, however, did not prevent the cultivation of the myth, which came to surround her, nor the explanations regarding her personal problems.

In a series of interviews with Aisha's dispatcher[19] who claimed to have conducted a number of conversations with the woman prior to dispatching her, and also relied on the account of his fiancée who was Aisha's close friend, there were no traces of the motives Victor mentions. It is not possible to completely rule out that Aisha had hidden her "true" motives from him or that he purposely avoided talking about them. However, the dispatcher presents the image of a normative, educated, and intelligent young woman who decided to carry out an attack due to the difficult personal circumstances of her life and her nationalist grievances. Aisha's male cousin, whom she was close to, was also dispatched on a suicide mission by the same dispatcher. Aisha reportedly became obsessed with getting the dispatcher to send her on a mission. According to the dispatcher, Aisha was determined to realize her death through an attack against Israel. When he rejected her many requests, she threatened that she would carry out an attack against soldiers with a knife, even if that would mean her death at their hands. As she would likely not harm any Israelis by doing so, Aisha asserted that her fruitless death would be on his conscience. In the end – and as the dispatcher had been searching for revenge for his friend's death, as well as revenge for the elimination of two leading Palestinian activists by Israel – the dispatcher overcame his initial decision and "surrendered" to her determination. According to what he claims to have heard from her, Aisha's main motive in carrying out a suicide attack was a mixture of deep personal trauma stemming from circumstances affecting herself, her family, and those close to her. Aisha was also said to perceive the acts of her cousin and Wafa Idris as models for emulation.

In interviews that were conducted with Ayat al-Akhras' cell leader,[20] as well as a few of his men, including the driver[21] who escorted Akhras to the site where she carried out her mission, there was no evidence that the main motive for her act was a desire to remove the stain cast upon her family – as Victor contended. It is once again possible that Akhras wanted to camouflage her true motive; a personal motive would of course defile her and her dispatchers, and cast the mission, not as an act of self-sacrifice in the service of God (*istishhad*) – a legitimate act in the eyes of many Palestinians – but as an act of "regular" suicide (*intikhar*), which is forbidden in Islam. According to interviews held with different members of the cell involved in the mission, Akhras, like Aisha, also turned to a cell commander a number of times but was initially rejected because she was a woman. The commander reported that Akhras was angry about being refused and told him that he did not have the right to decide for her what she should do with her life. She, too, threatened that she would carry out the attack by herself anyway.

When the commander finally accepted her request, he explained his acquiescence as the only way to smuggle a suicide bomber into Israel, since at that time men were not allowed in. Furthermore, he wanted to send a message to other Arab countries and the entire world that even women were participating in the struggle, and strove to spark interest in the reasons that women felt impelled to carry out suicide attacks. According to him, this was an especially significant message, and the proof of this lay in the fact that the entire world was interested in this case. He knew what message needed to be broadcast and projected to have a great influence on the Arab world. He therefore wrote the testimony that Akhras videotaped before her death.[22]

Henadi Jaradat detonated herself in the Maxim restaurant in Haifa in October 2004, leaving twenty-one dead and dozens wounded. In a series of interviews,[23] Jaradat's dispatcher rejected the claim that Jaradat had committed her suicide attack as a result of being unwed at twenty-nine. Jaradat was described by him as a special young woman, very strong in her personality ("like a man"), with a serious mind. She benefited from a higher education that she had acquired in Jordan. According to him, she did not marry due only to her sense of responsibility toward her family. He stated that she was responsible for the family's income since her father was a cancer patient. She postponed her personal plans so her brother could marry first and then planned to marry her fiancé. Jaradat's dispatcher also rejected the claim that, since her fiancé was married, he was in fact her lover (and herein lies the hint that she was not normative). He said that the possibility of Jaradat and her fiancé having had premarital relations was unlikely in their society:

> What drove her to commit suicide was anger and revenge over her brother and fiancé having been killed. In one moment everything was destroyed for her and in return she wanted to destroy for what they had done to her. Her idea was that they had ruined her life and thus she had to ruin life totally – this was pure revenge.[24]

He claimed that a large and central part of her decision was the desire for revenge and another part of it was based on religion:

> She was from a religious family, grew up on religion, read the Quran. After the death of her fiancé and the useless death of her brother who had no involvement in the conflict, she became highly sensitized to the idea that death could come to you at any place, even in your home, and unexpectedly. Every person's fate was determined by God and whatever one did, God would decide whether you die or live and she decided that she wanted to die at that time. We will all die at some point and it is preferable that we cause our enemies' deaths on their side.[25]

Jaradat's act can be seen as a striking example of the deadliest combination of sheer desire for personal revenge wrapped in nationalistic and religious terms. It seems to also reinforce Speckhard's perception that personal trauma is a central cause that drives female (as well as male) suicide bombers to their act of self-sacrifice – it produces a calming effect on their difficult emotional states and is an answer to the pain they cannot bear. Their refuge is found in relocating the personal pain to the nationalistic religious path.[26]

Interviews with failed female suicide bombers

My findings are based on seventeen interviews that were held with jailed women, eleven of whom were suicide bombers caught prior to having realized their mission, and two were chaperones of male suicide bombers. The ages of the interviewees ranged from seventeen to forty-four. Most of the women had completed high school and some went further in their education. Most were single, though one woman was divorced with a child, and another was the mother of four. The women that were interviewed were chosen entirely at random due to the shifting availability of prisoners and prison circumstances, which prevented systematic selection. The random nature of these interviews is a common and unavoidable constraint in the field of interviewing terrorists in general, and suicide bombers in particular. For most of the women I interviewed, their involvement in a suicide attack was their first and only experience of committing a serious violent act, and most were not previously affiliated with a militant organization. Together, these interviews suggest that a diverse set of motives drove the women to volunteer for this type of activity and, as has been argued with respect to their male counterparts, they claimed to have been driven by a deep sense of altruism, with deep nationalistic and, sometimes, religious roots. Among the women interviewed, some stressed religious reasons as the primary and distinct motive for their actions, while others expressed a desire to harm the Israelis in purely nationalistic terms. There were also cases that seemed to be classic examples of exploitation of the women's weaknesses in a manner that indeed correlated with the notion of "damaged goods."

Wafa Idris, whether or not she committed a premeditated suicide attack, was not the first Palestinian to volunteer for such a mission. A twenty-year-old named "Naima" was dispatched in 1987 to drive an explosives-filled car in front of Israeli government offices in Jerusalem. When interviewed[27] nearly twenty years later, "Naima" stated that her motivation to commit an attack was "irregular" in the context of the Palestinian struggle of the 1980s. By her own account, "Naima" was a devout and excellent student who decided that she wanted to participate in the struggle to free her birthplace and therefore joined the religious faction that operated within Fatah. "Naima" was part of a large family, and one of her brothers, to whom she was especially attached, was killed during a clash with the IDF. From her account, I was not able to identify any type of social or personal defect that could potentially have driven her to her act. From her current and more mature perspective, she asserted that what drove her to embrace such a mission was a blazing religious faith. Back then, she believed that it was the right path toward fulfilling her religious and nationalistic duties. However, she elaborated that, while still possessing the potent religious and nationalistic sentiments from her past, she would presently choose an alternative means to express her protest and beliefs. Naima" described her mood preceding the planned attack as follows:

> I was constantly praying and asking God that the time for "work" would arrive in order for me to be able to do it for Him. The most important thing for me was that I wouldn't commit any sin of foreign desire like heroism or revenge. Only for God. I felt like a young woman looking forward to a meeting with her beloved. I didn't even think about heaven. It was like wanting to think about a man that you would be close to. I was ready for it even if God would have put me in hell. I was ready provided that I would be close to Him. I wanted to be sure that I wouldn't be tempted by the devil that would steer me away from the pure thought of being with God.

In interviews with three women from the Islamic Student Union (the student offshoot of Islamic Jihad), two of whom were to be dispatched on suicide missions by Islamic Jihad, religious faith was cited as the main motivation. At the head of the group was the "recruiter,"[28] "Mariam," an honor student from al-Najah University and an active member of the Islamic Jihad student union. In 2003, after having assisted in transporting explosives for the organization, "Mariam's" operators proposed that she should commit a suicide attack on their behalf. "Mariam" refused, claiming she was afraid that her parents, who had labored to build their home and were in a difficult financial situation, would have their home damaged, and she added, "everyone has his/her role." However, she did volunteer to arrange for other female suicide bombers to take such steps in her place. To this end, she turned to two of her friends who she thought would be willing to carry out an attack.

The first girl she turned to was "Zahara," who was nineteen years old and from a Kabatia religious family. "Zahara" was born in Saudi Arabia and lived there until the age of ten, whereupon her family moved to Jordan and from there to the West Bank. In an interview, "Zahara"[29] said that the idea to commit a suicide attack preoccupied her for a long time while she was pursuing her religious studies. Through her studies she came to the conclusion that sacrificing their lives was the most exalted and obligatory duty of every Muslim. She said that this was especially due to the situation with Israel and to the "oppression of the Muslims in the world." Zahara's parents' suspicions about her intentions served to restrict her activities and prevented her from undertaking the attack.

With the urgent need to recruit another girl to volunteer for the attack, "Mariam" turned to "Karima," another female student[30] among her friends, who agreed to carry out the attack. "Karima" also cited religious motives as a primary factor. After she was petitioned by her friend, she reportedly prayed and did *istikhara* (a prayer that helps the person praying to sense whether the act he or she is considering is wanted by God). She decided to respond affirmatively and pursue what she deemed to be the path of God (*fi sabil Allah*). The arrests of the men who stood behind the planning led to the arrest of the recruiter and, a short time thereafter, to the arrest of the two potential female suicide bombers. As a result, the plot was thwarted.

"Najwa," a female suicide bomber[31] dispatched by Fatah to carry out an attack in a central Israeli city, regretted her decision at the last moment. In a series of conversations with her dispatchers (members of the same cell that had sent Ayat al-Akhras), the image of a normal, educated and articulate twenty-year-old girl (when she volunteered for the attack) emerged. "Najwa" made her decision to undertake a suicide mission following the killing of a close friend. This highly traumatic event, combined with a constant sense of humiliation and frustration that she, her friends, and nation were forced to endure, caused her to want to act. However, in the interviews I conducted with "Najwa," she fiercely denied that her motive for the mission was personal revenge. "Najwa" explained that her actions were in response to Israel's actions and based on her sense that there were no alternative ways of responding except with force against Israel. Of several failed female suicide bombers, "Najwa" came closest to realizing her intention. One can argue that her account is endowed with an even greater authenticity, by virtue of the independence she exhibited in exercising her own wishes against those of her handlers.

Though "Najwa's" personal history suggests its fair share of hardships – her father died when she was six months old, her mother did not remarry until she was ten, and she was raised in the home of her aunt and grandmother – these circumstances, while unfortunate, are not uncommon for many Palestinian families. Indeed, "Najwa" described her childhood and adolescence as happy and protected. She described the personal freedom that she had enjoyed at school, which included learning foreign languages (English and German), until the escalation of security measures came at the end of 2000, due to the political situation. The negative aspects of Najwa's childhood, in and of themselves, did not make her fit to be designated as "damaged goods."

In an interview with the woman referred to as "Zina" in Victor's book, nothing pointed to a son born out of wedlock or an affair with her dispatcher, Darlas.[32] Victor argued that the two together were the motives behind "Zina" volunteering to be the first Hamas female fighter to personally commit an attack and later the chaperone of male suicide bomber. "Zina," by her own account a religious girl, was impelled by a mixture of nationalistic and religious motives. The personal background that she reported included a life in Jordan and moving to the home of her relatives in the occupied territories. This process of seeing wounded Palestinians and experiencing a sense of opposition led to her increased political awareness and active involvement in protests against Israel. According to "Zina," the violence that Israel waged against the Palestinians demanded an especially violent counterattack. Hence her great disappointment when, on her first mission, the rigged beer bottle can that she had placed in a Jerusalem supermarket did not cause any injuries; and her immense joy when the suicide attack that she was involved in as a chaperone caused fifteen deaths.[33]

Irrespective of whether "Zina" had a child out of wedlock or had an affair with her operator, the filmed interview I conducted with her shows her to be an educated and opinionated young woman who, in the spirit of Islam and its decrees, clearly articulates the reasons that justify committing violence against Israel. Her hatred of Israel and her desire for revenge were expressed with self-control and chilling tranquility, as were her descriptions of what went through her heart as she returned home from the scene of the suicide bombing. She said that she longed to hear of the number of deaths that she was party to, especially in light of her disappointment with the outcome of her first attack, in which she acted alone. The quality of "Zina's" interpersonal skills, illustrated by her status in the Israeli prison as a spokesperson and representative for the female prisoners with prison authorities, makes it difficult to perceive her as "damaged goods" or as someone who was used unknowingly by others.

"Jamila," [34] an interviewee who escorted a male suicide bomber to Jerusalem where he killed two Israelis and wounded tens of others, is a married woman and mother of four children. Even though in her biography it is also possible to find the loss of a father at a young age and a marriage at the age of fourteen, she is not to be perceived as being socially aberrant. "Jamila" claimed that she did not initially intend to be a suicide bomber or assist one. The risk that she brought upon herself hiding wanted people and transporting arms for Palestinian militant groups, however, seemed to naturally progress toward taking the risk associated with escorting a male suicide bomber. For "Jamila," acting as such was the obvious thing to do in the struggle that her people were waging.

"Damara," [35] another potential female suicide bomber, was a thirty-year-old divorcee and a mother of a ten-year-old girl when I interviewed her (she was twenty-six when she undertook her mission). "Damara's" decision to commit a suicide attack grew out of the increased suffering of Palestinians she witnessed and the security escalation that intensified it. The escalation was largely a result of Operation Defensive Shield that followed the March 2002 chain of suicide attacks – the suicide attacks were in reaction to IDF forces targeting suicide bomber dispatchers living in the West Bank. "Damara" described her life before the outbreak of the second intifada as "good," both financially and personally. She explained that her divorce took place with her consent and to her satisfaction, and that she did not feel lacking because of it. She peacefully continued her life with her daughter and extended family in the large complex in which they lived until the violence around her intensified and became unbearable.

My interview with "Damara" revealed the emotional distress that she experienced related to the killing around her. "Damara's" younger brother had volunteered to perform a suicide attack that, in the end, did not come to fruition. The security closure and pressure around her, and the increase in suicide attacks committed by people from her camp – foremost among them, the suicide attack on the first night of Passover (March 27, 2002) that caused the deaths of thirty Israelis and the injuries of dozens more – were inspirational to her, and provided her with the final push to choose the path of a suicide attack.

It is impossible to ignore the fact that there are a considerable number of cases in which the main reason for selecting a woman was due to her having physical "defects" or "a lower social image." For example, Wafa al-Bas was a twenty-one-year-old girl from Gaza whose body was badly burnt. She underwent a series of treatments in Israel and was dispatched to commit a suicide attack there on June 20, 2005. Although al-Bas refused to speak with me directly on the advice of her prison friends who wanted to protect her from "the media," several of these same friends were willing to clarify the process of her recruitment. After she had suffered her burns, al-Bas was asked through the mediation of a female acquaintance if, due to her difficult personal situation, she would like to carry out a suicide attack that would award her great respect. al-Bas ostensibly replied positively, yet the acquaintance claims that she did not attribute importance and seriousness to what al-Bas said. This friend, whose brother was a member of Tanzim, invited al-Bas home to meet with a group of Fatah operatives who asked her if she was indeed willing to perform the attack. Al-Bas was allegedly nervous, though replied in the affirmative; they also told her that, since she had seen them and was able to identify them, that she did not have the option of regretting her decision. Indeed, al-Bas was ordered to blow herself up if she was discovered in order to ensure that she would not lead the authorities to those who sent her on her mission. This was the explanation al-Bas gave to her friends in prison when asked why she activated the explosive device, though it was clear that she had been discovered and was trapped within an area in which she could not harm Israeli security.[36] The short film in which Wafa al-Bas is shown being held at a distance from others, yet pressing the activation switch on the explosive belt she was wearing, received widespread media coverage. Her action was framed as revealing the irrationality of suicide attacks.

"Suaha,"[37] a thirty-eight-year old single woman with burn marks on her face and hands, needed ongoing medical treatments and was apparently not on the course to marriage and motherhood. In my interview with "Suaha," I got the impression that her difficult physical situation, in combination with the fact that she was dependent on receiving transit permits for treatment from Fatah members in the Palestinian Authority, aided in influencing her to carry out a suicide attack. In the interview, she spoke of her motives in nationalist terms – the struggle against the occupation and the desire for revenge against Israelis – but she also admitted that she had dreamt of reaching heaven and being one of the beautiful *khuriyat al-ain* ("virgins of heaven").

Similar instances of what clearly seem to be cases of exploiting the weakness and defects of miserable women are found in the attempts to dispatch Faiza Amal Jumaa and "Nazima" Jumaa. Faiza, a thirty-five-year-old woman whose appearance and behavior suggest a man trapped in a woman's body, volunteered herself as a suicide bomber for Hamas.[38] "Nazima" stated that she was coerced to commit a suicide attack by placing grenades on her body.[39]

Conclusion

The growing number of female suicide bombers, and especially Palestinian women who are caught on their way to an attack or in the advanced stages of one, presents an important research opportunity for understanding the motivations and circumstances leading women who undertake a suicide mission. Sweeping generalizations that advance the idea that Palestinian women largely pursue suicide attacks because they are "damaged goods" on the one hand, or because they possess super-human personality traits on the other, complicate the understanding of the phenomenon. From personal conversations conducted with female suicide bombers who failed to complete an attack, it is clear that they are neither "abnormal" nor do they possess meta-human qualities.

From interviews with the women, and dispatchers who sent women and were also imprisoned, it becomes clear that a variety of motives influenced the women to choose the path they did. For quite a few of them, being viewed as "damaged goods" by the society around them, or in their own eyes, was not the main prompt. Many phrased the women's motives in nationalistic and religious terms. Additional motives mentioned by the women were revenge and the desire to prove to Israel that Palestinians could fight back and force Israel to pay for the suffering that it had caused the Palestinians. Many of the women stated that they believed that a suicide attack was the only way open to them to take part in their national struggle. These arguments have likewise been heard many times from failed male suicide bombers who were not members of organizations and who did not possess any skill in using arms.

Given the traditional and conservative nature of Palestinian society, the choice by women to carry out suicide attacks, or for the men who set up such operations to dispatch them, was not simple. Though the dispatcher's initial reservations were overcome enough to send the women, there remained a sense of discomfort about sending women on these types of missions.[39]

The recent suicide bombing by Najar, a fifty-seven-year-old grandmother did not only set a new record for age by suicide bombers, but also represents another question mark regarding the proposition that women who agree to carry out suicide missions are socially anomalous in some important way and have little chance of fitting into the social fabric of the community. Najar's unique profile was followed by two other female bombers, both mothers who were intercepted at the Erez crossing in the Gaza Strip.

This is not to say that female suicide bombers, like their male counterparts, are not exploited. The situational weaknesses of the potential suicide bombers, even those who volunteered for their missions (and certainly those who were coerced into these actions), are neither disregarded nor channeled to less-destructive ends. Instead, they are seized upon and aggravated by those dispatching them for greater organizational purposes.

Since the phenomenon of suicide bombing in the service of terrorist organizations is widening across the globe, and women are being turned to more and more to carry out such missions, it is important not to misrepresent women's motives. Inaccurate stereotypes make it difficult to find effective ways to combat female suicide bombing and direct the women to alternative non-violent expressions of protest and opposition. Most of all, defusing this phenomenon requires attention to the greater organizational context of suicide bombers and those who sponsor them.

Notes

1 Yoram Schweitzer, "Introduction," in *Female Suicide Bombers: Dying For Equality?* Yoram Schweitzer (ed.), Memorandum no. 84, Jaffee Center for Strategic Studies at Tel Aviv University, 2006, p. 7.
2 For example: Harvey Gordon, "The suicide Bomber: is it a Psychiatric Phenomenon?" *Psychiatric Bulletin*, 26 (2002), pp. 285–287; Kaja Perina, "Suicide Terrorism – Seeking Motives Beyond Mental Illness," *Psychology Today* (January 9, 2002), p. 15; Jerrold M. Post, *"Killing in the Name of God: Osama Bin Laden and Radical Islam,"* Paper presented at the International Society of Political Psychology, 25th Annual Scientific Meeting, Berlin, Germany (July 16–19, 2002).
3 Raphael Israeli, "Palestinian Women: the Quest for a Voice in the Public Square Through 'Islamikaze Martyrdom'," *Terrorism and Political Violence*, 16, 1 (2004), p. 86.
4 Israeli, p. 87.
5 Cindy D. Ness, "In the Name of the Cause: Women's Work in Secular and Religious Terrorism," *Studies in Conflict and Terrorism*, 28 (2005), p. 366.
6 Memri, "Wafa Idris: A Female Suicide Bomber", February 5th 2002 (Hebrew document, no author specified).
7 Mira Tzoreff, "The Palestinian *Shahida*: National Patriotism, Islamic Feminism, or Social Crisis," in *Female Suicide Bombers: Dying For Equality?* pp. 19–20.
8 Barbara Victor, *Army of Roses: Inside the World of Palestinian Women Suicide Bombers*. Rodale Press, 2003, p. 50.
9 Victor, *Army of Roses*, p. 46.
10 Victor, *Army of Roses*, p. 100.
11 Victor, *Army of Roses*, p. 104.
12 Victor, *Army of Roses*, p. 109.
13 Victor, *Army of Roses*, p. 208.
14 Victor, *Army of Roses*, pp. 134, 140
15 Anat Berko, *On the Way to Heaven: the World of Female and Male Suicide Bombers and Their Dispatchers*. Miskal, Yediot Ahronot Books and Hemed Books, 2004, p. 22.
16 Berko, *On the Way to Heaven*, p. 20.
17 Shaul Kimhi and Shemuel Even, "Who are the Palestinian Suicide Bombers?" *Terrorism and Political Violence*, 16 (2004), pp. 815–840.
18 To protect the privacy of those women who failed to complete their missions, I have assigned them false names. Those who completed their missions have already been exposed, and hence the willingness to disclose the names of the men who sent them.
19 Interviews conducted with Naser Shawish, January 19, 23, 24, 2005.
20 Interviews with Ahmed Mugrabi, October 6, 9, 26, 2005.
21 Interviews with Ibrahim Sarhne, November 14, 2005.
22 Interviews with Ahmed Mugrabi, October 6, 9, 26, 2005.
23 Interviews with Amjad Ubeidi, January 21, 2005, November 2, 2005.
24 Interview with Amjad Ubeidi, November 2, 2005.
25 Interview with Amjad Ubeidi on January 24, 2005.
26 Anne Speckhard, "Understanding Suicide Terrorism: Countering Human Bombs and their Senders," *Topics in Terrorism: Toward a Transatlantic Consensus on*

the Nature of the Threat (Vol. I)*, Jason S. Purcell and Joshua D. Weintraub (eds), Atlantic Council Publication, 2005.

27 Interview with "Naima," June 19, 2006.
28 Interview with "Mariam," January 8, 2004.
29 Interview with "Zahara," April 2006.
30 Interview with "Karima," January 8, 2004.
31 Interview with "Najwa," March 2, 8, 22, 2005.
32 On November 21, 2006 there was an additional inquiry into the prior interviews that had been conducted with the dispatcher ("lover") Darlas, via an imprisoned trusted member of Hamas. In the interview he insisted that his relationship with "Zina" did not exceed the bounds of the operational connection and he claimed that, since she had been engaged, the notion never even crossed his mind according to the strict codes that exist in their society regarding such matters.
33 Interview with "Zina," April 18, 2006.
34 Interview with "Jamila," April 2, 2006.
35 Interview with "Damara," April 19, 2006.
36 Conversation on April 18, 2006.
37 Interview with "Suaha," April 25, 2006.
38 Smadar Peri, "A Female Suicide Bomber," *Yediot Ahronot*, June 18, 2004.
39 Berko *On the Way to Heaven*, pp. 20–25.
40 Yoram Schweitzer, "Palestinian Female Suicide Bombers: Reality vs. Myth," in *Female Suicide Bombers: Dying For Equality?*, pp. 28–30.

9 Martyrs or murderers? Victims or victimizers?

The voices of would-be Palestinian female suicide bombers

Anat Berko and Edna Erez[1]

Introduction

The January 2002 appearance of Palestinian women on the suicide bombing scene surprised players on both sides of the Israeli–Palestinian conflict. Offering a drastic deviation from their traditional roles in Palestinian society, women's involvement in violent resistance marked a turning point in the discourse and media representation of the suicide bombing phenomenon. Although women had been active in the Palestinian national struggle for a long time, their activities prior to 2002 were limited to actions short of violence. In the first *Intifada*, (uprising) ending with the Oslo Accords (1987–93), and the second *Intifada*, (2000 to the present), Palestinian women participated in demonstrations, were active members of popular committees, or assisted in the production of terrorist attacks. By and large, until 2002, the contribution of women to the military conflict had been mostly restricted to giving birth to sons – future soldiers – that could be dispatched to fight Israel (Tzoreff, 2006).[2] The entry of eight women into the exclusively male circle of Palestinian suicide bombers since January 2002 raises the question of whether the participation of females in such acts represents a shift in the status of women in Palestinian society.

Explanations in the literature of what motivates male suicide bombers have been both numerous and contradictory, and exist across a spectrum of cultural/religious, psychological and political theoretical frameworks. For example, some scholars have noted the role of religious beliefs and convictions in suicide bombing and the manipulation of these beliefs by suicide-producing organizations (Hafez, 2004). Others have presented suicide bombers as having a distorted sense of the world, and as pathological, brainwashed, or sexually deprived individuals (Fulford, 2001; Atran, 2003). Still others have attributed suicide bombing to frustrations related to political conditions – as a way to exact revenge, retaliate for group humiliation, and restore national honor (Crenshaw, 2002; El Sarraj, 2002a, 2002b; Rubenberg, 2001). Indeed, several scholars have suggested that feelings of hopelessness, despair, shame, or humiliation resulting from the occupation "makes living no better than dying" (El Sarraj, 2002a, 2002b; Shalhoub-

Kevorkian, 2003; Stern, 2003), particularly in Arab culture, which places much weight on "honor." Still others have argued that suicide bombing is not an act of desperation, but of struggle (Merari, 2004). Suicide bombing has also been presented as a means to achieve self-empowerment, redemption, and honor for individuals who experience powerlessness and humiliation (Juergensmeyer, 2000; Hassan, 2003). Finally, it has been understood as a way to guarantee access to sensual pleasures forbidden in this life, and as a hope for an attractive afterlife (Stern, 2003; Berko, 2004).

The explanatory framework most commonly applied by scholars to female suicide bombers has focused on gender. Within this framework, female suicide bombing is considered to be a way to resist patriarchal subservience, erase stains due to violations of sexual behavior, or restore a tarnished family or personal reputation (Victor, 2003; Patkin, 2004). More recently, however, some scholars have rejected or minimized the importance of gender-based explanations, arguing that suicide/martyrdom should be understood ontologically rather than strategically (Verancini, 2002/3: 43). They suggest reframing female suicide bombing as an act of anti-colonial (or anti-Zionist) resistance, and the only choice Palestinians have under the circumstances (Verancini, 2002/3; Hasso, 2005). According to this line of thinking, colonized Palestinian women refuse to internalize their subjugation. Through annihilating themselves, they take control of their bodies in defiance of what they see as a "Zionist" attempt bent on realizing their complete domination (Hasso, 2005).

The explanatory frameworks, related media presentations, and scholarly discussions surrounding the meanings, motives, and reasons for Palestinian women's engagement in suicide bombing have, for the most part, been based on two data sources: testimonials given by family members and other people in the women suicide bombers' lives that have been left behind (for example, see Victor, 2003) and farewell statements made by the women themselves prior to their departure. The latter have been played out in what has become the theater of suicide terrorism employed by terrorist organizations and the media for various political ends (Israeli, 2004; Bloom, 2005; Brunner, 2005; Hasso, 2005).

Each of these data sources provides a partial account of Palestinian women's decisions to engage in suicide bombing, or their experiences (Brunner, 2005; Schweitzer, 2006), and each embodies particular biases. The testimonials written by the women themselves are carefully self-edited and present an idealistic explanation that attempts to justify their suicide. Statements made after the fact by their friends, families, and in the media are likewise tainted with partiality, may at times contradict the women's testimonials or each other, and as a result raise questions about the value of pre-arranged testaments in uncovering women's motivations, thoughts, or feelings regarding such experiences (Patkin, 2004). Clearly, to understand these women's motives and experiences it is not sufficient to conduct a posthumous analysis of female suicide bombers' prepared testimonials; nor can the statements made by family and friends be considered uniformly reliable in shedding light on what brings a particular woman to suicide bombing. Fortunately a third source of information is available: the voices of women who have made the decision to become suicide bombers, but who, for various reasons, did not implement their plan.

The voices of unsuccessful bombers are likely to produce a more textured account for several reasons. First, the women are less likely to be in thrall to the political agenda of the suicide-producing organization once removed from its immediate influence. Their motives and reasoning are also not subject to the re-interpretations of well-meaning but self-interested family members who have a personal stake in the way their loved ones are portrayed.

In this chapter, we will present the voices of seven Palestinian women whose suicide mission was either thwarted[3] $(N = 4)$, failed[4] $(N = 1)$, or was aborted because the women changed their minds $(N = 2)$ prior to the operation. The chapter will display, in a woman's own words, how the decision to become a suicide bomber was arrived at, how she was recruited and deployed, how she remembers feeling regarding her mission, and her later reflections on her experiences.

To provide the social context in which Palestinian women navigate their daily lives, we will first discuss Palestinian society's gender-based structures and relations. We then will present in-depth interview data from seven Palestinian women who were about to execute suicide missions but for various reasons could not carry them out. We conclude with an analysis of the theoretical and policy implications regarding Palestinian female suicide terrorism.

Gender relations and women's status in Palestinian society

Palestinian society is a collective society based on the principles of tribalism and social homogeneity (Sharabi, 1975). Members' individual security, well-being, and survival derive from, and are guaranteed by, the protection provided by the group. Relations among nuclear and extended family members are highly valued and each member has the duty to care for the well-being and safety of other family members. The social order in Palestinian society, as in other collective societies, is hierarchical and fixed; individuals must adhere to the directions given by those with higher standing on the social scale, commonly determined by sex and age (Barakat, 1985; Ahmed, 1992).

Palestinian society is decidedly patriarchal; males occupy the highest stratum of the social hierarchy whereas women and children are placed at the base of the scale.[5] Young women must not only obey older women and males, but also males younger than themselves[6] (Sharabi, 1975). It is a grave offense for women to challenge male authority (e.g. a father, brother, husband). The patriarchal elements of Arab society emphasize the importance of preserving customs and traditions, while maintaining stability and harmony in the hierarchy of social relations (extended and nuclear) (Barakat, 1985).

Although variations[7] exist in Arab societies with respect to the status of the family, and of men and women, certain core cultural characteristics can be identified that structure Palestinian society (e.g. Barakat, 1985). One notable characteristic is that the family functions as the central social unit in the economic, social, and religious spheres of life. The family constitutes a source of support, unity, and cohesion that can sustain the individual socially, economically, and politically. Thus, it plays a crucial role in providing assistance and services such as employment, protection, mutual support in child rearing, financial support, etc. Family members are expected to be totally committed to the values of family protection, unity and reputation, which may require putting aside their own personal needs, aspirations, and desires in favor of the group's welfare. This collectivist orientation stresses self-sacrifice of individual members for the "common good," and lays out expectations to put the community's welfare and interests beyond one's personal happiness.

For women, this orientation means placing the family's welfare before their own, demonstrating an unconditional devotion to and continuous care for the family, and support for members of the family of origin (if unmarried) and the husband (if married).[8] For mothers, whose own happiness is determined by their children's happiness, growth, and achievement, success or failure in personal behavior in life choices in marriage and in child rearing is considered the success or failure of the family. What success the mother's influence has in this realm amounts to the success or failure of the family. It has been argued that the emphasis on a woman's central role in caring for her family results in a complete erasure of herself as a person and as a woman in her own right (Korbin, 2005).

All women are expected to preserve the family's reputation and "honor," which in Arab society is primarily connected to women's sexual conduct (Al-Khayyat, 1990). Women's chastity, modesty, and sexuality are extremely sensitive issues in the Arab world (including Palestinian society). If a woman is immodest or exhibits sexual behavior that is considered inappropriate, she brings shame and dishonor on all her kin. By and large, "family honor" for women means a chaste reputation, while for men it means courage, religiosity, and hospitality (Fernea, 1985). Women's "honor" is thus passive and can only be lost or tarnished, while "honor" for men is active, and can be retrieved, increased, and expanded (Hasan, 1999; Israeli, 2004).[9]

Social restrictions applicable to a woman include segregation from the public domain or confinement to the domestic sphere, and a prevailing morality that stresses traditional ideals of femininity, motherhood, and wifehood.[10] A woman's identity and worth are strictly defined in terms of her obedience, seclusion, and in producing male offspring (Rubenberg, 2001;

Israeli, 2004). The restrictions imposed by the patriarchal family, with its dual system of age and gender oppression, together with the translation of a woman's sexuality into a social norm of "honor," serve to control Palestinian women and strengthen men's domination over them (Hasan, 1999; Rubenberg, 2001).

Women's vulnerable position in Palestinian society is further exacerbated by Arab tribal notions that children or young adults are parental (father's) property, and that the welfare of the collective takes precedence over that of the individual, especially in times of crisis (Fernea, 1985; Al-Khayyat, 1990). When women's (or girl's) misbehavior (or abuse, see Shalhoub-Kevorkian, 2005) become known, it may be seen as an indication that their families failed to discipline (or protect) them. This in turn may call into question the power and privilege of male family members (particularly the father), demanding a response to restore their masculine status and protective capability (Hasan, 1999; Israeli, 2004).[11] The tendency to penalize violations of gender-expected behavior (in extreme cases by death) prevents women from disclosing to parents, siblings, and other family member such violations, particularly those involving unsupervised contact with men. It also stops women from turning to their families for help under such circumstances. As we will see, the collectivist nature of Palestinian/Arab society, its gender relations, male privilege, and female expected behavior illuminate Palestinian women's pathways to suicide terrorism as these emerge in the data.

Data-collection methods and procedures

These data are derived from in-depth individual interviews conducted with seven detained or incarcerated Palestinian female would-be suicide bombers who agreed to participate in the study.[12] The interviews took place between February 2003 and June 2006. Five of the women were interviewed in two separate wings of the prison for security offenders in which they were serving their sentences.[13] One woman was interviewed in the general prison to which she was transferred, after being assaulted by her fellow female security prisoners.[14] Another woman was interviewed while waiting for her military court arraignment. Protocols of human subjects' protection were strictly followed in the data-collection phase; participants were informed about their right to decline participation, to refuse to respond to specific questions, or withdraw at any point from the study without adverse consequences.

Dependent on the interviewee's preference and language proficiency, the interviews were conducted either in Arabic, Hebrew, English, or a mixture of these languages. Four of the participants were interviewed for at least two sessions separated by a period of a few days, weeks, or months. One participant was interviewed in a waiting room prior to her court hearing. Another interviewee, who was suffering from burns caused by a gas blast in her home, chose not to return to an additional interview session. Each interview session lasted between three and four hours (except the one in the court, which lasted for two hours).

The interview schedule included open-ended questions that soon became conversational interviews about the women's childhood and growing up, landmark events, and significant others in their lives, relationships with family and friends, and their personal aspirations during various life stages, including at the time of the interview. In all cases, during the second or third session, the participants volunteered to describe in detail the circumstances that led them to become involved in suicide terrorism and the reasons for their involvement. They described how they were recruited and deployed, how they felt about their involvement, and their views, beliefs, and expectations relative to their mission and its aftermath.[15]

The initial suspicion of the interviewees about being questioned, and the fear that it would be just another interrogation aimed at acquiring information on their mission or contacts, dissipated as the women realized that the questions focused on their private lives, social experiences, and personal views. Once they realized the personal/academic nature of the interview, they gradually opened up and provided comprehensive self-portraits.[16] Their stories, as reported in this chapter, provide insights into their world – their social history, experiences, beliefs and views, and the circumstances that resulted in their incarceration.

The interview data were analyzed through coding techniques for qualitative data described by Glaser (1992). As we read the transcripts, patterns and variations in participants' responses were identified, resulting in a set of conceptual categories or propositions. In analyzing the data, we applied the logic of analytic induction, which entails the search for "negative cases" that challenge the analyst to progressively refine empirically based conditional statements (Katz, 1983; Rubin and Rubin, 2004). As we encountered negative cases, we revised our propositions until we could identify patterns that were consistent throughout the data. Once no new conceptual categories could be added, and propositions did not require reformulation, it was assumed that "saturation" had been reached.

Findings

The social background of the women

The women came from seven different cities or villages in the Palestinian territories; one was born and raised in a neighboring Arab country until she was ten years old, at which time she had to move and live with her aunts in the territories. None of the women were citizens or residents of the State of Israel. The interviewees were not exposed to Israeli society or way of life, nor did any of them ever live or work in Israel. Some had taken day trips with their family or school to Israel before the *Intifada*.

At the time of the interview, the participants ranged in age from 20 to 30, with a mean of 23 and a median of 21. (At the time of their arrest, the age of the women ranged from 18–26.) For all participants, this was their first arrest. Their education level at their arrest was as follows: four were high-school students at the time of the incident (one had ten years and three had 11 years of schooling), two were university students (between the second and fourth year of their studies) and one had graduated from university. All the interviewees were single, never married, and without children.

All but one[17] of the interviewees grew up in large families (between six and nine children per family) in which the mother was a housewife and the father was the breadwinner. In one case, the father married a second wife. Two of the interviewees lost their fathers when they were young, one in a car accident, the other due to an illness. The father of a third participant suffered a heart attack two years prior to her arrest, and she blamed the Israeli military for causing the stress that presumably led to his premature death. The absence of a father–protector in the lives of three out of the seven women may have been a factor in their becoming involved in terrorism.

All but one interviewee spoke about their parents with warmth and appreciation. It was evident that the interviewees felt deep love toward their mothers, and affection fused with fear toward their fathers. One woman, who smoked incessantly during the interview, noted: "I would never dare smoking in front of my father." The interviewees who had a father discussed his tight control and close monitoring of their whereabouts, and how it was necessary to deceive him (or other family members) when they went out to participate in training, preparation, or the suicide mission itself. Mothers (or in one case the aunt who raised the interviewee) were described as particularly warm, hard-working, caring, and dedicated women, to whom the participants felt very close and in whom they confided.

The interviewee who did not express emotional affection for her parents stated that she felt they pushed her to become a suicide bomber (the explosive belt was placed on her body in her parents' presence at the family's home). The woman was raped by a family member during her childhood,[18] and in her twenties she was also injured from a blast of a gas pipe at her home. This accident left her body and neck seriously scarred[19] and she was undergoing treatment for her burns in an Israeli hospital, to which she was dispatched to blow herself up. She said that she felt uncomfortable talking about her parents because of their complicity in her being dispatched for the suicide mission.

Reasons for becoming suicide bombers

When describing their reasons for becoming suicide bombers, common themes emerged in the participants' interviews. They included a wish to help with the Palestinian national struggle, to contribute to the war efforts against Israel and the occupation, to follow the Qur'an's call for *Jihad*, to become a martyr (*shahida*), and to enjoy the pleasures awaiting martyrs in paradise. The statement that "everything that is prohibited in this world is permitted in paradise" was frequently mentioned in the interviews. As one woman elaborated: "We do not live the real life [in this world]; we are just by-passers. The real life is in paradise. Everything is there … the *shahida* is one of the 72 virgins[20] …"

The benefits that accrue to martyrs in paradise were described by one woman as follows:

> There is nothing that is missing in paradise; everything what I would need is within reach. You can see the prophet, Allah, and you save seventy relatives from the grave torment. Every *shahid* atones for the sins of family members. Every *shahid* liberates seventy relatives from suffering, and atones for their sins.

Another woman explained:

> Paradise is for Muslims and hell is for Jews. We have Allah and we believe in him. There are many beautiful things there [in paradise], the most important is that we see Allah and, god willing [*inshalla*], we see the prophet. The male martyrs [*shahids*] also have seventy virgins…

The decision to embark on a suicide mission was triggered by some problem for which the suicide operation became a solution, by a personal loss, or by both. For four women, the wish to avenge the death of a loved one was mentioned as a reason for the decision to perpetrate the suicide bombing, together with a desire to help the Palestinian cause. The loss of a family member (a brother or cousin), killed by the Israel Defense Forces (IDF) following involvement in terrorism, was mentioned by two interviewees; for two others, a death in similar circumstances of a fiancé or a young man whom the interviewee was hoping to marry provided the motivation to become a martyr. As two of the women put it: "My fiancé was the most beautiful man in the world and I loved him so much"; "There was someone who wanted to marry me but the Israelis killed him … I am being accused of martyrdom [*istishahad*]? I did not want to commit suicide, what kind of talk is it?"

One woman relayed how she was recruited by the friend of the man she was fond of and whom she was hoping to marry:

> There was a man who asked me, when we were alone, if I wanted to become a *shahida* [martyr]. I did not want to respond right away and told him that I need to think about it. He answered, "ok, think about it and get back to me." I knew this guy from before as we had social connections. This guy who recruited me knew someone who was close to my heart and who did martyrdom [*istishahad*]. The man who recruited

me knew me through this guy who wanted to get engaged with me, and then the IDF killed him with a helicopter. This guy [who was killed] wanted us to get engaged but I told him all the time "no," so he asked my uncle [for permission]. I was afraid that if I will marry him he will die because of his [military] activities ... But I thought I will meet him in paradise, I mean the guy who was killed ...

The cycle of violence in the Israeli–Palestinian conflict was well reflected in one woman's explanation of why she decided to perpetrate a suicide bombing:

My brother blew himself up because of my fiancé [who was killed by an IDF missile]. My brother loved him like a brother ... I raised my brother the *shahid*. Then my female cousin did a suicide bombing and another family member too and each one retaliated for someone [who was killed by the IDF].

This woman, determined to avenge the death of her loved ones, asked her deceased brother's dispatcher – when the latter came to pay a condolence visit to the mourning family home[21] – to send her on a suicide mission. The dispatcher responded that Islamic Jihad does not send women on suicide missions. She then shopped for another dispatcher, and found an activist who recruited her to find other women for terrorism-related work, for which she was arrested.[22]

One woman acknowledged that she decided to become a suicide bomber "to get back" at her father because he would not compromise about the dowry he expected to receive from the man she wanted to marry. She also stated that she had a cousin who was killed in the hostilities and her wish to become a suicide bomber was additionally "to avenge the killing of my cousin, who was a Hamas leader and the Israelis killed him with a helicopter."

Two women decided to volunteer for a suicide bombing mission because they were bored and wanted "to do something" or "get outside the house." The experience of being a suicide bomber is indeed associated with excitement and thrills that young women in a highly restrictive society are precluded from having. One woman explained:

When you participate in a mission you can take off the veil and wear pants. It is also allowed to travel alone with a guy and even a few guys, because they are the ones who drive you to the target. The goal is obvious, to implement a suicide bombing operation, therefore there is no need to worry about the [issue of] woman's honor.

One woman was recruited for the suicide bombing mission by a man with whom she corresponded over the Internet.[23] In a society that highly restricts social interaction between the sexes, the Internet provides an opportunity for secret, hard-to-detect "relationships" with men, which render naive and inexperienced women easy prey for recruitment into terrorism. This interviewee elaborated:

> It is easy to talk with someone on the Internet on various things in yourself [in your heart]. Sometimes he [the person you are corresponding with] knows you and sometimes not ... but perhaps he will help you, in some way.

She explained that the contact opened opportunities for her because "I want to have peace; I want to be able to go wherever I want and do whatever I want."

In one atypical case, as noted above, a female recruit's parents were complicit in dispatching her for a suicide mission. This woman was approached by activists about blowing herself up in the Israeli hospital where she was treated for her burns.[24] The interviewee described[25] the circumstances that resulted in her embarking on the mission, alluding to her sexual abuse by a relative – the family secret (see Shalhoub-Kevorkian, 2005) – and the difficulties that her burn injury posed for her family:

> I am a woman who suffered a huge blow in my life; and not only one, many blows ... I also failed in the university. And there were other problems. My father treated me badly and was constantly beating me. He told me I will never get married, and I will be a cripple for the rest of my life ...

Becoming a suicide bomber and reflecting on the experience

Four interviewees were eager to serve as suicide bombers, but others did not volunteer. One wanted to get trained to use weapons but was eventually compelled to agree to undertake a suicide mission because the activists who trained her were concerned about being identified or their location becoming known; one was recruited by activists for the mission, being convinced by her recruiters that taking part in a suicide bombing is important; and one was pressured by her parents to participate in a suicide operation, so that they "resolve" her from being a family embarrassment and burden. In most cases, the initial contact with the suicide-producing organization was facilitated by the candidate's social associates. The women who volunteered first expressed their interest to a friend or an acquaintance, requesting that they find ways to make contact with organizations that engage in suicide bombing. Once the connection was made, the women tried to convince the organization's representatives that they were committed to the cause and should be taken seriously. In three cases, the representatives first refused or hesitated to accept the volunteering woman; the initial decline of the offer was because they did not want a female, or because there was another *shahid* in the family, or due to the woman's young age. In some cases they were also concerned about the reaction of the women's nuclear family, particularly the father, who would consider it a misappropriation of his daughter from her male protector. In one instance, the organization asked the woman to sign a contract specifying that she volunteered for the operation. In all cases, upon the women's repeated appeals, the representatives agreed to send them on a mission, and their preparation was then undertaken.

The selection of the women who did not volunteer was not random. The activists who contacted them had knowledge about events in the women's biographies that were likely to render them willing recruits. The recruiters were also familiar with the women's social affiliates who made the contact with the women and offered them the opportunity to carry out a suicide bombing. The activists knew about the women's anger and anguish related to the loss of a loved one who was killed for being suspected of terrorist involvement. Whether it was a brother or other family relative, or a man with whom the women were planning their future, their loss generated anger and despair, predisposing the women to avenge their death through a suicide mission (see Fighel, 2003).

The antagonism that the women felt toward Israel was made clear by their willingness to kill and hurt Israeli/Jewish children. Although the interviewees viewed themselves first and foremost as women rather than terrorists, and considered their primary role as creating a family and raising children, they proudly noted how they were capable of killing Jewish Israeli children. In the words of one woman: "I do not feel any compassion toward the [Israeli] children. I can surely carry out a suicide mission in a kindergarten. I am capable of seeing your children playing or eating and blow myself up with them."

Other women elaborated: "Why should your children have everything and ours nothing?" "If I were able to cause a Jewish child to convert to Islam, I surely would do it." "I am capable of blowing myself up in a kindergarten because of what you have done to Muhammad Dura."[26]

At the same time, they felt compassion toward Palestinian children, wanting to protect them from the horrors of war.[27] Some also wanted to shield fellow-Palestinian youngsters from the prospects of being recruited for suicide operations. One woman who was designated to participate in a double suicide operation described how she felt toward the youngster with whom she was dispatched to the mission:

> I am something different [in regards to losing her life compared to his life] . . . I felt sorry for him. I was in pain because of him and felt the need to rescue him. He was just a kid. What did he see in his life? I also realized that he did not know or understand what he was about to do. He did not talk, was closed and sad . . . I had the need to save him . . .

Despite their love and close relationship with their parents, particularly their mothers, none of the interviewees disclosed to either parent their decision to embark on a suicide mission. They knew well that their family would object to their participation. As one woman noted: "my family is opposed to military work. The first thing they asked me is 'why did you do it?'" Another woman explained: "I reached the decision to become suicide bomber on my own. Had I told it to anyone [in the family] they would have prevented me from doing it. This is why I preferred not to tell anyone." One woman commented: "I did not tell my family anything ... My father would have killed me had he known I went with the guys [*shabab*] to the training." Another interviewee, who was raised by her aunts, noted that her family sensed some change in her behavior following the decision to become a martyr and confronted her with their observation. To allay their worries she told her uncle: "Do not worry about me doing something crazy; people who love their family would not blow themselves up."

By and large, the interviewees who volunteered to become suicide bombers were pleased with their decision to become martyrs. One woman described her decision to become a martyr as a high point in her life and one that distinguished her from other women:

> For a whole month, I was thinking about being a *shahida* ... This was the most beautiful month in my life ... I felt I was going to do something special and life will be easier ... It is more special when a woman is doing a martyrdom mission. We are oriental and women here are very restricted, so this makes a woman's mission special. In addition, the Qur'an allows it, as we are a situation of war and this is *jihad.*

Despite volunteering and being elated at being involved in the mission, one woman had second thoughts about her decision, as she saw her prospective victims. She thought that the baby in the carriage she was about to blow up resembled her nephew and decided not to follow through:

> I came to the target and I saw a baby with his mother in the carriage and he looked very similar to my beloved nephew. I felt I could not do it ... Paradise was then changed in my head. I thought that if I do it [blow myself up] I will go to hell and not paradise ... It could not be that Allah wanted me to do it ...

She then added an afterthought about the difficulties of bringing about change: "I know things will remain the same even after my death."

To implement a female suicide mission and get the operation to work, the involvement of another woman in the operation is often necessary. The additional woman is needed to give support to the prospective suicide bomber or otherwise assist the organization. Assistance involves providing a cover or an acceptable moral appearance to the social interaction that accompanies the dispatching of a female suicide bomber, to obviate any suspicion of prohibited contact with men. For instance, one woman who wanted to get out of the house and decided to "get trained with weapon" explained how, when she traveled to the training location, "there was always another woman in the car that picked me up for the training, so that I am not alone with the guy."

Providing emotional or moral support to the candidate is another important role that women provide in operations, assuring that a recruit does not regret her decision or back-peddle once she has agreed to participate. In the words of one interviewee:

> The older woman [at the apartment I was brought to before the operation] was patting me when things became difficult, and she told me that all members of my family will be proud of me and the honor that I would bring them.

In most cases, the time between recruitment and being dispatched to the target was minimal; it did not take more than a few days. Perpetrating a suicide mission does not require much expertise; the time from recruitment to the suicide bombing itself is rather short. As one of the interviewee explained: "It went so fast that I did not even have time to think. Within two days of my recruitment I was on my way to the target and to die."

Most of the women reported being elated about their decision to perpetrate suicide bombings. They felt they were doing a service to both themselves and their communities. As one woman put it: "I see myself as a white rose, even though I am dark. I give good scent to others. I feel it myself and others who look at me feel relaxed too." The interviewees stated that there was nothing that would have stopped them from carrying out their mission, except, in the words of one woman: "My mother is the only person that could have persuaded me not to carry out the suicide mission; I do not think I can bear the thought of my mother crying over me."[28]

The women prepared their farewell testaments and made final arrangements related to their imminent departure, including what should be done with their possessions or how their relatives should accept the suicide (for details on final arrangements of suicide bombers, see Hafez, 2004; Merari, 2004; Berko and Erez, 2005). Some interviewees noticed, however, differences between their preparations compared to that of their male counterparts. One woman stated:

> The men who recruited me advised me to give them all my money because after I am a *shahida* [martyr] I will not need the money as I will die, so it is preferable that I give them all the money I have ... They talked to me about paradise that is awaiting me, and also about the mission.

In listening to herself accounting the events prior to her being dispatched, she soon realized how "I was used and abused by the recruiters." Reflecting on giving her money to the activist who recruited her, she commented: "I know it is ridiculous, but luckily, since then my brain has grown bigger."

Another woman complained that she did not receive the standard treatment that is accorded to male candidates for suicide bombing. Alluding to the ceremonial videotaping of would-be suicide bombers' "famous last words," she noted: "I prepared the farewell will, but they did not do a video for me, they just took regular pictures." One woman discussed, with approval, her father's sentiments regarding dispatching suicide bombers, suggesting their exploitation in general: "every time my father would watch a suicide bombing operation on the television he would comment on how the dispatchers are merchants trading in the blood of *shahids*."

In retrospect, none of the women who lived to tell their stories were satisfied with how their loved ones reacted to their actions. Nor were they pleased to realize how little gratitude they received from their communities.[29] Although the women expected "respect" or praise for their actions, commenting that "people ought to respect me as I did not do it for myself," none experienced such a response. Instead, they were reminded by their communities that "it [military involvement] is not work for a woman but only for men because the woman has to be at home with her children, to raise her children." One woman elaborated:

> A woman is not a man [who is able] to do things like that [participating in terrorism]. A woman who succeeded or tried to do a suicide bombing they give her respect, but the older women in the man's [the prospective husband] family think that the woman who was in prison is like a man and they fear her, because in their time [when they were younger], young women would not go out of the house except to the hospital [to get medical treatment] ...[30]

Their deviations from gender-scripted expectations came back to haunt them, leaving them dismayed, disappointed, and determined not to venture again into the male-dominated world of terrorism. None of the women interviewed expressed a desire for a future in terrorist activities. Nor did any of the participants plan to return to what, in retrospect, comprised for them a double failure: as women and as terrorists. In the words of one woman: "I did not succeed even in blowing myself up. This is another failure [*fashla*] in my life."

Summary and conclusion

The interviews of would-be Palestinian female suicide bombers document a variety of circumstances, motives, and reasons that bring Palestinian women to suicide bombing. They include the need to fight political subjugation, the wish to retaliate for the loss of a loved one, or they comprise responses to events that have touched people's lives as members of the Palestinian community (see also Merari, 2004). Resisting gender oppression is another reason that brings Palestinian women to suicide bombing. In a society where women are rigorously controlled and monitored, suicide becomes a way to remove gender-based shackles, or loosen their grip. Suicide is used to get back at uncompromising disciplinarian male family members, or as a way to relieve boredom, escape a monotonous life, and have excitement and thrills that young women in restrictive Muslim society are precluded from experiencing. In sum, the data show that, for Palestinian women, becoming a suicide bomber comprises a measure to articulate political grievances and a way to express gender-based gripes. By becoming a suicide bomber, Palestinian women are as likely to make a statement about the colonization of their land (e.g. Hasso, 2005) as they are about the colonization of their female body by Palestinian patriarchal hegemony (e.g. Victor, 2003).

Palestinian women's entry to suicide bombing can also be compelled. For parents, the suicide mission can become an expedient, morally acceptable manner to remove a familial burden (i.e. an unmarriable daughter) or, for members of a suicide-producing organization, it can alleviate the concern that their activities, identity, or training location would become known.

The data also show that terrorism, particularly suicide bombing, has been integrated into the everyday life of the Palestinian community, comprising a focal point around which social interaction is developed and maintained. In a society that restricts opportunities for contact between the sexes, suicide operations create opportunities for networking, friendships, and romance, while simultaneously allowing participants to sustain the appearance of acting for a noble cause. Though the arrangement of a mission may only take a few days, for women who would otherwise not have such social opportunities, even this short period of time can be important. Some of the women also established Internet, or other, relationships with males for a substantial amount of time.

Lastly, the accounts that would-be Palestinian female suicide bombers provide about what brought them to suicide terrorism differ from the posthumous Palestinian official statements or media presentations that describe their motives (Israeli, 2004; Patkin, 2004; Brunner, 2005; Hasso, 2005). Another notable difference concerns the respect that failed female bombers are accorded by the community. The data show that, regardless of women's motives to commit suicide, and whether their participation was voluntary, followed active recruitment, or was compelled, the familial and social response to Palestinian women's attempted (but not completed) rendezvous with suicide terrorism is uniform. Female suicide bombers who do not manage to kill themselves receive little acclaim from their families or communities. In essence, if female suicide bombers die, they are praised – but not if they live.[31]

The observed differences between the interview data of would-be female suicide bombers and the testaments that actual suicide bombers have left behind raise questions about the adequacy of prevailing political and media discourses in explaining Palestinian female suicide bombing.[32] Further personal interviews of would-be female suicide bombers could be used to provide a window on competing interpretations of women's participation in suicide bombing. Personal interviews might also reinforce the finding about the diverse personal, political, and gender-related motives that trigger women's participation, and confirm the marginal status that female would-be suicide bombers occupy in Palestinian society, both inside and outside of prison walls.

Notes

1 We wish to thank the Israeli Prison Authorities for facilitating the interviews of the participants. The Office of Research and Sponsored Programs, Kent State University, provided financial support for travel expenses associated with the study. Cindy Ness made insightful suggestions and provided ample editorial help.
2 In addition, Palestinian women were commended for giving birth to many children to change the demographic composition of the area. Yassar Arafat had referred to the womb of the Palestinian woman as the best weapon of the Palestinian people.
3 In most cases where a mission was thwarted, it was due to the arrest of the would-be suicide bombers close to the mission, most commonly due to intelligence information about the planned event. Only in one of the cases reported here (the woman who was sent to blow herself up in an Israeli hospital that had treated her burn wounds) the woman was discovered at the border checkpoint, upon being asked to lift her outer clothing.
4 The woman who failed actually pulled the wire triggering the explosive; however, the device failed due to malfunction.
5 One of the ramifications of perceived inferiority of women in regard to terrorism is that families of female martyrs (*shahidas*) receive a substantially reduced amount of money for the death of their loved one (e.g. if she perpetrated suicide bombing) compared to families of male *shahids* (see Victor, 2003). This mode of thinking is practiced in other Islamic countries such as Iran, where the fine imposed for killing a woman is half the fine imposed for killing a man.
6 In cases where the man has multiple wives, the senior wife has to be obeyed by more junior wives. When a father marries another wife, often a younger woman than the first wife, the second marriage often leads to friction in the family, as the wives and their offspring compete for the husband/father's attention and family resources, causing the children of the first marriage to feel anger and bitterness toward the father. The interviewees whose mothers had to accept their fathers' second marriages expressed such sentiments.
7 It is also important to note that Arab society in general has undergone various economic and political changes over the last three decades that have transformed its social and familial organizations. Also, Arab society includes populations of various religious backgrounds (e.g. Christians, Muslims, and Druze). There are also variations by place of residence (urban, rural, or Bedouin localities), occupation or education level of family members, their national affiliation, and other factors influencing family lifestyle.

8 The family of origin continues to have certain obligations toward a married woman (daughter or sister); they will have to take her back if the husband divorces her, or will be the ones to protect the "family honor" if it has been violated through infidelity or other unbecoming behavior, as discussed later in the chapter.

9 In Arabic, a woman's honor is termed *ird*, whereas a man's honor is known as *sharaf*. As will be discussed later, the active nature of a man's honor is one reason why participation in terrorism increases men's prestige; it is viewed as a measure of male courage and dedication to the cause. For women, on the other hand, participation detracts from their reputation or honor, and may raise questions about the motives or reasons for engaging in terrorism.

10 In some places, additional restrictions apply to women, such as the imposition of veiling or clitorectormy (see Al Khayyat, 1990).

11 "Honor killings" by blood relatives of women are perpetrated in circumstances in which women have deviated from various gender related restrictions. For analysis of "honor killing" and the expansion of this practice in Palestinian society, see Hasan, 1999.

12 Since January 2002 – when Wafa Idris, the first time female suicide bomber, implemented her mission – there were 20 female would-be suicide bombers in different stages of preparation for the mission, who were arrested by the Israeli authorities. The women who were selected for the study were closer to perpetrating the suicide compared to those who were not included in the sample. In terms of their social and demographic characteristics, however, there were no differences between the two groups: those who were interviewed were similar by age (all in their twenties), marital status (single, no children), and educational background to the group that was not interviewed. All the women except for one were approached by the research team about whether they were interested in being interviewed for the study. One woman approached the interviewer when the latter was in the prison yard and requested to be interviewed.

13 In each prison, the women were housed in two different wings. The division was in response to the prisoners' wish to be separated, often according to their identification with a particular movement, although personal relationships and preferences played a role as well. One wing included women who were perceived as less religious, and who often had some affiliation with the Tanzim-Fattah organization. The other wing housed women who were perceived as more religious and were often connected with the Hamas or Islamic Jihad movements. The interviews took place in their respective wings. It should be noted that the "affiliations" the women acquired in the prison, with the Tanzim-Fattah, or Hammas–Islamic Jihad, had often more to do with liking a particular group leader rather than any ideological beliefs and conviction. Outside prison, when women became affiliated with a group, it was usually just prior to the operation in which they participated. In some cases, suicide-producing organizations claimed the operation as their own after it has been completed to increase the organization's stature and prestige.

14 A number of female security prisoners, including would-be suicide bombers, were transferred to a special wing in the general prison due to continuous disagreements and fights among various groups. Some of the transferred prisoners suffered severe injuries, including burn wounds on their face and body, after fellow inmates threw boiling margarine mixed with sugar on them.

15 Part of the results pertaining to four of the women who attempted suicide bombing was reported in Berko and Erez, 2005. In this chapter, three additional would-be female suicide bombers were interviewed. The reader is referred

to Hafez (2004), Berko and Erez (2005), and Merari (2004) for a more complete discussion of the (mostly male) Palestinian suicide bombing phenomenon.

16 The first author conducted individual interviews in a special room in the prisons that housed the participants. The interviewer's familiarity with Arab customs and the Arabic language, and her identity as a daughter of Iraqi–Jewish refugees, has helped in relieving the initial anxiety of the participants. At the end of each interview session, the participants stated that they looked forward to more interviewing time with the interviewer. They felt that the interviewer displayed a genuine concern for their well-being. In some cases, the participants were crying during the interviews, putting their head on the interviewer's shoulder or tightly holding her hands. The interviewer comforted the participants, and handed tissues to women who wept during the session. In some cases the interviewer held them until they regained composure and could continue with the interview. Prison staff were available in case the interviewees required professional assistance, but such services were not needed. Some of the participants invited the interviewer to visit them in prison and to maintain contact with them when they were released. The interviewer also spent time with the prisoners in the prison yard, drinking coffee with them while waiting for the individual interviews scheduled for that day to take place. It should be noted that the factual portions of the data collected through the interviews corresponded to the information in the interviewees' court documents.

17 The father of this woman was killed in a car accident when she was a baby, and because her mother remarried she had to move and live with her aunts (the sisters of the father, as a child belongs to the father's family) when her mother remarried. The mother subsequently had a son with her second husband.

18 Women in Arab –including Palestinian – society are reluctant to disclose or report sexual abuse to family members or authorities (see Shalhoub-Kevorkian, 2005). The sexual abuse issue was revealed in her trial.

19 During the period of the interview she still suffered from the burns, which interfered with her ability to move and to attend to basic needs, such as getting dressed. The accident also affected her self-image and made her prone to crying and self-imposed isolation.

20 There is a belief, which was expressed by the suicide bombers we interviewed, that in paradise the male martyrs will enjoy the company of 72 virgins. The female interviewees thought that the *shahidas* become one of these virgins.

21 Although family members of *shahids* are not "mourning" the death of their loved one, a tent is established to receive those who come to visit the family after their loved one has become a *shahid*. For the hardships experienced by *shahids*' mother due to the prohibition on mourning the death of a son who became a *shahid*, see Shalhoub-Kevorkian, 2003).

22 The woman stated in the interview that she was in love with her brother's dispatcher, whom she referred to as her "fiancé." She also commented that she was hoping to marry him once she completed serving her five-year prison sentence. The dispatcher was serving a life prison sentence in another Israeli prison.

23 On the use of the Internet for terrorism, see Weimann, 2006.

24 As the dispatchers learned that this hospital, located in the southern part of Israel, served a large Arab–Israeli population, she was ordered to blow herself up in another hospital in the center of Israel.

25 Some of the facts in this case, particularly the sexual abuse, were revealed during the court hearings; the woman was introverted during her interview and had difficulties verbalizing her experiences. Some of the quotations were submitted by her defense counsel for purposes of sentence mitigation.

26 Muhammad Dura was an 11-year-old child who was killed in September 2000,

allegedly in a cross-fire exchanged between the Palestinians and the IDF, while his father was trying to protect him. Various Arab TV stations presented a video of this incident, attempting to mobilize public opinion against Israel, and the IDF's presumably indiscriminate shooting of Palestinians. Analysis of the footage showed, however, that the shooting scene was staged by local organizations to acquire sympathy and support from the outside world. This phenomenon of manufacturing documentation about the conflict has been referred to as "Pallywood" (Palestinian Authority Hollywood). The analysis of the footage can be found on www.seconddraft.org/streaming/aldurah.wmv.

27 The tendency to have differential emotional responses to family or in-group members versus others was also evident in the interviews of dispatchers of suicide bombers – see Berko *et al.*, 2005.

28 A similar statement about the mother being the only one that could stop them from carrying out the plan was made by one of the male suicide bombers interviewed in the larger study – see Berko and Erez, 2005.

29 One of the incentives and rewards for suicide bombers is the respect and honor that their act will bring them and their families (e.g. Hafez, 2004; Pape, 2005). The interviews suggest that Palestinian women do not receive the same respect as their male counterparts, as their participation comprises deviation from gender role scripts (see Berko and Erez, 2007).

30 The tendency of older women to support and uphold traditional views of male hegemony is a well-recognized phenomenon. Patriarchal structures often rely on older women to help in preserving male-dominated social order and resist change – see for instance, Adelman, Erez and Shalhoub-Kevorkian, 2003.

31 The Palestinian community and family are highly sensitive to women (and other vulnerable populations) serving prison sentences due to their involvement in terrorism. The demand for freeing Palestinian women and juveniles serving sentences for security-related offenses pursuant to the kidnapping of the Israeli soldier Gilad Shalit in July 2006 well reflects this concern. However, underlying this concern is the need to exercise male protection rather than grant praise or appreciation to the efforts of women to help the cause. Informally, Palestinians we interviewed see them as stepping out of their female role and would "rather not see my son marry such a woman," commenting that "these women are not well-disciplined."

32 There is no doubt that testimonials can be analyzed to shed light on how the discourse of suicide bombing serves political agendas, on the personal concerns of the women involved or the organizations that produced the operations, or the political bodies behind them. However, to argue that these testimonials provide an "objective" or complete picture is inaccurate.

References

Adelman, Madelaine, Edna Erez, and Nadera Shalhoub-Kevorkian (2003) "Policing Violence Against Minority Women in Multicultural Societies: 'Community' and the Politics of Exclusion," *Police and Society*, 7: 105–133. Online, available at: *National Institute of Justice*, www.ojp.usdoj.gov/nij/specialissue/policesociety.html.

Ahmed, Leila (1992) *Women and Gender in Islam: Historical Roots of a Modern Debate.* Tel Aviv, IL: Yale University Press.

Al-Khayyat, S. (1990) *Honour & Shame: Women in Modern Iraq.* London: Saqi Books.

Atran, Scott (2003) "Genesis of Suicide Terrorism," *Science*, 299: 1534–1539.

Barakat, Halim (1985) "The Arab Family and the Challenge of Social transformation," in E.W. Fernea (ed.), *Women and the Family in the Middle East: New Voices of Change.* Austin, TX: University of Texas Press, pp. 27–48.

Berko, Anat (2004) *The Path to Paradise: the Inner World of Female and Male Suicide Bombers and their Dispatchers.* Tel Aviv: Yedioth Ahronoth Press (in Hebrew); in English (forthcoming), Praeger.

Berko, Anat, Yuval Wolf, and Moshe Addad (2005) "The Moral Infrastructure of Chief Perpetrators of Suicidal Terrorism: an Analysis in Terms of Moral Judgment," *Israel Studies in Criminology*, 9: 10–47.

Berko, Anat and Edna Erez (2007) "Gender, Palestinian Women and Terrorism: Women's Liberation or Oppression?" *Studies in Conflict and Terrorism*, 30(6): 493-519.

Berko, Anat and Edna Erez (2005) "'Ordinary People' and 'Death Work': Palestinian Suicide Bombers as Victimizers and Victims," *Violence and Victims*, 20(6): 603–623.

Bloom, Mia M. (2005) *Dying to Kill: the Allure of Suicide Terror.* New York: Columbia University Press.

Brunner, Claudia (2005) "Female Suicide Bombers – Male Suicide Bombers? Looking for Gender in Reporting the Suicide Bombing of the Israeli–Palestinian Conflict," *Global Society*, 19(1): 29–48.

Crenshaw, Martha (2002) "'Suicide' Terrorism in Comparative Perspective," in *Countering Suicide Terrorism.* Herzilya, Israel: The International Policy Institute for Counter-Terrorism, pp. 21–19.

El Sarraj, Eyad (2002a) "Suicide Bombers: Dignity, Despair, and the Need of Hope," *Journal of Palestine Studies*, 4: 71-76.

El Sarraj, Eyad (2002b) "Wounds and Madness: Why We've Become Suicide Bombers," *PeaceWork.* Online, available at: www.afsc.org/pwork/0205/020506a.htm.

Fernea, E.W. (1985) *Women and the Family in the Middle East: New Voices of Change.* Austin, TX: University of Texas Press.

Fighel, Yoni (2003) *Palestinian Islamic Jihad and Female Suicide Bombers.* International Policy Institute for Counter-Terrorism (ICT) website. Online, available at: www.ict.org.il/articles/articledet.cfm?articleid=499.

Fulford, R. (2001) "The Perverse Logic of Suicide Terrorism," *The National Post*, December: 6.

Glaser, Barney G. (1992) *Basics of Grounded Theory Analysis.* Mill Valley, CA: Sociology Press.

Hafez, Mohammed M. (2004) Manufacturing Human Bombs: Strategy, Culture, and Conflict in the Making of Palestinian Suicide Terrorism. A paper presented at the National Institute of Justice conference, Washington, DC: October 25–26, 2004.

Hasan, Manar (1999) "The Politics of Honor: Patriarchy, the State and Family Honor Killing. in D. Izraeli *et al.* (eds), *Sex, Gender and Politics.* Tel Aviv, Israel: Hakibutz Hameochad (in Hebrew), pp. 267–305.

Hassan, Riaz (2003) *Suicide Bombing Driven More by Politics than Religious Zeal.* Yale-Global Online. Online, available at: yaleglobal.yale.edu/article.print?id=3749.

Hasso, Frances H. (2005) "Discursive and Political Deployments by/of the 2002 Palestinian Women Suicide Bombers/Martyrs," *Feminist Review*, 81: 23–51.

Israeli, Raphael (2004) "Palestinian women: The quest for a voice in the public square through 'Islamikaze Martyrdom,'" *Terrorism and Political Violence*, 16(1): 66–96.

Juergensmeyer, Mark (2000) *Terror in the Mind of God: the Global Rise of Religious Violence*. Berkeley: University of California Press.

Katz, Jack (1983) "A Theory of Qualitative Methodology," in R. Emerson (ed.), *Contemporary Field Research*. Boston: Little, Brown Co., pp. 127–148.

Korbin, Nancy (2005) Countering Terrorists' Motivations. A paper presented at the Annual Conference of the International Policy Center for Counter-Terrorism, The Interdisciplinary Center, Herzelia, Israel.

Merari, Ariel (2004) Suicide Terrorism in the Context of the Israeli Palestinian Conflict. A paper presented at the Suicide Terrorism Research Conference, National Institute of Justice, Washington, DC, October 25–26, 2004.

Pape, Robert A. (2005) *Dying to Win: the Strategic Logic of Suicide Terrorism*. New York: Random House.

Patkin, Terri T. (2004) "Explosive Baggage: Female Palestinian Suicide Bombers and the Rhetoric of Emotion," *Women and Language*, 27(2): 79–88.

Rubenberg, Cheryl A.(2001) *Palestinian Women: Patriarchy and Resistance in the West Bank*. Boulder, CO: Lynne Rienner.

Rubin, Irene and Herbert J. Rubin (2004) *Qualitative Interviewing: the Art of Hearing Data*. Thousand Oaks, CA: Sage Publications.

Schweitzer, Yoram (2006) "Palestinian Female Suicide Bombers: Reality vs. Myth," in Y. Schweitzer (ed.), *Female Suicide Bombers: Dying for Equality?* Memorandum No. 84 (August). Tel Aviv, IL: Jaffee Center for Strategic Studies, Tel Aviv University, pp. 24–40.

Shalhoub-Kevorkian, Nadera (2003) "Liberating Voices: the Political Implications of Palestinian Mothers Narrating their Loss," *Women's Studies International Forum*, 26(5): 391–407.

Shalhoub-Kevorkian, Nadera (2005) "Disclosure of Child Abuse in Conflict Areas," *Violence Against Women*, 11: 1263–1291.

Sharabi, Hishan (1975) *Mukadimat li-dirasat al-mujtam'a al-Arabi (Introduction to Studies of Arab Society)*. Beirut: Dar Altali'a Liltiba'a Wa Al-nashr (in Arabic).

Stern, Jessica (2003) *Terror in the Name of God: Why Religious Militants Kill*. New York: HarperCollins.

Tzoreff, Mira (2006) "The Palestinian Shahida: National Patriotism, Islamic Feminism, or Social Crisis?" in Y. Schweitzer (ed.), *Female Suicide Bombers: Dying for Equality?* Memorandum No. 84 (August). Tel Aviv, IL: Jaffee Center for Strategic Studies, Tel Aviv University, pp. 12–23.

Verancini, L. (2002/3) "Suicide Bombers: a Colonial Phenomenon," *ARENA Journal*, 20: 37–43.

Victor, Barbara (2003) *Army of Roses: Inside the World of Palestinian Women Suicide Bombers*. Emmaus, PA: Rodale.

Weimann, Gabriel (2006) *Terror on the Internet: the New Arena, The New Challenges*. Washington, DC: the United States Institute of Peace.

10 Girls as "weapons of terror" in Northern Uganda and Sierra Leonean armed groups

Susan McKay

Introduction

Girls – both willingly and unwillingly – participate in terrorist acts within the context of contemporary wars. These acts range from targeting civilians for torture and killing to destroying community infrastructures so that people's physical and psychological health and survival are affected. Girls witness or participate in acts such as mutilation, human sacrifice, forced cannibalism, drug use, and physical and psychological deprivation. This chapter focuses upon girls in two fighting groups – the Lord's Resistance Army (LRA) in Northern Uganda and the Revolutionary United Front (RUF) in Sierra Leone – and their roles as combatants whose primary strategy is perpetrating terrorist acts against civilians. In analyses of gender and terrorism, girls are typically subsumed under the larger category of "female," which marginalizes their experiences and fails to recognize that they possess agency and power.

In the majority of contemporary wars, conflicts are internal to a nation, although often with regional and sub-regional involvement. Terrorist acts are implicit strategies used in fighting within rebel and opposition movements, although all sides of an armed conflict will perpetrate forms of terrorism. Such acts include torture and killing of parents, siblings, neighbors, and teachers, looting and burning property, amputations of limbs, disfigurement of body parts such as nose, lips, and ears, and gender-specific acts of rape and sexual mutilation that can be directed toward either sex, but are usually female focused.

During intra-state wars, civilians are the most frequent targets of such terror tactics. Civilian casualties, particularly women and children, are estimated to be as high as 90 percent.[1] Targeting civilians for horrific and capricious acts of terror conveys powerful political and psychological messages and creates widespread fear that is characteristic of terrorism. Such actions during armed conflicts are consistent with Deborah Galvin's definition of terrorism as

> those acts and events systematically protagonized for the purpose of instilling massive fear in individuals and/or the public at large, and

which are deliberately used for coercive purposes. Terrorists are those who engage in these activities, whatever form they take. Terrorism is never accidental ... [but] is deliberately aimed at the human mind through the calculated infliction of pain or loss or the threat of the same. ... Terrorism is something done by people to other people.[2]

In addition, purposeful destruction of the public health infrastructure – such as through damaging agricultural lands and water systems, looting health-care clinics, and destroying highways and electrical sources – jeopardizes civilians. This chapter argues that destroying such infrastructures also con-stitutes terrorist acts because of their powerful effects on people's physical and psychological health and survival. Also increasingly common is the ter-rorist practice of targeting humanitarian workers who, under threat of injury and death, are prevented from providing assistance in the form of food, water, and medical care.[3] Thus, terrorism as it occurs during civil wars is directed against people and also occurs indirectly by targeting their community infrastructures and those who work in humanitarian relief operations to make continued civilian existence possible.

Girls and terrorist acts

Although women and "females" are now more often identified as particip-ants in terrorism,[4] girls' experiences are poorly understood and only occa-sionally acknowledged. This is true regardless of whether they are socialized, volunteered, or coerced to participate in such acts. Also, girls' efficacy, actions, resistance, and survival skills within armed groups are inadequately appreciated.[5]

This chapter focuses on girls as actors within two armed groups known for directing terrorism at civilians. Within the context of rebel groups, girls are typically characterized as victims who lack agency although recent research indicates that girls in these groups, willingly or otherwise, also participate in terrorist acts.[6] As members of rebel groups, many witness and participate in terrorist mutilation, ritualistic murder (human sacrifice), forced cannibalism and drug use, and physical and psychological depriva-tion.[7] After situating girls' involvement as child soldiers in armed groups as a global phenomenon, including their recruitment and roles, this chapter details girls' participation, with a focus on their agency as fighters within armed groups in two African countries – Northern Uganda and Sierra Leone. It draws on data gathered between September 2001 and June 2002 when the author conducted field work in both countries.[8]

Girl child soldiers

Throughout the world, participants in armed conflicts involve children under 18 who are internationally referred to as "child soldiers." These children, boys in particular, have been a focus of international attention and advocacy on their behalf, largely because of the efforts of a child-advocacy consortium, the International Coalition to Stop the Use of Child Soldiers (hereafter, "the Coalition"). This group has systematically identified the use of girls and boys in armed groups, published, and publicized these data.[9] As a result of the Coalition's documentation, accurate estimates of the use of child soldiers are increasingly possible. Its *2004 Global Report* provides the most relevant and in-depth information on the worldwide use of children in armed forces and groups.

Just as women's war experiences have been overlooked until recently,[10] girls' presence in armed forces has received even less exposure. A long history exists of female participation in armed forces and groups, some of whom were girls – such as Joan of Arc who was 16 when her military career began in 1428.[11] Also, until recently and largely because of the emphasis placed on the girl child at the 1995 UN Fourth World Conference on Women,[12] girls were subsumed under the larger categories of "women" or "females" so that their presence in armed forces and groups was shrouded, and girls have been widely perceived as lacking agency in perpetrating acts of terror.

Some of girls' invisibility can be related to culturally specific definitions of who is a girl and who is a woman. For example, in some African countries where the Western cultural notion and rite of passage of being a teenager do not exist, pubescent girls are considered to be women after initiation rites. In contrast, in contemporary Western societies, females are normally thought of as girls when younger than 18 years of age. The definition, found in the Cape Town Principles, commonly accepted by the international community, is used in this chapter for defining a child soldier:

> any person under 18 years of age who is part of any kind of regular or irregular armed force in any capacity, including but not limited to cooks, porters, messengers, and those accompanying such groups, other than purely as family members. Girls recruited for sexual purposes and forced marriage are included in this definition. It does not, therefore, only refer to a child who is carrying or has carried arms.[13]

Global involvement

Throughout the world, from Colombia to Kosovo/a to Chechnya to Israel and Africa, girls are actors within armed forces and groups.[14] Between 1990 and 2003, girls were part of armed forces and groups in 55 countries. They were present in 38 armed conflicts in 13 African countries, seven countries in the Americas, eight countries in Asia, five countries in Europe, and five countries in the Middle East.[15] Most of these armed conflicts were internal to the country although, in some cases such as in Macedonia, Lebanon, Uganda, and Sudan, girls also fought in international conflicts.

Country-specific cases provide examples of girls' involvement in some of these armed forces and groups. During Cambodia's civil war, girls were used by both governmental forces and the Khmer Rouge. A 17-year-old girl taken as an òrphan into the Khmer Rouge when she was two years old reported that, together with a group of 300 to 500 girls, she was given military training from the age of five. Provided with guns and uniforms, they became active soldiers when they reached 14 years of age.[16] In the PKK, the Kurdistan Worker's Party, a 14-year-old Syrian national fought as a female guerrilla against the Turkish army. She received military and political training in Iraq. According to a report of the Coalition to Stop the Use of Child Soldiers, "In 1998 ... more than 10 percent of the PKK's total number of child soldiers were said to be girls."[17] In Asia, approximately 900 to 1,000 girls fought in the northeastern state of Manipur, India, constituting 6–7 percent of the total number of child soldiers fighting there. In Nepal, Maoist insurgents have used girls extensively in what they call "the People's War."[18] Similarly, in Sri Lanka, Tamil girls have been recruited into the Liberation Tigers of Tamil Eelam (LTTE) since the mid-1980s. In LTTE, girl fighters participate in grueling training and in fierce fighting.[19] According to government sources, because girls are less suspect than boys and less often subjected to body searches, girls in Sri Lanka have been chosen – or forced – to become suicide bombers at as young as 10 years old.[20] Of the LTTE fighting forces, 40–60 percent are estimated to be under 18 years of age, most being girls and boys aged 10–16.[21] However, these data lack precision and have been critiqued as needing reliable, field-based estimation.[22] In Colombia, 6,000 boys and girls are estimated to be involved in armed forces and groups. Again, although reliable statistics are unavailable, girls in Colombia are thought to constitute approximately 20 percent of children in guerrilla groups and 15 percent of children in paramilitary groups.[23]

In military forces in Ethiopia, Israel, the Philippines, Sri Lanka, and Colombia, girls have been highly respected and regarded as fighters. In Eritrea, where females comprised one-third of fighters, Veale[24] studied 11 former female participants. The girls' ages when recruited into the Tigrean People's Liberation Front (TPLF) averaged 12.68 years, with the youngest five years old and the oldest 17. On average, these girls spent 11.6 years as fighters, with a range of four to 18 years. In Liberia, older girls and young women in Liberians United for Reconciliation and Democracy (LURD) were reported as particularly fierce fighters who commanded respect from their male peers. A female commander reported that her unit entered combat clad only in undergarments due to beliefs that their appearance would intimidate enemies and strengthen their magical protection.[25] The terrorist elements of surprise and invoking fear as well as violating cultural taboos are strongly operational in this strategy, which has also been used by women as a form of non-violent protest.[26] Ellen S., a fighter and commander of girls for LURD, said that during attacks, girls and boys were captured for the group. She described how they would enter battle wearing yellow or brown T-shirts inscribed with the initials LURD. Ellen S.

also wore ammunition around her chest and carried an automatic weapon. She related how she terrorized captured enemies, "if my heart was there, I would bring them to the base for training. But if my heart was bad lucky [sic], then I would kill them right there."[27]

These data indicate that girls globally are actors in armed forces and groups, often because they were forced to participate, but they also volunteer for ideological or pragmatic reasons.[28] Regardless of their rank and situations in a group, girls participate in acts that terrorize civilians in countries where they fight. Perpetrating violence and torture become normal and routine within a culture of violence that pervades every aspect of daily routines and activities.[29]

Recruitment

Although the idea of children freely choosing to join a force or group is a contested one, girls may volunteer – meaning that they were not physically forced, abducted, or otherwise coerced. Some girls volunteered or were coerced into a force or group. Other entry points included being born of an abducted mother or captured by another armed force or group. They may enter a force or group for ideological reasons, to fulfill a compulsory obligation, escape poverty, and/or seek opportunities such as employment or sponsorship in school. They also join because of untenable family situations such as sexual abuse and overload of domestic work, and to find protection, join with other family members, and seek adventures.[30] Some girls find new freedoms and capabilities, with fewer gender restrictions and opportunities to exert authority that have not been previously possible.

Girls may be gang-pressed, meaning they are physically coerced into a force or group when they are in places such as schools, discotheques, and markets, or simply walking along a road or snatched from their homes. For example, during the war in Mozambique (1976–1992), the Frelimo government armed force recruited and gang-pressed girls to fight in the war against Renamo armed groups. Frelimo recruiters arrived with buses at schools where they asked girls to volunteer for the military. When few agreed, girls were forced onto buses and taken to a military base where they met with other "recruited" girls and began military training.[31] Girls also joined Frelimo because of the promise of new and emancipatory roles, to escape rural areas and expand traditional gender roles, and in hopes of improving their educational and career opportunities. In the Renamo armed group, most girls were abducted but some were recruited. Others joined because they felt discontent over Frelimo socialist policies, wanted to be with family members, or because they were lured into the armed group with the promise of educational opportunities.

In many rebel groups, notably in Africa, girls have entered involuntarily, usually by abduction. Cross-border abductions have also occurred in Sierra Leone and Northern Uganda, and other countries. Between 1990 and 2003, girls were abducted in 12 African countries, four countries in the Americas, eight Asian countries, three European countries, and two Middle-Eastern countries.[32] In some countries, boys and girls are taken from orphanages, as reported in Sri Lanka where the LTTE purportedly runs its own orphanages and uses these children as fighters.[33]

Roles

Girls' and women's participation within armed forces and groups are key because they carry on supportive tasks that maintain the armed force or group. Also, they are fighters, which can mean being sent to the frontlines as cannon fodder, sometimes with their babies drugged and strapped on their backs. Girls also conduct suicide missions, provide medical care, and serve as mine sweepers.[34]

Colombian ex-girl soldiers who joined as teenagers were taught how to care for and use guns, conduct military maneuvers and communications operations, and serve as bodyguards for commanders.[35] As such, girls' roles are multi-faceted and vary according to the force in which they are enrolled, their ages, and how gender is constructed within the armed force or group, such as whether girls are viewed as "equal" to boys (even though power differentials inevitably exist) or are treated as slaves and servants.

In some forces or groups where girls serve primarily as combatants, sex is consensual or forbidden, and severe punishment directed to sexual perpetrators was reported in Colombia, the Philippines, and Sri Lanka.[36] In many African armed groups, such as in Angola, Mozambique, Northern Uganda, and Sierra Leone, primary roles for pubescent girls are providing sex and being "wives" who give birth to children who are raised within a rebel group to be fighters.[37]

Regardless of whether they are primarily fighters or serve as spies, porters, or "wives" of rebel-captor "husbands," girls typically hide their involvement in terrorist acts when they come out of a force or group because they are reluctant to acknowledge roles that violate broader community and gender norms. They often feel shame, even though they acknowledge that they would have been killed had they refused to participate. Therefore, a veil of secrecy continues to surround their acts and experiences. Only recently have researchers focused on deconstructing their experiences and expanding the scope of their inquiry about child soldiers to include girls as both perpetrators of terror as well as terrorism's victims.

Northern Uganda and Sierra Leone

The Lord's Resistance Army in Northern Uganda

Since 1986, the Lord's Resistance Army (LRA), led by Joseph Kony, waged a war of terror in Northern Uganda and Southern Sudan against the governmental Ugandan People's Defence Force (UPDF). The primary victims have been the Acholi people whose community infrastructures have been shattered. Thousands of people have been displaced, often in camps for internally displaced people (IDPs). Until recently, they lived in terror of surprise LRA attacks in these highly vulnerable camps and in villages throughout Northern Uganda. In the main, the LRA force consisted of abducted children from Northern Uganda and Southern Sudan with 80 percent of the force estimated to be children. Girls comprised one-quarter or more of child soldiers, although actual numbers of children abducted into the LRA are imprecise.[38] Children were born into the LRA, fathered by rebel commanders and grew up in the LRA to become fighters. When they are taken into a force, girls (and boys) were immediately subject to intensive abuse and torture, and many were killed or died because of being unable to cope with the harsh circumstances of rebel existence.

After training in military tactics and use of weaponry, girls participated in frontline combat, with some holding command positions. They engaged in terrorist acts that created widespread fear, such as attacking their own families and neighbors, abducting other children, and killing civilians. Girls also performed support roles within the military bases such as raising crops, selling goods, preparing food, carrying loot, moving weapons, and stealing food, livestock, and seed stock.[39] They fetched firewood and water, cooked food, climbed trees to spy, transported ammunition, participated in guard duty, and fought during ambushes.[40] Younger girls were servants to commanders and their "wives," and they worked continuously.[41]

The Revolutionary United Front in Sierra Leone

Sierra Leone's 11-year war began in 1991 and officially ended in January 2002. The war pitted the Sierra Leone Army (SLA) and pro-government civilian militias such as the Civil Defense Forces (CDFs) against the rebel Revolutionary United Front (RUF) armed group. Gross human-rights violations were committed by all sides. The RUF was especially culpable because of its extensive abduction of children and adults, and of terror tactics that resulted in countrywide fear. These included attacking villages, destroying community infrastructures such as schools, homes, and health facilities, and perpetrating atrocities such as severing hands, arms, feet, and legs, cannibalism, and ritual murders.[42] The war was waged throughout the country, including trans-border regions. Girls fought on all sides and comprised an estimated 25 percent of the child soldiers in all armed forces and groups, with child soldiers estimated to constitute one-third of all fighters. An estimated 8 percent of the total armed forces and groups, both adults and children, during the Sierra Leonean war consisted of girls, although their use and numbers varied between forces and groups. For example, within the Revolutionary Unit Front (RUF) rebel group, girls are estimated to have constituted at least one-third of all child soldiers and approximately 16 percent of the total RUF.[43]

In Sierra Leone, girls' roles within the RUF were similar to those within the LRA. They were fighters, cooks, domestic laborers, as well as porters, "wives," and food producers. They cared for the sick and wounded, passed messages between rebel camps, served as spies, and some worked in diamond mining for their commanders or rebel-captor "husbands."[44] Ramata Y. was taken into the RUF when her mother and father were killed by the RUF. In the rebel group, she fetched water, cooked, and was a "wife." She reported that girls were trained to use guns. They killed people, stole property, and looted and burned houses.[45]

Victim, perpetrator, or both?

In the two rebel groups, the LRA and the RUF, most girls entered because they were abducted. Researchers studying 32 girls who were in the RUF in Sierra Leone found that all were abducted, often by children their own age who threatened them with death.[46] Sophia R.'s story is a typical one. At age 11, she was captured at school and spent the next nine years in the RUF. She was immediately "disvirginalized" by many men. Her leg was tattooed with the letters "RUF." In the RUF, Sophia R. was a "wife," but she also learned to use a gun and was given combat clothes. She was introduced to cocaine, which emboldened her to fight. She explained that the cocaine enabled her to destroy and "cause bad havoc."[47] Dorothy G. was 13 years old when she was abducted by the LRA. She was taken to Sudan and taught how to work a gun and to be a spy. She climbed trees to see when the Ugandan army was coming. She was also given as a "wife" and used for sex. She said that if a girl refused sex, she was beaten or killed.[48]

Given the realities of the almost-ubiquitous experience of girls being abducted into the rebel groups in Northern Uganda and Sierra Leone, a tension arises in explaining the paradox whereby victims of terrorist violence subsequently become perpetrators of similar violence. However, discrete categorization as "victim" or "perpetrator" fails to underscore the complexities of shifting roles and experiences such as the seeming paradox of girls becoming allies with individuals who were responsible for abducting and victimizing them, and who continue to sexually abuse them. Or, a girl who has never felt herself to be efficacious might experience the lure that can occur from the power of carrying a gun and defying traditional gender roles.[49] This dialectic has parallels with the abduction of Patricia Hearst in the 1970s, where she later became an actor in the Symbionese Liberation Army (SLA) and then came to be viewed as a perpetrator instead of a kidnapped and terrorized victim. Similarly, differentiating victim and perpetrator roles of girls is problematic because of the fluid roles and situations within a force or group and changes that can occur over time for impressionable children who are socialized, often for many years, into a culture of violence that encouraged perpetration of terrorist acts as a fighting strategy.

Girls in the Northern Ugandan and Sierra Leonean rebel groups have been victimized because they have been forced, at the threat of their lives, to participate in terrorist acts such as killing friends or family members and torching homes. Yet they also demonstrate resiliency, agency, and ability to resist – although usually not successfully – their oppressors. Over time, as they continue to participate in terrorist acts, some become combatants, spies, and communications personnel who hold key responsibilities within the group. Nevertheless, they remain relatively powerless and are coerced to participate. Except for the most powerful girls who hold commander status or are commanders' "wives," girls are subjected to abuse from men and boys – and, in some cases, women – because of their low status and traditional gender roles.

Boys' experiences are both similar to girls and also differ as an effect of gender. As young children taken into a group, boys may carry out domestic tasks, be porters, and participate in terrorist acts. Although some boys are thought to experience sexual abuse, little is known about the extent of sexual violence perpetrated against boys by male and female commanders; its occurrence is thought to be much less widespread for boys than for girls. Boys may also be forbidden to sexually approach girls and women until they attain rank, such as a commander, within the rebel group.[50]

Girls as fighters and resisters

Children abducted into the LRA before 2002 who spent time in Sudan were given long and formalized military training. Since 2002, training was sporadic, and some of the youngest abductees were not trained at all. Others were trained but not given uniforms or weapons.[51] In 2003, ex-LRA children told Human Rights Watch researchers that they were forced to participate in beatings or tramplings of other abductees. Susan A. told of being forced, along with three other girls, to beat and kill civilians in villages and internally-displaced-people camps.[52] Elizabeth B. was 12 when she was abducted into the LRA and was in the group for two years. Her father was killed trying to protect her from abduction. She described how another girl in her group was asked to beat somebody they [the LRA] wanted to kill. When the girl refused, she was killed. Elizabeth B. now becomes annoyed very quickly; when she's angry, she feels like killing somebody.[53] Another girl, Alice R., was abducted into the LRA when she was 17 years old. When Alice R. crossed into Sudan with the LRA, she carried guns and was subsequently trained to be a soldier. Although allocated to an army commander to be his "wife," she was also a fighter.[54] Janet M. was 15 when abducted into the LRA and spent nearly two-and-a-half years in southern Sudan. Her story is one of resistance to participating in violence and terrorist acts, although ultimately she became a fighter. Initially, she received training in Sudan after which time she was to be "allocated" to a commander to be his "wife." Because she was young and feared sexual abuse, she deceived her captors by saying she was [sexually] infected. Janet M. was next taken for a medical examination. When a report was given that she was not infected,

angry commanders ordered her killed. Kony, the LRA commander, inter-
vened to spare her life because, he said, her actions showed she was wise and
tricked people. She was then given to another commander but refused sex
with him. Beaten for six months as punishment, she was sent to fight the
Dinkas in southern Sudan. While fighting the Dinkas, she looted property
and foodstuffs; even minerals were taken. When she escaped the LRA, she
was in advanced pregnancy, evidence that despite her resistance she was subjected to forced sex.[55]

In Sierra Leone, girls also received military training. Many girls who were
with the RUF reported that although they learned to cock and load a gun,
they did not participate in combat.[56] It is possible that girls do not view
themselves as combatants, and few would self-identify as perpetrators of
terror unless they possessed and used guns or held commander rank within a
force. As in Northern Uganda, training could be intense and lengthy, and
consisted of how to use guns, engage in physical training, and to kill.[57]
Grace J. said that she was trained "on barbed wire." Trainees were put into a
kind of cage and told that if they managed to escape, they were perfectly
trained. Grace J. escaped whereas many others died during training exer-
cises.[58] Arlene N. was trained to hold a gun but did not handle [carry] a
gun. She explained that most girls were trained, and some participated in
terrorist acts such as shooting and killing, stealing properties, and looting
and burning houses.[59] Christine P. was young when she was abducted. She
stayed with the RUF throughout most of the war. When she was abducted,
the RUF force encountered her mother, in advanced pregnancy at the time,
and her father walking along the road. The rebels tied her father's hands
behind his back. Her mother was given a heavy load to carry that she threw
away because of its weight. The rebels then caught her mother, slit open her
abdomen, took out and killed the unborn child, and killed both her father
and brother.[60] Her story provides insights into the types of terrorist acts
perpetrated by the RUF, and in which girls participated.

Margaret C. recounted that she was trained and took part in fighting.
Within the force they would "kill and eat." In the jungle they ate humans
and reptiles; if she refused to eat, she would have been killed. She described
a terrorist ambush when a woman was killed, and they [commanders] told
them to eat this woman. So they opened the upper part of the body, cooked
it [presumably the heart] and threw away the other parts of the body.[61]

As noted by Denov and Maclure,[62] routinization of violence through
training and everyday experiences, such as these girls had, helps those who
perpetrate terrorist acts to see themselves as effectively performing a job.
Mary J., an ex-combatant in the RUF, explained that over time she came to
view her role of killing as normal and to understand that overcoming the
enemy was part of her job. Killing without a reason showed commitment
and willingness to work with other rebels. She was not allowed to show
remorse, sadness, or shame; brutal acts of torture and violence were encouraged and celebrated.[63] Girls have also reported that, by carrying small arms,

they gained power, status, and control – and they felt pride, self confidence, and a sense of belonging.[64] Also, when girls hold positions of power, such as being a military commander, feelings of pride may become more salient than identifying oneself as a victim.

Disarmament, demobilization, and reintegration (DDR)

Despite recent and increasingly robust data detailing girls in armed forces and groups,[65] the international community, governments, and militaries continue to ignore and deny the extent of girls' involvement and offer inaccurate and reductionistic explanations for their presence. Pervasive gender discrimination in war-affected countries, such as that existing in Northern Uganda and Sierra Leone, perpetuates the notion of girls solely as victims, most notably "sex slaves," and as having lesser agency in perpetrating violence and terror than boys. Girls, therefore, are not thought of as ex-combatants or as having held responsible positions within the rebel force. A consequence of "not seeing" girls as actors and perpetrators is that girls are seldom included in disarmament, demobilization, and reintegration (DDR) programs. Instead, boys and men are privileged in receiving DDR benefits, which typically include opportunities to enroll in skills training, attend school, or participate in rehabilitation programs. For example, in Angola, despite recognition that large numbers of girls were abducted into Angolan armed forces and groups, thousands of boys were formally demobilized although no girls were.[66] In Sierra Leone, 6,052 boys passed through DDR whereas only 506 girls did.[67] Reflecting the reality of their situations and without negating the knowledge that they also experienced sexual and other forms of gender-specific violence, girls should be recognized as serving in capacities that parallel or are complementary to those of boys.[68]

Community responses to girls' return

Community members often react with hostility and fear to girls coming back from a rebel armed group. This is understandable because these girls were among those who either witnessed or perpetrated acts of terror against community members and profoundly violated community norms of behavior.[69] Consequently, returning girls are often provoked, stigmatized, and poorly accepted by community members and at school, if they attend.

Girls returning with children conceived and born in a rebel group are especially stigmatized. The presence of these children makes explicit, regardless of forced maternity, that they have violated traditional gender norms that mandate girls should be virgins before they marry. Further, their children are often of unknown paternity or their fathers are rebel-captor "husbands." One effect is that some girls do not marry. Others eschew marriage because of the horrific sexual and other violence they have experienced from boys and men, and their lack of trust of them. This resistance to marriage can be construed as a radical act in some African societies, where marriage is perceived as mandatory to avoid being viewed as a social outcast.

Consequently, many girls leave their communities because they are poorly accepted, unable to adjust to community life, cannot marry, or find no way to secure an economic livelihood. Additionally, gender discrimination, such as the long hours girls must work at home or notions such as that education is more important for boys, affect returning girls' ability to attend school or learn skills or a trade. Returning girls also often experience gender-specific effects that reduce their life choices and span, such as sexually transmitted diseases resulting from forced sex within a force or group.[70]

Thinking about girls in rebel forces and terrorism

Terrorism, as construed in Western minds, is usually closely equated with 9/11 and similar episodic and unexpected acts that rivet the world's attention because of the magnitude of their effects. Girls and women are only occasionally seen as actors in these scenarios. Yet, history says that women, too, are involved, although usually with limited visibility. Within the context of rebel wars in Northern Uganda and Sierra Leone, as discussed in this chapter, girls' presence in these groups is pervasive and, as such, they routinely witness and experience violence and participate in terrorist acts. Their involvement is not isolated but occurs throughout the world, although with distinct experiences according to the group.

For some girls, often taken into the LRA at young ages and for relatively short periods, if they survived they may have been young enough to avoid full participation as terrorists in the group; instead they were first assigned to domestic work and serving as porters. Yet, they were inevitably witnesses, which has its own traumatic effects. In both Northern Uganda and Sierra Leone, large numbers of girls spent years in a group, and many grew into motherhood and adulthood within this context. They literally lost their childhoods and were socialized into a culture of violence where terrorist acts became normal. Further, their children were socialized into this same violent culture. When these girls, often now women, escaped or the war ends, as is occurring in 2007, they are ignored, stigmatized, and refused DDR benefits. Most go directly back to their communities, if these still exist, find relatives to stay with, or migrate to urban areas. Life does not continue as "normal" despite the changed circumstances of their lives. All are traumatized and often display inappropriate social responses or behavioral deficits. For example, community members in a village in Sierra Leone told of how returning girls would steal and kill neighbors' chickens and that some girls emotionally withdrew; others were belligerent and hostile – behavior that is consistent with the culture of violence in which they spent so much time. Yet, these same girls have been victimized and forced to participate in terrorist acts. This understanding must permeate initiatives to help them.

These girls can never "go back" to being innocents because they have experienced what most people cannot imagine, and they have also gained strengths from their survival. The challenge, therefore, is to empower them to use these strengths and to expand cultural definitions of gender to enable these strengths to be harnessed. Yet, so long as girls remain invisible within the programs and policies of international, national, and local groups, these steps will not be taken. One, then, must ask what the future may bring to these countries when girls become women after such socialization. How will gender roles be (re)constructed given their experiences and those of boys? What will happen to their children? Very little is known about the latter except for sporadic reports of "war babies" whose development shows aberrations and whose social adjustment is poor.

In addressing these questions, within the countries of Northern Uganda and Sierra Leone, much depends on empowering communities to work with these girls and their children. Because community is so central to the health and well-being of people in these two countries, Western-style individualistic approaches are usually inappropriate – including psychotherapeutic approaches that diagnose children as having PTSD. A key strategy in working with these girls is to enlist the leadership of women elders to talk and listen to their stories, and assist them in learning or re-learning normal behavior. These girls also need practical assistance. High priority must be given to their obtaining primary healthcare including, importantly, reproductive healthcare. They must be given opportunities to go to school or learn a skill and to participate in activities that foster healing if they are to be empowered to become citizens in a culture of peace.

So long as these girls continue to be hidden from the world's attention, and even invisible within their own communities except to be stigmatized and provoked, their strengths will not be realized. By calling their situations to attention within broader discussions of gender and terrorism, one step can be made in the right direction toward addressing the injustices they have experienced and advocating for international action on their behalf.

Notes

1 Barry Levy and Victor Sidel, *War and Public Health* (New York and Oxford: Oxford University Press, 1997); United Nations, *Women, Peace and Security* (New York: Author, 2002); United Nations (2004, June 14). *Renewed commitment to decision action for protecting civilians in armed conflict needed now more than ever, security council told: Emergency relief coordinator Jan Egeland urges new Council Resolution supporting further measures to improve civilian protection.* Security Council 4,990th Meeting. Press Release SC/8122. Online, available at: www.un.org/News/Press/docs/2004/sc8122.doc.
2 Deborah Galvin, "The female terrorist: a socio-psychological perspective," *Behavioral Sciences and the Law*, 1(2) (1983), p. 20.
3 UN, 2004.
4 See, for example, Karla Cunningham, "Cross-regional trends in female terrorism," *Studies in Conflict and Terrorism*, 26 (2003), pp. 171–195; Sharon Pickering

and Amanda Third, "Castrating conflict: gender(ed) terrorists and terrorism domesticated," *Social Alternatives*, 22(2) (2003), pp. 8–15.

5 For further discussion, see Dyan Mazurana and Susan McKay, "Child soldiers: What about the Girls?" *Bulletin of the Atomic Scientists*, 57(5) (September/October 2001), pp. 30–35; Dyan Mazurana, Susan McKay, Khristopher Carlson, and Janel Kasper, "Girls in fighting forces and groups: their recruitment, participation, demobilization, and reintegration," *Peace and Conflict: Journal of Peace Psychology*, 8(2) (2002), pp. 97–123; Susan McKay and Dyan Mazurana, *Where Are the Girls? Girls in Fighting Forces in Northern Uganda, Sierra Leone and Mozambique: Their Lives During and After War* (Montreal: Rights and Democracy, 2004).

6 For further discussion, see Myriam Denov and Richard Maclure, "Girls and armed conflict in Sierra Leone: victimization, participation, and resistance." In V. Farr and A. Schnabel (eds), *Gender Perspectives on Small Arms and Light Weapons* (Tokyo: United Nations University Press, in press). Yvonne Keairns, *The Voices of Girl Child Soldiers* (New York and Geneva: Quaker United Nations Office, October 2002); Susan McKay and Dyan Mazurana, *Where Are the Girls?*

7 McKay and Mazurana, *Where Are the Girls?*

8 This study's co-investigators were Susan McKay and Dyan Mazurana. It was funded by the Canadian International Development Agency's Child Protection Research Fund and implemented in partnership with Rights and Democracy, Montreal. The study examined the presence and experiences of girls in fighting forces and groups within the context of three African armed conflicts – Mozambique, Northern Uganda, and Sierra Leone. Also, funding was contributed for Susan McKay's research by the University of Wyoming Graduate School Research Office, the Women's Studies Program, the Office of the Dean of Arts and Sciences, the International Studies Program, the Provost's Office, and School of Nursing, and the Office of International Travel.

9 Coalition to Stop the Use of Child Soldiers. *Child Soldiers: Global Report 2004* (London: Author); McKay and Mazurana, *Where Are the Girls?*

10 Susan McKay, "The effects of armed conflict on girls and women," *Peace and Conflict: Journal of Peace Psychology*, 5 (1998), pp. 381–392; Elizabeth Rehn and Ellen Sirleaf, "Women, war and peace: the independent experts' assessment of armed conflict on women and women's role in peacebuilding" (United Nations Development Fund for Women (UNIFEM) report, 2002); Indai Sajor (ed.), *Common grounds: violence against women in war and armed conflict situations* (Quezon City, Philippines: Asian Center for Women's Human Rights, 1998); United Nations, *The Impact of Armed Conflict on Children: Report of the Expert of the Secretary-General, Ms. Graça Machel* (New York: Author, 1996).

11 Linda DePauw, *Battle cries and lullabies: women in war from prehistory to the present* (Norman: University of Oklahoma Press, 1998).

12 See United Nations, *Beijing Platform for Action* (New York: Author, 1995).

13 United Nations Children's Fund (UNICEF), *Cape Town Annotated Principles and Best Practices* (April 30, 1997). Adopted by the participants in the Symposium on the Prevention of Recruitment of Children into the Armed Forces and Demobilization and Social Reintegration of Child Soldiers in Africa, organized by UNICEF in cooperation with the NGO Sub-group of the NGO Working Group on the Convention on the Rights of the Child, Cape Town, South Africa, p. 1.

14 Coalition (2001); Mazurana *et al.*, "Girls in fighting forces and groups"; McKay and Mazurana, *Where Are the Girls?*

15 McKay and Mazurana, *Where Are the Girls?*

16 Coalition, *Asia Report: Executive Summary, Child Participation in Armed Conflict in Asia* (May 2000). Online, available at: www.child-soldiers.org.

17 Coalition, *Girls with Guns: an Agenda on Child Soldiers for "Beijing Plus Five,"* (2000). Online, available at: www.child-soldiers.org/reports/special%20reports.
18 Coalition, *Asia Report: Executive Summary* (May 2000).
19 Keairns, *The Voices of Girl Child Soldiers* (New York and Geneva: Quaker United Nations Office, October 2002).
20 Coalition, *Girls with Guns* (2000); Cunningham, "Cross-regional trends in female terrorism."
21 Coalition (2001).
22 This observation was written in an unpublished draft document (July 2000) by Ken Bush who has worked extensively on the issue of child soldiers in Sri Lanka. *Stolen Childhood: the Impact of Militarized Violence on Children in Sri Lanka.*
23 Erika Páez, *Girls in the Colombian Armed Groups, a Diagnosis: Briefing* (Germany: Terre de Hommes, 2001).
24 Angela Veale, From child soldier to ex-fighter, a political journey: female fighters, demobililisation, and reintegration in Ethiopia. Monograph No. 85, Institute of Security Studies, South Africa (2003).
25 Human Rights Watch, *How to Fight, How to Kill: Child Soldiers in Liberia* (New York: Author, 2004, February). Online, available at: hrw.org/report s/2004/liberia0204/6. htm#_Toc61673969.
26 Dyan Mazurana and Susan McKay, *Women and Peacebuilding* (Montreal: Rights and Democracy, 1999).
27 Human Rights Watch, *How to Fight, How to Kill.*
28 Rachel Brett and Irma Specht, *Young Soldiers: Why They Choose to Fight* (Geneva: ILO and Boulder, CO: Lynne Rienner, 2004); Páez, *Girls in the Colombian Armed Groups.*
29 Denov and Maclure, "Girls and armed conflict in Sierra Leone."
30 Brett and Specht, *Young Soldiers*; Keairns, *The Voices of Child Soldiers*; Paez, *Girls in the Colombian Armed Groups.*
31 McKay and Mazurana, *Where Are the Girls?*
32 Ibid.
33 Coalition (2001); Mazurana and McKay, *Child Soldiers.*
34 Mazurana and McKay, *Child Soldiers.*
35 Yvonne Keairns, *The Voices of Girl Child Soldiers: Colombia* (New York, Geneva, and London: Quaker UN Office and Coalition, 2003).
36 See for example, ibid.; Yvonne Keairns, *The Voices of Child Soldiers: Angola* (New York, Geneva, and London: Quaker UN Office and Coalition, 2003); Yvonne Keairns, *The Voices of Child Soldiers: the Philippines* (New York, Geneva, and London: Quaker UN Office and Coalition, 2003); Yvonne Keairns, *The Voices of Child Soldiers: Sri Lanka* (New York, Geneva, and London: Quaker UN Office and Coalition, 2003); Veale, *From Child Soldier to Ex-fighter.*
37 Keairns, *The Voices of Child Soldiers*; McKay and Mazurana, *Where Are the Girls?*; Veale, *From Child Soldier to Ex-fighter.*
38 McKay and Mazurana, *Where Are the Girls?*
39 Ibid.
40 Interview conducted in Northern Uganda by Dyan Mazurana and Susan McKay on November 26, 2001.
41 Human Rights Watch, *Stolen Children: Abduction and Recruitment in Northern Uganda*, 15(7A) (March 2003), pp. 1–24.
42 McKay and Mazurana, *Where Are the Girls?*
43 Ibid.
44 Ibid.
45 Interview conducted in Sierra Leone by Susan McKay on June 11, 2002.
46 Denov and Maclure, "Girls and armed conflict in Sierra Leone."

47 Interview conducted in Sierra Leone by Susan McKay on May 31, 2002.
48 Interview conducted in Northern Uganda by Dyan Mazurana and Susan McKay on November 26, 2001.
49 Denov and Maclure, "Girls and armed conflict in Sierra Leone"; V. Sherrow, *Encyclopedia of Youth and War: Young People as Participants and Victims* (Phoenix: The Oryx Press, 2000).
50 McKay and Mazurana, *Where Are the Girls?*
51 Human Rights Watch, *Stolen Children.*
52 Ibid.
53 Interview conducted in Northern Uganda by Dyan Mazurana and Susan McKay on November 27, 2001.
54 Ibid.
55 Interview conducted in Northern Uganda by Dyan Mazurana and Susan McKay on November 28, 2001.
56 McKay and Mazurana, *Where Are the Girls?*
57 Denov and Maclure, "Girls and armed conflict in Sierra Leone."
58 Interview conducted in Sierra Leone by Susan McKay on June 6, 2002.
59 Ibid.
60 Interview conducted in Sierra Leone by Susan McKay on June 11, 2002.
61 Interview conducted in Sierra Leone by Susan McKay on June 6, 2002.
62 Denov and Maclure, "Girls and armed conflict in Sierra Leone."
63 Ibid.
64 Ibid.; McKay and Mazurana, *Where Are the Girls?*
65 Ibid.
66 Mazurana, McKay, Karlson, and Kasper, "Girls in fighting forces and groups."
67 McKay and Mazurana, *Where are the Girls?*
68 Coalition (2000); Keairns, *The Voices of Girl Child Soldiers* (New York and Geneva: Quaker United Nations Office, October 2002); Isobel McConnan and Sara Uppard, *Children, Not Soldiers* (London: Save the Children, 2001); McKay and Mazurana, *Where Are the Girls?*
69 Elise Fredrikke Barth, *Peace as Disappointment: the Reintegration of Female Soldiers in Post-Conflict Societies: a Comparative Study from Africa.* PRIO Report 3/2002. Online, available at: www.prio.no/publications/reports/female soldiers; Susan McKay, Mary Burman, Maria Gonsalves, and Miranda Worthen, "Known but invisible: girl mothers returning from fighting forces," *Child Soldiers Newsletter*, 11, pp. 10–11. McKay and Mazurana, *Where Are the Girls?.*
70 Coalition (2000); McKay and Mazurana, *Where Are the Girls?*

11 From freedom birds to water buffaloes

Women terrorists in Asia

Margaret Gonzalez-Perez

Like traditional warfare, terrorism is associated with males more than with females, despite the fact that women have long been active in violent political conflict. Indeed, women played a central role in one of the earliest manifestations of political terror – the French Revolution – and have participated in other terrorist movements throughout history (Levy 1997). The participation levels of female members in terrorist organizations vary dramatically, however. In an earlier examination of women in Latin-American guerrilla movements (Gonzalez-Perez 2006), I argued that women tend to be more active in organizations that promote a domestic agenda and less active in those seeking change on an international level. Moreover, I argued that women were more apt to attain higher levels of responsibility, both in combat and with respect to policy-making, in groups with a domestic agenda, whereas women in international terrorist organizations typically filled only subordinate roles.

The study I present here draws on this same basic argument, but with respect to terrorist groups. In this study, I will examine six terrorist groups with documented female activity and show how levels of female participation are linked to the groups' domestic or international orientation. To reduce the influence of cultural and regional differences, all six cases are drawn from Asia. The Liberation Tigers of Tamil Eelam (LTTE) of Sri Lanka, the Naxalites of India, and the People's Liberation Army of Nepal (PLA) are advanced as examples of domestic terrorist organizations in which females play an important role and participate in large numbers. In contrast, the People's Liberation Army Front (PLAF), the Viet Minh of Vietnam, and the Red Army of Japan represent international terrorist groups where women served primarily in support-level activities rather than combat and command positions.

Terminology

As the current study is based on arguments I have put forth pertaining to the roles that women play in guerrilla organizations, it is important to begin by underscoring that important philosophical differences exist between guerrilla and terrorist groups, particularly with regard to violence. Generally speaking, guerrilla organizations engage in violence for political objectives, but typically limit their attacks to military targets or targets associated with the government of a state. Terrorist organizations, on the other hand, are philosophically more willing to conduct violent attacks against civilians and non-combatants. Whereas many guerrilla groups are known to routinely attack civilians, guerrilla groups typically do not openly justify killing civilians to reach their stated goals. However, despite their differences, the fact that both guerrilla and terrorist groups engage in violence for political purposes leaves each a legitimate subject for comparison where females are concerned.

As this chapter undertakes to comment on a broad range of political violence in which women are involved, it is important to also comment on the definitional and conceptual lack of clarity that surrounds the term "terrorism." As Eileen MacDonald states, "Those who deal with terrorism on a daily basis are keenly aware that the terminology is a problem" (1991, xiii). Scholars, military agencies, and international organizations often identify terrorism by different characteristics, such as the group's goals, methods, or ideologies, but most definitions have a common core. Counter-terrorist security specialist Brian Jenkins and terrorism scholar Walter Laqueur provide some of the most widely accepted definitions. Jenkins defines terrorism as the threat or use of force for the purpose of political change (White 2002, 8). Laqueur's definition adds the illegitimate use of force as well as the targeting of innocent people (1987, 72). Laqueur also includes peasant wars, general wars, civil wars, revolutionary wars, wars of national liberation, and resistance movements as possible contexts in which terrorism can be used (1977, 7). In addition, Laqueur notes that new terms related to terrorism with a range of associated nuances are constantly emerging, such as "asymmetric warfare" (2004, 58), causing further obstacles to the formation of a standard definition.

Like Jenkins' and Laqueur's, many other definitions revolve around the central theme of violence against civilians for a political purpose (Kapitan 2003, 48; Snow 2003, 71; Sterba 2003, 206; Pillar 2001, 14–15; Terrorist Research Analytical Center 1995; Georges-Abeyies 1983, 71). Drawing upon characteristics common to the above definitions, this study defines terrorism as the use or threat of violence against non-combatants by individuals, groups, or state governments for political objectives; these activities may include guerrilla warfare, revolutions, state-sponsored terrorism, separatist movements, and organized militia movements.

The distinction between domestic and international terrorism is less volatile, but deserves clarification, nonetheless. In this examination, domestic terrorist groups are those who seek change *within* their nation or state. Whether the terrorist agenda involves mere reform or total revolution, its focus is on a transformation of internal characteristics or perceived forces of oppression within the state rather than foreign influences. As such, a domestic terrorist group is more inclined to challenge traditional gender roles and restrictions on women's activity, and to provide far more opportunities for females to actively participate in the organization through guerrilla warfare, policy formation, and even leadership roles. Such access to greater participation should not be confused with a primary commitment to gender equality, however. Some domestic terrorist movements take advantage of women's participation as a resource, yet abuse female members. Just as women are traditionally exploited in many societies, they suffer from similar exploitation in most terrorist organizations. The degree to which they are exploited differs, however, based on the domestic or international focus of the terrorist group. Women tend to gain greater access to opportunity in domestic terrorist movements, while they experience far less in international terrorist groups.

It is important to note that, although women may gain rights within a domestic terrorist movement, these reforms rarely translate to the society at large. Women are drawn to domestic terrorist groups because they can gain upward mobility and leadership positions, yet many domestic terrorist organizations offer women this power and equality out of self-interest rather than a long-term commitment to societal change. Particularly in the Asian case studies of this analysis, female members of terrorist groups have failed to maintain their enhanced status beyond the terrorist movements, suggesting that the higher levels of women's participation in Asian domestic terrorism is another form of the gender exploitation found in traditional society.

International terrorists typically oppose external forces, such as imperialism, globalization, capitalism, or Western culture in general. Any change within their own state, including gender roles, is incidental to the primary objective of combating foreign political, economic, or societal influences. Although some may espouse gender equality as part of some broader platform, they rarely put these philosophies into practice within their own organizations. In internationally oriented terrorist groups, women function almost exclusively in supportive roles, cooking, sewing uniforms, providing shelter and sometimes sex to the males in the organization. The terrorist group as a whole devotes little effort to addressing women's policy concerns, as its energies are directed toward combating an external force. The entrenched gender roles that keep women in traditionally subservient roles also inhibit their participation and limit recruitment potential. Because female participation is restricted, few women perceive any advantage to membership in international terrorist groups and female recruitment remains low.

Liberation Tigers of Tamil Eelam (LTTE)

Since 1983, the Liberation Tigers of Tamil Eelam (LTTE), or Tamil Tigers, have been fighting to separate the 13 percent of Sri Lanka's Hindu Tamil population from the majority Buddhist Sinhalese society and establish an independent homeland of Eelam, or "Freedom" (Cunningham 2003, 180; Alison 2004, 450). Despite their colonial past under the Dutch (1505–1656), Portuguese (1656–1796), and British (1815–1948), the Tamils are not an internationally oriented terrorist group. They do not seek to eliminate Western imperialism, globalization, or any of the other popular international targets. While the LTTE espouses a Marxist ideology, it never enjoyed Soviet support, nor, unlike Vietnam's National Liberation Front, was Tamil terrorism ever part of an international Cold War strategy (Grosscup 1998, 244). Admittedly, the LTTE was responsible for assassinating a foreign head of government, Indian Prime Minister Rajiv Gandhi, in a 1991 suicide bombing; however, even this operation was domestically motivated as an act of retaliation for India's provision of peace-keeping forces to Sri Lanka from July 1987 to March 1990 (Joshi 1996, 21) and the LTTE's numerous other assassinations have been directed at Sri Lankan officials (Sambandan 2002). Thus, it would be fair to conclude that the LTTE is primarily a domestic terrorist group that opposes only the government of its state.

Notably, although both the Sinhalese and Tamils have previously resisted imperial rule under three different foreign powers, none of these resistance efforts was characterized by a significant female presence (Jayawardena 1986, 115; Grosscup 1998, 235). Tamil women were an oppressed minority under imperial rule, but remained inactive during the anti-colonial resistance movements. Women had little to gain from international struggles if they were to overthrow a repressive external power only to be repressed by an internal state. Tamil women only grew more politically active in the 1960s with the advent of a domestic secessionist movement against Sri Lankan authority (Maunaguru 1995, 160–162).

Women comprise one-third to one-half of the LTTE's key weapon, the commando elite unit known as the Black Tigers. The Black Tigers conducted over 168 suicide attacks between 1980 and 2002, more than any other terrorist organization, killing approximately 1,500 people in these attacks alone (Reuter 2004, 26). The Sea Tigers are a similar specialized unit of women and men who conduct attacks against the Sri Lankan navy, bridges, and merchant vessels. Because such units require specialized instruction, the presence of a large female contingent suggests that the LTTE views women as valuable comrades and worthy of the training investment. Within the LTTE as a whole, female membership in the 15,000-member terrorist militia grew from 3,000 in 1992 to almost 5,000 by 2001 (Goldstein 2001, 83; Xinhua News Agency 9 September 1992). These women gather intelligence, engage in combat, conduct suicide bombings, and lead attacks on civilians (Goldstein 2001, 83; Samuel 2001, 185; de Silva 1999, 61–62). In addition to combat duties, women are also active in policy-making and leadership roles in the LTTE. In 1994, three members of the LTTE's highest organ, the 12-member Central Committee, were women (Bose 1994, 108–109) and the number had increased to five by 2002 (Alison 2003, 47).

Within the regular LTTE militia, the women's branch is called *Suthanthira Paravihal* (Freedom Birds), the Women's Front of the Liberation Tigers, or the Women's Wing. LTTE members began recruiting women as early as 1979 and established the first women's training camp in 1984. As part of their training, women endure six months of boot camp and gain expertise in combat, explosives, and strategy. Although the first female suicide bombing occurred in Lebanon in 1985, the LTTE is the first terrorist organization to institutionalize this practice. Since 1987, LTTE women have engaged in 30 to 40 suicide bombings, making the Tigers the most prolific female suicide bombers of the modern era, and providing a model for other terrorist groups (Zedalis 2004, 2). The use of women as suicide bombers has proven to be even more effective than that of male suicide bombers because the practice contrasts so sharply with most gender stereotypes. Female terrorists attract more media attention, and perhaps inspire more fear, because they are unexpected and contrary to traditional female gender roles. Female suicide bombers take this strategy to the next level, garnering even more notice from the media and further publicizing the demands of the LTTE.

Women have come to share all of the tasks that men perform within the LTTE, and virtually all of the militant Tamil organizations emphasize the need for women to participate alongside the men (Maunaraguru 1995, 164). In one of the more notorious attacks, 75 to 100 cadres stabbed, shot, hacked to death, and slit the throats of 57 sleeping Sinhalese villagers; witnesses reported that women led the attack and 20 of the terrorist troops were reported to be female (Cruez 1999; Balachanddran 1999). The brutal attack attracted considerable public attention, in large part due to the fact that it was led predominantly by women.

Tamil women have also taken the lead in assassination plots against more than a dozen public figures. In 1991, a young female Black Tiger called Dhanu presented former Prime Minister Rajiv Gandhi of India with a flower garland and detonated explosives strapped to her waist, killing them both. According to investigative reports, the assassination attempt was plotted by Lieutenant Colonel Akhila, the female deputy chief of the Freedom Birds (Agence France Presse 20 May 1992). In addition, the women of the Black Tigers participated in the murders of Sri Lankan President Ranasinghe Premadasa in 1993, former Prime Minister Dissanayako in 1994, constitutional expert and Tamil parliamentarian Neelan Tiruchelvam, former Cabinet Minister C.V. Gooneratne in June 2000, and a suicide bombing that claimed the lives of four Colombo policemen in July 2004 (Sambandan 2002). While assassinations of political leaders and governmental authorities are routine among terrorist groups, the participation of women in such terrorist acts defies traditional gender roles and emphasizes women's commitment to LTTE objectives.

The strong presence of women in the LTTE is particularly noteworthy in light of the many societal restrictions they endure. Both Tamil and Sinhalese social structures still relegate women to a traditional, subordinate role

(Jayawardena 1986, 111, 113–114; de Alwis 1995, 141; Maunaraguru 1995, 169). In defiance of cultural prohibitions, women have challenged their conventional gender roles and joined the LTTE, which promises a "radical transformation of women's lives and social attitudes towards women" (Maunaraguru 1995, 165). Whether the LTTE delivers on these promises remains to be seen, but the women of the Tamil Tigers have actively committed to the domestic goals of this terrorist organization.

Naxalites of India

In 1967, long-standing conflicts between tribal farmers and large landholders in the Naxalbari region of West Bengal, India, gave way to an uprising of farmers, led by communist activists. The clash spawned the term "Naxalite," describing a merger of India's communist party and peasant farmers into a violent political force that has grown far beyond the borders of Naxalbari. As a terrorist organization, the Naxalites focus on internal targets that represent domestic oppression, such as political leaders, police stations and informants, government buildings, and development projects. Naxalite goals include the elimination of India's caste-based society, implementation of land reforms for the poor, and enfranchisement of the oppressed, all of which are domestic objectives (Indian Elections 2005; Diwanji 2003).

The Naxalite movement exhibits a high degree of female participation and women have been active from its inception (Singha Roy 1992, 60). Not only do women comprise a large percentage of the membership (33 percent), they also hold high-ranking organizational positions as combat leaders and policy-makers. The Naxalites do not actively promote women's equality as a separate agenda, but the agrarian and leftist origins of the group have led them to encourage egalitarianism and equality of opportunity across caste and gender divisions, and this practice has helped Naxalites to enjoy widespread support from women at all levels of their hierarchy.

At the support levels, women carry supplies and act as informants and spies; at the combat level, women are often in charge of planting mines and detonating explosives (Sreedharan 1998). A group of 300 Naxalites, including 50 women wielding hand grenades, bombs, and AK-47 assault rifles, attacked the Karnataka State Police Reserve camp in February of 2005 in retaliation for the police killing of a Naxalite leader (Nayak 2005). Naxalite women also serve in leadership roles within the guerrilla army, acting as squad commanders over male guerrillas and formulating policy. While some terrorist groups have been accused of high female casualty rates and recruiting women for their expendability, Naxalite women have a comparatively greater longevity, with some serving as many as 11 years in the terrorist militia (Sreedharan 1998).

The Naxalites consider women to be better guerrillas than the men because of their greater commitment to the egalitarian goals of the group. Its leftist focus on equity and redistribution of resources are domestic objectives that appeal to many women in the poorer regions of India. Extreme poverty, combined with a severe lack of public services, provides a niche for the Naxalite presence. In areas where the government has failed to provide adequate infrastructure in the form of roads, schools, and clinics, the Naxalites have created a Compact Revolutionary Zone (CRZ), stretching from India's border with Nepal to the southernmost state of Tamil Nadu (Reddy 2004). Within the CRZ, the Naxalites operate a parallel administration, providing public services and maintaining some level of order, albeit through brute force (Gupta 2005; Sahni 2005). The Naxalites also engage in large-scale destruction of government projects, bombing large factories and dams, murdering police, threatening missionaries, disrupting elections, and taking command of roadways (Gupta 2005; Nayak 2005; Ray 2002). Such anti-state activities discourage the government from investing in rebuilding and reinstating political control in the CRZ, which only increases the opportunity for Naxalite governance.

Women in the CRZ are often more amenable to Naxalite programs because these programs reduce women's social burdens. Women are typically responsible for the education of their children, family healthcare, and the care of the sick and elderly.

Naxalite clinics help women to deal with such duties. In addition, women traditionally gather firewood and water for the family and are often responsible for providing part or all of the family income – duties that require access to safe roadways and marketplaces. Naxalite control of roads, bridges, and gathering places can ensure safety for women who are compliant with the group. Women have become an integral part of the Naxalite movement, making the militants an even greater threat to India's national security than the Kashmir crisis, according to India's Prime Minister, Manmohan Singh (Sahni 2005).

People's Liberation Army of Nepal (PLA)

The Communist Party of Nepal-Maoist (CPN-M) emerged from a realignment of Nepal's leftist parties in 1991 following the collapse of democracy in 1990. The CPN-M and its guerrilla branch, the People's Liberation Army (PLA), initiated the People's War in 1996 through guerrilla attacks on government installations and terrorist assaults on non-compliant civilians (Watt 2002). The overriding goal of the CPN-M is the ouster of Nepal's monarchy. Equality and land redistribution are high priorities as well, but the CPN-M believes that these secondary objectives can be achieved only through the removal of the current government. The CPN-M's opposition to internal forces and the prevailing domestic agenda demonstrate that the CPN-M's PLA is a domestic terrorist organization. Its primary target is the domestic government, and while it may support forays across the border into India or China, its chief objectives lie within its own state.

Other goals of the CPN-M include equal rights for women and an end to exploitation and injustice (Onesto 2001, 3). In light of the opportunities granted to women within the CPN-M, it is little wonder that many women in impoverished and patriarchal Nepal view the PLA terrorist organization as the most credible guarantor of equal rights (Pradhan Malla 2001). To the extent that any basic services like schools, medical care, and legal services are provided in these areas, they are provided by the CPN-M (South Asia Forum for Human Rights 2000). In the absence of such social programs, the burden for providing education, medical treatment, childcare, elder-care, as well as basic food and shelter, falls on the shoulders of women (Gupta 2005). Thus, many women have become ardent supporters of the CPN-M and PLA.

Many women who have joined the local PLA militias have become guerrillas who participate in combat. PLA women have seized banks, conducted assassinations, and engaged in strategic bombing. According to PLA Commander Parvati, "Their participation has been phenomenal, sometimes even surpassing that of men" (Parvati 1999). PLA forces are estimated at 12,000 trained guerrilla troops and militia (Tiwari 2001). The PLA requires that each guerrilla squad of the PLA must contain at least two female members but, by 2005, one-third of all PLA troops were women, with many female commanders, vice commanders, and political commissars throughout the various battalions, platoons, squads, and militia (Onesto 2004; Parvati 1999). CPN-M Chairman Prachanda states, "Our Party considers women as [a] basic revolutionary force" and the organization uses every opportunity to mobilize Nepali women (Portland Independent Media Center 2004).

The CPN-M and PLA also demonstrate a strong presence of women in leadership and policy-making bodies, as well (Thapa 2003). Within the Party administration, there are "several women in the Central Committee of the Party, dozens of women at the regional level, hundreds in the district levels, and several thousands in the area and cell levels in the Party" (Onesto 2004). Data from the Institute for Conflict Management (2001) indicates that half of lower-level political cadres and 30 percent of upper-level cadres are women. The CPN-M also contains the Women's Department, an upper-level leadership council that formulates policy for the Party, the military, and allied organizations. The All Nepalese Women's Revolutionary Organization is an organization for mass participation (Portland Independent Media Center 2004). Women who are not directly involved in terrorist warfare serve as propagandists, nurses, and organizers for the CPN-M and PLA (Onesto 1999).

Because the majority of households are headed by women, the CPN-M is dependent upon the women to wage a Maoist agrarian revolution. As Hsila Yami, the highest-ranking woman in the CPN-M, stated, "The women have more to gain than men from the People's War" (Online Pioneer and Ideals World News 2004). According to PLA Commander Parvati, women join the CPN-M because its anti-class agenda "directly address[es] the oppressive socio-economic relation ... from which women are the worst sufferers" and Nepali women have no other alternatives (Parvati 1999). The women of

Nepal have limited property rights, even after the 1990 reforms, cannot inherit land, and cannot conduct banking transactions. They cannot choose their own husbands, and marriages are arranged for the mutual benefit of the families. Divorce and remarriage are forbidden, and widows are expected to honor the memory of their husbands by remaining in mourning for the rest of their lives (Onesto 2001; Pradhan Malla 2001; South Asia Forum for Human Rights 2000)

The CPN-M contends that "the fight for women's equality and liberation is woven into the very fabric of this People's War" and "women are seeing some concrete outlines of a new society" that does not oppress its people (Onesto 2001, 5). Due to the internal characteristics of the Nepali state, the PLA "has become an attracting point for women" (Portland Independent Media Center 2004) and CPN-M Chairman Prachanda commented that the party was "overwhelmed by the unexpected response of women to join the armed struggle" (Online Pioneer and Ideals World News 2004).

The National Liberation Front (NLF) of Vietnam and the Japanese Red Army (JRA) are also terrorist groups, but the role of women in these organizations is very different from the heightened participation of women in the Tamil Tigers, Naxalites, and Nepalese PLA. The NLF and JRA were predominantly international terrorist groups with international objectives and international targets. The NLF sought to remove French and, later, American political control, and to institute a communist regime within not only Vietnam but in neighboring Cambodia as well. The JRA's goals were more nebulous, espousing the creation of a World Army to lead a World Revolution, but with little thought given to practical implementation. The two groups share the adoption of terrorist tactics and strategy, however, and reliance on an international network of assistance. Due to their international nature, the women of both groups had little to gain from increased participation and remained at lower support-level positions, rather than ones related to combat, leadership, or policy-making.

Vietnamese People's Liberation Armed Front (PLAF) and the Viet Minh

The Viet Minh formally began in 1941 as a nationalist Vietnamese resistance movement against France's colonial government. By the early 1950s, the communist Vietnamese People's Liberation Armed Front (PLAF) had absorbed much of the Viet Minh and assumed the leadership of the anti-French terrorist movement. Although many scholars may disagree with the characterization of the Vietnamese insurgency against French colonial rule as a terrorist action, the rebellion meets the definition of terrorism used in this study in that it employed violence against non-combatants for political objectives, including the use of guerrilla warfare and suicide bombs. Guerrillas attacked villages, murdering local leaders, and detonated bombs in the larger cities to incite terror and induce civilian compliance (Parry 1976,

418). Within a single 24-day period in February 1968, the Viet Minh and PLAF militia "systematically and deliberately shot to death, clubbed to death or buried alive some 2,800 individuals ... government personnel, administrative personnel, students, teachers, priests, rural-development personnel, policemen, foreign medical teams" (Jones 1974, 93).

This conflict was not merely a quest for independence, however; it was also an international power struggle between the communist and democratic superpowers over influence in Asia. Rife with insurgent attacks on civilians and complicated by the official and unofficial participation of the U.S., Soviet Union, China, Cambodia, Laos, and other states, the conflict in Vietnam became perhaps the most international of all terrorist movements of the twentieth century.

The women of Vietnam had no part in politics, education, or professional careers (Duiker 1982, 109). Rather, they were expected to observe the "three submissions" of obedience to the father, then the husband, then the oldest son, in addition to the "four virtues": hard work, proper appearance, submissive speech, and subservient behavior. The traditional view of women is perhaps best described by the Vietnamese proverb, "A hundred daughters are not worth a single testicle" (Marr 1981, 193). The struggle against French and American forces promised no change in this status and Vietnamese women responded by participating at much lower levels of activity than NLF propaganda indicated.

Many studies of the insurgency in Vietnam refer to women as guerrillas or soldiers, when in fact they engaged only in support activities. One source states that, "about 840,000 female guerrillas operated in the north and some 140,000 in the south," serving in "community mobilization, intelligence gathering, and the transport of materiel" (Tetrault 1994, 115), adding that women's most significant role was that of food production, and that unarmed women had the moral authority of passive resistance (Tetrault 1994, 118–119). While these activities were important, they were not equivalent to guerrilla warfare or offensive attacks on civilians or state forces. The phrase "Long Haired Army" added to the confusion. It originally referred to 5,000 women and children who marched on government buildings in South Vietnam to protest corruption, the poor economy, and government atrocities in 1960 (Duiker 1982, 114). By 1967, the term was being used to describe all female PLAF, NLF, and Viet Minh, with propaganda claiming that they numbered two million, a wild exaggeration (Taylor 1999, 72; Tetrault 1994, 121).

Certainly, it was not unknown for women to join the PLAF, but it was nonetheless uncommon (Taylor 1999, 82; Duiker 1982, 112). Male soldiers were often resentful of women and considered them a liability in combat (Goldstein 2001, 80; Duiker 1982, 115). The few female PLAF members served not in guerrilla units, but in special units such as the medical corps, liaison work, or bomb-defusing teams. General policy discouraged female participation beyond the support level (Duiker 1982, 117). A small number of women acted as snipers, but most women who fought did so as unarmed village militia, standing in front of U.S. tanks with picks and hoes to stop troops from destroying rice fields (Taylor 1999, 82, 38). News reports of the day indicated that women rarely served in combat, and then only as a last resort after male troops had been depleted (*New York Times* 11 November 1969; Wiegersma 1988, 209; Gottschang Turner 1998, 20, 23, 33).

Women were noticeably absent in the leadership of the NLF and PLAF. A small number of women gained national acclaim, but they were very few in number and were usually second-in-command to male leaders (Turley 1972, 797, 803). Moreover, their "leadership" duties consisted of organizing meetings, arranging for couriers, and other logistical tasks rather than actual policy and decision-making (Taylor 1999, 40).

The best known of these leaders was Madame General Nguyen Thi Dinh, the Deputy Commander of the PLAF and the President of the Vietnamese Women's Union. NLF propaganda portrayed Dinh as a warrior, but other reports of Dinh transporting rifles and participating in mass marches are likely a more accurate representation of her duties (Duiker 1982, 114–115). In a 1987 interview, Dinh even complained about the lack of women's rights and status in Vietnamese society. Recalling the Vietnam war, she stated that even among the guerrilla troops, men were hostile to women and she acknowledged the widespread discrimination among the leadership. Dinh said that many women were promoted as mere recruitment symbols (Jones 1987).

It can be hypothesized that the women themselves did not seek greater levels of participation because they realized that they battled external forces in this international conflict, and a victory would not change the societal restrictions that had lingered over them for ten centuries. The PLAF doctrine on women followed societal conventions, establishing three aspects of women's 'combat' role much like the Confucian three submissions. Female soldiers had to provide labor (usually agricultural) for national defense, women over age 40 had to care for wounded soldiers and boost troop morale, and young women had to serve in the village defense militias, usually armed only with farming tools (Turley 1972, 802). A common NLF propaganda cartoon portrayed a tiny Vietnamese woman holding a powerfully built American G.I. captive. Although, at first glance, this could be interpreted to show the strength of Vietnamese women, it more probably embodied an attack on the strength of the U.S., demonstrating that "even a woman" could wage battle against it (Tetrault 1994, 122). Even in 1970, the Vietnamese Women's Liberation Association considered embroidering napkins with revolutionary mottoes as achievements worthy of reward (Taylor 1999, 90), suggesting that higher levels of activity were simply non-existent among women.

The women in the PLAF and other insurgent militia units played an important part in the Vietnamese insurgency, but "primarily as support staff" (Taylor 1999, 27). Even in civilian roles, women were employed at the lowest levels of agriculture, industry, and military production (Duiker 1982, 118–119). Their principal military function was the transportation of supplies and equipment. Women reportedly carried 200-pound loads of weapons, munitions, and supplies, on foot or by bicycle through mountains, monsoons, and darkness, all the while evading detection (Taylor 1999, 12; Tetrault 1994, 114). The Dan Cong battalion, two-thirds of whose members were women, was responsible for transporting virtually all the PLAF's front-line supplies during the battle of Dien Bien Phu (Tetrault 1994, 115). Although men were stronger, women complained less and had greater stamina, leading Douglas Pike to describe them as "the water buffalo of the revolution" (1966, 178).

In addition to transport, Viet Minh and PLAF women also provided other support services. Female cadres were almost solely responsible for agricultural production, as well as the preparation and delivery of food to fighting forces. As one PLAF member stated, "to produce is to fight" (Eisen Bergman 1974, 127). They also gathered intelligence information, dug tunnels and bunkers, hid insurgents, provided clean clothes for male insurgents, diverted enemy troops from strategic sites, built coffins, buried the dead, wove cloth, nursed the wounded, carried messages, distributed propaganda, and built roads (Taylor 1999, 72; Gottschang Turner 1998, 15, 20–23, 33, 76, 93, 149; Eisen Bergman 1974, 103–107, 127, 142; Turley 1972, 797). Although women suffered high casualty rates, which could suggest participation in combat, the majority of women were engaged in road construction and were killed in bombing raids on the road system (Eisen Bergman 1974).

There is no doubt that the women of the PLAF and Viet Minh participated in the insurgency in Vietnam and contributed to the maintenance of the rebel infrastructure, but the evidence clearly shows that women were not active in combat, leadership, or policy-making roles. The international focus of the conflict promised nothing for Vietnamese women. Even the PLAF's own doctrine offered no improvement upon conventional gender roles. Therefore, women participated only at support levels, providing services in the insurgency that were virtually the same as those they performed in their daily lives. Unlike women in domestic terrorist groups, the women of the PLAF and Viet Minh were not recruited with promises of equality and opportunity. Rather, they were exploited by the terrorist system much as the traditional Vietnamese society exploited them.

The Japanese Red Army (JRA)

In 1972, fringe members of two radical student organizations in Japan formed the Japanese Red Army (JRA). The organization viewed itself as an elite student vanguard that would lead a World Red Army in a World Revolution of the proletariat (Kuriyama 1973, 336; Parry 1976, 433–434; Steinhoff 1989, 724). Like many other radical leftist student movements of the 1970s, the JRA "placed heavy emphasis on internationalism" (Kuriyama 1973, 342). Its efforts to coordinate a global communist party and a global army that would conduct a global revolution clearly reflected an agenda that focused on international issues almost to the exclusion of domestic politics. The JRA's commitment to international goals presents itself even more clearly in its terrorist activities, which included the establishment of cells in Europe and Palestine, as well as collaborations with other terrorist groups such as Germany's Baader–Meinhoff Gang, the Popular Front for the Liberation of Palestine, Libya, North Korea's Intelligence Service, and even the Black Panthers of the U.S. (Parry 1976, 433; Farrell 1990, vii). Evidence suggests that the Red Army even established ties with the notorious international terrorist, Ilyich Ramirez Sanchez, known as Carlos the Jackal (Farrell 1990, 158).

As an international terrorist group, the JRA offered little opportunity to change the rigid societal roles of women in Japan and "had a fairly traditional view of male–female relations. Women were to be the supporters, while soldiering was left to the men" (Farrell 1990, 10). The women of the JRA

> were not true leaders but simply surrogates for male leaders who were temporarily unavailable.... Shiomi Kazuko was simply a stand-in for her imprisoned husband, Nagata for a whole string of males (Kawashima, Sakaguchi, and then Mori), and Shigenobu for the deceased Okudaira until other males were brought to the organization who could take over.
>
> (Steinhoff 1996, 317)

Intrigued with the unconventional image of female terrorists, the media glamorized the women of the JRA, particularly its leader, Fusako Shigenobu. However, the women reputed to be the powerful leaders and anarchic masterminds of Red Army terrorism were, in fact, engaged primarily in support functions for the JRA, while men held the decision-making roles (Steinhoff 1996; Farrell 1990, 10, 12, 16; Parry 1976, 434; Kuriyama 1973). Shigenobu exercised her leadership by arranging meetings, providing first-aid kits at protests, fund-raising, creating promotional leaflets for which "she was much in demand because of her beautiful handwriting," selling the organization's newspaper, and arranging a phone signal system (Steinhoff 1996, 313, 301, 730). Shigenobu and the other leaders, Shiomi and Nagata,

> did the feminine jobs that keep a political movement going, and they had significant personal relationships with men in leadership positions.... but were only thrust into externally visible positions of leadership when the men around them disappeared for one reason or another.
>
> (Steinhoff 1996, 317)

Even the terminology of "leadership" is misleading due to the fact that the JRA, though active, was extremely small. The membership of the JRA never reached beyond 40 individuals and was often half that number (MIPT 2005). At its height, the leadership core only held 15 members (International Policy Institute for Counterterrorism 2003). It is true that "women invariably formed between one-third to half of the organization" (O'Ballance 1979, 149), but male leaders were the norm in the JRA and its precursors, the United Red Army and Red Army Faction (Steinhoff 1996, 315). Shigenobu became the leader of the JRA only after the original male leader, Takanari Shiomi, was killed (Parry 1976, 434).

In spite of the reported presence of women in the JRA, the majority of JRA terrorist operations were planned and conducted by male members of the JRA and other terrorist organizations. Indeed, the undertakings conducted in cooperation with the Palestinian Front for the Liberation of Palestine (PFLP) were referred to as *Sons* of the Occupied Territories operations. The JRA's deadliest terrorist act was the 1972 attack on the Lod Airport in Tel Aviv, Israel, that killed 26 and injured 80. William Farrell contends that this operation was a precursor to the 1972 Munich Olympics massacre as well as the subsequent terrorist assaults of the 1970s and 1980s, and was thus "a seminal event in the history of modern terrorism" (1990, 141). Yet, this pivotal act was conducted by three men of the JRA with no female participation whatsoever.

In the 1973 hijacking of a Japanese Airlines flight from Paris to Tokyo, only one of the five hijackers was female – and this Iraqi woman was not even a member of the JRA. The 1974 attempted bombing of the Shell Oil refinery in Singapore was conducted entirely by men (O'Ballance 1979, 156–159). Women of the JRA provided support for the group's operations, facilitating meetings and communication, but female participation was limited almost exclusively to support roles.

Despite the group's espoused left-wing proclivities, the JRA operated within the traditional norms of Japanese gender roles and women "achieved their positions of prominence by performing distinctly female roles in male-dominated organizations" (Steinhoff 1996, 302–303).

Conclusion

The post-World War II era has seen the emergence of many distinct terrorist organizations throughout the world that have used innumerable methods of combat. Among those groups that are characterized by female participation, the levels of women's contributions vary widely. Even in a single region, the differences between women's roles in the domestic and international terrorist organizations of Asia emerge clearly.

Scholars have argued that class differences, feminist movements, liberal democracy, or religion determine the level of women's participation in terrorism. Though both were characterized by limited, support-level, activity among women, the women in Vietnam's peasant-based PLAF and those in Japan's university-educated JRA were from distinctly different socio-economic classes.

The presence or absence of feminist movements also fails to explain varying levels of participation. Of the countries studied, only Japan, at the time, had experienced even the beginning of a feminist movement, and its terrorist movement presented some of the lowest levels of female leadership or policy-making. However, the JRA's views of women remained rooted in Japanese patriarchal tradition; thus, the international nature of the organization gave little hope to JRA women of any change in their status. As such, their fight against the external forces of capitalism and imperialism was waged only with limited support from the female members.

The presence of a liberal democracy seems unrelated to the emergence of female terrorist activity in a particular setting. Sri Lanka, India, and Japan, countries referred to in this study, are all democratic states, yet only Sri Lanka and India saw the emergence of a strong female terrorist presence. The non-democratic regimes of Vietnam and Nepal offered similarly disparate results in that Vietnam's female terrorists were active only at lower support levels, while Nepal's terrorist women engage in the higher levels of combat and policy-making.

Religious doctrine also failed to predict any patterns of female terrorist activity. The Tamil of Sri Lanka and the Naxalites of India are both Hindu and exhibit high levels of female terrorist activity, but no aspect of Hinduism emerges to explain this. The Nepali, Vietnamese, and Japanese are predominantly Buddhist, yet, among them, the Nepali are the only group to demonstrate female terrorist activity at the higher levels of combat and command.

In sum, the domestic/international model of women and terrorism may be criticized for its simplicity, but its clear structure provides a functional analysis to help to understand and explain why women participate in terrorist organizations at varying levels in different environments.

References

Alison, Miranda, 2003. "Cogs in the Wheel? Women in the Liberation Tigers of Tamil Eelam," *Civil Wars* 6(4): 37–54.

Alison, Miranda, 2004. "Women as Agents of Political Violence: Gendering Security," *Security Dialogue* 35(4): 447–463.

Balachanddran, P.K., 1999. "Women Warriors Form Core of LTTE Operations," *Hindustan Times*, 30 September.

Bose, Sumatra, 1994. *States, Nations, Sovereignty: Sri Lanka, India, and the Tamil Eelam Movement*. New Delhi: Sage Publications.

Cruez, Dexter, 1999. "Women Lead Rebel Carnage," *The Daily Telegraph*, 20 September: 19.

Cunningham, Karla J., 2003. "Cross-Regional Trends in Female Terrorism," *Studies in Conflict and Terrorism* 26(3): 171–195.

de Alwis, Malathi, 1995. "Gender, Politics and the 'Respectable Lady'," in Pradeep Jeganathan and Qadri Ismail, eds, *Unmaking the Nation: The Politics of Identity and History in Modern Sri Lanka*. Colombo: Social Scientists Association, pp.137–156.

de Silva, Chandra, 1999. "A Historical Overview of Women in Sri Lankan Politics," in Sirima Kirimabune, ed., *Women and Politics in Sri Lanka: A Comparative Perspective*. Kandy: International Centre for Ethnic Studies.

Diwanji, A.K., 2003. "Who are the Naxalites?" *The Rediff Special*. Available at: www.rediff.com/news/2003/oct/02spec.htm.

Duiker, William J., 1982. "Vietnam: War of Insurgency," in Nancy Loring Goldman, ed., *Female Soldiers – Combatants or Noncombatants: Historical and Contemporary Perspectives*. Westport, CT: Greenwood, pp.107–122.

Eisen Bergman, A., 1974. *Women of Vietnam*. San Francisco: People's Press.

Farrell, William R., 1990. *Blood and Rage: The Story of the Japanese Red Army*. Lexington, MA: D.C. Heath and Company.

Georges-Abeyie, Daniel E., 1983. "Women as Terrorists," in Lawrence Zelic Freedman and Yonah Alexander, eds, *Perspectives on Terrorism*. Wilmington, DE: Scholarly Resources, Inc.

Goldstein, Joshua, 2001. *War and Gender*. Cambridge: Cambridge University Press.

Gonzalez-Perez, Margaret, 2006. "Guerrilleras in Latin America," *Journal of Peace Research* 43(3): 313–29.

Gottschang Turner, Karen, 1998. *Even the Women Must Fight: Memories of War from North Vietnam*. New York: John Wiley & Sons, Inc.

Grosscup, Beau, 1998. *The Newest Explosions of Terrorism*. Far Hills, NJ: New Horizon Press.

Gupta, Kanchan, 2005. "Maoists threaten India's internal security," *Intro-Asian News Service*. Available online.

Institute for Conflict Management, 2001. "Nepal Terrorist Groups – Communist Party of Nepal-Maoist," *South Asia Terrorism Portal*. Available at: www.satp.org.

International Policy Institute for Counterterrorism, 2003. "Terrorist Organization Profiles," *International Terrorism*. Available at: www.ict.org.il/.

Jayawardena, Kumari, 1986. *Feminism and Nationalism in the Third World*. London: Zed Books, Ltd.

Jones, Clayton, 1987. "Vietnam Fighter Up in Arms Again," *Christian Science Monitor*, 4 November.

Jones, James, 1974. *Viet Journal*. New York: Delacorte Press.

Joshi, Manoj, 1996. "On the Razor's Edge: The Liberation Tigers of Tamil Eelam," *Studies in Conflict & Terrorism* 19: 19–42.

Kapitan, Tomis, 2003. "The Terrorism of Terrorism," in James P. Sterba, ed., *Terrorism and International Justice*. Oxford and New York: Oxford University Press, pp. 47–68.

Kuriyama, Yoshihiro, 1973. "Terrorism at Tel Aviv Airport and a 'New Left' Group in Japan," *Asian Survey* 13(3): 336–346.

Laqueur, Walter, 1977. *Terrorism*. Boston: Little, Brown and Company.

Laqueur, Walter, 1987. *The Age of Terrorism*. Boston: Little, Brown and Company.

Laqueur, Walter, 2004. "The Terrorism to Come," *Policy Review* 126: 49–64.

Levy, Darlene Gay, 1997. "A Political Revolution for Women? The Case of Paris," in Renate Bridenthal, Susan Mosher Stuard, and Merry E. Wiesner, eds, *Becoming Visible: Women in European History*. New York: Houghton Mifflin, pp.265–294.

MIPT Terrorism Knowledge Base, 2005. "Japanese Red Army," *Terrorist Group Profile*. Available at: www.tkb.org/Group.jsp?groupID=59.

MacDonald, Eileen, 1991. *Shoot the Women First*. New York: Random House.

Marr, David G., 1981. *Vietnamese Tradition on Trial, 1920–1945*. Berkeley, CA: University of California Press.

Maunaguru, Sitralega, 1995. "Gendering Tamil Nationalism: The Construction of 'Woman' in Projects of Protest and Control," in Pradeep Jeganathan and Qadri Ismail, eds, *Unmaking the Nation: The Politics of Identity and History in Modern Sri Lanka*. Colombo: Social Scientists' Association, pp.156–175.

Nayak, Nihar, 2005. "Naxalites: The Economy at Risk," *Dysfunctions*. Available at: www.ocnus.net/cgi-bin/exec/view.cgi?archive=63&num=16534&printer=1/.

O'Ballance, Edgar, 1979. *Language of Violence: The Blood Politics of Violence*. San Rafael, CA: Presidio Press.

Onesto, Li, 1999. "Nepal: Women Hold Up Half the Sky!" *Revolutionary Worker*. Available at: www.rwor.org/a/v22/1090-99/1094/nepal_women.htm/.

Onesto, Li, 2001. "Nepal: Intrigue and Insurgency," *Asian Week*. Available at: www.asianweek.com/2001_07_06/opinion3_voices_nepal.html.

Onesto, Li, 2004. "Taking it Higher: Women's Liberation in Nepal," *Revolutionary Worker*. Available at: www.home.clear.net.nz/pages/wpnz/mar11-04nepal.women.htm/.

Online Pioneer and Ideals World News, 2004. "Women Flocking to Ranks of Maoist Rebels." Available at: ins.onlinedemocracy.ca/index.php?name=News&file=article&sid=3913.

Parry, Albert, 1976. *Terrorism: From Robespierre to Arafat*. New York: The Vanguard Press.

Parvati, Com, 1999. "Women's Participation in People's Army," *The Worker*, 5. Available at: www.cpnm.org/worker/issue5/article_parvati.htm.

Pike, Douglas, 1966. *Viet Cong: The Organization and Techniques of the National Liberation Front of South Viet Nam*. Cambridge: MIT Press.

Pillar, Paul R., 2001. *Terrorism and U.S. Foreign Policy*. Washington, D.C.: Brookings Institute Press.

Portland Independent Media Center, 2004. "Interview with Women's Leader in Revolutionary Nepal." Available at: portland.indymedia.org/en/2004/02/281672.shtml.

Pradhan Malla, Sapana, 2001. "Property Rights of Nepalese Women," *Nepal Democracy*. Available at: nepaldemocracy.org/gender/property-rights.htm.

Ray, Bikramjit, 2002. "A Band of Maoist Rebels Terrorizes an Indian Region," *The Christian Science Monitor*. Available at: www.csmonitor.com/2002/0813-p07s02-wosc.html/.

Reddy, Balaji, 2004. "Naxalites and Al-Qaeda Cooperation for Terror in India?" *India Daily*. Available at: www.indiadaily.com/editorial/07-01d-04.asp/.

Reuter, John, 2004. *Chechnya's Suicide Bombers: Desperate, Devout, or Deceived?* Washington, D.C.: The American Committee for Peace in Chechnya.

Sahni, Ajai, 2005. "Naxalites: What, Me Worry?" *South Asia Intelligence Review* 3(29). Available at: www.satp.org/satporgtp/sair/Archives/3–29.htm.

Sambandan, V.S., 2002. "LTTE Releases Casualty Figures," *The Hindu*, 23 November.

Samuel, Kumudini, 2001. "Gender Difference in Conflict Resolution," in Inger Skjelsbaek and Dan Smith, eds, *Gender, Peace and Conflict*. London: Sage Publications, pp. 184–204.

Singha Roy, Debol ·K., 1992. *Women in Peasant Movements: Tebhaga, Naxalite and After*. New Delhi: Manohar.

Snow, Donald M., 2003. *Cases in International Relations: Portraits of the Future*. New York: Longman. ,

South Asia Forum for Human Rights, 2000. "People's War in Nepal," 1(3): 1–8.

Sreedharan, Chindu, 1998. "Women Make Better Guerrillas than Men," *Rediff on the Net*. Available at: www.rediff.com/news/1998/aug/28pwg.htm.

Steinhoff, Patricia G., 1989. "Hijackers, Bombers, and Bank Robbers: Managerial Stylein the Japanese Red Army," *The Journal of Asian Studies* 48(4): 724–740.

Steinhoff, Patricia G., 1996. "Three Women Who Loved the Left: Radical Women Leaders in the Japanese Red Army Movement," in Anne E. Imamura, ed., *Re-Imaging Japanese Women*. Berkeley, CA: University of California Press, pp. 301–322.

Sterba, James P., 2003. "Terrorism and International Justice," in James P. Sterba, ed., *Terrorism and International Justice*. Oxford and New York: Oxford University Press, pp. 206–228.

Taylor, Sandra C., 1999. *Vietnamese Women at War: Fighting for Ho Chi Minh and the Revolution*. Lawrence, KS: University Press of Kansas.

Terrorist Research and Analytical Centre, 1995. *Terrorism in the United States 1995*. Washington, DC.

Tetrault, Mary Ann, 1994. "Women and Revolution in Vietnam," in Mary Ann Tetrault, ed., *Women and Revolution in Africa, Asia, and the New World*. Columbia: University of South Carolina Press.

Thapa, Manjushree, 2003. "Girls in the War," *Centre for Investigative Journalism*. Available at: www.countercurrents.org/gen-thapa170603.htm

Tiwari, Chitra K., 2001. "Maoist Insurgency in Nepal: Internal Dimensions," *South Asia Analysis Group*. Available at: www.saag.org/papers2/paper187.htm/.

Turley, William S., 1972. "Women in the Communist Revolution in Vietnam," *Asian Survey* 12(9): 793–805.

Watt, Romeet Kaul, 2002. "The Himalayan Blunder," *The Kashmir Telegraph*, May. Available at: www.kashirtelegraph.com/nepal.htm/.

White, Jonathan R., 2002. *Terrorism: 2002 Update*. Belmont, CA: Thomas/Wadsworth.

Wiegersma, Nancy, 1988. *Vietnam: Peasant Land, Peasant Revolution: Patriarchy and Collectivity in the Rural Economy*. New York: St Martin's Press.

Zedalis, Debra, 2004. "Female Suicide Bombers," *Strategic Studies Institute*, June. Available at: www.strategistudiesinstitute.army.mil/ssi/.

12 Women and organized racial terrorism in the United States

Kathleen M. Blee

In April 2003, 28-year-old Holly Dartez of Longville, Louisiana, was sentenced to a year and a day in prison and fined $1,000 for her part in a Ku Klux Klan (KKK) cross-burning the previous year. Ms. Dartez, whom the U.S. Attorney's Office characterized as secretary to the local Klan chapter, pled guilty to conspiracy for driving four other KKK members to the residence of three African-American men, recent migrants from Mississippi, where a cross was erected and set ablaze. Among the Klan members convicted in this episode was her husband, Robert, described as a leader of the local Klan, who received a 21-month sentence and a $3,000 fine. Despite these arrests and convictions, the African-American men targeted in the attack clearly received the message intended by the Klan's action. All abandoned their desire to move their families to Longville and returned to Mississippi.[1]

That same year, 23-year-old Tristain Frye was arrested for her part in an attack and murder of a homeless man in Tacoma, Washington. The attack was carried out by Ms. Frye and three men, among them her boyfriend, David Pillatos, with whose child she was pregnant, and Kurtis Monschke, the 19-year-old reputed leader of the local neo-Nazi Volksfront. The four, all known racist skinheads, had set out to assault a Black drug dealer, but instead attacked Randy Townsend, a 42-year-old man suffering from paranoid schizophrenia. Frye's involvement in the attack was apparently motivated by her desire to earn a pair of red shoelaces, a symbol of her participation in violence against a minority person. Although Frye reportedly made the initial contact with Townsend and admitted to kicking him in the head, hard, three or four times, her agreement to testify against Monschke and the prosecutors' conclusion that she had not been dedicated to White supremacy – despite the Nazi and racist tattoos on her back – were sufficient to get her charges reduced to second-degree murder.[2]

A year earlier, Christine Greenwood, 28, of Anaheim, California, and her boyfriend, John McCabe, already imprisoned for a separate offense, were charged with possessing bomb-making materials, including 50 gallons of gasoline and battery-operated clocks that could be used as timers. Greenwood was described as the co-founder of "Women for Aryan Unity," a group to integrate women into White supremacism, and a member of the militant racist skinhead gang "Blood and Honor." She pled guilty to this charge as well as an enhancement charge of promoting a criminal gang and received a short sentence and probation. She has not been visible in racist activities

since her arrest, but both groups with which she was associated continue, with elabor-
ate websites claiming chapters and affiliates across the globe.[3]

The women in these three vignettes were arrested for very different kinds of racist violence. Holly Dartez was involved with a Ku Klux Klan group in a cross-burning, an act whose violence was symbolic rather than physically injurious. Tristain Frye took part in the murder of a homeless man – an act of brutal physical violence – with a racist skinhead group, but the victim was White. Christine Greenwood – with her White-supremacist group affiliations and bomb-making equipment – seemed intent on racial mayhem, although her target was unclear. As these cases suggest, women in the United States today participate in acts of racial-directed violence whose nature, targets, and social organization vary considerably.

This chapter explores women's involvement in racial violence associated with the major organized White-supremacist groups in the United States: the Ku Klux Klan, White power skinheads, and neo-Nazis.[4] Such violence is best understood as *racial terrorism*. As commonly specified in the scholarly literature and by federal counterterrorist agencies, terrorism requires three components: acts or threats of violence, the communication of fear to an audience beyond the immediate victim, and political, economic, or religious aims by the perpetrator(s) (Cunningham 2003, 188; Hoffman 1998, 15; see also Crenshaw 1988), each of which is characteristic of White supremacist racial violence. Racial terrorism, then, is considered here as *terrorism under-*
taken by members of an organized White-supremacist or pro-Aryan group against
racial minorities to advance racial agendas.

Considering the violence of organized racist groups as a form of racial ter-rorism brings together scholarships on terrorism and organized racism that have largely developed in parallel tracks. With few exceptions (e.g., Blazak 2001; Cunningham 2003), research on terrorism has paid relatively little attention to the growing tendency of White supremacism in the United States to adopt the organizational structures, agendas, and tactics more com-monly associated with terrorist groups in other places. Similarly, studies of U.S. organized racism have rarely portrayed racist groups as perpetrating racial terrorism, although at least some of their actions clearly fall under the U.S. State Department's definition of terrorism as "premeditated, politically motivated violence perpetrated against noncombatant targets by subnational groups or clandestine agents, usually intended to influence an audience."[5]

To analyze the nature and extent of women's involvement in U.S. racial terrorism, it is useful to consider two dimensions of terrorism. The first is the nature of the intended ultimate target; what organized racist groups consider their enemy. Some acts of racial terrorism are "intended to coerce or to intimidate"[6] governments; others are directed toward non-state actors such as members of minority groups. The second dimension is how violence is organized. Some acts of racial terrorism are strategic, focused on a clear target and directed by the group's agenda. Others are what the author terms

"narrative," meant to build solidarity among racist activists and communic-
ate a message of racial empowerment and racial vulnerability but instigated
outside of a larger strategic plan (Blee 2005b; Cooper 2001; Perry 2002).
This chapter explores women's roles in racial terrorism from the immediate
post-Civil War era to the present along these two dimensions. It concludes
with a proposition about the relationships among women's participation,
definitions of the enemy, and the organization of terroristic violence in the
U.S. White-supremacist movement.

Perceptions of the enemy

Organized White supremacism has a long history in the United States,
appearing episodically in response to perceptions of gains by racial, ethnic,
or religious minorities or political or ideological opportunities (Chalmers
1981). White supremacism is always organized around a defined enemy.
African Americans have been the most common enemy of organized racists
over time, but other enemies have been invoked on occasion. The massive
Ku Klux Klan of the 1920s, for example, targeted Catholics, Jews, labor
radicals, Mormons, and others, in addition to African Americans. Today's
small and politically marginal KKK, neo-Nazi, and White-supremacist
groups express little hostility toward Catholics, Mormons, or labor radicals,
focusing their anger instead on Jews, Asian Americans, gay men and lesbians, and feminists, in addition to African Americans and other persons of
color.[7]

Each wave of organized White supremacism has been accompanied by
terrorist acts against its enemies, although the nature of such violence has
varied considerably over time and across groups. The KKK of the 1920s, for
example, amplified its periodic and vicious physical attacks on African
Americans, Catholics, Jews, and others with frequent terrifying displays of
its economic and political strength, including rallies and parades, boycotts
of Jewish merchants, and electoral campaigns (Blee 1991; Chalmers 1981).
Today, a few White-supremacist groups, particularly some KKK chapters
and Aryan-rights groups such as the National Association for the Advancement of White People (NAAWP), a former political outlet for racist media
star David Duke, follow the lead of the 1920s Klan in seeking public legitimacy for agendas of White rights, but most openly advocate or engage in
physical violence against enemy groups. The form of such racial terrorism
ranges from street-level assaults against racial minority groups to efforts to
promote a cataclysmic race war.

Women's involvement in racial terrorism is strongly associated with how
organized White supremacists define the nature of their enemies. Although
variation in the racist movement, even within a single historical period,
makes it impossible to make broad generalizations that hold for every racist
group, there have been changes since the Civil War in how racist groups
define their enemies. Particularly important for understanding women's

involvement is the changing focus on members of racial/ethnic groups versus institutions of the state as the primary enemy of organized racist groups. The following sections focus on definitions of the enemy in three major periods of racial terrorism: the immediate postbellum period, the first decades of the twentieth century, and the present.

Postbellum racial terrorism

Most White-supremacist groups in the immediate postbellum period directed their violence at racial minority groups, but the ultimate target of their actions was the state apparatus imposed on the defeated southern states during the Reconstruction era. The quintessential White-supremacist organization of this time – the Ku Klux Klan – emerged in the rural south in the aftermath of the Civil War, inflicting horrific violence on newly emancipated African Americans and their White, especially northern, allies. Organized as loose gangs of White marauders, the first Klan may have had a chaotic organizational structure, but its goals and efforts were focused and clear – to dismantle the Reconstructionist state and restore one based on White supremacism. Women played no direct role in this Klan. Indeed, its mob-like exercise of racial terrorism on behalf of traditional southern pre-rogatives of White and masculine authority left no opening for the partici-pation of White women except as symbols for White men of their now-lost privileges and lessened ability to protect "their" women against feared retali-ation by former slaves (Blee 1991).

Racial terrorism in the early twentieth century

The first wave of the KKK collapsed in the late nineteenth century, but its legacy of mob-directed racialized violence continued into the first decades of the twentieth century through extra-legal lynchings and racially biased use of capital punishment to execute African Americans.[8] The re-emergence of the Klan in the late 1910s (a Klan that flourished through the 1920s) sub-stituted political organization for mob rule, enlisting millions of White, native-born Protestants in a crusade of racism, xenophobia, anti-Catholi-cism, and anti-Semitism that included contestation of electoral office in some states. The violence of this second Klan also took a new form, mixing traditional forms of racial terrorism with efforts to instill fear through its size and political clout and create financial devastation among those it deemed its enemies (Blee 1991).

The targets of lynchings, racially biased capital punishment, and the 1920s Klan were mostly members of racial, ethnic, and religious minority groups; they also constituted its primary enemies. The racial terror of lynch-ing and racially biased capital punishment both depended on state support, either overtly or covertly. Similarly, for the second Klan, located primarily in the north, east, and western regions rather than the south, the state was not an enemy; instead, it was a vehicle through which White supremacists could enact their agendas. Rather than attack the state, in this period organized racism was explicitly xenophobic and nationalist, embracing the state through an agenda they characterized, in the Klan's term, as "100% American."

Women were active in all aspects of racial terrorism in the early twentieth century, including lynchings and the public celebrations that often accompanied, and added enormously to the terror of, these events. It is difficult to assess the precise role of women in such forms of violence because the historical record is mute about how often a woman tied the noose around a lynched person's neck or struck the match to burn an African-American corpse, or a living person. Yet, it is clear that women were integrally and fully involved in these events. Photographic records of lynchings, often the only means by which these were recorded, show large numbers of women, often with their children, gathered around lynched bodies, partaking in the spectacle with a fervor and brutality that shocks contemporary observers (Allen 2000). The inclusion of women and children helped to make such racial murders possible, even respectable, in many areas of the country.

Women were also active in the second KKK, adding more than half-a-million members to its ranks in female-led chapters, the Women of the Ku Klux Klan. They participated actively and avidly in the terrorist actions of this Klan which, unlike Klans that preceded and followed it, practiced racial terror largely through mechanisms of exclusion and expulsion. Women Klansmembers were instrumental, even leaders, in the effort to rid communities of Jews, Catholics, African Americans, and immigrants through tactics such as financial boycotts of Jewish merchants, campaigns to get Catholic schoolteachers fired from their jobs, and attacks on the property and sometimes the bodies of African Americans and immigrants (Blee 1991).

Part of the explanation for women's increased involvement in racial politics and terror in the early decades of the twentieth century lies in changing gender roles and possibilities in this time. The granting to women of the right to vote in all elections in 1920 made women attractive recruits for the second Klan as it sought to increase its size, financial base, and electoral strength. At the same time, women's increasing involvement in other forms of public life, including prohibition politics, the paid labor force, and civic improvement societies, made women more likely to join racist groups. But women's participation was also the result of tactics of racial organization and violence that were more compatible with the lives of (White) women than had been the case in previous decades. Women could, and did, contribute to the Klan's strategy of creating economic devastation, for example, by spreading vicious rumors about Catholic schoolteachers or Jewish merchants without stepping far from their roles as mothers and consumers. Such factors also made women's participation in mob-directed racial terrorism like lynching more likely. The rigid patriarchal ideas that precluded White southern women's entrance into the first Klan had crumbled significantly by the 1920s, making more acceptable the notion that women could act in the public sphere. Moreover, racial lynchings and other forms of mob-directed racial terrorism were often enacted as large-scale community events in which women could join without straying from their primary roles as mothers and wives, for example, by bringing their children to what Tolnay and Beck (1995) termed the "festival of violence " of lynching (see also Allen 2000; Patterson 1998).

Racial terrorism today

In the later decades of the twentieth century, the nationalist allegiances of many White-supremacist groups began to crumble. Much of this shift can be traced to the widespread adoption of new forms of anti-Semitic ideology, especially the idea that the federal government[9] had been compromised by its allegiance to the goals of global Jewish elites. This understanding, commonly summarized in the belief that the United States is a "Zionist Occupation Government (ZOG)," shifted the central axis of organized White supremacism. Additional pressures toward global pan-Aryanism diminished the allegiance of U.S. White supremacism to nationalist agendas and, increasingly, Jews became the focus of its vitriol, with African Americans and other persons of color regarded as the lackeys or puppets of Jewish masters. With this ideological shift – codified in the precepts of the widely embraced doctrines of "Christian Identity," a vicious racist theology that identifies Jews as the anti-Christ – the U.S. government itself became a target of White-supremacist violence. The bombing of the Oklahoma City federal building, assaults on federal land-management agencies in the West, and a series of aborted efforts to attack other government installations were the outcome of this shift toward the U.S. state as an enemy of White supremacism.

Identifying the state as a primary enemy has had complex effects on the participation of women in organized White supremacism and racial terrorism. Some racist groups have made considerable effort to recruit women in recent years (Blee 2002; Cunningham 2003), especially those, like some chapters of the KKK, that want to develop a durable and intergenerational racist movement. These groups see women as key because of their centrality in family life and their (perceived) lesser likelihood to become police informants. Some neo-Nazi and Christian Identity groups are also recruiting women heavily, but generally to create a more benign image for White supremacism (Blee 2002).

Following the influx of women into racist groups, there has been an apparent rise in the participation of women in racist terrorism, as suggested by the vignettes at the beginning of this chapter. However, the number of women involved appears to be relatively low, despite their increasing numbers in racist groups. Firm statistics on the gender composition of perpetrators of racially motivated violence are not available (see FBI 2002), but reports compiled by the Southern Poverty Law Center in Montgomery, Alabama (SPLC 2004),[10] the most highly regarded non-official source of such data, indicate that the clear majority of perpetrators are still male. In particular, the SPLC reports indicate that, relative to men, women have low levels of involvement in racial terrorism targeted at state institutions, with somewhat greater involvement in violence directed at racial minority groups.

What can be concluded from this brief history? Although any generalization needs to be treated with caution, given the heterogeneity of organized White supremacism, the historical data examined suggest that, in the United States, *women are more likely to be involved in organized racial terrorism that is directed at racial/ethnic minorities than racial terrorism directed against the state.*

The organization of racial terror

White supremacism has taken a variety of organizational forms in the United States, each typically associated with a particular form of violence. Much organized White supremacism is highly structured and hierarchical, with clear (if often violated) lines of authority, like the second and subsequent Ku Klux Klans. However, some White-supremacist groups are very loosely organized with highly transient memberships and little hierarchy, such as contemporary racist skinheads, which operate like gangs bound together by ideology rather than territory. The following sections consider how the form of racist organization is associated with the level and nature of women's involvement in racial terrorism, although particular racist groups may be involved in different forms of violence. What is proposed is an analytic abstraction meant to highlight specific aspects of racial terrorism rather than a firm typology of racial violence and racist groups.

Structured, hierarchical organization

White supremacism is an ideology that puts tremendous value on ideas of hierarchy. Indeed, the very premise of modern-day Western racism is the idea that human society is naturally divided into racial categories that can be ranked by their moral, political, cultural, and social worthiness (Frederickson 2003; Winant 2002). This ideology is mirrored in how racist groups are typically constituted, with strong demarcations between leaders and followers, a high valuation on acceptance of internal authority, and firm boundaries against participation by those of inferior categories, including not only those from enemy groups, but also, at many times, White Aryan women. This form of organization is characteristic of racist groups like the second and subsequent Ku Klux Klans, World War II–era Nazi groups, and some racial terrorist groups in the late twentieth century.

In recent years, a number of those involved in the racist movement have embraced a new structure known as "leaderless resistance," a concept developed in response to racist groups' desires to shield themselves from authorities. The principle of leaderless resistance is simple: the activities of racist activists are coordinated by their allegiance to a set of common principles rather by than communication among groups. In practice, leaderless resistance requires that racist activists develop very small cells in which plans are developed and enacted, with little or no communication between cells that would allow the police to trace a chain of racist groups.

Strategic racial terrorism is generally, although not always, associated with structured, hierarchical groups, including those that follow the model of leaderless resistance. This is violence that is planned, focused on precise targets, and calculated to have predictable consequences. Typically, such violence is developed in a small leadership group and disseminated to members for activation, or, in the case of leaderless resistance, created and executed by a small, tightly knit group. Strategic racial terrorism is exemplified by efforts to foment race war or to terrorize racial-minority communities by burning crosses, scrawling swastikas on buildings, or assaulting racial-minority persons. It also includes attacks on government agencies or efforts to precipitate cataclysmic economic collapse and social chaos, thereby hastening the demise of the Jewish-dominated government. One example in which a number of women were implicated was a paramilitary survivalist, Christian Identity-oriented group known as the Covenant, Sword, and Arm of the Lord (CSA). Insisting that Jews were training African Americans to take over the nation's cities, CSA members initiated a series of strategic terrorist activities, including firebombing a synagogue and a church and attempting to bomb the pipeline that supplied the city of Chicago with natural gas. When the FBI raided the CSA compound in 1985, they found supplies for further terrorism: weapons, bombs, an anti-tank rocket, and quantities of cyanide apparently intended for the water supply of an undisclosed city.

One woman from a highly structured racist group talked of her involvement in terms that succinctly summarize strategic racial terrorism. In an interview conducted for a study of women in contemporary racist activism (Blee 2002), she told me that she felt it was necessary to

> prepare yourself for war constantly – don't speak if you can't defend yourself in every way. Prepare by knowing – first of all, then work on guns and ammo, food and water supply, first aid kits, medication, clothing, blankets, try to become self-sufficient and [move] away from the city, if possible. Don't get caught into the "debit" or "marc" cards, etc – [that is, in the] new world order.

This woman, as well as Christine Greenwood whose efforts on behalf of the Women for Aryan Unity included making bombs, are examples of women who participate in strategic racial terrorism. But men are far more likely than women to be arrested for direct involvement in such acts. The strict principles of social hierarchy embraced by most tightly organized racist groups tend to exclude women from leadership, even from inclusion, and thus from a role in executing violence (also see Neidhardt 1992; Neuburger and Valentini 1998; Talbot 2000). Women's involvement in strategic racial terrorism is generally indirect, like Holly Daretz's role as a driver for the Klansmen arrested for the Louisiana cross-burning. This indirect involvement in strategic racist terrorism takes three forms: serving as legitimation, promoting group cohesion, and providing abeyance support. Women are used to *legitimate* strategic racial terrorism by creating an air of normalcy that belies the violence of organized racism (Blee 2002; Dobie 1997), a tactic increasingly common among terrorist groups across the globe (Cunningham 2003). In the United States, this legitimation role can be seen in efforts like those of the Women's Frontier/Sisterhood, female affiliates of the violent World Church of the Creator (WCOTC), whose Web publications stress benign topics like motherhood that serve to blunt the violent activities of its members, including Erica Chase and Leo Felton, arrested for attempting to detonate bombs to incite a "racial holy war" (Ferber 2004, 7; Rogers and Litt 2004; see also Bakersfield *Californian* 24 July 2004). Women also function to *promote group cohesion* in organized racism – making possible its agendas of strategic terrorism – by working to create solidarity within existing racist groups and recruit new members (Blee 2002). An example of this cohesive function is the effort of Women for Aryan Unity's campaign "White Charities – by Whites for Whites"[11] to provide support to imprisoned White racists. This campaign, one of a number in which racist women are involved, target those they term "prisoners of war" through pen-pal programs, prison visitation, and aid to the families of POWs, as well as by reintegrating former prisoners into the racist movement. And, finally, women create *abeyance support* (Taylor 1989) by standing in for male racist leaders when they die or are in prison. One example is that of Katja Lane, whose husband David was arrested for murder and other crimes during his involvement in the underground Aryan-supremacy group, Silent Brotherhood. During David's imprisonment, Katja has risen to prominence in the racist movement for her work in maintaining movement publications and a prison outreach program for White-supremacist prisoners (Dobratz and Shanks-Meile 2004; Gardell 2003).

Loose organization

White-supremacist groups that operate with loose, gang-like forms of organization typically exhibit high levels of violence. Indeed, such groups often eschew tighter forms of organization in the effort to avoid detection and arrest for their violent actions.[12] Klansmen who terrorized African Americans and their allies in the immediate postbellum period operated in this way, as do racist skinheads whose thinly linked groups operate under names like "Confederate Hammerskins" or "Blood and Honor."

Loosely organized White-supremacist groups often practice what can be termed *narrative* instead of, or in addition to, strategic racial terrorism. Narrative racial terrorism is at least somewhat spontaneous, in which victims are chosen impulsively and without clear purpose, and whose consequences are rarely calculated by the perpetrators in advance. Practices of narrative racial terrorism include street assaults on African Americans, gay men or lesbians, or Jews, like the description of the actions of one racist woman who would provoke her husband to go with her to "find a homosexual or someone and beat them up" (ABC News.com 2004a), or the acts of brutality inflicted on African Americans by the night-riders of the first Klan. It also includes acts of violence that seem inexplicable, like the murder of the White homeless man by Tristain Frye and her fellow skinheads, or those that seem attributable to the immaturity or psychological pathologies of their perpetrators, such as violence and savagery against fellow White supremacists or self-inflicted violence (Blee 2002; Christensen 1994; Hamm 1994).

What distinguishes narrative from strategic racial terrorism is not the character of the acts of violence, but its incorporation into a larger set of plans and tactics. Strategic racial terrorism is intensely focused on disabling, undermining, or exterminating those considered to be the enemies of White supremacism. Narrative racial terrorism is less clearly focused on specific enemies; it targets enemies for violence, but that violence also has an internal purpose: to strengthen, sometime even to create, organized White supremacism, to attract new members, to instill a sense of collective identity among existing members and bind them closer to each other, and to instill the passion and commitment that will sustain their efforts into the future.

Women are directly involved in narrative racial terrorism, although in lesser number than are male racists (Christensen 1994; Dobie 1997; but see Blazak 2004). Yet, there is evidence that women's role in narrative racial terrorism may be increasing, as racists skinheads and similar groups attract larger number of women who see themselves as empowered through the enactment of physical violence (Blee 2002). A description of narrative racial terrorism was related by a racist activist, in response to the present author's question about whether she had been involved in physical fights:

Yes. [With] about 20–25 women, six men. Some of who were non-whites, i.e., gangbangers – people who don't like people like me so they start trouble with me – and others were White trash traitors who had either screwed me over, started trouble because they don't believe in my ways or caused trouble in the movement. Some were hurting, physically, friends of mine, so I involved myself in it.

It is unclear whether women's increasing participation in groups that practice narrative racial terrorism is due to pull or push factors. It is likely that both are operating. Women may be attracted to groups that undertake such violence since, although both groups may carry out each kind of terrorism to some degree, groups that practice narrative violence are less likely than those engaged in strategic violence to have the rigid ideological and organizational structures that have excluded women from power and decision-making in the U.S. White-supremacist movement since its inception. Indeed, there have been at least fledgling attempts to organize all-women racist skinhead groups under the joint banner of "White power/women power" (Blee 2002), efforts that would be unimaginable in other parts of the White-supremacist movement. But it is also the case that groups that practice narrative racial terrorism, like White-power skinheads, can be surprisingly receptive to the inclusion of women because their boundaries are loosely guarded, relatively permeable, and often fairly undefined. For example, it can be more difficult to ascertain who is a member of a group that is bound together by the practice of violence and often-fragile and superficial connections between people than a group that has a more clearly defined agenda, strategy, and sense of what constitutes membership. There are instances in which White-power skinheads have later become active in anti-racist skinhead groups that fight racist skinheads, often with a great deal of violence. Such ideological switching is an indication that commitment to violence may outweigh commitment to racist ideas, a phenomenon rarely found among those who practice strategic racial terrorism.

What can be concluded about the relationship between gender and the organization of racial terror? Again, the diversity within organized racism means that any generalization can only be provisional, but the evidence presented here suggests that *women participate in strategic racial terrorism to a lesser extent than they do in narrative racial terrorism, and women participate in strategic racial terrorism largely through indirect means, whereas women participate in narrative racial terrorism more directly.*

Conclusion

Thus far, the relationships of gender to definitions of the enemy and to the organization of racial terror have been considered separately. The brief case studies of White-supremacist groups can also be used to think about the three-way relationships among gender, enemies, and violence, as presented in Table 12.1.

The case in which the state is perceived as the main enemy and violence is narrative in nature (cell A) is rare in the history of modern U.S. White supremacism. The first Ku Klux Klan is the paradigmatic example, and in this Klan, women had no direct involvement either as members or as participants in Klan violence. For the first KKK, women's exclusion is explicable by the specific historical and sociopolitical situation of the

Reconstruction-era South and by this Klan's intense emphasis on White men as the protector of vulnerable White women. Whether women would always be excluded from this type of racial terrorism is unclear because there are no major subsequent racist movements that have this set of characteristics. Indeed, this form of racial terrorism is unlikely to recur in the foreseeable future in the United States as it is associated with situations of profound political uncertainty and fluctuations in the organization of the state, as in the Reconstruction era. With the consolidation of federal state power, racial terrorism directed at the state is much more likely to be strategic in nature, both because the enemy is more clearly defined and because the state has the power to monitor and suppress its opponents.

The case in which racial minorities are the primary enemy group and violence is expressed in a narrative form (cell B) is exemplified today by racist skinheads. In these groups, women generally participate substantially less than do men, but women's role appears to be increasing in recent years. A similar situation exists when the state is the enemy, but violence is strategic in nature (cell C). This is the case with many racial terrorist groups today, especially those that target the state as an agent of Jewish domination. For these groups, too, women tend to participate at considerably lower rates than men, but their participation has increased in recent years and is likely to continue to increase. Both require very public and assertive actions – the street-level violence of skinheads or bombing campaigns of ZOG-focused groups – that contradict traditional ideas about women's passivity and subservience. Further, participation in these forms of racist terrorism challenges the traditional male leadership and public image of such groups. Yet, it is likely that the barriers to women's participation in these forms of racist terrorism will decline over time. Gender ideologies are crumbling in racist groups as elsewhere in U.S. society (Blee 2002). Moreover, media attention to recent instances of women in gender-traditional societies who are involved in terrorism against the state, in such places as Chechnya, Israel, Germany, and Sri Lanka (ABC News 2004b; Cunningham 2003), as well as women's involvement in domestic terrorism against the U.S. government by groups such as the Weather Underground and Black Panther Party (Brown 1994; Zwerman 1994) have provided models for the incorporation of women into these forms of organized racial terror. These factors are likely to result in an increase in women's activity in narrative forms of terror against racial minorities and strategic forms of terror against the state.

The case in which racial minorities are the enemy and violence is expressed in a strategic form (cell D) is different. This is characteristic of groups like the Klan in the 1920s or some Klans and other White-supremacist groups today. In these, women's participation is often high – although always lower than men's – as this organization of racial terror provides structural openings for women to participate without challenging existing ideas about gender hierarchies. Women in these groups often work to facilitate and promote violence behind the scenes or in less directly confrontational

Table 12.1 Gender, enemies, and violence

Type of violence	Definitions of the enemy	
	State	Racial minorities
Narrative	A (no women)	B (some women, increasing)
Strategic	C (some women, increasing)	D (many women, steady)

ways. They recruit and cultivate new racist group members and steer them toward ideas of strategic violence, spray-paint swastikas on houses and cars of new immigrants to convince them to move, and burn crosses in the yards of interracial couples. All of these forms of racial terrorism can be under-taken from within the perimeters of the group's existing gender hierarchies, resulting in a level of women's participation that is higher than other forms of racial terrorism, although unlikely to increase further in the future.

This brief history of women's role in organized U.S. racial terrorism sug-gests that women are fully capable of participating in the most deadly kinds of terrorist activities on behalf of agendas of White or Aryan supremacy. But it also points to the variability of women's involvement in racial terrorism. Although women's participation in racist terrorism has increased over time in the United States, it is not the case that there is a simple temporal pattern to women's involvement in such violence. Rather, the conditions under which women are likely to become involved in racist terrorism reflect not only broader societal changes in the acceptability of women's involvement in politics and in violence, but also the strategic directions and tactical choices of organized White supremacist groups.

Notes

1 *State-Times Morning Advocate*, Baton Rouge, Louisiana, 19 April 2003; online, available at: www.lexis-nexis.com/universe.
2 Heidi Beirich and Mark Potok, "Two Faces of Volksfront." Online, available at: www.splcenter.org/intel/intelreport/article.jsp?aid=475@printable=1; "'To Do the Right Thing.' A Guilty Plea," *News Tribune* (Tacoma, Washington), 26 Feb-ruary 2004.
3 "Domestic Terrorism Ties?" NBC 4, 18 November 2002. Online, available at: www.nbc4.tv/prnt/1793308/detail.html; "ADL Assists in OC White Suprema-cists Arrest," *The Jewish Journal of Greater Los Angeles*. Online, available at: www.jewishjournal.com/home/print.php?id=9642; "Out of the Kitchen: Has the Women's Rights Movement Come to the Extreme Right?" ABC News, 12 December 2003. Online, available at: abcnews.go.com/sections/us/DailyNews/extreme_women021212.html.
4 This excludes individual acts of racial violence, such as hate crimes.
5 Title 22 of the United States Code, Section 2656f(d). Online, available at: www.state.gov/s/ct/rls/pgtrpt/2003/31880.htm.
6 From the DoD definition of terrorism, cited in Cunningham (2003, 188, n. 4).

7 The idea that racist movements express sentiments of anger needs to be used with caution. For a discussion of the theoretical and political implications of understanding emotions such as anger as expressions of individual sentiment versus group-level emotions, see Blee (2005a); see also della Porta (1992).

8 The exact number of lynchings is difficult to determine, both because of the extralegal, secret nature of most lynchings and because of the overlap of lynchings with legal forms of execution of African Americans such as misapplications of the death penalty – what George C. Wright (1990) terms "legal lynchings" (see also Tolnay and Beck 1995).

9 Some groups, especially those who regard local and county government as less likely to be under the control of ZOG, support devolving government power to these levels. Some of these complexities are explored by Levitas (2002).

10 Analysis not reported, but available from the author.

11 Online, available from: www.faughaballagh.com/charity.htm.

12 In this sense, there is a continuum from the loose organization of groups like racist skinheads to the very ephemeral racist groups that operate with little or no lasting organization such as lynch mobs, but this chapter considers only groups with some level of organization.

References

ABC News. 2004a. "Out of the kitchen: has the women's rights movement come to the extreme right?" Accessed from ABCNEWS.com, 5 August 2004.

ABC News. 2004b. "Black Widows: Hell hath no fury like Chechnya's ruthless widows of war." Accessed from ABCNEWS.com, 4 September 2004.

Allen, James. 2000. *Without Sanctuary: Lynching Photography in America*. Santa Fe: Twin Palms.

Bakersfield *Californian*. 2004. "Making fascist statements over frappuccinos," 24 July.

Blazak, Randy. 2001. "White boys to terrorist men: target recruitment of Nazi skinheads," *American Behavioral Scientist*, 44(6), (February), pp. 982–1000.

Blazak, Randy. 2004. "'Getting it': the role of women in male desistence from hate groups," in *Home-Grown Hate: Gender and Organized Racism*, edited by Abby L. Ferber. New York: Routledge, pp. 161–179.

Blee, Kathleen. 1991. *Women of the Klan: Racism and Gender in the 1920s*. Berkeley: University of California Press.

Blee, Kathleen. 2002. *Inside Organized Racism: Women in the Hate Movement*. Berkeley: University of California Press.

Blee, Kathleen. 2005a. "Positioning hate," *Journal of Hate Studies*, 3(1), pp. 95–106.

Blee, Kathleen. 2005b. "Racial violence in the United States," *Ethnic and Racial Studies* 28(4), (July), pp. 599–619.

Brown, Elaine. 1994. *A Taste of Power: a Black Woman's Story*. New York: Anchor/Doubleday.

Chalmers, David M. 1981. *Hooded Americanism: the History of the Ku Klux Klan*. Durham, NC: Duke University Press.

Christensen, Loren. 1994. *Skinhead Street Gangs*. Boulder: Paladin Press.

Cooper, H. 2001. "Terrorism: the problem of definition revisited," *American Behavioral Scientist*, 45, pp. 881–893.

Crenshaw, Martha. 1988. "Theories of terrorism: instrumental and organizational approaches," in *Inside Terrorist Organizations*, edited by David C. Rapoport. New York: Columbia University Press, pp. 13–31.

Cunningham, Karla J. 2003. "Cross-regional trends in female terrorism," *Studies in Conflict and Terrorism*, 26(3), (May–June), pp. 171–195.

Della Porta, Donatella. 1992. "Introduction: on individual motivations in underground political organizations," in *International Social Movement Research*, Vol. 4, *Social Movements and Violence: Participation in Underground Organizations*, edited by Donatella Della Porta. London: JAI Press, pp. 3–28.

Dobie, Kathy. 1997. "Skingirl mothers: From Thelma and Louise to Ozzie and Harriet," in *The Politics of Motherhood: Activist Voices from Left to Right*, edited by Alexis Jetter, Annelise Orleck, and Diana Taylor. Hanover, NH: University Press of New England, pp. 257–267.

Dobratz, Betty A. and Stephanie L. Shanks-Meile. 2004. "The white separatist movement: worldviews on gender, feminism, nature, and change," in *Home-Grown Hate: Gender and Organized Racism*, edited by Abby L. Ferber. New York: Routledge, pp. 113–142.

Federal Bureau of Investigation (FBI). 2002. Hate Crime Statistics. Online, available at: www.fbi.gov/ucr/hatecrime2002.pdf.

Ferber, Abby L. 2004. "Introduction," in *Home-Grown Hate: Gender and Organized Racism*, edited by Abby L. Ferber. New York: Routledge, pp. 1–18.

Fredrickson, George M. 2003. *Racism: a Short History*. Princeton: Princeton University Press.

Gardell, Mattias. 2003. *Gods of the Blood: the Pagan Revival and White Separatism*. Durham, NC: Duke University Press.

Hamm, Mark S. 1994. *American Skinheads: the Criminology and Control of Hate Crimes*. Westport: Praeger.

Hoffman, Bruce. 1998. *Inside Terrorism*. New York: Columbia University Press.

Levitas, Daniel. 2002. *The Terrorist Next Door: the Militia Movement and the Radical Right*. New York: Thomas Dunne Books/St. Martin's Press.

Neidhardt, Friedhelm. 1992. "Left-wing and right-wing terrorist groups: a comparison for the German case," in *International Social Movement Research*, Vol. 4: *Social Movements and Violence: Participation in Underground Organizations*, edited by Donatella della Porta. London: JAI Press, pp. 215–235.

Neuburger, Luisella de Cataldo and Tiziana Valentini. 1998. *Women and Terrorism*. New York: St. Martin's Press.

Patterson, Orlando. 1998. *Rituals of Blood: Consequences of Slavery in Two American Centuries*. Washington, DC: Calvados Counterpoints.

Perry, Barbara. 2002. "Defending the color line: racially and ethnically motivated hate crime," *American Behavioral Scientist*, 46(1), 72–92.

Rogers, Joann, and Jacquelyn S. Litt. 2004. "Normalizing racism: a case study of motherhood in White supremacy," in *Home-Grown Hate: Gender and Organized Racism*, edited by Abby L. Ferber. New York: Routledge, pp. 97–112.

Southern Poverty Law Center (SPLC). 2004. On-line copies of the SPLC *Intelligence Report* and other publications, accessed 5 September 2004. Online, available from: www.splcenter.org.

Talbot, Rhiannon. 2000. "Myths in the representation of women terrorists," *Beire-Ireland: a Journal of Irish Studies*, 35(3), pp. 165–186.

Taylor, Verta. 1989. "Social movement continuity: the women's movement in abeyance," *American Sociological Review*, 54, pp. 761–75.

Tolnay, Stewart E. and E.M. Beck. 1995. *A Festival of Violence: an Analysis of Southern Lynchings, 1882–1930.* Urbana: University of Illinois Press.

Winant, Howard. 2002. *The World is a Ghetto.* New York: Basic Books.

Wright, George C. 1990. *Racial Violence in Kentucky, 1865–1940: Lynchings, Mob Rule, and "Legal Lynchings."* Baton Rouge: Louisiana State University Press.

Zwerman, Gilda. 1994. "Mothering on the lam: politics, gender fantasies and maternal thinking in women associated with armed, clandestine organizations in the United States," *Feminist Review*, 47, pp. 33–56.

13 The portrayal of female terrorists in the media

Similar framing patterns in the news coverage of women in politics and in terrorism

Brigitte L. Nacos

"Her nails manicured and hair pulled back from her face, the Palestinian woman asks that she be called by an Arabic name for a faint star – Suha." Following this opening sentence, the next paragraph revealed that Suha, a future suicide bomber for the Al Aqsa Martyrs Brigade, "is barely 5 feet tall, fair-skinned and pretty, with a quick smile and handshake." The up-front sketch of a beautiful young woman, determined to become a human bomb in order to kill others, was contrasted with the description of her bodyguard as "grim-looking."[1] Whether intended or not, the reader of this article, published in April 2002 in one of the leading U.S. newspapers, was left with the paradox of a pretty girl as suicide terrorist and a tough-looking male as presumably content to live. Three months earlier, an American news magazine published an article that linked terrorism to male hormones. The authors wrote, "Testosterone has always had a lot to do with terrorism, even among secular bombers and kidnappers like Italy's Red Brigade and Germany's Baader–Meinhof gang."[2] Here the reader was explicitly told that terrorism is the domain of men. The implicit message was inescapable as well: females do not fit the terrorist profile.

Contrary to the gender stereotypes in the earlier citations and contrary to conventional wisdom, women terrorists are neither misfits nor rare. Throughout the history of modern terrorism, females have been among the leaders and chief ideologues (i.e., in the American Weather Underground, in Italy's Red Brigade, and Germany's Red Army Faction) and followers in terrorist groups. And today, according to Christopher Harmon, "more than 30 percent of international terrorists are women, and females are central to membership rosters and operational roles in nearly all insurgencies."[3] Other estimates range from 20 percent to 30 percent for many domestic and international terrorist groups. Typically, left-wing organizations have far more female members than conservative organizations. Yet, whenever women commit acts of terror, most people react with an extra level of shock and horror.

There is no evidence that male and female terrorists are fundamentally different in terms of their recruitment, motivation, ideological fervor, and brutality – just as there is no evidence that male and female politicians have fundamentally different motivations for seeking political office and abilities in different policy areas. Yet, the media's treatment of female terrorists is consistent with the patterns of societal gender stereotypes in *general*, and of gender biases in the news coverage of female politicians in particular. In other words, gender stereotypes are found in the news about non-violent and violent political actors.

Research has demonstrated that mass-mediated societal gender stereotypes affect the behavior of female politicians and the campaign tactics of their advisers.[4] Similarly, there is also evidence that gender clichés influence the tactical considerations and decisions of terrorist groups and the behavior of female terrorists. Therefore, the intelligence community, law enforcement, and others involved in the implementation of anti- and counterterrorism would benefit from understanding and highlighting the gap between the stereotypical female terrorist and the reality of gender roles in terrorist organizations.

The research presented here is based on a content analysis of U.S. and non-American English-language print and broadcast news and, to a lesser extent, on an examination of the relevant literature in the field.[5] As an aside, this material also allowed a comparison between American and European reporting. Although European women have won elective and appointed offices in far larger numbers than their American counterparts and increasingly served in the highest-ranking government and party posts (i.e., British Prime Minister Margaret Thatcher), male and female media sources and commentators in Europe are just as likely as their American counterparts to see female terrorists through the prism of gender stereotypes.

Of news frames and stereotypes

Whether print or television, the media tend to report the news along explanatory frames that cue the reader, listener, and viewer to put events, issues, and political actors into contextual frameworks of reference.[6] Framing can and does affect the news in many ways, for example in the choice of topics, sources, language, and photographs. According to Entman, "a frame operates to select and highlight some features of reality and obscure others in a way that tells a consistent story about problems, their causes, moral implications, and remedies."[7] Accordingly, reporters, editors, producers, and others in the news media make constant decisions as to what and whom to present in the news and how. Some framing patterns seem especially important with respect to terrorism news because they have strong effects on the perceptions and reaction of news receivers.

Iyengar, for example, found that in the United States TV-network coverage of terrorism is overwhelmingly episodic or narrowly focused on who did what, where, and how, rather than thematic or contextual, which would explore why terrorism occurs. Furthermore, his research demonstrated that

narrowly focused coverage influenced audiences to hold individual perpetrators responsible, whereas thematic reporting was more likely to assign
responsibility to societal conditions and the policies that cause them. By
highlighting and dwelling on the fact that a woman perpetrated a horrific
act of terrorism, the media frames such news inevitably in episodic terms
and affect news consumers' attribution of responsibility: when exposed to
episodic framing of terrorism, people are more inclined to support tougher
punitive measures against individual terrorists; when watching thematically
framed terrorism news, recipients tend to be more in favor of policies
designed to alleviate the root causes of terror.[8]

A generation ago, Gans concluded that, in the United States, "the news
reflects the white male social order. ..."[9] Although contemporary newsrooms
are more diverse than 25 years ago, entrenched prejudices and stereotypical
perceptions have not disappeared. As one newsman observed more recently,
"Newsrooms are not hermetically sealed against the prejudices that play per-
niciously just beneath the surface of American life."[10] The result is that the
media continue to use different framing patterns in the news about women
and men. Research revealed, for example, that "journalists commonly work
with gendered 'frames' to simplify, prioritize, and structure the narrative
flow of events when covering women and men in public life."[11] Norris found
evidence for the prevalence of sex stereotypes, such as the female compassionate nature and the male natural aggressiveness, that lead people to
expect men and women to behave differently. As a result, "Women in politics are commonly seen as compassionate, practical, honest, and hardwork-
ing, while men are seen as ruthless, ambitious, and tough leaders."[12]
Moreover, by perpetuating these sorts of stereotypes, the news magnifies the
notion that the softness of female politicians qualifies them for dealing
capably with social problems and policies, such as education and welfare,
but not with national security and foreign relations – areas best left to tough
males. Although preferring "stereotypes of women politicians as weak, inde-
cisive, and emotional," the news sometimes reflects the opposite image of
the mean and tough female politician, the "bitch," who does not fit the conventional profile of the soft woman. Or female politicians are portrayed as
"outsiders," the exception, not the norm.[13] Indeed, women are "most newsworthy when they are doing something 'unladylike.' "[14] Researchers found
furthermore that the media report far more on the physical appearances
(their figure, hairstyle, make-up, attire, overall look) and the personal traits
of female candidates and office holders, whereas male politicians receive
more issue-oriented coverage.[15] Female politicians are far more often defined
by their family status than male politicians, and typically identified as the
wives of a multimillionaire husband, the daughters of a well-known politician, the unmarried challengers of male incumbents, the mothers of several
children, and so on.[16] Finally, even after reporting the initial news that a
woman has accomplished another "first," the media tend to forever identify
these females as trailblazers (i.e., Geraldine Ferraro, the first female nominee

for vice-president of a major political party; Madeline Albright, the first female secretary of state).

When we cannot understand women in roles that cultural norms and prejudices perceive as inherently male (i.e., women as political leaders, women as violent political actors), there is a tendency to resort to stereotypical explanations (i.e., her good looks opened doors; her family affected her path; she is tough like a man, not a real woman).

Women terrorists and the media

In the early 1980s, Crenshaw noted that there was "considerable speculation about the prominent position of women in terrorist groups" and that it would be "interesting to find out if female participation in violence will have an effect on general social roles or on the stereotyping of women."[17] To what extent the roles and images of women in social, political, and professional settings have been affected by female terrorist leaders, and perhaps of male terrorists' acceptance of women in leadership roles, is difficult to assess – if there have been such effects at all. But a survey of the limited literature on female terrorists reveals that a number of explanations have been advanced to understand what kind of woman becomes a terrorist and why. Although some of these explications reflect reality, others are rooted in conventional gender stereotypes. More importantly, an analysis of pertinent material in the news media demonstrates that similar framing modes are found in the news about female politicians and female terrorists. The following reporting patterns, images, and stereotypes are most obvious in the way the media portray female terrorists.

The physical appearance frame

In 1995, a year after Idoia Lopez Riano of the Basque separatist organization ETA was arrested and charged with 23 assassinations, Anne McElvoy reported in the *Times* of London that the female terrorist, known as The Tigress, "has the looks of a Mediterranean film star" and "is one of the few women who manages to look good even in a police shot."[18] The Tigress was furthermore described as "wearing hefty eye make-up, fuchsia lipstick and dangling earrings that tinkle as she tosses her hair of black curls."[19] When reading these kinds of descriptions of female terrorists, nobody could be less surprised than women in public life, especially politicians, because they know about the media's interest in the way they look and dress. U.S. Senator Barbara Mikulski of Maryland, for example, has noted that the Baltimore press always described her as "short and round" when she first ran for a seat in the upper chamber of the U.S. Congress. By emphasizing her physical characteristics, the news perpetuated the idea that this candidate did not fit the profile of a United States senator – a tall, trim gentleman.[20] Other female politicians learned, too, that the press paid a great deal of attention to their appearance and that this reporting reflected the predominant cultural sentiments. Thus, after Blanche Lincoln was elected to the U.S. Senate in 1998, she remarked that "it doesn't matter what I say about an issue. If I have a run in my panty hose, that's all anybody will talk about."[21] In other words, when it comes to women, their appearance is deemed more important than their ideas, policies, and positions. This coverage pattern differs from the way the news reports about male politicians.

Just as the media find the physical appearance of women in politics especially newsworthy, the news dwells on the looks, the ready smiles, or the carefully chosen apparel of female terrorists that seem in sharp contrast to the image of a tough terrorist. Thus, a newspaper article about the first female Palestinian suicide bomber, Wafra Idris, began with the sentence, "She was an attractive, auburn haired graduate who had a loving family and likes to wear sleeveless dresses and make-up."[22] In another report, Idris was described as a woman with "long, dark hair tied back with a black-and-white keffiyeh."[23] A report about the wave of "Palestinian women strapping explosives to their bodies and becoming martyrs" on the website of the Christian Broadcasting Network was headlined "Lipstick Martyrs: a New Breed of Palestinian Terrorists."[24] An article in the *New York Times* that emphasized the similarities between a Palestinian suicide bomber and her Israeli victim, both girls in their teens, began with the following words: "The suicide bomber and her victim look strikingly similar. Two high school seniors in jeans with flowing black hair..."[25] A would-be suicide bomber who got cold feet and ended up in an Israeli prison was described in one news account as a "petite, dark 25-year-old with an engaging smile and an infectious giggle" and as a woman who "was well-suited to her job arranging flowers for weddings in her village near Jenin in the West Bank."[26] This attention to the appearance of female terrorists in the news is not a recent trend. More than 30 years ago, Leila Khaled of the Popular Front for the Liberation of Palestine was described as a trim and dark-eyed beauty with sex appeal. Even three decades after Khaled's involvement in terrorism, reporters dwelled on the attention she received as the first female hijacker because of her "beauty," her "pin-up" looks, and her "delicate Audrey Hepburn face."[27] One interviewer told Leila Khaled three decades after her career as a hijacker ended, "You were the glamour girl of international terrorism. You were the hijack queen."[28] And well after Khaled had retired from active terrorist duty, "a Norwegian newspaper made jokes about her 'bombs' [Norwegian slang for breasts] ..."[29]

Not only "The Tigress" Lopez Riano, but other especially brutal women members of ETA have frequently been described as beautiful by reporters themselves, and by the sources they cited. Thus, according to one story, a Spanish man who had met her years ago described Lierni Armendariz, an ETA leader, as "flirtatious, pretty and the furthest away from someone you would think of as a terrorist."[30] As one European reporter put it, "Female terrorists, from Palestinian Leila Khaled to German Ulrike Meinhof, have long fascinated the popular imagination with their frequent combination of feminine charms and ability to kill in cold blood."[31] After her indictment as co-conspirator in a bombing plot in Boston and the revelation that she moved in White-supremacy circles, the news media described the accused young woman as "bright-eyed" and so "attractive" that she "caught the eyes of many men, including World Church founder Matt Hale."[32]

If one takes the news at face value, female terrorists are almost always good-looking, trim, and pleasant. Aside from one reference to the nickname "Fatty" of a leading woman in the Basque separatist organization ETA, there were simply no descriptions of less than pretty women terrorists. Although this focus helps to dramatize the contrast between these women and their violent occupations, readers, listeners, and viewers do not always appreciate such emphasis. As a reader of the *Los Angeles Times* wrote in a letter-to-the-editor, "Your article affectionately describes this particular day's suicide bomber with 'doe-brown eyes and softly curled hair.'... How desensitized are we readers expected to become to these continuing satanic acts, this one committed by a woman?"[33] But such protests have not diminished the media's attention to female terrorists' physical attributes.

To be sure, at times news stories do mention details about the physical characteristics of male terrorists − most of the time in order to explain a particular facet of their actions or of police investigations. When a report on a male terrorist's prison breakout says that he is very slim, this information may explain how he could escape through a small window. Information about a male terrorist's hair color is most likely discussed in the context of color change on the part of a fugitive or captured perpetrator.

The family connection frame

Even though women in politics are no longer the exception in the United States and in comparable liberal democracies, the news media tend to define female politicians based on their family status. When Christine Todd Whitman, who had long been active in New Jersey politics, ran for governor in her state, an article in a leading newspaper characterized her as "the preppy wife of a multimillionaire investment banker." Along the same lines, a female columnist described U.S. Senator Kay Bailey Hutchison as a "typical Republican housewife."[34] In view of this kind of media focus, it is hardly surprising that the news pays a great deal of attention to the family backgrounds of female terrorists. When women terrorists are especially pretty, reporters wonder why they are not married or engaged. The young Leila Khaled preempted such questions when she declared that she was engaged to the revolution. This statement was often cited in reports about the "glamorous" Palestinian terrorist.[35] In the case of the unmarried ETA terrorist Idoia Lopez Riano, the media linked the fact that this beauty was single to her "mythical sexual prowess"[36] and her alleged habit to "picking up police officers, normally ETA targets, in bars and having one-night stands with them."[37]

But just as common are reporters' references to and explorations of female terrorists' family backgrounds that might explain, or not explain, their violent deeds. One instructive example is the catchy sound bite "Black Widows" that the news media coined and repeated over and over again, when reporting on female Chechen terrorists. By invoking the image of the widow, clad from head to toe in black, the news perpetuated the image of the vengeance-seeking widow who becomes a terrorist because her husband was killed by Russian troops – a woman with a strong personal rather than political motive. To be sure, some of these women lost their husbands and others reacted to the violent death or disappearance of their sons, brothers, or fathers. But by lumping them together as "Black Widows" with personal grievances, the media ignored that some, perhaps many, of these women were motivated instead by political grievances.

What the news revealed about Wafra Idris, the female Palestinian suicide bomber who started a wave of similar attacks in January 2002, was based on interviews with her parents, siblings, cousins, other relatives, and her ex-husband. But an allegedly grief-stricken husband seemed more compelling in a human-interest story than one who had divorced the female "martyr." As one correspondent reported, "Ahmed Zaki is a very proud husband indeed – he is the husband of the first female Palestinian suicide bomber, Wafa Idris." By not reporting up front that he had divorced Wafa Idris against her wish because she could not bear him children, and had married another woman, the reporter presented Zaki as the person that knew why Wafa became a suicide bomber: she was "a nationalist," he said. The article mentioned eventually in passing that the couple had separated six months ago, but that the husband (as he was called in the headline) still loved her.[38]

Even in scholarly writings, the family background of female terrorists tends to get far more attention than that of male members of the same organizations. With respect to the Red Army Faction in Germany, for example, references to the parents of Ulrike Meinhof, one of the group's co-founders, have been far more common than similar information about Andreas Baader, also a co-founder. When writing about another leading RAF member, Gudrun Ensslin, experts rarely failed to mention that her father was a Lutheran minister.[39]

Terrorist for the sake of love

Related to the previous category is the popular image of the women terrorist for the sake of love – not for deeply held political reasons. Although seemingly without a parallel in the cliché of female politicians, one can actually construe even a "politician for the sake of love" frame in admittedly extra-ordinary cases: When a woman is appointed to serve out the term of her deceased husband, the widow tends to enjoy – at least initially – a great deal of sympathy in her home district or state, and even beyond. In such situations, political opponents tend to temper their behavior. Although not explicitly stated, there is the notion that a loving wife continues her husband's work after years of supporting him. This, in turn, tempers the behavior of political opponents. But the stereotype of the female terrorist following her lover or husband, or perhaps her father, brother, or cousin, into terrorist groups and activities transcends by far the special circumstances of some female politicians. The "politician for the sake of love" frame differs also from the stereotype of the women who resort to political violence in the wake of personal tragedies or disappointments. Although the idea of terrorism for the sake of love or because of lost love "diminishes women's credibility and influence both within and outside organizations,"[40] as Karla Cunningham has suggested, it has been a common theme emphasized by experts in the field, by reporters, and even by female members of extremist groups. Supporting the notion that females are drawn to terrorism by the men they love, Robin Morgan has argued that most women do not want to admit to that connection. According to Morgan, "These women would have died – as some did – rather than admit that they had acted as they did for male approval and love."[41] Surveying a host of female terrorists and their relationships with male colleagues as well as the many affairs enjoyed by "Carlos, the Jackal" and other male terrorists, Morgan concluded that women in terrorist organizations, whether followers or leaders, are involved in a "rebellion for love's sake [that] is classic feminine – not feminist – behavior."[42] Morgan told an interviewer that female terrorists are "almost always lured into it by a father, a brother or most commonly by a lover."[43] In her view "Carlos, the Jackal" is the perfect example of a pied piper attracting females as a free man, fugitive, and prisoner. As Morgan described it:

> In 1994, after a worldwide manhunt and numerous escapades, the notorious "Carlos, the Jackal" was caught and sentenced to prison for life, following several already incarcerated members of his "harem," his many female lovers (some of whom were aware of his exploits – and each other – and some of whom weren't).[44]

Just as telling was the fact that Carlos's attraction did not wane behind bars: in 2002 he announced his engagement to and plan to marry his French attorney Isabella Coutant, a high-society figure, who characterized their love according to news accounts as a "meeting of hearts and of minds."[45]

The "love connection" has been a frequent theme in the media's coverage of gender terrorism. To explain the large number of female members of the German Red Army Fraction in the 1970s, the news cited male criminologists who said that "a few male terrorists and extremist lawyers in West Germany have had the fanatical devotion of female gang members" and that women join because they "admire someone in the terrorist movement."[46] Female members in White-supremacy organizations, such as the Ku Klux

Klan, also spread the word that most of them joined because of their husbands or boyfriends. According to one long-time female KKK member, a woman who uses the pseudonym Klaliff, "My introduction into the White Pride Movement [WP Movement] was in college where I fell in love with another college student, a man who had been an activist in the WP Movement." She reveals that many women got involved because they had a boyfriend in the Movement. "I cannot speak for all women in the WP Movement," she wrote, "but I see the men in the WP Movement as manly men with strong ideals and courage."[47] The writer notes furthermore that she married her husband because of "his [WP] beliefs."[48] In the recent case of a young woman in Boston, accused of participating in a White-supremacy bomb plot, the media reported that it was her romantic involvement with a former prison inmate that pushed her into a federal conspiracy."[49] Although true in many instances, but not in many others, the media's emphasis on the love connection has produced the cliché of the female "demon lover" following Morgan.

The flip-side of the coin is the girl or woman who acts because of a lost love. When a 20-year-old Palestinian student was recruited as a suicide bomber, she was reportedly "out to avenge the death of her fiancé, a member of a terrorist group." She was said to believe that the young man had been killed by the Israeli military even though the Israelis reported that he had blown himself up in an accident.[50] When reporting on one of ETA's leaders, Maria Soledad Iparaguirre, the news media rarely failed to mention that she allegedly became a brutal terrorist after her boyfriend was shot by the police in the early 1980s.[51]

It has been the exception, not the rule, for the media to scrutinize this conventional image. The writer of one such exceptional article stated,

> There remains a misleading, but popular Patty Hearst image of female terrorists. The idea of women only killing, maiming and bombing when duped by a boyfriend or partner is an alluring one. It allows us to believe that the sexes are different, and to fall in behind all the cosy [sic] discriminations which flow from such a fallacy. Women are not simply brainwashed molls desperate to please hardened criminal lovers. On an individual level, this may hold true for some, but it is insulting to suggest women are so easily led that they will commit murder simply for a partner's approval.[52]

In sum, then, the mass media reinforce the stereotype of the female terrorist for the sake of love. In reality, when it comes to the recruitment of terrorists, both males and females are typically inspired and enlisted by relatives, friends, and acquaintances. In her study of Italy's Red Brigade, della Porta found, for example, that "in as many as 88 percent of the cases in which the nature of the tie with the recruiter is known, she or he is not a stranger; in 44 percent, she or he is a personal friend, and in 20 percent, she or he is a relative."[53] There were no gender differences with respect to recruits and recruiters. Because "the presence of strong affective ties is ... a powerful explanation of individual motivation [to join a terrorist organization],"[54] it can be assumed that some male terrorists, just as their female counterparts, were recruited by their lovers as well. But the news is silent on this angle. It may well be that far fewer men are recruited by women than the other way around. But even when it comes to Muslim extremists, this is not out of the question. The author has seen websites with text that tells "sisters" why they should encourage their husband to join *jihad*.

The women's lib/equality frame

In the past, far more than today, many female politicians tried to perform balancing acts in order to cultivate a positive, mass-mediated image of the capable candidate or office holder and, at the same time, avoid the negative stereotype of the overly aggressive feminist. Seemingly not at all concerned about their public image, female terrorists have often been described as women's lib extremists. Although this was very common in the past, the contemporary news still quite frequently explains the motives of female terrorists as the expression of gender equality or the struggle to achieve gender equality. During the 1970s, when it became clear that women played starring roles in leftist terrorist groups in the United States, Europe, Latin America, and Japan, media sources often explained this phenomenon as a manifestation of women's liberation. Thus, *Newsweek* quoted an expert on the prevention of crime who had said, tongue-in-cheek, "You might say that women terrorists have passed the Equal Rights Amendment and now play a variety of prominent roles."[55] Mentioning in particular the role of females in the Weather Underground and the Symbionese Liberation Army, the article's authors concluded:

> Inevitably, some scholarly analysts claim to see a connection between the recent flowering of the feminist movement and the dramatic upsurge in violent crimes attributed to women since the 1960s. First, the civil rights movement drew women students into the vortex of direct social action; later, anti-war protests baptized them in the harsher politics of confrontation. Before the decade was out, the logic of liberation brought women into the Weather Underground and other terrorist organizations.[56]

Similarly, criminologist Freda Adler explained female terrorist activity, in an interview with the *New York Times*, as a "deviant expression of feminism."[57] According to the *Times*, Dr. Adler said that the publicity surrounding terrorism gives female terrorists "a platform to say, 'I am liberated from past stereotypes, I am accepted in the ultimate masculine roles.'"[58] Earlier, in her book *Sisters in Crime*, Adler wrote, "Despite their broad political pronouncements, what the new revolutionaries [such as the Weather Underground] wanted was not simply urban social gains, but sexual equality."[59] Pointing in particular to the female terrorists of the Symbionese Liberation Army, she added:

> That such women turned so drastically toward a new and highly volatile identity caused a good portion of the nation to ask incredulously, "How could women do this sort of thing?" Perhaps the question itself was the very point of the episode. The fires which consumed the ramshackle Los Angeles house where the small band staged its last shoot-out also burned away a large part of the prevailing American illusion about women.[60]

In Europe, experts provided similar explanations for the large number of female members in terrorist organizations, such as the Red Brigades in Italy and the Red Army Faction in West Germany. According to one news account in 1977, "Italian and German sociologists and news commentators, all of them men, have suggested over the last few weeks that the significant female membership in radical and terrorist groups was an unwelcome consequence of the women's liberation movement."[61] Male sociologists and commentators in Europe were not the only ones to blame women's lib. Sharing this view, a female German politician told the media, "These women demonstratively negate everything that is part of the established feminine character."[62] A male professor in Munich wondered whether these female terrorists "see violence in society as prerogative of males and ask, 'Why shouldn't we participate?' "[63] *Newsweek* quoted the former neighbor of German terrorist Susanne Albrecht as complaining, "She sang Communist songs all night and never cleaned the stairs."[64] Given the prevalence of such attitudes, one West German criminologist told a reporter, "Maybe we are paying the price a little bit for having such a male-dominated society."[65]

In the early 1990s, an American reviewer of British journalist Eileen MacDonald's book *Shoot the Women First* wrote:

> There is no question that most of these women – particularly the younger generation – identify with feminism and with a larger struggle against political oppression. One young Basque woman says, "Men are used to being seen as strong and macho and women are expected to follow them.... But in revolutionary groups, the basic understanding is that we are equal."[66]

More recently, there were many media accounts that explained female terrorists in traditionally male-dominated countries and regions as expressions of gender equality. In early 2002, following the first lethal bombing inside Israel proper by a female suicide attacker, some observers seemed not terribly surprised because, as the media reported, "Palestinian women have been

the most liberated [compared to other Arab societies]" in spite of the fact
that Palestinian society remains male-dominated.[67] For Abdel Hamuda, the
editor of an Egyptian weekly, the first female suicide bombing was a monu-
mental event in that it "shattered a glass ceiling" and "elevated the value of
Arab women and, in one moment, and with enviable courage, put an end to
the unending debate about equality between men and women."[68] His col-
league Mufid Fawzie wrote in the Egyptian daily *Al Aalam al Youm*, "She
bore in her belly the fetus of rare heroism, and gave birth by blowing herself
up. What are the women of velvet chatting in the parlors next to the act of
Wafa Idris?"[69] Although declaring that her purpose was not to "morally
justify" female suicide bombers, the writer of a paper, available on the Internet, wrote nevertheless:

> As an American woman, I rejoice at the implementation of the female
> suicide bomber for the same reason Muslim women rejoiced. It is the
> purest form of enactment and dissention against Islamic fundament-
> alism. Moreover, the female suicide bomber empowers Muslim women
> to no longer accept their inferior status. But while western societies hail
> the trend of gender equality in Muslim society, the use of the female
> suicide bomber as a way to achieve gender equality is not comprehended
> nor accepted.[70]

In a lengthy commentary in the *Chicago Tribune*, a terrorism expert noted
that by "attacking the Israelis, these female suicide bombers are fighting for
more than just national liberation; they are fighting for gender liberation."[71]
She pointed out that the funeral held for Wafa Idris, the first Palestinian
woman to carry out a successful suicide mission, "looked like a feminist
rally, with hundreds of women paying her homage. Female students all over
the West Bank and Gaza City say they want to be next in line for a bombing
mission." But in the end, the female commentator rejected suicide bombing
as a means to advance the women's-rights movement and recommended
"peaceful resistance and civil disobedience" as appropriate strategies, not
human rights violations.

The tough-as-males/tougher-than-men frame

When female politicians rise to the very top, they are often described as
particularly tough females. Thus, British Prime Minister Thatcher was frequently called "the Iron Lady." Similarly, there is the mass-mediated notion
of the female terrorist who, in order to prove that she belongs, tends to be
more fanatical, more cruel, more deadly. More than 25 years ago, a female
German politician said in an interview about female terrorists in West
Germany and Italy, "Women, unfortunately, can be particularly fanatical."[72]
At least some former terrorists seem to agree. Matias Antolin, the author of
a book about female members of the Basque ETA organizations, told a

correspondent, "Once in an active service unit they tend to be more cold-blooded and more lethal than the men because they have to prove their worth."[73] Reports about the violent take-over of a Moscow theater by heavily armed Chechen men and women emphasized that the females were "the most determined and aggressive of the hostage takers" and that they were especially "cruel and threatening and eager to die. ..."[74]

Another image creeps into the tough-as-male frame – that "of the terrorist as lesbian, because everyone knows no 'real woman' would hijack planes or cripple middleage men by shooting them in the kneecaps."[75] But apart from the lesbian label, the idea that terrorists are not "real women" tends to be expressed especially in the context of the mother who chooses political violence over her own children. Such was the case of the Red Army Faction's Ulrike Meinhof and Gudrun Ensslin who reportedly "put contacts with their children completely out of their minds, presumably because they interfered with their soldierly poses, Ensslin from the beginning and Meinhof from Christmas 1973."[76] It speaks to the prevalent double standard with respect to gender roles that similar issues have not been raised in the media or the scholarly literature with respect to male terrorists who happen to be fathers.

The bored, naive, out-of-touch-with-reality frame

This last stereotype seems the only one without obvious parallels in the mass-mediated depiction of women politicians. With respect to female terrorists, the notion of the naive, bored, non-political, out-of-touch-with-reality woman who turns to terrorism is perpetuated in the media – mostly by news sources, sometimes by reporters themselves. In the late 1970s, a female criminologist said in an interview:

> Sometimes a woman turns to terrorism out of simple boredom. It sounds strange, I know, but boredom is one of the pathetic rights and privileges of the middle-class woman. What does a middle-class woman do who doesn't happen to be interested in a career or college? What does she do in 1978?[77]

Around the same time, a male professor in West Germany said that women who become terrorists have "deficiencies in their socialization process."[78] Probably because most of the females in the Baader–Meinhof group were former students, this professor described West Germany's females in general as "unpolitical" and his own female students as "sort of educated housewives."[79]

More than 20 years later, after interviewing two young women who had been recruited by a male cousin to plant incendiary devices in a store in Bahrain, the interviewer wrote a story that was headlined, "From Boredom to Bombs: Two Female Terrorists." The report described the women as non-political and clueless about the motives of the young man who had recruited them. Pondering what he called a "naïve response," the male interviewer wrote, "I concluded half-way through the interview, there is no crusade here to spread the word of Islam, or to overthrow the regime then! I had the strong suspicion that many arson attacks are copycat attacks by bored kids."[80] Not surprisingly, there are no comparable news accounts of male terrorists whose motivation is said to be boredom.

Implications of the "feminine paradox" for anti- and counterterrorism

Gender stereotypes persist in the mass-mediated portrayal of women, whether they are involved in legitimate political activities (campaigning for and filling public offices) or in political roles that are widely perceived to be illegitimate (joining terrorist groups and carrying out terrorist acts). But whereas the stereotypical framing patterns of female politicians weakened somewhat in the last two decades or so, the entrenched gender cliches have proved far more enduring in the mass-mediated portrayal of women terrorists. Women in politics have come a long way. Today, many people can imagine a female U.S. president some time in the future. Strangely, however, although women figure prominently into the history of terrorism, the female terrorist continues to be perceived as an exception to the rule. In a welcome departure from the common coverage patterns, the writer of an article in USA Today asked readers to close their eyes "and imagine a woman – perhaps of slight build, perhaps a young mother – piloting American Airlines Flight 11 into the World Trade Center."[81] Although deeming the scenario difficult to imagine, the writer concluded that "it can happen, and we need to think about the possibilities."[82]

Even in the recent past, realistic assessment of female terrorists and the threats they pose were rare in the media. Instead, the news has continued to frame these stories along the lines of traditional stereotypes that portray the female terrorist as a paradox. Because these clichés tend to cue readers, viewers, and listeners to resort to deeply ingrained gender stereotypes in order to process and make sense of the news, they are likely to affect the opinions and attitudes of the general public and people charged with fighting terrorism as well. As a result, women are thought to have a far better chance than their male comrades to carry out terrorist attacks without being suspected and intercepted. According to one expert:

> Women are able to use their gender to avoid detection on several fronts: first, their "non-threatening" nature may prevent in-depth scrutiny at the most basic level as they are simply not considered important enough to warrant investigation; second, sensitivities regarding more thorough searches, particularly of women's bodies, may hamper stricter scrutiny, and third, a woman's ability to get pregnant and the attendant changes to her body facilitate concealment of weapons and bombs using

maternity clothing as well as further impeding inspection because of impropriety issues.[83]

Terrorists have been aware of these tactical advantages for a long time. With respect to the Red Army Faction, Harmon wrote:

> German male terrorist "Bommi" Bauman of the late Second of June Movement has observed that "Women can get closer to the target. If a man in a high position, perhaps knowing that he may be a target for terrorists, is approached by a woman, he may think, she is a prostitute. Women can go straight to the target's doorstep; sometimes they do it in pairs, two women, saying they are lost. If two men approached him, he would be suspicious."[84]

What Bauman described was precisely the script for several of the kidnappings and assassinations conducted by West German terrorists in which women exploited the fact that they were not as suspicious as men – although it was well known that females were well represented in these groups. Terrorists elsewhere followed this blueprint as well. Before Dhanu, a female member of the Black Tiger's, assassinated Rajiv Gandhi, she had "garlanded him, bowed at his feet, and then detonated a bomb that killed them both. . . ."[85] Playing the role of a female admirer of Gandhi, she did not have any problem getting close to him. It is telling that one of the members of a two-person back-up team was a young woman as well. The Kurdish Workers Party, too, decided to use female members for suicide attacks because of their tactical advantages. More recently, a wave of attacks against Russian targets by female Chechen suicide bombers succeeded because these women were able "to move more freely than Chechen men, who are routinely harassed by Russia's police and security services."[86]

Groups that have shied away from recruiting female terrorists in the past manage to surprise their targets when they make changes in this respect. In early 2004, after Hamas claimed responsibility for dispatching the first female suicide bomber to kill Israelis, the group's spiritual leader, Sheik Ahmed Yassin, cited "purely tactical reasons," when asked why his organization had decided on selecting a woman, saying, "It could be that a man would not be able to reach the target, and that's why they had to use a woman."[87] For the same reason, Al Qaeda and similar groups are likely to recruit women to carry out terror attacks. Indeed, in early 2003, American law-enforcement officials learned that bin Laden's organization planned to enlist women to infuse an element of surprise into the terror war against the United States.[88] In early 2004, European intelligence services monitored a conversation between Al Qaeda terrorists in which the ringleader revealed that a female operative had been discovered, but that there were other female recruits.[89]

Security officials in some societies came to understand over time that female terrorists were just as likely as their male comrades to commit deadly acts of terrorism. When West Germany was faced with a wave of terror by the Red Army Faction and its successor groups, the country's anti-terrorism units were allegedly ordered by their superiors to "shoot the women first."[90] In responding to the increased attacks by Chechen females, Russian authorities expanded their security checks to women in traditional Muslim attire. One wonders, therefore, whether the gender advantage of female terrorists will disappear altogether. For this to happen, it is not enough for top officials to understand that the female paradox in terrorism is a myth – rather, the men and women who implement anti- and counterterrorist policies day-in and day-out must have this understanding as well and must act accordingly.

Unfortunately, even in societies that have experienced repeated attacks by women terrorists, there remains a tendency to view and treat males and females differently. Israel is a perfect example here. After the country was hit repeatedly by female suicide bombers, Israeli security personnel still made a gender distinction, as demonstrated in January 2004: when a 22-year-old Palestinian woman, pretending to be crippled, told Israelis at a Gaza checkpoint that she had metal plates in her leg that would sound the alarm, they allowed her to wait for a woman to search her in a special area. Moments later, the woman blew herself up and killed four Israelis. Lamenting the cynical exploitation of his soldiers' consideration for the dignity of women, the officer in charge said:

> We're doing our best to be humanitarian, to consider the problems associated with searching women. She said she had a medical problem, that's why the soldiers let her in, to check her in private because she is a woman. That's a very cruel, cynical use of the humanitarian considerations of our soldiers.[91]

Conclusion: gender stereotypes and counterterrorism

In conclusion, then, there is no doubt that gender clichés persist in the mass-mediated portrayal of women, whether they are involved in legitimate political activities or in political roles widely perceived to be illegitimate. But whereas the stereotypical framing patterns of female politicians weakened somewhat in the last several decades, the entrenched gender frames have proved more enduring in the mass-mediated portrayal of women terrorists. Because these kinds of news frames reflect and reinforce deep-seated societal attitudes, terrorist groups are able to take advantage of their target societies' gender prejudices. Therefore, the lesson is that gender reality must inform the measures designed to prevent and respond to terrorism and, perhaps more important, the implementation of anti- and counterterrorist policies. Otherwise, terror groups will increasingly exploit the tactical advantages of female terrorists in target societies that deem women far less suspect and dangerous than men.

Notes

1 Greg Zoroya, "Her decision to be a suicide bomber." *USA Today*, 22 April 2002, p, A1. Retrieved from the ProQuest archive on 1 November 2003.
2 Christopher Dickey and Gretel C. Kovach, "Married to Jihad." *Newsweek*, 14 January 2002, p. 48.
3 Christopher C. Harmon, *Terrorism Today* (London: Frank Cash, 2000), p. 212.
4 Kim Fridkin Kahn, *The Political Consequences of Being a Woman: How Stereotypes Influence the Conduct and Consequences of Political Campaigns* (New York: Columbia University Press, 1996).
5 I used "female terrorist," "woman (as) terrorist," "women (as) terrorist," and "female suicide bomber" to retrieve articles and transcripts from the LexisNexis and ProQuest archives for all available dates.
6 See, Pippa Norris, ed., *Women, Media, and Politics* (New York: Oxford University Press, 1997).
7 Robert M. Entman, "Reporting environmental policy debate: the real media biases." *Harvard International Journal of Press/Politics*, 1(3), (1996), pp. 77, 78.
8 Shanto Iyengar, *Is Anyone Responsible?* (Chicago: University of Chicago Press, 1991), pp. 26–45.
9 Herbert J. Gans, *Deciding What's News* (New York: Vintage Books, 1980), p. 61.
10 David K. Shiper, "Blacks in the newsroom." *Columbia Journalism Review*, May, June 1998, p. 28.
11 Norris, *Women, Media, and Politics*, p. 6.
12 Ibid., p. 7.
13 Maria Braden, *Women Politicians and the Media* (Lexington: University of Kentucky Press, 1996), especially chapter 1.
14 Braden, *Women Politicians and the Media*, p. 4.
15 Braden, *Women Politicians and the Media*; James Devitt, "Framing gender and the campaign trail: women's executive leadership and the press" (Washington, DC: Women's Leadership Fund: 1999).
16 For examples, see Braden, *Women Politicians and the Media*; and Devitt, "Framing Gender and the Campaign Trail."
17 Martha Crenshaw, "Introduction: reflection on the effects of terrorism," in *Terrorism, Legitimacy and Power: The Consequences of Political Violence,* Martha Crenshaw, ed. (Middletown, CT: Wesleyan University Press, 1983), p. 24.
18 Anne McElvoy, "The Trapping of a Tigress." *The Times* (London), 9 September 1995.
19 Ibid.
20 Braden, *Women Politicians and the Media*, pp. 5, 6.
21 Cited in Sean Aday and James Devitt, "Style over substance: newspaper coverage of female candidates." The Second in the White House Project Education Fund Series: Framing Gender on the Campaign Trail, 2000, p. 5.
22 Christopher Walter, "Twisted by anger, she turned to terror." *The Times* (London), 31 January 2002.
23 National Public Radio's program, "All Things Considered," 7 February 2002.
24 CBN.com, retrieved 4 November 2003.
25 Joel Greenberg, "2 girls, divided by war, joined in carnage." *New York Times*, 5 April 2002, p. A1.
26 Media organizations in Europe and in North America frequently reported on the Chechen "black widows," especially after a large group of heavily armed Chechen women and men seized a Moscow theater with hundreds of Russians inside in October 2002.
27 Katharine Viner, "Palestinian liberation fighter Leila Khaled." The *Guardian* (UK), 26 January 2001.

28 Philip Baum interviewed Khaled for *Aviation Security International*. See www.avsec.com/editorial/leilakhaled.htm.
29 Viner, "Palestinian liberation fighter Leila Khaled."
30 Antonella Lazzeri, "They're deadly, they are ruthless, they're women." The *Sun* (UK), 4 August 2002.
31 Sinikka Tarvainen, "The life of female terrorists: guns, reluctant sex, and longing." Deutsche Presse Agentur, 2 November 1997, BC Cycle.
32 Thanassis Cambanis, "Witness tells of accused pair's ties." *Boston Globe*, 17 July 2002, p. B4. The full name of Hale's white-supremacist hate organization is "World Church of the Creator."
33 The letter-to-the-editor appeared in the *Los Angeles Times* on 2 February 2002, p. M4, in response to an article headlined "Palestinian bomber stood out from the rest," published on 31 January 2002.
34 Braden, *Women Politicians and the Media*, pp. 150, 162.
35 See, for example, Bernard Weintraub, "Woman hijacker feels 'engaged to the revolution.'" *New York Times*, 9 September 1970, p. 19.
36 McElvoy, "The Trapping of a Tigress."
37 Giles Tremlett, "ETA brings women fighters to the fore." The *Guardian* (UK), 27 August 2002, p. 13.
38 Alex Williams, "Exclusive: suicide bomber's husband on why he is proud of her military act." The *Mirror* (UK), 1 February 2002, p. 15.
39 See, for example, Thomas G. Otte, "Red Army Faction: the Baader–Meinhof Gang." In *Encyclopedia of World Terrorism, Volume 3*, Martha Crenshaw and John Pimlott, eds (Armonk, NY: M.E. Sharpe, 1997), pp. 552–556.
40 Karla J. Cunningham, "Cross-national trends in female terrorism." *Studies in Conflict & Terrorism*, 26(3), (May–June 2003), p. 163.
41 Robin Morgan, *The Demon Lover: the Roots of Terrorism* (New York: Washington Square Press, 2001), p. 204.
42 Ibid., p. 208.
43 Judy Mann, "Terrorism and the cult of manly men." *Washington Post*, 19 December 2001, p. C10.
44 Morgan, *The Demon Lover*, p. xv.
45 Ibid.
46 Michael Getler, "Women play growing role in slayings by West German terrorist groups." *Washington Post*, 6 August 1977.
47 Klaliff, "Women in the White Pride Movement." Online, available at: women.stormfront.org/writings/women.htm (accessed 20 October 2003).
48 Ibid.
49 Thanassis Cambanis, "Witness tells of accused pair's ties." *Boston Globe*, 17 July 2002, p. B4.
50 James Bennett, "Rash of new suicide bombers exhibit no patterns or ties." *New York Times*, 21 June 2002, p. A1. Arien Ahmed did not go through with the suicide mission and ended up in an Israeli jail.
51 See, for example, Tremlett, "ETA brings women fighters to the fore."
52 Linda Watson-Brown, "Gender warriors." The *Scotsman*, 26 September 2000, p. 4.
53 Donatella della Porta, "Left-wing terrorism in Italy," in *Terrorism in Context*, Martha Crenshaw, ed. (University Park: Pennsylvania State University Press, 1995), p. 141.
54 Ibid.
55 Kenneth L. Woodward and Phyllis Malamud, "Now, the violent woman." *Newsweek*, 6 October 1975, p. 29.
56 Ibid.
57 Judy Klemesrud, "A criminologist's view of women terrorists." *New York Times*, 9 January 1979, p. A24.

58 Ibid.
59 Freda Adler, *Sisters in Crime* (New York: Waveland Press, 1975), p. 20.
60 Ibid., pp. 21, 22.
61 Paul Hofmann, "Women active among radicals in Western Europe." *New York Times*, 14 August 1977, p. 7.
62 Hanna-Renate Laurien, a conservative, was quoted by Kim Wilkinson, "The hit women." *Newsweek*, 15 August 1977, p. 30.
63 Getler, "Women playing growing role in slayings."
64 Ibid.
65 Ibid.
66 Susan Jacoby, "Terrorism is women's work too." *Washington Post*, 2 October 1992, p. C8.
67 Libby Copeland, "Female suicide bombers: the new factor in Mideast's deadly equation." *Washington Post*, 27 April 2002, p. C1.
68 James Bennett, "Arab press glorifies bomber as heroine." *New York Times*, 11 February 2002, p. 8.
69 Ibid.
70 Laura Ann Trombley, "Female suicide bomber: the newest trend in terrorism." Online, available at: www.nyu.edu/classes/keefer/joe/tromb1.html.
71 Stephanie Shemin, "Wrongheadedness of female suicide bombers." *Chicago Tribune*, 18 June 2002, p. 23.
72 Hofman, "Women active among radicals."
73 Tremlett, "ETA brings women fighters to the fore."
74 Peter Goodspeed, "Cruel 'black widows' eager to die." *National Post* (Canada), 30 October 2002, p. 3.
75 Jacoby, "Terrorism is women's work too."
76 Peter H. Merkl, "West German left-wing terrorism," in *Terrorism in Context*, Martha Crenshaw, ed. (University Park: Pennsylvania State University Press, 1995), pp. 161–210.
77 Klemesrud, "A criminologist's view of women terrorists."
78 Getler, "Women playing growing role in slayings."
79 Ibid.
80 Adel Darwish, "From boredom to bombs – two female terrorists." *WIN Magazine*, April 1999.
81 Patricia Pearson, "Hard to imagine female bad guy? Think again." *USA Today*, 30 January 2002, p. 13A.
82 Ibid.
83 Cunningham, "Cross-national trends in female terrorism," pp. 171, 172.
84 Harmon, pp. 219, 220.
85 Cunningham, "Cross-national trends in female terrorism," p. 180.
86 Steven Lee Myers, "Female Suicide Bombers Unnerve Russians." *New York Times*, 7 August 2003, p. 1.
87 Hamas's first female suicide bomber was Reem al-Reyashi, a 22-year-old mother of two small children. Yassin was quoted in Greg Myre, "Gaza mother, 22, kills four Israeli soldiers." *New York Times*, 15 January 2004, p. A3.
88 Online, available at: stacks.msnbc.com/news/888153.asp.
89 Elaine Sciolino, "Terror suspect in Italy linked to more plots." *New York Times*, 11 June 2004, p. A3.
90 "Shoot the Women First" was therefore chosen as the title of a book exploring the phenomenon of female terrorists. See Eileen MacDonald, *Shoot the Women First* (New York: Random House, 1992).
91 Brigadier-General Gadi Shamni, the Gaza divisional commander, was quoted in Chris McGreal, "Human-bomb mother kills for Israelis at Gaza checkpoint." The *Guardian* (UK), 15 January 2004, p. 17.

Index

9/11 54, 60, 128

ABC News 210, 212
abductions 16–17, 171–2
abeyance support 209
Abu Aisha, Darin 133–4, 135–6
academic theory 74, 79–82
Addario, L. 94
Addelson-Payne, K. 74
Adler, Freda 226–7
Afaq Arabiya 27
Afghanistan 86
Africa 171–2
age 107–8; *see also* children
Agence France Presse 187
Ahmed, Lynsey 148–9
Aisheh, Dareen Abu 27
Akhmedova, Khapta 6, 91, 100–18
Akras, Ayat 11
al Alan al Youm 228
al Aqsa Martyrs Brigade 5, 26, 89, 217
al Jazeerah News 21, 94
al Khansa 6, 93
al Sharq al-Awsat 28
al-Akhras, Ayat 134, 136
al-'Ayyiri, Yusuf 44, 45–6, 85
al-Amaliyyat al-istishhadiyya fi al-mizan al-fiqhi 42–3
al-Bas, Wafa 141–2
al-Batsh, Majeda 88
al-Ghani, Abd 38
al-Hassan, Sheikh Abu 27, 28
al-Jihad wa-l-qital fi al-siyasa al-shara'iyya 41–2
al-Khayyat, S. 149, 150
al-Mawlawi, Faysal 43
al-Najar, Fatma Omar 90, 131
al-Nakbah women's movement 25
al-Qadir, Nizar abd Riyyan 43
al-Qaeda: attacks against US 51, 231; and

Chechnya terrorism 128-9; expansion of
network 53, 59–60; Saudi Arabian branch
45–6; training bases 93; women's roles 6,
20–1
al-Qaradawi, Yusuf 43
al-Rishawi, Sajida Mubarak 95
al-Riyashi, Reem 28, 29
al-Riyyan, Nizar 44
al-Sha'ab 49
al-Takruri, Nawaf 42–3
al-Tamimi, Ahlam 89
al-Taqatiqah, Abndalib Suleiman 28
al-Zarqawi 95
al-Zawahiri, Ayman 93
Albrecht, Susanne 227
Aldrovandi, Mara 14
Ali-Khansa 61
Alison, Miranda 185
All Nepalese Women's Revolutionary
Organization 190
Allen, James 205, 206
Amnesty International 70
analysis, suicide bombers: initial anaylsis
50–1; overview 49–50; projections
59–62; recent activity 51–6; way ahead
62–4
analytical gaps 56–9
anti-Semitism 206
anti-terrorism, implications of "feminine
paradox" 230–2
Antolin, Matias 228–9
Arafat, Yasser 26–9
Ardovini-Brooker, J. 13
Aretxaga, Begoña 81
Armendariz, Lierni 221
Army of Roses (Victor) 133
Arquilla, John 13
Asha, Iman 26
Asharq al-Awsat 20–1
Asia 183–97

assassination plots 187
assistance 157–8
Atran, Scott 52, 136

Bader-Meinhof group 1, 13, 229
Bairakova, Zareta 125
Balachanddran, P.K. 187
Balasingham, Adele 24–5
Baraev, Arbi 113
Barakat, Halim 148–9
Barayev, Hawa 19–20, 43, 45–6
Barayev, Movsar 128
Barayeva, Khava 91, 100, 113
Basayev, Shamil 128–9
Basque ETA organizations 228–9
Bauman "Bommi" 231
Beck, E.M. 206
behavior, understanding of 58–9
Beichman, Arnold 93
Berko, Anat 8, 135, 146–61
Beslan school incident 100–17, 124, 128–9
betrayal 69–72
Bhatia, Shyam 94
bin Laden, Usama 94–5
Bizleva, Zura 113
Black Tiger suicide unit, LTTE 24, 186, 187, 231
"Black Widows" 19–20, 100–18, 122–30, 223
Blazak, Randy 202, 210
Blee, Kathleen 9, 201–13
Blood Rites (Ehrenreich) 69, 79–80
Bloom, Mia 52, 147
boredom 229–30
Bose, Sumatra 186
Bosnians, religious sentiments 52
Brown, Elaine 212
Brunner, Claudia 147, 160
Buddhist Sinhalese society 185–8
Bush, George W. 11

Californian 209
Cambodia 170
Cape Town Principles (UN) 169
casualties, women as 72–4
Chalmers, David M. 203
Chase, Erica 209
Chechnya: Black Widows 122–30; Nationalism and Salafi/Wahhbibism 90–2; tandem bombings 60; women's roles 2, 5–6, 52, 84–6, 231, 232
Cherkizov, Andrei 123
Chicago Tribune 228
childbearing 107–8

children 17, 61–2; in rebel forces/terrorism 178–9; in Sierra Leone/Uganda 172–8; as soldiers 168–72; and terrorist acts 167–79
Christensen, Loren 210
Christian Broadcasting Network 221
classical background, Islam 38–9
classical *jihad* material 39–41
CNN 28, 57
coercive recruitment 16–17, 155–9
collective past 22
Colombia 170
Communist Party of Nepal–Maoist (CPN–M) 189–91
community responses, child soldiers 177–8
community support 55–6, 63
Compact Revolutionary Zones (CRZs), West Bengal 189
conservative societies 15–18
contemporary legal literature, Islam 41–3
Cook, David 7, 20, 37–47, 84–5, 93
Cooper, H. 203
counterterrorism: and gender stereotypes 232; implications of "feminine paradox" 230–2
Covenant, Sword, and the Arm of the Lord (CSA) 208
Crenshaw, Martha 146, 202, 220
Cross Regional Trends in Female Terrorism 56, 60, 62
Cruez, Dexter 187
Cunningham, Karla 7–8, 84–96, 186, 202, 206, 212, 224

Daghles, Mohamed 89
damaged goods, women as 131–44
Daraghmeh, Hiba 5
Dartez, Holly 201, 202, 209
Davis, Joyce 3
Dawr al-nisa' fi jihad al-'ada' 45
de Alwis, Malathi 188
de Certeau, Michel 81–2
de Silva, Chanrda 186
Degauque, Muriel 6, 95
della Porter, Donnatella 225–6
demobilization, child soldiers 177
demographic data 107–8
Dickey, Christopher 93
diplomacy 63–4
disarmament, child soldiers 177
dispatchers 135–7, 158–9
Diwanji, A.K. 188
Dobie, Kathy 209, 210
Dobratz, Betty A. 209
domestic terrorism 184–5

Dubrovka theatre siege 5, 100–17, 128–9
Duiker, William J. 192, 193, 194
Duke, David 203
Dura, Muhammad 156
Dying to Kill (Bloom) 52

early modern terrorism 13–15
Echo of Moscow 123
economic support 64
education 108
Ehrenreich, Barbara 69, 79–80
El Sarraj, Eyed 146
emotional support 157–8
employment 108–9
enemy, perceptions of 203–7
Ensslin, Gudrun 223, 229
Entman, Robert M. 218
Erez, Edna 146–61
Eritrea 170
Ethiopia 170
Eubank, William 13

failed suicide bombers 137–42
family commitments 136–7
family connections 222–3
family, importance of 148–50
Faranda, Adriana 13
fard 'ayn 41, 45, 85–6, 92, 93, 95–6
fard kifaya 41, 85
Farrell, William R. 195, 196
Fatah 26
fatwas 20, 43, 85, 92
Fawzie, Mufid 228
FBI 207, 208
Federal Security Board (FSB), Russia 128
Felton, Leo 209
Female Suicide Bombers 49
"feminine paradox" 230–2
Ferber, Abby L. 209
Fernea, E.W. 149, 150
Ferrandi, Mario 14
Fighel, Yoni 156
fighters, child soldiers as 175–7
fighting back 74–7
Frederickson, G.M. 207
Frye, Tristain 201, 210
fugitive status 111

Gadzhiev, General Gaidar 125
Galvin, Deborah 167–8
Gandhi, Rajiv 186, 187, 231
gang-pressing 171
Ganleva, Fatima and Khadjat 113
Gardell, Mattias 209

Gazueva, Aiza 114–15, 124–5
gender relations, Palestine 148–50
gender roles, US 205–6
gender stereotypes 220–30; and
   counterterrorism 232
gendered war 69–82
Georges-Abeyies, Daniel E. 184
Glaser, Barney G. 151
global expansion 53
global involvement, child soldiers 169–71
global *jihadi* movement (GJM) 84–96
Goldstein, Joshua 186, 192
Gonzalez-Perez, Margaret 9, 183–97
Gottschang Turner, Karen 193, 194
Greenwood, Christine 201–2, 208–9
Grosscup, Beau 186
group cohesion 209
guerrilla groups, definition 184
Gupta, Kanchan 189, 190
Gurr, Ted 13

Hadid, Diaa 90
Hafez, Monhammed M. 146, 158
hajj 45–6, 85
Hale, Matt 222
Hamas: analysis of 21–2, 26–9; and *fatwas*
   44–5, training 52–3; women's roles 12,
   231
Hamm, Mark S. 210
Hammami, Rema 88
Hammer, Julianne 89
Hamuda, Abdel 228
Handel, Joel 13
Harmon, Christopher 217, 231
Hasan, Manar 149, 150
Hassan, Riaz 147
Hasso, Frances H. 147, 160
Haykal, Khayr Muhammad 41–85
Hearst, Patricia 174, 225
Helie-Lucas, Marieme 15, 17, 18
hierarchical organization 207–9
High Islamic Council, Saudi Arabia 20, 85
"*Hijab* Campaign" 88–9
Hindi Tamil society 185–8
Hindu culture 23–5
Hizbollah 18, 19
Hoffman, Bruce 18, 19, 23, 202
Human Rights Watch 175–6
Hutchison, Kay Bailey 222

Ibn Abi al-'Asim 40
Ibn al-Nahhas al-Dumyati 40–1
Ibn Babawayhi 39–40
ideological range, Islamist groups 87

Idris, Wafa 1, 4–5, 26, 27, 28, 89, 132, 133, 135, 138, 221, 223, 228
India 170, 186, 188–9, 197
Indian National Army 23
information operations 64
Institute for Conflict Management 190
Institute for Counter-Terrorism (ICT) 49, 50
International Coalition to Stop the Use of Child Soldiers 169, 170
International Policy Institute for Counterterrorism 196
international terrorism 184–5
Internet 60–1, 154–5
interviews: failed suicide bombers 137–42; friends/relatives of Chechen martyrs 124–50; Palestinian would-be suicide bombers 150–1; psychological autopsy method 105–6
intra-state wars 167–79
Iparaguirre, Maria Soledad 225
Iran–Iraq War 19
Iranian revolution (1979) 18, 19
Iraq 59, 60
Islam 5–6: classical background 38–9; classical *jihad* material 39–41; contemporary legal literature 41–3
Islamic groups, political/ideological range of 87–90
Islamic Ruling on the Permissibility of Martyrdom Operations 43–4, 46
Islamic Student Union 139–40
Israel 170; antagonism towards 156
Israel Defense Forces (IDF) 141, 153–4
Israeli, R. 147, 149, 150, 160
Israeli–Palestinian conflict 25–9
Italian Marxist/Communist armed resistance 14
Iyengar, Shento 218–19
Izvestya 129

Jadarat, Hanadi 28
Jamaat-i-Islami 94
Jane's Intelligence Review 15
Japanese Red Army (JRA) 13, 191, 194–6
Jaradat, Henadi 136–7
Jayawardena, Kumari 186, 188
Jenkins, Brian 13, 184
jihad 5, 12, 19–22, 26–9, 37–47, 53; and women 85–6; *see also* global *jihadi* movement
jihadist ideology as psychological first aid 115–17
Jones, Clayton 193
Jones, James 192
Joshi, C.L. 24, 186

Juergensmeyer, Mark 147
Jumaa, Faiza Amal 142
justification, rhetorical strategies for 21–9

Kadyrov, Akhmad 127
Kapitan, Tomas 184
Katz, Jack 151
Kazuko, Shiomi 195
Khaled, L. 15–16, 17, 221, 222
Khalid, Leila 1, 4, 13, 88
Khandaq, Battle of (627) 38
Khildekhoroeva, Lida 113
Khmer Rouge 170
Khomeini, Ayatollah 19
Kirk, Robin 17
Korbin, Nancy 59–60, 149
Ku Klux Klan 201–2, 203, 204–7, 209–12, 224–5
Kurdistan Workers Party (PKK) 2, 16, 63–4, 170, 231
Kuriyama, Yoshihiro 194, 195

Laqueur, Walter 184
Laronga, Bruno 14
"leaderless resistance" 208
leaders, women as 61
left-wing groups 13–15, 84
Levy, Darlene G. 183
Liberation Tamil Tigers of Eelam (LTTE): and children 170, 172; gendered war 69–72, 74; leadership 61; and secular terrorism 12, 16, 18, 21–5, 197; women's roles 2, 62, 185–8
Liberians United for Reconciliation and Democracy (LURD) 170–1
life trajectories 100–18
Lincoln, Blanche 221
Litt, Jacqueline S. 209
"Long Haired Army" 192
Lopez Riano, Idoia 220, 221, 222–3
Lord's Resistance Army (LRA), Uganda 167–73, 174–6, 178
love, terrorism for sake of 223–6

McCormick, Gordon 23
MacDonald, Eileen 1, 184, 227
McElvoy, Anne 220
McKay, Susan 8–9, 16–17, 167–79
Magomadova, Luisa 91, 100, 113
Manaqib al-sahabiyyat 38
marital status 107–8, 134–5
Marr, David G. 192
martyrdom, rhetorical strategies for justification 21–9

Maskadov, Aslan 128
Masoud, Marwa 131
Maunaguru, S. 186, 187, 188
media 40, 57–8, 217–20; and female
    terrorists 220–30
Meinhof, Ulrike 1, 13, 223, 229
Merari, Ariel 54, 147, 158, 160
Middle East Media and Research Institute
    90
Mikulski, Barbara 220
MIPT 196
Mishandling Suicide Terrorism (Atran) 59
moral support 157–8
Morgan, R. 1, 224
motivations 56–7, 110–13, 152–5; and
    gender stereotypes 220–30; lethal mix of
    113–15
Mouhadly, Sana'a 1–2
Mozambique 16–17, 75–9, 171
Ms. Magazine 13
Mubarak, Aliyya Mustafa 38
Muhammad, Prophet 27, 37, 38–9
Mujikhoeva, Zareema 113
Munich Olympics massacre 196
Musleh, Isam 15
Muslims, attitudes towards American
    culture 64
Mutaeva, Malija 113
My Life is a Weapon (Reuter) 52

Nabulsi, Randa 88
Nacos, Brigitte 9, 217–32
naivety 229–30
National Association for the Advancement of
    White People (NAAWP) 203
National Liberation Front (NLF) of Vietnam
    191
nationalism 15–16; blend with
    Salafi/Wahhabism 90–2; as motivational
    factor 112; religious and secular 87–90
Naxalite movement 188–9, 197
Nayak, Nihar 188, 189
Neidhardt, F. 209
Nepal 170, 197
Ness, Cindy 1–9, 11–30, 84, 86
networked recruitment 112, 113
Neuberger, Luisella De C. 1, 14, 209
news frames 218–20
Nezavissimaya 123
Nivat, Anne 8, 91, 122–30
non-combatants, women as 71–2, 80–1
Nordstrom, Carolyn 7, 69–82
North Ossetia 100–17, 124
NTV 129

Nyiramasuhuko, Pauline 3–4

O'Ballance, Edgar 196
Oklahoma City bombings 206
Omar, Mullah Mohammed 93
Onesto, Li 190, 191
Online Pioneer and Ideals World News 190,
    191
Operation Defensive Shield 141
organization, racial terrorism 207–11
organizational security 63
organizational support 50–1
organizations, importance of 52–3

Pakistan 131–44
Palestinian Centre for Research and Cultural
    Dialogue 15
Palestinian Front for the Liberation of
    Palestine (PFLP) 196
Palestine: characteristics of suicide bombers
    3; children 61; Sabena Airlines hijacking;
    would-be suicide bombers 146–61;
    women's liberation 227–8
Palestine Liberation Organization (PLO) 88
Palestinian Islamic *jihad* 5, 53
Palestinians, religious sentiments 52
Parry, Albert 191, 194, 195, 196
Parvati, Com 190
Patkin, Terri T. 147, 160
patriarchal societies 148–50, 205–6
Patterson, Orlando 206
Paz, Reuven 53, 64
People's Liberation Army Front (PLAF),
    Vietnam 183
People's Liberation Army of Nepal (PLA)
    183, 189–91
perpetrators, child soldiers as 174–5
Perry, Barbara 203
personal search 110–11
Pew Research Center 55
Philippines 170
physical appearance 220–2
Pike, Douglas 194
Pillar, Paul R. 184
Pirabaharan, Velupillai 23
political range, Islamist groups 87
political transformation 81–2
Popular Front of the Liberation of Palestine
    (PFLP) 1, 13, 15, 88
Portland Independent Media Center 190, 191
post-traumatic stress disorder (PTSD) 179
postbellum racial terrorism, US 204,
    209–10
power 81–2

Pradhan Malla, Sapana 190, 191
pregnant women 62, 70
Premadasa, Ranasinghe 187
profiling 54
psychological autopsy 105–6
psychological contagion 112–13
psychological first aid 115–17
Putin, Vladimir 122–3, 128, 129, 130

Quayle, Ethel 13
Qur'an 39, 94, 95, 152–3, 157

racial terrorism, US 201–13
Ramirez Sanchez, Ilyich 195
Rantisi, Abd al–Aziz 27, 28
Ray, Bikramjit 189
Razawi, Ayman 89
recruitment 50, 54, 63, 154–5; child
    soldiers 171–2; *see also* coercive
    recruitment; networked recruitment
Red Army Faction, Germany 223, 224, 227,
    232
Red Army, Japan 183
Red Brigade, Italy 225–6, 227
Reddy, Balaji 189
Reeves, Minou 15, 19
Reeves, Phil 89
regeneration 77–9
reintegration, child soldiers 177
religion 109–10
religiosity 111–12
religious discourse 85–6
religious nationalism 87–90
religious terrorism 11–12, 18–21, 25–9
resisters, child soldiers as 175–7
Retreat of the State (Strange) 81
Reuter, Christoph 52, 53–4
Reuter, John 186
Revolutionary Armed Forces of Columbia
    (FARC) 16
Revolutionary United Front (RUF), Sierra
    Leone 167–72, 173–5, 176–7
rewards 44–5
rhetorical strategies for justification 21–9
riots, Sri Lanka 70
Rogers, Joann 209
roles: child soldiers 172; loss of 113
Ronfeldt, David 13
Rosenthal, John 95
Rubenberg, Cheryl146, 149, 150
Rubin, Herbert J. & Irene 151
Russia 5, 90–1, 100–17, 122–30

sacrifice 28–9

Sahabiyyat mujahidat 38
Sahni, Ajai 189
Salafi Wahbabism 91–5
Salafis 85, 86
Salamah, Dr. Salam 44
Sambandan, V.S. 187
Samuel, Kumudini 186
Sana, Khyadali 49
Sassoon, Siegfried 69
Saudi Arabia 20, 45–6, 85
Schalk, Peter 12, 21–2, 23–4
Schweitzer, Yoram 8, 18, 90, 131–44, 147
secular nationalism 87–90
secular terrorism 11–18, 21–5
selection 156
separatism 91–2
sex stereotypes 219–20
sexual purity 19
Shalhoub-Kevorkian, Nadera 146–7, 150,
    155
Shalinsky, Audrey C. 86
Shamsie, Kamila 11
Shanab, Isma'eel Abu 90
Shanks-Meile, Stephanie L. 209
Sharabi, Hishan 148
shari'a 43
Shi'ite tradition 39–40
Shigenobu, Fusako 1, 13, 195–6
Shikali, Kahlil 53–4
Shining Path 16, 17–18
Shiomi, Takanari 195–6
Shomaly, Walid 15
Shoot the Women First (MacDonald) 227
Sierra Leone 167–79
Singh, Manmohan 189
Singha Roy, Debol K. 188
"Sister's Role in Jihad" 42
Sisterhood 90, 209
Sisters in Crime (Adler) 226–7
Snow, Donald M. 184
social background 151–2
social image 141–2
social opportunity 17–18
socio-economic status 108–9
soldiers, children as 168–72
South Asia Forum for Human Rights 190,
    191
Southern Poverty Law Center (SPLC),
    Montgomery 207
Speckhard, Anne 6, 8, 91, 100–18
Sreedharan, C. 188
Sri Lanka 69–72, 74, 170, 185–8
    status of women 17–18; in Palestine 148–50
Steinhoff, Patricia G. 194, 195, 196

Sterba, James P. 184
Stern, Jessica 147
Strange, Susan 81
strategic racial terrorism 208–9
Studies in Conflict and Terrorism 1, 6
suicide bombers, analysis of 49–59; *see also*
    failed suicide bombers; would-be suicide
    bombers
suicide terrorism, types of 100–4
Sunni tradition 40
Suthanthira Paravihal see Women's Front,
    LTTE
Symbionese Liberation Army (SLA) 174,
    226, 227
Syrian Social Nationalist Party (SSNP) 1–2

Tamil culture 23–5
Tamil Tigers *see* Liberation Tamil Tigers of
    Eeelam (LTTE)
Tamini, Ahlam 26
tandem bombings 60
Taylor, Maxwell 13
Taylor, Sandra C. 192, 193, 194
Taylor, Verta 209
terminology 183–5
terrorist groups, definition 184
Terrorist Research Analytical Center 184
Tessler, Mark 64
Tetrault, Mary A. 192, 193, 194
Thapa, Manjushree 190
Thatcher, Margaret 228
Thi Dinh, Nguyen 193
Tigrean People's Liberation Front (TPLF)
    Eritrea 170
Tiruchelvam, Neelan 187
Tiwari, Chitra K. 190
Tolnay, Stewart E. 206
"total war" 85
toughness 228–9
trauma 110–11, 178–9
traumatic events 113–15
Turkey 63–4
Turley, William S. 193, 194
TV5 129
Tzoreff, Mira 133, 146

Uganda 167–79
Ugandan People's Defence Force (UPDF)
    172–3
Uhud, Battle of (626) 38
UN Fourth World Conference on Women
    (1995) 169
US: counter-terrorism 63–4; media 219–20;
    racial terrorism 59–60, 62, 201–13

US State Department 202
Usher, Graham 88

Valentini, Tiziana 1, 14, 209
Verancini, L. 147
victims, child soldiers as 174–5
Victor, Barbara 3, 17, 24, 26, 28, 133–6,
    140–1, 147, 160
Viet Minh 191–4
Vietnam 197
Vietnamese Women's Liberation Association
    193
virtuous heroines, women as 131–44
volunteering 155–9
Vremya Novosty 123

Wahhabis/Wahhabism 20, 91–5, 107, 109,
    110, 112
war: gendered 69–82; intra-state 167–79
Watson-Verran, Helen 74
Watt, Romeet K. 189
Weather Underground 13, 226, 227
Weinberg, Leonard 13
West Bengal 188–9
White Pride (WP) Movement 225
White, Jonathan R. 184
Whitman, Christine Todd 222
Wiegersma, Nancy 193
Winant, Howard 207
Women and Terrorism (Neuberger/ Vanentini)
    1
Women for Aryan Unity 201–2, 208–9
Women's Front, LTTE 187
Women's Frontier 209
women's lib/equality 226–8
Women's Media Bureau 93
World Church of the Creator (WCOTC) 209
would-be suicide bombers 146–61

Xinhua News Agency 186

Yadlin, Rivka 85
Yami, Hsila 190
Yasin, Ahmad 44–5, 89–90
Yassin, Sheik Ahmed 231
Younes Habib, Rawda Ibrahim 143
Younes Hassan Zaq, Fatima 143
Yusef, Sheikh Hassan 90

Zedalis, Debra 7, 49–64, 187
Zwerman, Gilda 212